POWER AND CHANGE

INDIANA SERIES IN MIDDLE EAST STUDIES

Mark Tessler, *General Editor*

POWER AND CHANGE IN IRAN

Politics of Contention and Conciliation

Edited by Daniel Brumberg
and Farideh Farhi

Indiana University Press

Bloomington and Indianapolis

This book is a publication of

Indiana University Press
Office of Scholarly Publishing
Herman B Wells Library 350
1320 East 10th Street
Bloomington, Indiana 47405 USA

iupress.indiana.edu

The paper used in this publication meets the minimum
requirements of the American National Standard for Information
Sciences—Permanence of Paper for Printed Library Materials,
ANSI Z39.48-1992.

Manufactured in the United States of America

Library of Congress Cataloging-in-Publication Data

Names: Brumberg, Daniel, editor. | Farhi, Farideh, editor.
Title: Power and change in Iran : politics of contention and
    conciliation / edited by Daniel Brumberg and Farideh Farhi.
Description: Bloomington ; Indianapolis : Indiana University Press,
    [2016] | Series: Indiana series in Middle East studies | Includes
    bibliographical references and index.
Identifiers: LCCN 2015046017 | ISBN 9780253020680 (cloth : alk.
    paper) | ISBN 9780253020765 (pbk. : alk. paper) |
    ISBN 9780253020796 (ebook)
Subjects: LCSH: Iran—Politics and government—21st century.
Classification: LCC DS318.825 .P69 2016 | DDC 320.955—dc23 LC
    record available at http://lccn.loc.gov/2015046017

1 2 3 4 5   21 20 19 18 17 16

Contents

Acknowledgments

THIS BOOK WAS MADE possible by the support and enthusiasm of family members, friends, colleagues, and institutions whose backing over a four-year period was essential to completing the work. The editors would like to thank the US Agency for International Development for supporting the original study group, whose essays formed the basis for the book, as well as the US Institute of Peace (USIP), which provided an outstanding umbrella for the group's endeavors. Daniel Brumberg would also like to thank the Department of Government at Georgetown University for encouraging his multiple scholarly efforts on and off campus over the duration of this project. We are of course grateful to all our superb contributors, who not only met regularly to discuss their work in a spirit of scholarly exchange and intellectual openness but generously responded to our many questions, suggestions, and edits, some of which were surely quite demanding as we moved forward. Appreciation is also due to Semira Nikou and Tara Nesvaderani, who as program assistants at the USIP kept tabs on funding, meetings, and chapter revisions. Daniel Brumberg would like to thank his wife, Laurie, and son, Gabriel, for their love and support as he juggled a busy schedule to help codirect the project while Farideh Farhi's gratitude abounds to Ardalan, Semira, and Kaveh for sharing their insights about Iran over the dinner table and in long walks and for making her feel lucky everyday. From the outset this project was animated by the belief that the political and social struggles that are central to the Islamic Republic of Iran have echoes in all societies and thus mirror global challenges, aspirations, and even dreams. Dan and Farideh brought this shared conviction to their fruitful and often joyous partnership, for which they are and will long remain very much grateful. Finally, we would like to thank all our comrades at Indiana University Press who have worked so hard to make this book a reality, with a special thanks to Mark Tessler, the general editor of the Middle East series, whose enthusiasm for the project helped make it possible in the first place; Rebecca Tolen, who as the sponsoring editor initiated the editing process; as well as David Miller and Jay Harward, who saw it finish.

Note on Transliteration

PERSIAN WORDS AND NAMES have been transliterated so as to follow modern Persian pronunciation, and with the exception of *ayn* ('), diacritical marks have been omitted. In cases where Persian names and words are already established in English, the spelling used in the mainstream media has been adopted. For Arabic terms like *ijtihad* and *fiqh* the standard used by the *International Journal of Middle East Studies* has been used.

Introduction

Politics of Contention and Conciliation in Iran's Semiautocracy

Daniel Brumberg and Farideh Farhi

Two signal events bracket this extraordinary collection of essays on political and social change in contemporary Iran. The first was the hotly contested reelection of Mahmud Ahmadinejad in June 2009, and the second was the surprise election of Hassan Rouhani to the presidency in June 2013. The 2009 poll precipitated massive demonstrations, as reportedly more than three million Iranians protested what they perceived as massive electoral fraud. For an exhilarating moment, it seemed as if the country's robust authoritarian institutions were backing down in the face of the spontaneously formed Green Movement. But this was not to be. Instead, the security forces moved aggressively to complete a campaign of political repression that over the previous four years had nearly decimated President Mohammad Khatami's left-of-center Reformist Movement. Leaders of the Green Movement were imprisoned or placed under house arrest, and the circle of repression was widened by a series of televised show trials that were reminiscent of Stalinist Russia, followed by the banning of two key reformist political parties: Islamic Iran's Participation Front and Mojahedin of Islamic Revolution. But if these events seemed to usher in a new era of political darkness, Rouhani's election in June 2013 shined an unexpected light on what had seemed like an endlessly dark tunnel. A veteran politician relying on open support from former presidents Akbar Hashemi Rafsanjani and Khatami, he assembled an embryonic alliance of reformists, centrists, and even some veteran conservatives. Uniting behind his candidacy, this coalition helped Rouhani defeat a divided field of hard-liners and conservatives in a campaign that exposed serious disagreements within the regime regarding the direction of the country. After securing a first-round victory with 51 percent of the vote, Rouhani promised his supporters a new era of "moderation and prudence," entailing a more conciliatory foreign policy abroad and greater political openness at home. Thus politics in Iran seemed to witness a resurrection and a burst of cautious optimism that surprised Iranians as much as it did the rest of the world.

This sense of astonishment was understandable. After all, the four years that preceded Rouhani's victory were grim. During these years, the arena of political participation and debate not only came under the thumb of hard-line conservative politicians, clerics, and newspaper columnists but was increasingly dominated by a new generation of Revolutionary Guards (IRGC) and their affiliated troops—the Basij Resistance Force. The IRGC had existed since the early days of the Islamic Republic, and had always played a special role—endorsed by Article 150 of the Constitution—as the official defender of "the revolution and its achievements." However, by the late 2000s, the IRGC's political and economic clout reached new heights. This shift stemmed from a host of domestic and international facts. On the domestic front, the rise of a new generation of political activists who had fought in the 1980–1988 Iraq-Iran War but had remained outside—and even estranged from—the dominant political and economic elites, generated pressure to open up political and business opportunities to this rising elite. The latter's efforts were abetted by escalating regional and global conflicts. In the wake of the 2003 US invasion of Iraq and the further deterioration of US-Iranian relations, security-minded leaders argued that military, cultural, and ideological threats from the US justified a clampdown on domestic political forces that hard-liners deemed sympathetic to the US and political liberalism.

These efforts succeeded: by the mid-2000s, the IRGC's growing influence not only worried many Iranian mainstream political leaders, but in the US it helped solidify the view of an increasingly influential group of academics, policy experts, and media pundits, all of whom argued that Iran had transformed into a veritable "security state." With Iran's political system seemingly shorn of the quasi-pluralistic institutional mechanisms that had long supported a complex system of state-controlled political competition and conflict management, some of these US-based observers asserted that the Iranian state had become a wholly owned subsidiary of a new generation of IRGC leaders and the institution they headed. Allied with an ultra hard-line wing of Parliament's conservative "principlist" faction, this new cadre of apparatchiks, paranoid ideologues, and allied businessmen had seemingly not only suffocated independent political life and competition; it had captured a wide number of institutions, thus assuring the long-term sustenance of this new security state.

As this grim view of Iran's politics took hold, the focus of US-based academic and policy work on Iran often narrowed to two subjects: the security apparatus and the new state it supposedly had created, and the regional and global security implications of Iran's assumed transformation into a full-fledged security state. Set against a backdrop of escalating tensions between Iran and the US, this narrowing research agenda reinforced the view that Iran was condemned to the bleakest of futures.[1] Even the sudden outbreak of Arab political rebellions in 2011—with their inspiring images of mass protest and falling (or shaken) autocratic regimes—did little to mitigate the sense that while parts of the Arab world might now witness a new spring, Iran's political system would remain frozen in a near-permanent winter.

The key puzzle this volume addresses is whether the growing power of the security-oriented forces presaged the emergence of a qualitatively different and far more closed regime or whether these centralizing trends obscured enduring dynamics of political and social struggle, political contestation, and even political bargaining that might eventually pull Iran in a more promising direction. Thus we treat the security state argument as a hypothesis that requires close empirical scrutiny and testing. To that end, the contributors have undertaken detailed case studies of political, social, or ideological contestation and competition in a diverse set of formal and informal arenas that since 2005 have received little serious attention from scholars and policy experts. The essays cannot possibly cover all the arenas of contentious politics that have been largely overlooked in recent scholarship. Nevertheless, these chapters illuminate the most hard-fought and important contests that Iran has witnessed: over privatization, social welfare reform, university education, human rights, the rule of law, electoral dynamics, the emergence of the Green Movement, and the institutional reach of the Leader and his Office. Written by Iranian and Iranian American scholars, including several who conducted field research in Iran during the crucial 2009–2013 period and others who were important political actors during the early 2000s, these studies highlight the persistence of contentious political debate, competition, and negotiation during a period of political darkness—dynamics that might explain the rise of, and popular and elite support for, Rouhani's platform of moderation in reaction to what he identified as extremism and imprudence.

The continued relevance of economic, political, and social struggles in Iran suggests lessons that extend far beyond the borders of the Islamic Republic itself. Indeed, far from offering another example of Islamic, Shi'ite, or Middle East "exceptionalism," the Iranian case is important precisely because it illuminates the complex and often contradictory dynamics of political change—and continuity— in what political scientists call "hybrid" or semiauthoritarian systems. Thus while the case studies in this book focus on Iran, we will begin by setting out some of the broader conceptual puzzles posed by processes of political change in hybrid regimes. This brief theory-focused discussion suggests wider lessons of concern to both scholars and policy makers. We then provide a concise analytical map of Iran's political system as a framework for reading the more detailed case studies to follow. Having set out this map, we briefly discuss the case studies themselves, highlighting specific themes and insights that we believe illuminate important political and social dynamics in present-day Iran. As to the significance of these chapters for Iran's evolving society and politics, we will address this crucial question in the epilogue.

Dilemmas of Transition in Iran's Semiautocracy

During the difficult years of 2000–2013, Iran endured a concerted bid by an increasingly powerful security sector to weaken—and, some would argue, destroy—the various institutional channels through which political leaders had long competed, negotiated, and even clashed. Apart from the human suffering that this narrowing of the political arena engendered, it also threatened to denude Iran of the suppleness, political energy, and vitality that had helped sustain the Islamic Republic for more than thirty years. Iran, after all, was never a totalitarian state or theocratic despotism. On the contrary, its ideological heritage comprised a hodgepodge of ideas, symbols, and traditions taken as much from the idea of constitutionalism as from the notion of clerical rule (if not more so). The resulting "dissonance"—as Daniel Brumberg has called it—was channeled through a host of competing institutions and arenas that coexisted under the umbrella of a system that was surely authoritarian in terms of significant limits on civil liberties and political and cultural expression, but that tolerated and even relied on a measure of state-managed political competition to negotiate over policies and actions that affected the direction of the country.[2] For Iran's leaders—including the *Rahbar* or Leader (discussed shortly)—to abandon or eradicate the flexibility that this system afforded required silencing some of the leaders and groups representing a rising urban middle class that has expanded under the umbrella of the state's modernizing project and whose contribution to that very project was central to the creation of the Islamic Republic of Iran (IRI).[3] In Iran—as in many other modernizing development-oriented autocracies—the dilemma facing regime leaders was to reap the modernizing economic potential of these rising middle classes while limiting the latter's capacity to challenge the fundamental institutions and rules of the political system.

In Iran, efforts to address this familiar dilemma were exacerbated by the perception that the rapid rise of Khatami's Reformist Movement during the late 1990s and early 2000s posed a threat to the material and ideal interests of hard-line leaders and conservative institutions. They deemed—and many of them continue to deem—reformism a "soft" revolution or "sedition" that if not controlled would eventually undermine the Islamic Republic and its core institutions, not least of which was the Office of the Leader. This fear drove hard-liners to launch a campaign of repression that by 2010 had shut out many of the social forces and leaders who in the 1980s had played a key role in creating the Islamic Republic. The resulting alienation of these Children of the Revolution (as they were sometimes called) widened the arena of would-be reformists while swelling the ranks of a largely urban population whose young people were questioning the conduct and even legitimacy of the IRI. This dynamic generated a tricky dilemma for Iran's reformists: how to channel popular disaffection in ways that would engage support from elements within the regime—without provoking lethal retaliation from hard-liners, including the Leader himself.

If Khatami's reform efforts during 1997–2005 highlighted the opportunities and the dangers that came with every bid to walk this fine line, the post-2009 clampdown seemed to suggest that by 2012 the reformists had decisively lost the final battle for any kind of limited political change or pact. This is certainly the key thesis, as we have noted, of the securitization literature. But as we have also noted, Rouhani's 2013 election hinted at another possibility: namely, that the institutional, social, and human capital required for building a wider form of political consensus had survived despite—or perhaps because of—escalating efforts to centralize power. Rather than generate an irreversible transition to a new security state, it is possible that the hard-liners' power grab might have also stimulated counterefforts to reassert long-standing dimensions of Iran's dissonant political system. Although it may sound counterintuitive, centralizing dynamics may have also sparked efforts at reinvention, revival, and reopening, particularly if they provoked elite conflicts which threatened the political system itself. That said, this unintended "boomerang effect" would not necessarily indicate some kind of decisive "liberalizing response" to centralization. Instead, it may have also unfolded in tandem with other centralizing dynamics—thus creating a messy and contradictory political field. How one sorts out this messy picture and assesses its implications for Iran's political development is the central empirical puzzle that this volume addresses.

The multiple consequences issuing from the drive to centralize power in Iran suggest wider conceptual lessons, particularly in regard to the study of transitions and/or political change in what political scientists have called semiauthoritarian, competitive authoritarian, or hybrid regimes.[4] While scholars disagree regarding their precise meanings, all of these related terms hint at political orders that do more than merely mix mechanisms of democracy, political pluralism, and autocratic rule: they do so in ways that give ruling elites an array of tools—constitutionally sanctioned or via informal prerogatives given to certain elements within the state—to manage, co-opt, or divide potential opposition movements or challenging elites. This is why, to varying degrees, efforts to force political centralization in semiautocracies can be destabilizing. Such efforts not only rob the system of some of the supple mechanisms that had facilitated regime survival; they can also create a rigid and narrow arena of elite competition that can magnify conflicts among the remaining players. What is unclear, however, is how the increasing centralization of power affects the nature, dynamics, and fate of semiautocracies. Is there a critical threshold whose crossing precludes reviving elements of the previous semiautocracy, thus assuring a permanent transition to full autocracy? Or does centralization pull in the opposite direction by giving estranged elites impetus to stop the hemorrhaging and even reopen the system?

To address these questions we must consider the tensions and contradictions that semiauthoritarian political systems generate and the wider implications of these tensions for the forging of political accommodation or pacts in semiautocracies.

Exiting Protection Rackets: Pact-Making Dilemmas in Semiautocracies

The fundamental problem of transitions in all autocracies is how to move from a system of authoritarian to democratic protection. After all, as Charles Tilly once noted, modern states have their origins in a "protection racket system" by which ruling elites extended social, economic, or security benefits and rights to specific constituencies in return for the latter's loyalty—or at least acquiescence—to the authority of the rulers.[5] In democracies this bargain was often secured through prolonged political and even violent conflicts that produced institutions and procedures that made elected rulers and ruling institutions accountable to a broader public and to the rule of law. In autocracies, by contrast, protection pacts were achieved through a more coercive exchange sustained and enforced from above by imposition or fiat or, as Dan Slater has reminded us in his study of successful counterrevolutions in Southeast Asia, through the active participation of a broad array of elites "from captains of industry to captains in military" threatened by the radicalism of other groups.[6] Aside from the political freedoms and civil liberties that democracies promise and autocracies abjure, one key if related difference between these two kinds of regimes is especially relevant to this book: the mechanisms that democracies use to secure and legitimate the protections they offer create a political arena that is sufficiently open or uncertain enough that all groups can reasonably expect that their representatives might win positions of influence or authority.[7] By contrast, in autocracies the mechanisms used to secure the ruling bargain between regimes and constituencies—including elections—are designed to guarantee ruling elites the certainty of ultimate victory and power. This is why at their core, transitions to democracy entail a process by which ruling elites are either forced by popular rebellion to abandon the mechanisms that are supposed to secure certainty of rule or compelled to negotiate agreements with opposition elites. The latter, either by design or unintended default, allows for a shift to democratic uncertainty. Regime collapse or regime-opposition negotiations are the principal ramps along which leaders and oppositions often exit onto the path of potential democratic change.

Negotiated or "pacted" transitions can be notoriously uncertain and unstable affairs. In the first instance, they require forging a tricky alliance between regime soft-liners and opposition moderates. What brings these two together is the realization—usually brought about by years of conflict—that they are better off finding a political compromise that allows for state-controlled political and social détente rather than returning to a violent status quo that denied full victory to either regime or opposition. But to strike such a compromise, each side must contain hotheads in their own camps. After all, regime hard-liners see even the smallest opening like a slippery slope to political oblivion, while opposition militants view any compromise as a ruse that is bound to reinforce the power of regime hard-liners. In negotiated transitions, the move away from autocracy depends partly on the capacity of regime soft-liners and opposition moderates to find enough common ground to fend off pressures from their own hard-line allies to either stop all change or rapidly push for a complete collapse of the regime.[8]

Such pacts are necessary but far from sufficient conditions for regime change or transformation. Indeed, even when regime reformists and opposition moderates are smart and/or lucky enough to walk this fine line, there is no guarantee that a political pact that allows for state-controlled opening will by itself produce one inevitable outcome or trajectory of change. In fact, the experiences of the Soviet Union and Poland show that state-initiated openings undertaken by regime soft-liners are highly contingent: in the Soviet Union they led to the collapse of the Communist Party, while in Poland they opened the path for the creation of a competitive democracy. By contrast, in Egypt, Algeria, Jordan, Morocco, and other Arab states, and in Brazil as well, state-managed openings were a regular feature of authoritarian survival.[9] As for Iran, the efforts of former president Khatami from 1997 to 2005 to forge a new political consensus in favor of a political opening provoked a hard-line campaign that threatened to drag Iran into a new political system—one bereft of the mechanisms of state-managed conflict and completion that had existed previously.

In semiauthoritarian regimes, the previously discussed phenomenon of uncertainty presents complicated challenges and dilemmas that merit further comment. In contrast to full autocracies, which tolerate no uncertainty, the operation and even survival of semiautocracies depends on a kind of implicit bargain or protection pact between regimes and opposition according to which the latter is allowed to organize, mobilize, and even participate in state-controlled elections providing that opposition groups, parties, or associations never try to use the space accorded to them to undermine the power of the ruling elite and its key institutions. Thus the key question facing regimes and their potential opponents is how to sustain state-enforced political competition that is robust enough to sustain the leverage of moderate actors in regimes and oppositions but sufficiently constrained to deflect intervention from hard-line regime actors—especially those who might favor moving to a fully authoritarian system. The answer to this question is not clear, if only because the "red lines" in semiautocracies are notoriously ambiguous and constantly shifting. Thus the chances of provoking retaliation from hard-liners is always present, a consideration that often invites a game of cat and mouse, as opposition elites test the boundaries of acceptable dissent and regime actors signal the consequences of violating these boundaries and/or move to impose stricter political controls to punish transgressors.

To get a better grasp of these particularly complex dynamics, we can distinguish between *hegemonic* and *diffused semiautocracies*. In the first, formal mechanisms of party competition and elections provide the principal site of political contestation and competition.[10] Thus when it comes to regime survival, what counts is the capacity of ruling regimes to dominate and control these formal institutional arenas so that electoral outcomes assure the ruling party of victory. Party unity is crucial: parties that remain united are more capable of both mobilizing constituencies and sustaining the divide-and-rule strategy necessary for weakening opponents, whereas parties that endure significant splits can suffer defections to the opposition, thus undermining control. Intimately intertwined with the issue of formal party and electoral dominance is the importance of constitutionalism and the rule of law. Rival leaders seeking to sustain or undermine the political machinery of a dominant party can—and often do—invoke constitutional and legal principles so long as both provide a set of legitimate, coherent, consistent, and widely accepted rules of the game.[11] By contrast, in diffused-power semiautocracies, power and authority is unevenly spread and concentrated among formal and informal mechanisms and arenas. In these systems formal parties and elections sometimes exist and have a role. But that role is largely confined to channeling a more fluid and informal dynamic by which factions, cliques, and networks jockey for influence through other arenas—while collaborating to deflect challenges coming from outside the ruling elite or family. Moreover, in diffused systems, constitutions and legal systems do not provide a broadly agreed-upon template of principles for the exercise of political or constitutional rights. Instead, they either constitute a hodgepodge of conflicting principles that are subordinated to the informal rules and norms of competition, or they are selectively manipulated by competing elites to rationalize political actions that are usually arbitrary rather than grounded in any clear and broadly shared constitutional or legal principles. These fluid institutional and legal mechanisms create a hobbled or "feckless" pluralism (to use Tom Carothers's evocative term), one that seems to be incoherent, disorganized, and constantly improvised but uses such suppleness to channel, contain, or diffuse challenges to regime domination and elite unity.[12]

Examples of such diffused-power systems are legion: variations include the "liberalized autocracies" of the Arab world, the semiauthoritarian junta that ruled Brazil from 1964 to the late 1970s, and the IRI itself, a point to which we shall return shortly. Diffused-power systems have elements that both facilitate and limit the impact of elite efforts to negotiate the political and social terrain. On the one hand, these systems usually promote and even celebrate a continuous dynamic of regime-led dialogues through a host of institutions, including elected parliaments. These dialogues channel and contain elite conflict, thus giving regimes additional room to maneuver and a basis to claim popular support and legitimacy. On the other hand, because they lack institutionalized parties or parliaments with authority and power to legislate significant political change, the opportunities for and capacity to channel dialogue and negotiations to facilitate and sustain elite-initiated pacts are limited. In short, diffused systems are a double-edged sword, cutting both against and in favor of political accommodation and change.

Given that the blade of participation can cut both ways, scholars want to better understand the factors that either undermine or sustain the level of power fluidity and diffuseness on which the equilibrium of diffused semiautocracies depend. Compiling a comprehensive list—much less "testing" it—in ways that would demonstrate the relative effect of these factors is beyond the scope of this study. Nevertheless, three factors loom large in any effort to trace the evolution of political competition and elite accommodations in diffuse semiautocracies.

The first of these factors is the nature and strength of the security sector. Militaries, security forces, or police forces that have extensive economic, institutional, or ideological investments in the survival of the political system or state constitute a powerful hard-line block. As a result, they can either limit the boundaries of political participation, or if necessary push for a move toward full autocracy when and if they perceive their fundamental interests threatened. The latter dynamic emerged in Iran during the 2000s, but it has analogues in other semiautocracies such as Egypt, where a powerful military that saw itself as the guarantor of the economic, strategic, and ideological foundation of the state itself presided in 2013–2014 over a shift from semiautocracy to full autocracy.

The second factor has already been mentioned but merits elaboration, and that is ideology. Complex, elusive, and thus not easily grasped by the most astute scholars, ideology can play a crucial part in either undermining or sustaining accommodations between regimes and estranged elites. Indeed, the more a regime or state has constructed its rule around a doctrine whose defense it equates with its or the state's survival, the more intolerant a regime will be of opposition efforts that challenge that creed.[13] Thus while there may be room for debate about political matters, the more that elites are seen by regimes as challenging or effectively corroding the ruling ideology, the more likely hard-line retaliation becomes. This rule of thumb was amply displayed in Egypt, where escalating challenges from Islamists from within and outside the regime regularly provoked clampdowns on the opposition (and finally, of course, an effective coup d'état in 2013), and Iran, where challenges by critics of the official doctrine of the Guardianship of the Jurisprudent (*velayat-e faqih*) fed the determination of hard-liners to narrow the field of political debate and competition. The fact that in both cases the security sector viewed itself as the ultimate "guard" of the state and its ruling ideology created a deep structural incentive to view even tepid ideological challenges as a potentially existential threat.

The third factor that can complicate or undermine regime-opposition entente is external pressures or threats from state and/or from nonstate actors. Regional and global dynamics that ruling regimes see as endangering their very survival tend to increase the political leverage of hard-liners and thus hinder regime-opposition accommodation. In the Middle East, this dynamic is manifest in the arena of US-Iranian conflict, which has magnified the fears of regime hard-liners; in the arena of Egyptian-Persian Gulf conflict—which in the wake of the 2011 Arab rebellions fed the fears of Egypt's military that Islamist movements were directly or indirectly controlled and financed by several Arab Persian Gulf states; and lastly, in the arena of Iranian-Saudi conflict, whose strategic and sectarian features have played into the hands of more hard-line leaders in both countries while narrowing the room for maneuver of more conciliatory leaders. Indeed, the increasingly sectarian nature of this conflict and its escalation into violent confrontations in Lebanon, Bahrain, Syria, and Yemen (particularly after the 2011 Arab uprisings) undermined elite accommodation in all four countries.[14] Meanwhile, only time will tell whether the easing of external economic pressures and military threats against Iran, made possible by the July 2005 nuclear agreement—known as the Joint Comprehensive Plan of Action (JCPOA)—between Iran and five permanent members of the United Nations Security Council plus Germany (P5+1), will have a positive impact on the country's domestic dynamic (a question that we will briefly address later in this introduction and in the epilogue of this book as well).

The preceding observations regarding the nature and impact of security sector, ideology, and regional/global conflicts suggest an intersecting field of multiple forces that can either widen or narrow the boundaries of regime-opposition accommodations in semiautocracies. In Iran, the evolution, intersection, and clash of these and other forces beginning in the late 1990s generated storms of increasing intensity. Indeed, by the early to mid-2000s a "perfect storm" was creating widespread damage to the fabric of a diffused array of institutions and mechanisms that had supported a dynamic of elite accommodation and negotiation within the ruling revolutionary family since the consolidation of the IRI in the mid-1980s. Next we provide a concise map of the central institutions and mechanisms that constitute Iran's diffused semiautocracy power system, followed by a rapid but essential account of the diverse array of centralizing forces that by the mid-2000s were undercutting the delicate ecology of semiauthoritarian governance.

Mapping Iran's Diffused Semiautocracy

Iran's diffused-power semiautocracy crystallized during the mid-1980s, after a period of revolutionary state-building and consolidation. In its macro-contours, political contestation in the IRI unfolds through cliques and factions rather than organized parties. Factionalism allows for a dynamic of elite conflict and negotiations fluid enough to contain, channel, or mediate numerous elite conflicts, but sufficiently institutionalized to sustain political accommodation, alliance building, and negotiation among competing elites and the social forces that often support them.[15] But while factional politics necessitates informal elite negotiations, it can also hinder efforts by regime soft-liners and opposition moderates to challenge the foundations of power and authority in the political system.[16] In short, the system's fluidity is its great advantage and its Achilles' heel.

One source of this fluidity stems from the complex intersection of economic and ideological-identity conflicts. As in many states, elite struggles in Iran mirror and channel significant differences (and interests) in the society regarding the role of state versus market forces in the economy. But this familiar structural cleavage is matched—and sometimes overtaken—by political-ideological conflicts over the proper nature of state authority in regulating beliefs. On one side of this political divide are elites who hold that democratic elections and the institutional-legal infrastructure of popular sovereignty are the best mechanisms for adapting to the changing sentiments of the society; even a religious one. On the other are elites who do not necessarily reject democratic procedures but insist that in the final analysis, a state-supported clerical elite is the best guide of popular sentiments and should impose ideological conformity from above. Because this ideological-political cleavage also cuts across the statist/private economy divide, Iran's factional politics is characterized by a multiplicity of conflicting forces and groups whose changing memberships and priorities can inhibit the formation of stable elite alliance and elite negotiation that is a necessary if insufficient condition for elite pact making. The resulting fluidity can be functional and useful for containing elite conflicts and thus sustaining the system. But it also has its limits. Indeed, when the ideological divide becomes the driver of factional disputes, it can pose a near existential threat to the system, sharply narrowing the room for elite compromise.[17] This was precisely the kind of polarizing political-ideological dynamic that Iran witnessed in the early 2000s, a point to which we return shortly.

Factional competition, negotiation, and conflict have all unfolded through formal and informal forums including the media, clerical schools and associations, the security sectors, and the electoral system itself. But the authority of elected institutions—the presidency, Parliament, the Council of Experts, and municipal councils—is ultimately limited. Legislative authority is severely restricted by the Leader and by the Guardian Council. A body whose six clerical members—half of its membership—are chosen directly by the Leader, the Guardian Council has the constitutional authority to veto any legislation it deems unconstitutional or un-Islamic. In the early 1990s, the council's checking power expanded, as it interpreted the Constitution to give itself vetting powers over who can become a candidate for elected offices, including Parliament (municipal councils excepted). Nevertheless, within these constraints, Parliament provides an important arena through which factions compete for popular support, and through which they can debate national policy—so long as these debates are not viewed as violating the institutional and ideological foundations of the Islamic Republic (an often murky standard that is in a constant state of flux—at times tending toward more openness and less doctrinaire and at other times moving in the opposite direction).

A similar checking logic has applied to the role and authority of the president. He is the only political leader who is elected directly and who represents the nation as whole. By contrast, the Leader is indirectly elected by the clerical Council of Experts. While in theory the authority of the council's eighty-six members comes from their direct "election" every eight years, in practice after the Guardian Council appropriated vetting powers over this body in 1991, the Council of Experts has become a body that merely confirms the Leader's actions rather than, as envisioned in the Constitution, ensures accountability to his conduct. From the outset of the IRI, this arrangement created the structural preconditions for a difficult and possibly conflict-ridden relationship between the president and the Leader. This tension was amply displayed by the imminent impeachment and subsequent escape 1981 of Seyyed Abolhassan Banisadr, Iran's first elected president. It intensified after the position of prime minister was abolished in 1989, thus creating a two-headed executive, one elected, the other not, and both with quite a bit of power. Indeed, in the IRI's original Constitution, the fact that the president was the only directly national leader also gave him authority to serve as arbiter among the branches of the government, an authority that was taken away in the amended 1989 Constitution and vested in the office of the Leader. The president, instead, became fully in charge of Iran's state bureaucracy and resources, including oil revenues. The problem—as the experience of Khatami illustrated after he was elected president in 1997—was that the president's ultimate authority was formally or informally checked by (or subordinate to) the Leader himself, who is commander in chief and exclusively endowed with the power to appoint military chiefs as well as the head of the judiciary. Indeed, any pact-making effort undertaken by the president that runs afoul of the Leader and his subordinate but nevertheless robust military and judicial institutions is probably doomed to failure.

This sobering constraint is underscored by the authority of the Leader. Indeed, the IRI's first Constitution (1980–1989) was designed to tightly fit the country's founding father, Ayatollah Ruhollah Khomeini. A genuinely charismatic leader, he advocated and simultaneously held two constitutionally mandated positions: *vali-ye faqih* or religious guide, which gave him ultimate religious authority, and the Office of Rahbari or Leadership, which made him the highest political authority. These cojoined positions created a Leader/*Faqih* whose authority in practice derived from his role as a kind of Ultimate Arbiter over Iran's factionalized system. But thus structured, this arbitrating role did not give the Leader the kind of supranational or symbolic authority that, for example, in Spain helped King Juan Carlos preside over the negotiation of a pro-democratic political pact in the late 1970s. After all, the doctrine of the divine right of kings was long dead by then, whereas in the case of the IRI, the Leader's religious authority makes him a kind of Shi'ite pope ruling over a country that had yet to experience its own Reformation. This level of unchecked semidivine power not only limits the Leader's capacity to act as a disinterested shepherd guiding his fractious flock; it ensures that factions that fear any effort by their rivals to change—or even modestly open up—the political system must eventually enlist the Leader either to quash such reforms or become the force that pushes them through. These dynamics ensure that the Leader's primary role is to act as a kind of Ultimate Enforcer rather than Ultimate Arbiter.

Those forces that depend on—and in turn support—the Leader's role as Ultimate Enforcer include the IRGC. While the Constitution in its original and amended versions stated that "the Islamic Revolution's Guards Corps . . . is to be maintained so that it may continue in its role of guarding the revolution and its achievements," and that "the government must during peacetime utilize the technical personnel and resources of the military in aid relief, education, production, and construction Jihad while following principles of Islamic justice in full," in practice, the extent of the IRGC's power and authority has been at least partly conditioned by changing historical contexts and the relevant strength of different politics. For example, the Constitution did not allow for the IRGC to intervene in everyday factional politics, and Khomeini himself counseled against political involvement in his last will and testament.[18] In time, however, the role given to the IRGC as protector of the revolution's achievements—as well as a resource to rely on as part of the military infrastructure during times of crisis and for the promotion of the country's development—not only opened the door to assigning the IRGC a significant role in economic projects, it also ensured that the IRGC would provide the Ultimate Enforcer and commander in chief with the coercive power needed to enter the fray in order to protect the "achievements of the revolution."[19] Indeed, precisely because Khomeini's successor lacked his charismatic authority, Ayatollah Seyyed Ali Khamenei increasingly depended on the IRGC's coercive clout to defend the Office of the Leader as his role as Chief Enforcer.

That role has also been considerably enhanced by the Leader's constitutionally mandated authority to direct the judiciary. This interdependent relationship between Leader and Judiciary is rooted in an official state ideology enshrined in the Constitution itself. While a myriad of religious and political doctrines inspired Iran's state builders—including Khomeini—the doctrine of *velayat-e faqih* or the Guardianship of the Jurisprudent (as interpreted and shaped by him) provides a near-sacred foundation of state legitimacy. As with all sacred or semi-sacred creeds, this doctrine requires a chief interpreter and enforcer, hence the enormous—and in many ways arbitrary—power conferred in Iran's political system to the judiciary. As detailed in the Constitution, those powers ensure that the judiciary—especially at its commanding heights—serves as an adjunct to the Leader's authority and power. Indeed, the Leader appoints the head of the judiciary for a five-year term, which has historically been extended once. The head of the judiciary is in charge of a top-down system of appointments, including prosecutor general and the leadership and membership of the Court of Cassation (effectively the Supreme Court), designed to ensure the political loyalty—or at least compliance—of judges. This system is buttressed by other "special" courts and includes the Revolutionary Court, which deals with charges such as blasphemy and incitement against the state, and the Special Court of Clergy, which met on an ad hoc basis in the early 1980s and then was permanently established in 1987. The existence of these two special courts testifies to the judiciary's enforcer role: they provide an institutional apparatus by which the state manipulates laws and judicial procedures to protect the unelected executive and counter dissent and challenges to the status quo. In Iran, as in many autocracies, the ruling apparatus uses "rule by law" rather than the "rule of law" to give a legal blessing to its actions.

The Constitution provides ample language to facilitate this subordination of law to the dictates of power politics, even as it spells out other articles and provisions that support a democratic system of rights and countervailing authorities.[20] But the latter provisions coexist with a myriad of other articles whose vague if not contradictory wording offers Iran's hard-liners ample justification for invoking the Constitution to limit political debate or competition.[21] As a result, the Constitution—as with so much of the apparatus of diffused-power semiautocracy in Iran—provides a messy, contradictory legal framework that can be invoked for multiple purposes and goals in a system of factional competition; one that is ultimately enforced by powerful institutional enforcers that can invoke the Constitution to justify the legal measures needed to quash the efforts of disaffected elites or factions to open the political system.

Dynamics of Political Centralization and Elite Conflict, 1990–2012

The system just described never achieved an easy or durable equilibrium at any point in the short history of the IRI. On the contrary, the political and social struggles that have animated Iran's politics since the mid-1980s have been supercharged with conflicts that undermined Khomeini's own efforts from 1979 to 1989 to institutionalize the revolution. But if he openly expressed his unhappiness with the failure to achieve *esteqrar* (stability or settlement), it was not until the mid-2000s that the system began to veer in a more sustained and decisive manner from semiautocracy to what looked to many scholars like full autocracy.

The seeds of Iran's drift to a more closed system were planted as far back as 1988, when Khomeini and his disciples began to address the tricky question of succession. Under his rule, Khomeini had invoked his considerable personal and charismatic authority to arbitrate factional conflicts and thus keep them from threatening the stability of system. His capacity to play this role was assisted by the fact that during the 1980s, factional disputes largely pivoted around economic issues, with the Islamic Leftists pushing for more state intervention in the economy in contrast to the private sector inclinations of the forces to the right of the political spectrum. Generally avoided were explicitly political/ideological questions—especially those that touched on the very nature of state authority. Indeed, although factional competition and political disagreements doomed the fate of Ayatollah Hossein-Ali Montazeri—Khomeini's designated successor as *vali-ye faqih*, as long as Khomeini ruled—no political or social actor who wanted to remain within the official political system (or avoid its wrath) dared question the doctrine of *velayat-e faqih*, much less the specific way that the office and authority of the Leader had been rendered in the 1979 Constitution. But as Khomeini's health declined, Iran's leaders could no longer ignore or skirt fundamental political issues, particularly those that related to—or touched on—the role and authority of the Rahbar himself.

Khomeini may have anticipated such issues in a remarkable speech that he gave on January 6, 1988. In that speech he argued that the ultimate authority of the Leader rested on the practical requirements of state interest (*maslahat-e nezam*) rather than on God's timeless religious laws or principles. As he put it, "Government . . . is one of the foremost injunctions of Islam and has priority over all other secondary injunctions, even prayers."[22] But because the speech was far from clear as to whether the Leader or the government (or state) determined these interests, it did not clearly resolve the question of who or what institution should exercise ultimate (or shared) political authority after Khomeini. The February 1988 creation of the Council for the Discernment of State Interest, usually translated as the Expediency Council, seemed to provide at least one plausible solution. This body was charged with resolving disputes between the Majles and the Guardian Council, thus providing a new forum and mechanism for adjudicating institutional disputes that was not dependent on the personal or institutional authority of the Leader. The council—all of whose members are appointed by the Leader for extendable five-year terms—also provided the Leader with a consultative mechanism in his delineation of the general policies of the Islamic Republic as well as its *maslahat*. The following year this process of debating and redefining the authority and role of the Leader widened with the series of amendments to the Constitution. Among other things, these amendments dropped the requirement that the Rahbar also be a leading "source of (religious) emulation" or *marja'*, thus effectively defining the Leader's authority in explicitly political rather than religious (much less charismatic) terms. Indeed, to compensate for the reworking of the Leader's authority, the 1989 Constitution expanded the official institutional powers and reach of his Office to include "resolution of disagreements and regulation of relations among the three branches" and "resolution of problems that cannot be resolved through regular means through the Expediency Council."[23]

But if these changes gave Khamenei, the new Leader, greater formal power, it would be incorrect to conclude that the framers of the amended 1989 Constitution sought to free the Leader of any and all constraints. On the contrary, they maintained the critical role of the Council of Experts, an eighty-six-member body whose official role was to supervise the Leader. At least in theory, this supervisory role included the assessment of the Leader's capacity to carry out his duties. The council was given two other roles: the right to remove him for such reasons as lack of "proper political and social insight, prudence and courage," and the task of selecting a new Leader when the previous Rabhar dies or becomes incapacitated (Article 109). Presumably, the council's seemingly ample and even extraordinary capacity to check the power of the Leader flows from the fact that the council is directly elected by popular vote, thus—once again in theory—creating a mechanism that should secure a diversity of opinions and voices in the council, rather than reducing it to a mere mouth piece of the Leader himself. But in practice, as Farideh Farhi has noted, during Khamenei's twenty-five-plus years (and counting), the body served as a rubber stamp for his authority, if for no other reason than this: the candidates who competed in elections to be members of the Council of Experts were vetted by the Guardian Council, thus ensuring that the Council of Experts was made up of members loyal to Khamenei.[24] In this way, and over time, the fates of both Rahbar and the council were each made reliant on the other, thus creating a powerful but potentially constraining alliance between the two. While their mutual dependency may have limited the capacity of the Leader to rise above the political fray and thus play the role of Ultimate Arbiter, it also highlighted the distinctly political—as opposed to religious authority or role—of the new Leader. Indeed, given that the amended 1989 Constitution removed the requirement that he also have the official qualifications of a *marja'*—and what is more, emphasized that the "Leader is equal with the rest of the people . . . in the eyes of the law" (Article 107)—the document provided an unclear and potentially contentious vision of the source and nature of his authority.

This novel if confused situation opened the door to an unprecedented political debate that put enormous strain on IRI's factional system. With a Leader whose ability to mediate factional conflicts was yet to be tested, elites from the left of the political spectrum now began making bold comments that seemed to question Khamenei's authority as Leader.[25] This defiance provoked retaliation from conservative clerics, who in the lead-up to the 1992 parliamentary elections passed a new law that made the Guardian Council the "source of assertion" in determining the eligibility of candidates to run for office. Supported by then president Hashemi Rafsanjani and Khamenei, the council used its new vetting power to disqualify a large number of Islamic Leftists. This action threatened a key wing of the Revolutionary Family that had helped to build the IRI and had long played a vital part in sustaining (and legitimizing) Iran's competitive semiautocracy. These events in turn provoked a brief but telling ideological crisis, as prominent leaders from the Islamic Left—including Khatami—warned that the effort to banish the Children of the Revolution could harm the legitimacy of the IRI.[26]

The 1990–1992 assault on the Islamic Leftists foreshadowed the instability that can flow from any bid to replace accommodation with the more abrasive instrument of permanent political expulsion. In this case, the left suffered a temporary suspension rather than permanent expulsion. Many of its leading lights took refuge in universities, research institutes, or the press, only to return in smaller numbers during the 1996 Majles elections. Their return was facilitated by then President Hashemi Rafsanjani. His right-of-center Servants of Construction Party of mostly technocrats provided a useful ally—and cover—for an opening to estranged Republican Leftists, one of whom was Khatami. Khatami ran and scored a landslide victory in the 1997 presidential election.

This narrative of political closure, conflict, and reopening underscores the fragile and constantly changing equilibrium of Iran's semiautocracy. On the one hand, powerful conservative enforcers such as the Guardian Council were ready to narrow the boundaries of elite competition and debate. On the other hand, such efforts intensified elite conflict at the pinnacle of the state, creating an impetus to reopen the political arena to estranged elites and stabilize the system, always with an eye to maintaining relatively high participation rates in the electoral process as a reflection of the legitimacy of the Islamic Republic. But far from securing equilibrium, Khatami's 1997 victory opened the door to a ten-year struggle during which elite battles to either open up or close the political system reached unprecedented levels of political—and even ideological—polarization.

Paradoxically, this polarizing dynamic owes much to the successes of the reformists, the new brand name for Islamic Leftists. By flooding proposed candidate lists with their supporters, the reformists were able to circumvent the Guardian Council, which accepted nearly 84 percent of the reformist registrants, thus allowing Khatami's allies to secure control of the Majles in 2000. But this was a Pyrrhic victory, as it provoked a sharp counterreaction from their conservative rivals. Although the conservative camp was divided by competing economic agendas and interests, during 2000–2009 period there was no soft-line faction that had either the institutional capacity or will to pursue a serious political dialogue with the Reformists. On the contrary, escalating political differences between reformists and conservatives regarding basic questions such as the constitutional authority of the Sixth Majles highlighted the enduring ideological constraints of the IRI system. For no matter how much the reformists in control of the government insisted that they wanted to slowly reform rather than topple the political system, for the Iran's hard-liners, any opening—no matter how narrow—seemed to threaten the founding ideology of the state. Khatami tried to mitigate this dilemma by reasserting his commitment to the system, even as he called for more openness, democracy, and rights. But he could not control the more radical wing of the opposition, which was spearheaded by university students and members of the press, nor impel reformist leaders to forge a unified strategy. Thus the 2000 electoral victory only egged on the most hard-line of political rivals, inviting a campaign of repression that accelerated over the next five years. This campaign resulted in the shuttering of nearly all the reformist papers and the March 2000 attempted assassination of Tehran municipal council member Saʻid Hajjarian, a veteran political actor and leader of Islamic Iran's Participation Front, whose musings on the theory and practice of political change premised on the general notion of "bargaining at the top and pressure from below" had influenced many reformist leaders.

This repressive campaign had the Leader's clear support. Indeed, Khatami's efforts to reach an understanding with Khamenei had clearly failed by 2000. One year before that, student protests at the University of Tehran over the closure of the *Salam* newspaper, which was close to the reformists, had provoked a violent attack on a Tehran University dormitory by the riot police, which in turn sparked six days of student protests. The protests, which were the largest since the inception of IRI, elicited a letter by several IRGC commanders who warned Khatami of their "patience coming to an end" and for allowing "shouting slogans against the Leader" and "practice of democracy laden with chaos and insult."[27] The tying of student protest to a challenge to the *nezam* (order) and the Leader himself clearly placed the IRGC on the side of Khamenei, thus underscoring his determination to silence the "radical" wing of the reformist movement, not to mention moderate reformist leaders who had depended on the students' mobilizing capacity to enhance their leverage in the wider arena of factional competition. With the university arena increasingly repressed, the reformists were poorly positioned to stand up to powerful institutional enforcers such as the Guardian Council. Flexing its muscle, the Guardian Council disqualified 33 percent of registrants—up from 17 and 16 percents in the previous two elections and including almost all the sitting reformist members of Parliament—from running in the 2004 Majles elections, thus ensuring that the conservatives would regain control of the Majles.[28] This victory set the stage for the 2005 election of Ahmadinejad, and with that, the rise of a new generation of political elites who posed an unprecedented threat to the viability of the factional system itself.

This shift to a more closed form of autocracy was brought about by two intersecting dynamics, one of which was domestic and the other regional and even global. The regional/global dynamic stemmed from the intensifying cold (and sometimes hot) war between Washington and Tehran, particularly following the US-led invasion of Iraq and toppling of Saddam Hussein in 2003. As numerous studies show (including several in this volume), the invasion—and even more so, the decision by the administration to place Iran at the heart of what President George W. Bush in 2002 called the "Axis of Evil"—reinforced the perception of many Iranian leaders that Washington was determined to topple the regime.[29] This perception intensified in tandem with the rise of a new cadre of security apparatchiks and political operators. Many of these actors were veterans of the Iran-Iraq War who had suffered on the front but had not reaped the benefits of the economic opening that Hashemi Rafsanjani had advanced during the early and mid-1990s. Resentful of the perks that had accrued to Iran's existing elites—including those in the IRGC itself—this rising cadre of "neo-principlists," as they were often called, made significant gains in the heavily vetted 2004 elections. All of this occurred in the context of further deterioration of US-Iranian relations during 2006–2008 and in wake of the Colored Revolutions in Georgia and Ukraine in 2003 and 2004. These political uprisings rang alarm bells in Tehran, reinforcing the determination of many of these security-minded new leaders to thwart any "soft revolution" in Iran.[30] Indeed, this security outlook was abetted by all enforcer institutions including the Leader's office, the Guardian Council, and the judiciary. As the first of these institutions is examined at length in this volume, we will limit ourselves to some brief comments on the Guardian Council and the judiciary.

The widening reach of the Guardian Council was manifest in the increasingly obstructive role that it played in choosing who could and could not run in Majles and presidential elections. Though constitutionally mandated to supervise these polls, over time the council argued that this mandate gave it a right to impose a test of the revolutionary credentials of candidates and, on this basis, to disqualify them. The Guardian Council first made this case during the 1991 Council of Experts elections, when it obtained parliamentary approval to vet the Islamic "credentials" of candidates running for the Council of Experts. With Parliament's support, it then asserted a similar vetting power in the lead-up to the 1992 election for the Fourth Majles, a move that provoked widespread criticism and even a partial boycott of the election by the Islamist leftists.[31] The council was not restrictive in the elections for the Fifth and Sixth Majles, but after the success the reformists had in the Sixth Majles (2002–2004), it maintained a close supervisory watch, thus preventing most prominent reformists from standing in Majles elections. As a result, the Seventh Majles was retaken by an alliance of veteran principlists and neo-principlists—the new brand name for an array of conservatives and hard-liners bonded by their opposition to the reformists.

Still, if the 2004 Majles was now controlled by an overwhelming majority of conservative deputies, the public debate generated by the highly politicized nature of the Guardian Council's actions further undermined the credibility of IRI's electoral system, not to mention its capacity to mediate and contain elite conflict. This development may help explain the fact that in the lead-up to the 2005 presidential election—which put Ahmadinejad into the presidency—even Khamenei ended up challenging the council by reversing its decision to disqualify two reformist candidates. Eight years later, the Guardian Council's decision in the 2013 presidential election to disqualify no less a regime stalwart than former president Hashemi Rafsanjani further eroded the council's reputation. Although the council was apparently not bothered by the negative publicity, its politicized vetting cudgel remained and was a source of continued friction.[32]

Another conservative institution, the judiciary, was more sensitive to criticism. Although the judiciary is constitutionally structured to serve as a powerful adjunct of the unelected executive, in its broader ensemble the many courts that constitute its vast domain are not necessarily presided over by judges and prosecutors who see themselves as mere political tools of the Leader and his allies. Anecdotal evidence—and the few systematic studies that exist—offer an image of a judiciary that was politicized in its dealing with political dissent. But the judiciary was also institutionally overwhelmed by the task of dealing with a rising number of cases that have their roots in economic disputes, drug offenses, family disputes, and petty crimes as opposed to distinctly "political crimes." Although the number of political prosecutions continued in the mid-2000s—along with the dispensing of punishments that violated international human rights norms and the increasing use of specialized courts in the early and mid-2000s (such as the Special Court of Clergy)—these dynamics were part of a wider institutional and bureaucratic crisis that sapped the legitimacy of the judiciary in almost every domain of its work. This crisis proved so embarrassing that even prominent members of government acknowledged growing disarray in the Judiciary and the public criticism that it had provoked. Thus in 1999, newly appointed judiciary chief Mahmud Hashemi Shahrudi called the judiciary a "ruin" and promised that the "judiciary will not enter any political disputes or factionalism" and that he would seek "clean and brave judges" to ensure "supervision over all the organs of the judiciary."[33] Toward this end, he reportedly removed several hardline judges linked to the Haqani Seminary in Qom and proposed several penal and institutional reforms. Two years later these efforts remained moribund, thus prompting 151 members of the reformist-dominated Majles to send him a letter in April 2001 demanding "an end to the exiting lawlessness" in the judiciary. But whether by inclination or bureaucratic resistance—or as a consequence of his personal and institutional dependence on the Supreme Leader—Hashemi Shahrudi failed to enact serious changes. Thus while as late as May 2005 he decried the use of "detention centers that violate Islamic and ethical principles to elicit confessions," he had neither the will nor the ability to pry the judiciary from the hands of its hard-line enforcers. Indeed, both the 2009 Decriminalization Bill and the reform of the Iranian Bar Association in that same year only aggravated the situation.[34] In the latter case, the government effectively stripped the bar association of its independence, further eroding the capacity of lawyers to defend their clients from a system of justice that was increasingly politicized.

This apparent slide into the abyss of full-fledged autocracy unfolded through the intensified efforts of Iran's political leaders from 2005 to 2011 to strengthen ideological indoctrination in the public universities, and especially in the institutions of higher education that were affiliated with the IRGC and the militia force, the Basij, which formally came under the command of the IRGC commander in 2007. While studies of this dynamic do not tell us how successful it was, the fact that state leaders felt it was necessary to recharge the IRI's ideological batteries attests both to the perception of vulnerability within the regime and to the commitment of its ideologues and enforcers to ensure that the leaders of organizations such as IRGC and Basij remained loyal and committed.[35] Similarly, during the same period the Guards gained more control over public and privatized enterprises, even if this scope and depth remains a matter of legitimate debate. By the eve of Iran's 2009 presidential elections, key elements of this system were drifting in the direction of full autocracy.

Ahmadinejad signaled this shift when he assailed key founders of IRI. In the lead-up to the June 2009 elections, his televised accusations of corruption, verbal assaults on Hashemi Rafsanjani, and his criticism of Ali-Akbar Nateq Nuri—the conservative cleric whom Khatami had defeated in the 1997 election—suggested that Ahmadinejad was the lightning rod for a project aimed at drastically reducing the arena of political competition. The subsequent controversy over the election results provided the pretext to advance some of these goals, as the regime arrested many leaders or associates of the Green Movement, a diverse grouping of urban professionals, students, workers, and intellectuals who came in the streets. In his July 17, 2009, speech, Hashemi Rafsanjani's unprecedented chastising of the securitization of the political environment further demonstrated the polarizing dynamic provoked by the widening net of repression. Caught in the middle was the Leader. While he openly backed Ahmadinejad and condoned the crackdown, Khamenei could not foresee the effect that his own words and actions would have on the legitimacy of the system, not to mention his own Office. Hashemi Rafsanjani's speech telegraphed some of the potential costs, as his words seemed to imply that Khamenei was abusing his powers in ways that the Prophet Mohammad himself warned against in his discussions with none other than Ali Ibn Abi Talib, the rightful heir to the position of caliph according to the Shi'ite faith. Thus, Hashemi Rafsanjani argued, the prophet himself had reminded Ali:

> You are the Guardian of this Ummah [community]; this is a Guardianship
> that belongs to you, and is something that God has given you. . . . If the major-
> ity coalesced around you . . . you will become the Guardian and see to their
> day to day affairs and resolve their problems. . . . If you saw that they opposed
> you, and that they do not come along with you, then you have to leave them.
> Let them do what they want to; they know themselves what they need to do
> with their lives.[36]

Hashemi Rafsanjani then went on to warn that if the Islamic Republic "loses its
republican aspect . . . it will not be realized," thus clearly articulating the profound challenge that the June 2009 election and the immediate crackdown had
provoked. These events, he claimed, had damaged the "trust of the people in the
polls"—a trust that he insisted must be restored.[37]

Multiple Dynamics in Iran's Semiautocracy: Insights from the Field

All of this may seem to suggest that the process of securitization and closure
had reached its culmination by 2009. But as we have noted—and as Guillermo
O'Donnell demonstrated in his studies of military juntas in Latin America—
regimes that drift toward full autocracy give up the symbolic, cultural, or religious "mediations" without which they cannot forge any wider moral foundation
for their rule. That said, and as Adam Przeworski also argued, legitimacy is a
necessary but far from sufficient condition for rule. What counts is the capacity of alienated leaders or groups to organize a credible alternative, one that has
the means—and perhaps even the moral authority—to compel regime leaders to
reopen the political arena and thus regain some measure of popular legitimacy.[38]

Przeworski's argument is especially relevant to semiautocracies, and particularly to those that maintain a system of diffused-power politics, such as Iran.
As we noted earlier, in these systems efforts to reduce the multiple channels of
elite conflict and negotiation that animate and sustain political life and elite competition can be highly destabilizing Thus while we cannot exclude a priori the
possibility that Iran's system was moving toward full autocracy by the late 2000s,
we also need to understand the parallel efforts to revive or rebuild elements of
the former semiautocratic system and whether such efforts helped create a basis
for a new elite accommodation or pact—one that could repair the growing state-
society breach that Hashemi Rafsanjani addressed so passionately spoke in July
2009, and to which Rouhani alluded in the presidential campaign that led to his
surprise election in 2013. To offer a tentative answer to these questions, we look
to the contributions in this volume for much-needed insight and illumination.

In examining the overall dynamics of socioeconomic and political change,
the first three chapters, written by scholars who have done extensive field research

in Iran, offer three distinctive approaches that in many ways challenge each other. In chapter 1, Payam Mohseni's study places regime power struggles and shifting factional conflict and negotiations over key economic disagreements in a comprehensive conceptual framework that anticipates many of the themes and dynamics that are explored in other chapters of this volume. For this purpose, he divides factional positioning along two competing axes. The first is distinctly political, as it highlights an ideological divide between republican concepts of political order and those oriented to a theocratic vision of authority. The second axis is economic, as it highlights a familiar left-right spectrum distinguished by support for state-led development versus commitment to free-market capitalism. This differentiation between political and economic orientations produces a four-part factional map that features the theocratic left and right and the republican left and right. This categorization allows him to make a basic distinction between institutional shifting and system transformation. Mohseni argues that these four camps are institutionalized in the system in ways that support a constantly shifting architecture of factional politics, accommodation, and negotiation. These dynamics, he argues, absorb and channel conflict—while at the same time inhibiting dramatic, systemwide change *of any kind*, be it a full-scale shift to classic despotism or a transition to fully competitive democracy with more or less guaranteed civil rights for all citizens. Iran's competitive politics endures— and monopolistic drives by any one faction or institution are checked—because factional competition works in tandem with the veto role of key institutions such as the Leader and the Guardian Council to block fundamental changes of the status quo. This does not mean that the Islamic Republic is a static system. In fact, a weak party system sustains the constant fluctuation of powers and positions of factions, with some groups becoming more ascendant than others at different times. But multiple institutional checks and balances also promote a balancing act, with the Leader as the ultimate veto player who prevents any one group from attaining political hegemony. This dynamic not only ensures that multiple voices and interests are incorporated and accommodated in the policymaking process; Mohseni's most salient point is that this factional system also creates an incentive *not* to make the political exclusion of any one faction a permanent outcome of any specific political or social battle. Mohseni examines this fluid factional dynamic in the midst of a strategic transformation of economic institutions and policy through the detailed analysis of the prolonged negotiations that took place among all factions regarding privatization policy in the first decade of the new millennium. Privatization was not blocked but was significantly modified by forces concerned by the ascent of neo-liberal economics as well as the expansion of the power base of the proponents of privatization and economic liberalization.

Mohseni's thesis is provocative: he argues that the results of the 2005 and 2009 presidential elections did not signal a hegemonic bid for power by Ahmadinejad and new elites in the security sector but was rather a reaction to the hegemonic drive of former president Hashemi Rafsanjani and his supporters to impose their own pro-market economic agenda. While this analysis will surely elicit much debate, it nevertheless highlights a key theme in this book, and that is the ways in which efforts by any faction to corner or expel its rivals eventually produces a counterpunch. Indeed, as Mohseni notes, the election of Rouhani seems to demonstrate the resilience of the system and could even portend "the possibility of piecemeal reform within the context of the Islamic Republic."

Kevan Harris, like Mohseni, examines intra-elite conflicts through the prism of interactions and negotiations over specific policies in chapter 2. But by focusing on pressures from below, instead of broader political debates over democracy or authoritarianism, he sheds light on changes, accommodations, and intra-elite bargaining that are constantly at play not only as intrinsic features of the Islamic Republic but also in interplay with robust social forces that have been unleashed by the 1979 revolution. He challenges the oft-repeated claims, even by secular middle-class Iranians who cite demonstrations of regime supporters on various occasions of the Islamic Republic as evidence, that Iran's extensive patronage and welfare system is organized to sustain authoritarian governance and targets only those groups loyal to the system or enlisted to defend it. Because these two assumptions do not grasp the multiple constituencies and purposes that welfare policies serve, they also sustain basic misunderstandings regarding the ever-changing dynamics of factional alliances, negotiations, and conflicts in the country. Instead, through careful examination of negotiated policies regarding war veteran benefits, family planning and rural health policy, and subsidy reform, Harris shows how coalitions backing specific policies are formed when there is a perceived broad and shared threat to power either from below or from outside the country. Harris's provocative take regarding these threats is that those coming from outside Iran have tended to centralize state power through state-promoted nationalism intended to extract compliance from potentially dissident groups. Conversely, domestic threats encourage state leaders to reorder socioeconomic policies in ways calculated to deflect political challenges or actually address grievances and inadequacies. However, shifts in socioeconomic policies—particularly welfare policies—often invite renewed demands for political change. Thus struggles over the social compact are not simply a top-down method of state control or merely the result of factional accommodations at the top. Rather, they constitute an arena that is always up for grabs, thus assuring that economic and political struggles are joined at the hip and are constantly renewed. Change in the Islamic Republic thus comes the same way it comes in many other upper-middle-income countries—through the constant interplay of powerful and varied domestic social forces and a differentiated and bureaucratized state with multiple constituencies. Most crucially, the evolving interaction of these two arenas—from below and from above—is shaped by outside regional and global pressures. For this reason, Harris concludes that prospects for "future democratic challenge" will depend in no small measure on shifting "the balance of external and internal pressure" so that the room for the latter can expand in a normal fashion and in ways that "will assuredly come at moments we cannot predict."

In chapter 3, Shervin Malekzadeh offers yet another take on dynamics of change and transformation in Iran. He urges the reader to see students and not the student movement as the source of change and transformation in the Islamic Republic. Malekzadeh lays out in detail the extent to which schooling in Iran has become part of the state's strategy for securing the quiescence of Iranian youth and a growing urban middle class, thus tying the latter's fortunes to the state. Instead of producing loyal citizens of the Islamic Republic, the country's secondary and postsecondary school systems provide a coveted private resource, and this in turn provides an opportunity for the state to recapitulate its authority in a distinctly pragmatic fashion. By expanding the student ranks of this growing urban middle class—one whose career trajectories depend on their successful completion of studies and exams—the state strives to create a basis for accommodation with a huge public sector, some of whose cadres might otherwise pose a political threat. Two dynamics—aggressive expansion of the university system and enthusiastic response of ordinary citizens to this expansion—explain why students and former students, not student movements, will likely be among the key actors in any future conflict between state and society. Indeed, Malekzadeh's analysis suggests that in the coming years, the student population will emerge— as it did with the Green Movement's brief emergence—as a spontaneous and wide-reaching phenomenon, incorporating many segments of Iranian society. "Rather than university students leading mass protests, demonstrations are more likely to feature protesters who happen to be students."

Examination of social forces that underpin institutional adjustments and transformations is essential to understanding contemporary Iran. But so are institutional dynamics themselves—particularly those designed to sustain the regime and limit the capacity of social forces to undermine the workings of the political system. The two chapters by Mehrzad Boroujerdi and Kourosh Rahimkhani and by Yasmin Alem examine these institutional dynamics through two key institutions: the Office of the Leader and the electoral system. The legitimacy of both of these institutional arenas suffered after the 2009 contested election: the Office of the Leader because of its occupant's inability or unwillingness to stay above the factional fray, and the electoral system because of the doubts surrounding the fairness of the election and the mass protests such doubts provoked following Ahmadinejad's reelection.

Chapter 4, by Boroujerdi and Rahimkhani, goes to the core of this book's investigation of formal centralization of political power and its wider implications for the political system. Indeed, the increasing appropriation of power and resources by the Office of the Leader, some constitutionally sanctioned by the 1989 amendments and some informally gained through individual perseverance and characteristics of the person occupying the office, is something that any discussion of the political evolution of the Islamic Republic must address. Boroujerdi and Rahimkhani lay out the paradox of increased powers of the Office in the face of its declining legitimacy due to 2009 events. The economic power and reach of the Leader is impressive, as the authors explain in some detail. That said, their analysis does not support the argument—set out, as we have noted earlier, by some Washington-based analysts—that the Leader and his Office are now subordinate to the security apparatus. The authors are not convinced that Khamenei is "cuckolded by the IRGC" or that his "political cost-and-effect calculations" are "the same as those of the Revolutionary Guards." Indeed, they assert, while Iran has elements of both "Sultanism and Praetorianism," the system retains a distinctive logic that defies subordinating ultimate authority to one person or to a military-security apparatus. While for the time being "no position is more secure" than that of the Leader (and the man who occupies that post), Boroujerdi and Rahimkhani's analysis points to the destabilizing consequences for the system that have ensued with the expanding powers of the Leader. Lacking his predecessor's charisma, Khamenei may have overreached, prompting "insubordination of his underlings" in a system whose "cacophony . . . will not end anytime soon." The apparent paradox of a Leader whose increasing power makes him vulnerable to wider political dynamics, not least of which is increased elite conflict, has opened the door to a myriad of scenarios. How these scenarios play out will depend on the ability and desire of, as well as pressures on, the Leader (or his successor) to walk a different path and engage in institutional adjustments and bargaining with other forces that see the post-2009 direction of the country as dangerous to the survival and legitimacy of the Islamic Republic. Whether such institutional adjustments, bargaining, and pressures occurred during the period leading up to the 2013 presidential election is an issue our readers will certainly ponder and to which we will return in the epilogue.

A similar assessment awaits Iran's electoral system. There is little doubt, as Yasmin Alem shows in chapter 5, that presidential and especially parliamentary elections have long been key instruments in what she calls a system of guided competition and limited contestation. That system was designed to give some measure of popular legitimacy in ways that nevertheless strengthened the ultimate power of the ruling elite. This tricky effort to have it both ways—to reap the legitimizing benefits of controlled elections without opening the political arena to systemwide change—became more complicated with the emergence of Khatami's reform movement in the late 1990s. Indeed, the reformists' success during the 2000 parliamentary elections provoked a sustained campaign by the

Guardian Council to prevent reformists from running in the 2004 and 2008 parliamentary elections. But if the council's efforts opened the door to the rise of Ahmadinejad and his neo-principlist allies—who together with more mainstream conservatives took commanding control of the Majles—the contentious presidential election of 2009 and the protests that followed created a crisis for the regime. Despite or perhaps because of this very crisis, in 2011 Ahmadinejad made the mistake of openly challenging the Leader, a move that shifted "political boundaries . . . overnight, pushing Ahmadinejad and his associates to the circle of outsiders." In the subsequent 2012 parliamentary elections, allies of the Leader won a majority of the seats, whereas reformists took only 6.6 percent and Ahmadinejad's allies about 1 percent more. While Alem holds that these events confirm the increasingly exclusionary nature of the electoral system, she nevertheless argues the 2013 presidential poll produced a fundamentally different result—a president who, "despite being a consummate insider, was a critic of the country's trajectory." These observations suggest a situation in which "elections are far from becoming irrelevant." Indeed, despite a trend toward excluding radical challenge on the left and the right, the authority and role of elections will likely be affected by shifting dependent domestic, regional, and even global conditions. Indeed, such contextual volatility was amply demonstrated in 2012 when, Alem notes, "escalating tensions between Iran, Israel, and the United States . . . created a climate of fear," which the regime used to "persuade the electorate to participate in elections." Whether a shift in the opposite direction on the global plane might open the domestic space for the reformists to launch a serious challenge in the 2016 parliamentary elections remains to be seen. Such an outcome—rather than the abolishing of the post of president—cannot be ruled out in an electoral system that has now become rationalized to occur every two years, and whose "boundaries," as Alem puts it, "will likely remain in constant flux," thus challenging both those forces who wish to narrow the political field and those who wish to open it up.[39]

Elections are not the only challenge the conservative guardians of the Islamic Republic must manage. Broader societal challenges to the constantly "in flux" parameters of the Islamic Republic are the subject of the next section of this book. The three chapters by Mehrangiz Kar and Azadeh Pourzand, Fatemeh Haghighatjoo, and Shadi Mokhtari examine the legal, political, and discursive challenges respectively. In chapter 6, Kar and Pourzand look at the arguments and strategies used by the reformists to push for key changes in religiously inspired laws. Drawing from Kar's experience on the ground as a leading human rights lawyer, they argue that the reformist efforts to invoke existing constitutional principles to advance the rights of citizens produced paradoxical results. On one hand, these efforts provoked a securitization of the judiciary by hardliners determined to discredit any effort to use the Islamic Republic's own laws to defend human rights. Moreover, the reformists also compelled authorities to enshrine the principle of state interest (*maslahat*) and to assert their uncontested right to invoke this principle against all efforts to circumvent state authority. Not surprisingly, the conservatives in charge of the judiciary and various security services ended up working hard to transform rule *of* law into rule *by* law. On the other hand, on top of their success in pushing authorities to accept a few changes in important arenas of social legislations such as family, law, age of marriage, and child custody, the reformists' efforts to defend rights from within the existing system demonstrated to the wider public and to the ruling elite that Islamic principles could—in theory—provide a religious and culturally authentic basis for advancing democracy, rule of law, and human rights. That said, if the authors' detailed examination of these contradictory dynamics illuminates both failures and some limited successes in the effort to defend human rights and the rule of law, they nevertheless argue that the "reform era brought about transformations that have proven impossible to undo in the collective memory of Iranian society," among them "awareness about the capacities of the existing laws," which has "rendered repression even more complicated for conservatives."

The capacity of Iranian leaders in civil society and the electoral arena to sustain such potential through organized collective action is the subject of Haghighatjoo's study of the Green Movement in chapter 7. A political activist who was a prominent and outspoken member of the Sixth Majles (2000–2004), the author begins with a brief analysis of the divisions with the reformist camp during this time before turning to the largely spontaneous mass protests that erupted following the 2009 presidential elections. She argues that the failure of the Green Movement was largely due to the unprecedented repression visited upon its leaders and its followers. But, she asserts, it was also the consequence of tactical and strategic divisions within the reformist leadership that hampered its coherence and undermined the movement's ability to take advantage of what was an unprecedented moment—that is, the sudden emergence of a mass movement that had the potential to enhance the leverage of opposition elites, and in so doing "[convince] the incumbent elite to be more responsive to at least some of [its] demands." The shift to a more closed authoritarian system suggests "that the possibility for reconciliation . . . rested largely" on the shoulders of the Leader. Paradoxically, while his highly personalized power threatens society, it makes him "capable of mustering political consensus." The question is, what forces would compel the Leader to use this power, and more importantly, toward what aim? As Haghighatjoo's essay shows, the Leader's ambivalence is matched by the opposition's ambivalence over the desired objective of political action: reforming the Islamic Republic or transitioning out of it. This ambivalence keeps the reformists *in* politics, contesting for political power within the confines of the Islamic Republic and in the face of constant threat of disqualification. At the same time, it keeps them accused of either not being true to their reformist or gradualist tactics and objectives or unable to control the people whom they mobilize to vote for them in the hope that the reformists will transform the Islamic Republic. These internal tensions are likely to remain, undermining the capacity of reformists to advance a coherent program or find reliable interlocutors among the conservatives. Moreover, Haghighatjoo argues, these tensions are sure to be sustained and even magnified by the persistence of US-Iranian conflict. For this reason she not only believes that US policies "undermined the reform movement, either intentionally or inadvertently," she also asserts the corollary position, that "the more the threat of force was employed, the less the likelihood that the support base of the movement would expand." Indeed, she writes, "possibilities for accommodation between the regime and opposition" will hinge as much on the readiness of the reformists to overcome their own divisions and find a greater degree of unity as they will on the diminishing of an international conflict that has only strengthened hard-liners and the readiness of the Leader to support them against the reformists.

Mokhtari's discussion of the responses to the post-2009 crackdown in chapter 8 challenges us to see the Green Movement beyond its impact in street protests on the one hand or internal elite struggles on the other. Because Iran's leaders assert that their right to rule derives from their defense of an ethically based religious order, she argues that they are vulnerable to both popular and elite claims that their failure to defend religious values renders their rule illegitimate. The Islamic Republic is by its ideological nature prone to questions regarding to the legitimacy of its conduct that can open up space for a variety of outcomes and dynamics, including popular challenges to the regime itself, or political openings initiated by disaffected elites trying to reassert the legitimacy of the Islamic Republic. State-led repression following the June 2009 elections produced a widely diffused human rights narrative, two elements of which have endured to this day: first, that in their exercise of power, Iran's rulers have strayed from the Islamic Revolution's own ideals; second, that repression amounts to a grave injustice that violates inherent human rights deriving from both Islam *and* universal norms. More than ever before, growing segments of the Iranian population came to view Iran's rulers as adhering neither to the revolution's promise of politics guided by religious morality and the tenets of Islam nor its promise of republicanism and rights. Through meticulous research Mokhtari uncovers the different rhetorical instruments used to challenge the ethical foundations of inhumane practices of the Islamic Republic, many times by the participants and children of the revolution themselves. The political potency of these challenges is derived in part from their reliance on existing constitutional norms and laws and their "unrealized potential." Such morally potent critiques have not ended the imprisonment of political opponents or practices such as torture. Still, because these critiques have been broadly disseminated in the public arena, the legacy of the 2009–2011 period has created a symbolic and ideological resource or repertoire that can be invoked to push for political change or at least serve to limit state repression in a system whose leaders still claim to defend both Islamic and republican values. Indeed, Mokhtari argues, the repression of 2009 and beyond "backfired to the extent that discontent surrounding hard-liners' use of repression in the aftermath of the 2009 elections continued to simmer . . . [being] widely viewed as unjust not only by opposition figures but also by large segments of the Iranian population." This creates opportunities for the opposition and promoters of civil rights in Iran. But the author ultimately speculates that the capacity of reformist elites to take advantage of these dynamics will be shaped—and perhaps constrained—by their effort to walk a difficult path between their declared allegiance to operating "within the parameters of maintaining an Islamic state and the key vocabulary of Islamist ideology" on one hand, and their need to sustain popular legitimacy by challenging or impugning that ideology and its institutional foundations. This is a dilemma with which all reformists in autocracies must grapple—and one that the 2009 repression sharpened, thus opening potentials that Mokhtari argues were partially capitalized upon in Rouhani's 2013 campaign for political change but are yet to be fully realized.

The studies collected here trace dynamics of conflict, negotiation, conciliation, and contention. These processes have not unfolded at the same pace or even in the same directions. Instead, the picture that emerges reflects trajectories of both centralization and contentious competition—a mixed and even contradictory dynamic whose ultimate fate and meaning will be determined by factors national, regional, and global in the coming years. Indeed, many of our contributors' observations suggest that the prospects for political, social, and even ideological reopening may ultimately depend as much on the evolution of Iran's conflicted relations with the US and the wider international arena as on Iran's internal politics. This is one among several themes to which we return in the epilogue.

Notes

1. The quality of these publications differ immensely, with some of this work striving—with varying degrees of success—for objectivity and balance, and other studies taking an implicitly (and sometimes explicitly) political stance. The former would include Frederic Wehrey, Jerrold D. Green, Brian Nichiporuk, Alireza Nader, Lydia Hansell, Rasool Nafisi, and S. R. Bohandy, *The Rise of the Pasdaran: Assessing the Domestic Roles of Iran's Islamic Revolutionary Guards Corps* (Washington, DC: Rand, 2009); Elliot Hen-Tov and Nahan Gonzalez, "The Militarization of Post-Khomeini Iran: Praetorianism 2.0," *Washington Quarterly* 34, no. 1 (Winter 2001): 3–59; Kazem Alamdari, "The Power Structure of the Islamic

Republic of Iran: Transition from Populism to Clientelism, and Militarization of the Government," *Third World Quarterly* 26, no. 8 (2005): 1285–1201; Roozbeh Safshekan and Farzan Sabet, "The Ayatollah's Praetorians: The Islamic Revolutionary Guard Corps and the 2009 Election Crisis," *Middle East Journal* 64, no. 4 (2010): 543–558, and Ali Alfoneh, "The Revolutionary Guards' Role in Iranian Politics," *Middle East Quarterly* 15, no. 4 (2008): 3–14 (a piece that takes a hard position but nevertheless resists polemics). By contrast, see Michael Rubin, "Can Iran be Deterred?" *Middle Eastern Outlook* no. 8 (2008): 1–9; and Mohebat Ahdiyyih, "Ahmadinejad and the Mahdi," *Middle East Quarterly* 15, no. 4 (2008): 27–35. Both pieces draw a rather unclear if not misleading line between the rise of the Revolutionary Guards, the supposed emergence of a new millennarian ideology, and the implications of these trends for Iran's nuclear program.

2. Daniel Brumberg, *Reinventing Khomeini: The Struggle for Reform in Iran* (Chicago: University of Chicago Press, 2001).

3. Kevan Harris, "The Brokered Exuberance of the Middle Class: An Ethnographic Analysis Of Iran's 2009 Green Movement," *Mobilization: An International Quarterly* 17, no. 4 (2012): 435–455.

4. The literature on hybrid regimes has now become as confusing as it is voluminous. We are compelled by the proliferation of terms and their multiple usages to choose in favor of simplicity. We use the term "hybrid" or "semiauthoritarian" to denote a wide category of regimes that blend elements of democracy, elections, pluralism, centralized or state control, autocratic mechanisms and the like, while eschewing terms such as "electoral autocracy" or "competitive authoritarianism," which are associated in the literature with more specific types of hybrid regimes. On hybrid or semiauthoritarian regimes, see Larry Diamond, "Thinking about Hybrid Regimes," *Journal of Democracy* 12, no. 2 (2002): 21–55, and Marina Ottaway, *Democracy Challenges: The rise of Semi-Authoritarianism* (Washington DC: Carnegie Endowment for International Peace, 2003). On the term "competitive authoritarianism" and its application to systematic research, see, among others, Steven Levitsky and Lucan A. Way, *Competitive Authoritarianism, Hybrid Regimes after the Cold War* (Cambridge: Cambridge University Press, 2010).

5. Charles Tilly, "War-Making and State-Making as Organized Crime." In *Bringing the State Back In*, edited by Peter Evans, Dietrich Rueschemeyer, and Theda Skocpol (Cambridge: Cambridge University Press, 1985), 169–187.

6. Dan Slater, *Ordering Power: Contentious Politics and Authoritarian Leviathans in Southeast Asia* (Cambridge: Cambridge University Press, 2010), 31.

7. In some democratic systems a significant number of people often opt out or lose confidence in representation. But in established democracies they are either unable or unwilling to assert their marginalization—if they see it as such—as a challenge to the legitimacy of the rules of democratic game which only function when political outcomes are to one degree or other *uncertain*.

8. This, of course, is the essence of the argument that animates the "transition paradigm" and the work, in particular, of Guillermo O'Donnell and his colleagues during the mid- to late 1980s. See Guillermo O'Donnell and Philippe Schmitter, *Transitions from Authoritarian Rule: Tentative Conclusions about Uncertain Democracies* (Baltimore: Johns Hopkins University Press, 1986).

9. Daniel Brumberg, "Liberalization versus Democracy: Understanding Arab Political Reform," Carnegie Endowment for International Peace, Working Papers Middle East Series no. 37 (May 2003).

10. We use the term "hegemonic" in a manner that evokes the formal institutional dynamics Schedler associated with "electoral authoritarianism." See Andreas Schedler, ed., *Electoral*

Authoritarianism, The Dynamics of Unfree Competition (Boulder: Lynne Rienner, 2006). In this sense, as we suggest, Iran is *not* an electoral autocracy.

11. This is precisely what happened, for example, in Mexico, where a "quiet revolution" that unfolded through rather than against the prevailing party, electoral, and constitutional system undermined the electoral dominance of the Revolutionary Institutionalized Party (PRI).

12. See Thomas Carothers, "The End of the Transition Paradigm." *Journal of Democracy* 13, no. 1 (2003): 15–21.

13. This rule of thumb is especially manifest in revolutionary regimes but can apply to regimes that protect the interest of minority sectarian groups, as has been the case in Syria, in Iraq under Saddam Hussein, and in Bahrain. On revolutionary regimes, see Steven Levitsky and Lucan A. Way, "The Durability of Revolutionary Regimes," *Journal of Democracy* 24, no. 3, (2013): 5–17.

14. Genieve Abdo, "The Arab Uprisings and the Rebirth of the Shi'a-Sunni Divide." Brookings Center for Middle East Policy Analysis Paper no. 29 (April 2013). http://www.brookings .edu/~/media/research/files/papers/2013/04/sunni%20shia%20abdo/sunni%20shia%20abdo.

15. See Arang Keshavarzian, "Contestation without Democracy: Elite Fragmentation in Iran." In *Authoritarianism in the Middle East*, edited by Marsha Priepstein Posusney and Michele Penner Angrist (Boulder: Lynne Rienner, 2005), 63–88.

16. Kazem Alamdardi puts it well: "The political structure of the IRI is . . . built on many independent, rival, parallel columns of power that hold the system together . . . Paradoxical actions of numerous groups holding various centres of power and resources bring conflicts and disorder . . . but at the same time the diversified and vast engagement of various groups bring internal collaboration that resists the intrusion of political outsiders." See his "The Power Structure of the Islamic Republic of Iran," 1299.

17. The chapters by Payam Mohseni and Kevan Harris illustrate this fluidity and its advantages for the ruling elite. But at times this fluidity has been undercut by the increasing saliency of the ideological divide. Whether a pact can be negotiated when elemental political cleavages prevail is a fundamental question.

18. "My emphatic counsel to the armed forces is to observe and abide by the military rule of non-involvement in politics. Do not join any political party, group or faction. No military man, security policeman, no Revolutionary Guard or Basij may enter into politics. Stay away from politics and you'll be able to preserve and maintain your military prowess and be immune to internal division and dispute. Military commanders must forbid entrance into political ties by the men under their command." http://www.alseraj.net/maktaba/kotob/english /Miscellaneousbooks/LastwillofImamKhomeini/occasion/ertehal/english/will/lmnew2 .htm.

19. According to former interior minister Ali-Akbar Nateq Nuri, the Supreme National Security Council has made clear distinctions among four categories of social disturbances: protest, riot, revolt, and crisis. Each of these situations also have a clear line of command with the police force in command in dealing with protests, riots, and even revolts, although in the latter category both the Basij and IRGC forces can come in for assistance. In a crisis situation, however, the IRGC will take command and all other forces must operate under its direction. Morteza Mirdar, ed., *Khaterat-e hojjatoleslam valmoslemin ali-akbar nateq nuri* (Memoirs of hojjatoleslam valmoslemin ali-akbar nateq nuri), Vol. 2 (Tehran: Markaz-e Asnad-e Enqelab-e Eslami, 1384/2005), 275.

20. Chapter III of the Constitution, which entails principles 19 to 55, is titled "People's Rights" and includes clauses that are absolute, such as prohibitions against torture and prosecution based on one's beliefs, while other rights such as freedom of press and association are guaranteed so long as they do not undermine "Islamic principles."

21. Asghar Schirazi, *The Constitution of Iran: Politics and the State in the Islamic Republic of Iran* (London: Tauris, 1997).

22. See Brumberg, *Reinventing Khomeini*, 135.

23. Article 110.

24. Farideh Farhi, "The Assembly of Experts," US Institute of Peace, *The Iran Primer*, http://iranprimer.usip.org/resource/assembly-experts.

25. Mehdi Moslem, *Factional Politics in Post-Khomeini Iran* (Syracuse, NY: Syracuse University Press, 2002), 142–179.

26. See Brumberg, *Reinventing Khomeini*, 172–184. Nearly one third of the 3,150 candidates were rejected, including 39 incumbents, most of them linked to the Islamic Left. Hashemi Rafsanjani supported this effort because he resented the Islamic Left's mobilization against his pro-market reform program.

27. The IRGC commander's letter can be found at http://www.princeton.edu/irandata portal/laws/proclamations/icrg-letter/ICRG_Letter_Persian.pdf. The translation is at http://www.princeton.edu/irandataportal/laws/proclamations/icrg-letter/.

28. In the 2008 Majles election, the percentage of disqualified registrants was even higher, reaching 41 percent.

29. See Wehrey et al., *The Rise of the Pasdaran*, 32–34.

30. Farideh Farhi, "Iran's Security Outlook." *MERIP Online*, July 9, 2007. http://www.merip.org/mero/mero070907.

31. Because of the boycott, the council ended up not using its vetting powers extensively and only disqualified 15 percent of the candidates who chose to run.

32. The council disqualified 41 and 36 percent of candidates respectively in the 2008 and 2012 parliamentary elections. For data regarding Iran elections, see Princeton University's Iran Data Portal: http://www.princeton.edu/irandataportal/elections/.

33. See Jonathan Lyons, "New Justice Chief Faces Reform Battle," *The Iranian*, September 9, 1999. http://iranian.com/News/1999/September/chief.html.

34. See "Iran's Judiciary Chief, Ayatollah Shahroudi Admits Human Rights Violations in Iran," *Payvand*, May 6, 2005. http://www.payvand.com/news/05/may/1044.html. On the Iranian Bar Association, see "Disqualification of Lawyers and the Iranian Bar Association's Demise: An Interview with Abdolsamad Khorramshahi, International Campaign for Human Rights in Iran, http://www.iranhumanrights.org/2010/03/disqualification-of-lawyers-and -iranian-bar-associations-demise-an-interview-with-abdolsamad-khorramshahi/.

35. See Saeid Golkar, "The Ideological-Political Training of Iran's Basij," *Middle East Brief*, no. 44 (September 2010). http://www.brandeis.edu/crown/publications/meb/MEB44.pdf.

36. Rafsanjani's Friday Prayers Sermon, July 2009. http://www.cfr.org/iran/rafsanjanis -friday-prayers-sermon-july-2009/p19877.

37. Ibid.

38. Guillermo O'Donnell, "Tensions in the Bureaucratic-Authoritarian State and the Question of Democracy." In *The New Authoritarianism in Latin America*, edited by David Collier (Princeton, NJ: Princeton University Press, 1980), 285–318; Adam Przeworski, "Some Problems in the Study of the Transition to Democracy." In *Transitions from Authoritarian Rule: Comparative Perspectives*, edited by Guillermo O'Donnell et al. (Baltimore: Johns Hopkins University Press, 1986), 47–63.

39. The Islamic Republic has had an election almost every year since its inception, requiring massive mobilization of resources to conduct them. But beginning with the 2013 elections, the electoral process has shifted to a two-year system in which presidential and provincial council elections are held jointly while elections for Parliament and Council of Experts will also be held jointly.

PART I

THE CONTESTED TERRAIN

1 Factionalism, Privatization, and the Political Economy of Regime Transformation

Payam Mohseni

THE CONTESTED IRANIAN presidential election of 2009—which ignited the most serious challenge to the authority of the Islamic Republic since the revolution—seemed to be a turning point in Iranian politics. The violent repression of the Green Movement by the coercive forces of the state and the timely inauguration of President Mahmud Ahmadinejad to his second term in the presidency were ominous signs of a closing of the Iranian regime and a turn toward military dictatorship.[1] The expanding role of the Islamic Revolution's Guard Corps (IRGC) in the economic and political realms, the strengthening of the Supreme Leader's power and position, and the sidelining of the reformists from the ruling elite all pointed to a fundamental change in the nature of the regime. Indeed, that US Secretary of State Hillary Clinton declared Iran to be "morphing into" a dictatorship[2] demonstrates the significance of this issue for both contemporary world affairs and domestic Iranian politics, presenting a bleak image of the future evolution of its political system. The specter of Iranian dictatorship thus came to loom prominently in both Western policy and academic circles alike.

The unexpected election of moderate candidate Hassan Rouhani to the presidency in June 2013, however, has brought this thesis under serious question. Despite the strength and attraction that such a view may have held earlier, these striking developments did not necessarily add up to a reworking of the logic of the political system as was commonly assumed. While there is no doubt that we were witnessing a transformation in the political order of the country, the same pieces of evidence pointing to Iranian dictatorship simultaneously presented a completely different image of the state of Iranian affairs. The ongoing shifts and changes begun with the election of Ahmadinejad in 2005 were instead internal transformations within the confines of the same system of multiple contentious power centers that had been established with the revolution. In other words, to recognize institutional modifications and shifts in power within the regime is one thing—and to argue that these institutional alterations produce a change of regime type to dictatorship is another. To avoid conflating these two seemingly similar—yet vastly different—processes, our knowledge of the precise institutional sites of transformation and the exact mechanics by which these changes have been occurring within the Iranian regime needs to be more fully developed.

This chapter explores the complexity of these processes and assesses the degree of change and continuity in the Iranian political system in light of the tumultuous events unfolding since 2009. Why have elite power relations in Iran been unsettled, and what is the impact of these factional fluctuations of power and processes of change on the institutional structure of the Iranian regime itself? It is critical to ask whether the manner by which institutional alteration occurs within the regime was conducive to the long-term monopolization of power by a single political faction. If so, has the multifactional and competitive nature of the regime been replaced by one of dictatorship, as may have appeared to be the case? Or, is the regime's system of elite conflict management and institutional restraint a durable feature that will persist in the foreseeable future?

A central issue that may illuminate these political trends is the country's shift toward economic privatization, which represents the most important case of strategic institutional change undertaken since the 1979 revolution. My analysis, accordingly, does not involve an examination of the purely economic dimension or material result of privatization per se but rather the intricate and highly contentious policy making and implementation stages that constitute its political facet. Privatization, in other words, allows me to explore the built-in regime mechanisms that produce institutional change in the country—to fully expose the impact of the institutional architecture of the Iranian political system on elite contestation. Such a study will increase our understanding of how the regime's institutions function and will delineate the manner by which the power of political factions guides and influences policy. This dynamic can be very revealing—both in terms of the sources and sites of elite contestation as well as the institutional restraints placed on elite power struggles. It will show us the contours and limits of transformation within the Iranian political system.

This analysis focuses on two levels: the regime's internal factional composition and its external institutional framework. These levels reflect Iran's political party capacity and its state institutional capacity, respectively—the two dimensions that political scientists argue must be addressed in order to assess the capability of state elites to monopolize power and construct dictatorship.[3] Iran's factionalized political scene and high degree of regime checks and balances safeguard not only the competitive and inclusive nature of the Iranian regime but also the system's adeptness in restraining and inhibiting monopolistic drives for power by any one faction. In other words, the regime legacy of elite conflict management via multiple institutionally embedded power centers has endured, and it will likely define the parameters of Iranian politics for years to come. Moreover, my analysis of institutional change and factional contestation in the Iranian privatization program reveals that—far from being an effort to construct dictatorship—the rise of Mahmud Ahmadinejad and the theocratic hard-liners represents a systemic move for survival by the revolutionary and clerical power base of the regime that counterintuitively integrates them more fully within the multifactional order of power. The economic privatization policies and "China model" of development pushed by other regime elites—particularly former president and current chair of the Expediency Council Akbar Hashemi Rafsanjani—were viewed as existential threats that had to be resisted but yet, at the same time, adapted to. The politics of privatization thus unleashed serious challenges to the political and economic order of the country—the reverberations of which continue to this day.

The transformation we are witnessing in Iran therefore stems from a reworking of the Islamic Republic's factional architecture rather than its institutional metamorphosis to dictatorship. In a comparative perspective, unlike many Arab countries that have witnessed regime-opposition dynamics of street mobilization with the Arab Spring, the contentious politics of the 2009 Iranian elections represented a fierce intraregime elite struggle over the nature of the country's shifting economic order that spurred factional mobilization. The political uncertainty that pervades the factional scene today is thus a result of the relatively weakening power of old-guard political elites and the opening of regime gateways to the incorporation of new and rising social forces. The ensuing expansion and growth of the ruling elite circle of power will simultaneously reshape and transform the power dynamics and relationships among the country's power holders. In this fluid and competitive environment, the prospects of greater political accommodation of multiple social forces within the current regime will be more probable given a conducive international environment—a conclusion that has only been further confirmed by the election of Rouhani to office.

The Iranian Political System

Iran's Architecture of Power

Before delving into an examination of the factional struggle over economic privatization, I begin with a brief overview of the Iranian political system in order to introduce the larger theoretical framework guiding this analysis. The Islamic Republic of Iran is a quintessential hybrid regime whose institutional structure spans the blurred boundary between democracy and dictatorship. Political scientists have defined this regime category as any political system that resists classification as either a democratic or authoritarian regime by standard definitions, and it has received a diverse set of labels ranging from "illiberal democracy" and "semidemocracy" all the way to "semiauthoritarian" and "competitive authoritarian" regimes.[4] Iran is classified as a hybrid regime because it holds popular competitive elections for both the executive and the legislature and has been witness to frequent turnover in both branches of government—a condition that is starkly absent in dictatorial regimes. At the same time, however, it is not a democracy because of the poor enforcement of individual civil liberties and the intrusive role of religious authorities who interfere in democratic processes of decision making.[5] The Guardian Council, for example, is an Iranian body charged with vetting parliamentary laws that are deemed in violation of Islamic law and with assessing the qualifications of individuals running for political office.

Institutionally, however, Iran is particularly striking not just because it is the world's only electoral theocracy but because of the high degree of checks and balances its regime architecture provides. Its structure is characterized by many parallel institutions that accommodate multiple overlapping power centers—both institutional and factional—within the regime. It is composed, more precisely, of the three executive, legislative, and judicial branches of government rooted in Western constitutional design as well as unique political bodies including the Guardian Council, the Expediency Discernment Council of the System (Expediency Council for short), the Council of Experts, and the position of the Supreme Leader. Iran's institutional architecture contains many decision-making centers that share the responsibility of state policy formulation directly or indirectly—significantly more so than many other autocratic regimes.

These various regime bodies act as veto players, which are "individual or collective actors whose agreement is necessary for a change of the status quo."[6] In the United States, for example, the President, Congress, and the Supreme Court each represent a veto player, as they can effectively block or impede the decisions of another branch of government. Institutional checks and balances indicate the degree to which power is distributed in a political system. States with more veto players have stronger checks and balances that can prevent the monopolization of power in the hands of a single group and that impede significant institutional modifications.

Iran's complex and multifaceted regime architecture comprising many veto players thus generates a robust system of institutional checks and balances. Undertaking major institutional change in Iran is time- and cost-intensive because of the multiple channels by which policy can be blocked. A single group or faction cannot easily alter the institutional structures or even major policies of the regime. Iran's seemingly "stubborn" yet durable policy in the nuclear field and the difficulty facing Western states in negotiating with the Islamic Republic is another illustrative example of the thorny consequences posed by multiple veto players that represent different elite power centers. There is always another veto-playing institution and center of power blocking abrupt and significant regime alterations or policy U-turns. If significant change does come about—as is the case with privatization—it is a long, conflict-ridden process that includes the input and acquiescence of most if not all major political Iranian factions and institutions. The prospects of dictatorship are therefore much weaker for a regime like that in Iran.

The most important veto player, and the ultimate arbitrator, is the position of the Supreme Leader. In other words, this one veto right is more significant than all the others. The minimum requirement to partake in the political game or the "authoritarian bargain" of the Islamic Republic is to accept the legitimacy of this supreme veto player—the fundamental position of the *velayat-e faqih*. This veto power, however, does not mean that the Supreme Leader can single-handedly dictate all policy and actively undertake day-to-day governance. Rather, the Leader resolves elite conflict between other veto players and balances the interests of different political groups within the regime.

Such a balancing act, however, does not preordain or verify that there is a natural equilibrium of factional power within the political system. Factional power and positions constantly shift and fluctuate in the regime, with some groups becoming more ascendant than others at different times. Rather, the balancing role of the Leader means that the ultimate veto player should both prevent any one group from attaining political hegemony over government institutions for an extended period of time and ensure the meaningful incorporation of multiple voices and interests in the policy-making process of the state. Policy making, in other words, should not be a unilateral affair. To provide further explanation, we must first understand the nature of Iranian political factions and the history of electoral turnover and factional inclusion in the Islamic Republic prior to the 2009 election.

The Fluidity of Iranian Politics

In contrast to its vigorous system of checks and balances, Iran has a weak—if not nonexistent—political party system. Instead, the Iranian political landscape contains a disarray of associations, parties, and individuals loosely affiliated over ideological and socioeconomic issues in the form of factions. The absence of Iranian party capacity is an important factor inhibiting the regime's move toward dictatorship. No single political group in the country can monopolize power and order political rule. As a power ascends, other factions form alliances to upend the other's growing ambitions, while factions themselves also splinter internally and dissolve in light of the changing political issues of the day and shifting conflicts of interest. And the fate of factional struggles is even more unpredictable given the uncertainty of competitive elections and popular input. The fluid condition makes constructing a dictatorship in Iran like building a house on quicksand.

Indeed, a hegemonic political party is often the defining feature of modern dictatorial regimes, as it provides an effective and durable means of elite management with which dictators can organize their rule.[7] It limits competitive participation in the electoral arena and streamlines decision making among a like-minded cadre of ruling officials.[8] Mexico's Institutional Revolutionary Party (PRI), the Nazi Party in Germany, and the Communist Party of the Soviet Union and that of China are all examples of party rule.

With the revolution of 1979, Iran interestingly tried its hand in creating just such a ruling party, the Islamic Republic Party (IRP), to dominate the political scene like other classic dictatorships, but the attempt quickly failed. The IRP initially provided the clergy with an effective vehicle to sideline liberal and Marxist forces from the political scene and to consolidate the revolution in the form of a theocracy. The IRP, however, was disbanded without heavy popular opposition or violence in 1987, with only eight years of rule. Intraparty elite conflicts and factional bickering—with stark policy disagreements on various political, economic, and even cultural issues—resulted in constant political deadlock and forced then Supreme Leader Ayatollah Ruhollah Khomeini to frequently intervene. In other words, the absence of a clear programmatic ideology and political platform within the party and even among the revolutionary clergy—a condition that remains true up to the present day—prevented a totalitarian ordering of power. In stark contrast to the experience of other modern revolutions,[9] no group of Iranian elites had the power, authority, or institutional capacity to eliminate their rivals irrespective of their desire to do so.

The era of relatively open and competitive factional politics—exemplary of the hybrid nature of the regime—was consequently unleashed with the party's abolishment in 1987. Since that time, factional formations have largely taken shape according to the two most salient dimensions of Iranian politics: the theocratic-republican regime divide and the left-right economic scale. The first dimension refers to the primary source of legitimacy for the regime, particularly the institution of the Supreme Leader—the guardianship of the jurisprudent, *velayat-e faqih*. The theocrats argue that this type of rule and guardianship is divinely ordained. While popular sentiment and approval is important to varying degrees, ultimately the power and decision rests with God and not with the people. For the republican factions, however, the ultimate authority rests squarely with the people. If the Islamic institutions of the regime and the leadership are legitimate, they are so because of popular approval and belief in them. Republicans, as a result, aim to reform the current Islamic system from within to make it more accountable to the people.

While the first dimension is unique to the Islamic Republic of Iran, the second left-right economic dimension is a standard political measurement of elite economic preferences across the world. In Iran, those on the left generally support the state's redistribution of wealth and hold a critical view of capitalism, particularly neo-liberal economic policies such as free trade and privatization, to various degrees. In contrast, those on the right support a free market, a capitalist economy, and a smaller and less interventionist state. Economic variance within the right usually revolves around the type of economic policy instruments advocated and the precise function of the state itself—some support state developmental policies along the lines of the World Bank and International Monetary Fund (IMF) while others want a more minimalist state with a traditional economy of Islamic charities linked with private businesses.

These two dimensions accordingly form the conceptual and theoretical space for classifying four political positions: the theocratic right, the republican right, the theocratic left, and the republican left (see figure 1.1). The actors and factions working within the regime navigate and maneuver across these four fields. While shifts in individual positions are common over time, four factions largely occupy each of the quadrants identified in the figure. The theocratic right mainly consists of the *Bazaari* merchants and the traditional clergy who drove the revolution and supported the creation of an Islamic state. Parliament Speaker Ali Larijani, former judiciary chief Ayatollah Mahmud Hashemi Shahrudi, and the deceased chair of the Council of Experts Mohammad-Reza Ayatollah Mahdavi Kani represent important figures within this camp. Important associations include the Society of Combatant Clergy (*Jame'eh-ye Rohaniyat-e Mobarez*), the Islamic Coalition Party (*Hezb-e Motalefeh-ye Eslami*), and the Society of Qom Seminary Teachers (*Jame'eh-ye Modarresin-e Howzeh-ye Elmiyyeh-ye Qom*). And noteworthy newspapers are *Resalat*, *Quds*, and *Jomhuri-ye Eslami*.

In contrast to the theocratic right, the theocratic left favors state intervention in the economy to promote social justice and equal welfare. They hold strong anticapitalist views, believing Islam and capitalism to be antithetical, and look

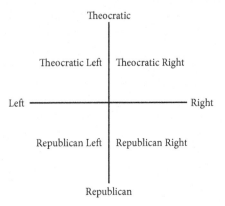

Figure 1.1 Classification of political factions in the Islamic Republic of Iran

upon the nouveau riche elite produced by the Islamic Republic with suspicion. Many of the supporters of the faction include war veterans, members of the Basij and Islamic Revolutionary Guards, the urban poor and lower-middle classes, and the provincial classes. President Ahmadinejad, for example, belongs to this faction. Important associations and parties include the Developers of Islamic Iran (*Abadgaran-e Iran-e Eslami*), the Supporters of Hezbollah (*Ansar-e Hezbollah*), the Society of War Veterans (*Jame'eh-ye Issargaran*), and the University Students' Basij (*Daneshjuyan-e Basiji*). Representative publications have included *Keyhan*, *Shalamcheh*, *Sobh*, and *Vatan-e Emruz*.

The republican right is the main advocate of the "China model" for Iran, and their discourse primarily deals with modernization and economic growth rather than social justice. Supporters of this faction mostly include Western-educated technocrats as well as *Bazaari* merchants and capitalists loosely affiliated around Akbar Hashemi Rafsanjani, president from 1989 to 1996 and the chairman of the Expediency Discernment Council of the System, a body charged with mediating conflict between the Guardian Council and Parliament as well as drawing macro policy proposals for the state. Other influential figures, however, include Mohsen Rezaei and Hassan Rouhani. The major parties of this faction are the Executives of Construction Party (*Hezb-e Kargozaran-e Sazandegi*), the Islamic Work Party (*Hezb-e Eslami-ye Kar*), and the Moderation and Development Party (*Hezb-e E'tedal va Tose'eh*). Important media outlets include *Kargozaran*, *Ettela'at*, and *Shahrvand*.

Out of all the factions, the republican left has undergone the most significant ideological change throughout the course of the revolution—slowly exchanging their revolutionary anticapitalist and anti-Western ideology for international political détente, liberal economics, and democracy. Referring to figure 1.1, the elites of the republican left faction have largely shifted right on the left-right economic continuum toward the republican right quadrant in the 1990s, thus largely abandoning the republican left conceptual space—a significant phenomenon with far-reaching implications for the political scene, as will be described later. Important figures of this faction include former president Mohammad Khatami, former parliamentary speaker Mehdi Karrubi, and former prime minister Mir-Hossein Mussavi. Important social bases of the republican left, particularly during the reform period of former president Mohammad Khatami, can be found in the urban middle classes, more secular-minded university students and intellectuals, and women's rights groups. The faction comprises associations and parties, some currently banned, such as the Mojahedin of Islamic Revolution (*Mojahedin-e Enqelab-e Eslami*), the Association of Combatant Clergy (*Majma'-e Rohani-yun-e Mobarez*), the Office for the Consolidation of Unity (*Daftar-e Tahkim-e Vahdat*), the National Trust Party (*Hezb-e E'temad-e Melli*), and Islamic Iran's

Participation Front (*Hezb-e Mosharekat-e Iran-e Eslami*). Significant publications have included *Aftab-e Yazd, E'temad-e Melli, Mardomsalari, Shargh,* and *Asr-e Ma.*

In the 1980s, disagreements between the republican left and the theocratic right factions led to serious tensions within the Islamic Republic Party and were an important reason why the party was disbanded. One of the main sources of contention concerned land reform, as then prime minister Mussavi of the republican left supported the cause, while others including members of the Guardian Council, dominated by the theocratic right, opposed it. Figure 1.2 presents the factional composition of the regime under formal party rule.

In the post-IRP era, Iranian factions have coalesced in different ways—because of electoral outcomes and frequent turnover—to form tactical political alliances for controlling the regime. These alliances distinguish three distinctive periods of political rule in the country. The first represents the alliance of the right between the theocratic right and the republican right from 1989 to 1996, depicted in figure 1.3. Under the revised constitution ending the state's semipresidential system, the victory of Hashemi Rafsanjani's election to the presidency marked an electoral turnover in which the executive switched hands from the republican left, with Mussavi, to the republican right. This event was followed by the 1992 parliamentary election changing the republican left–dominated Majles to one controlled by the theocratic right. Accordingly, Ali-Akbar Nateq Nuri replaced Mehdi Karrubi as the new speaker of Parliament.

The next period of rule was marked by the alliance of the republicans, from 1997 to 2004. Figure 1.4 illustrates this coalition, which has been broadly referred to as the reformists. The surprise electoral victory of Khatami on the republican

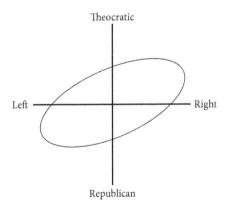

Figure 1.2 Factional alliance from 1980 to 1988 in the Islamic Republic of Iran

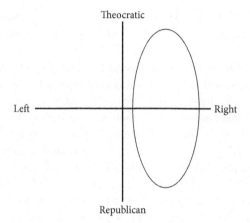

Figure 1.3 Alliance of the theocratic right and the republican right from 1989 to 1996

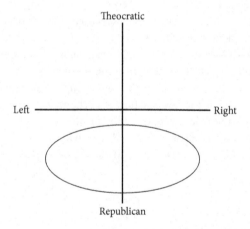

Figure 1.4 Alliance of the republican left and the republican right from 1997 to 2004

left to the executive in 1997 and the defeat of Nateq Nuri marked a significant setback for the theocratic right, as it had hoped to capture the executive branch. The republican right formed an alliance with the republican left prior to the election and was critical for mobilizing institutional and popular support for Khatami's candidacy against the looming threat of, as Sa'id Hajjarian put it, the "monopolization of power" in the hands of the theocratic right.[10] Later, in 2000, the theocratic right's grip on power was even further weakened by the electoral victory of the republican left to the legislature and the return of Karrubi as head of Parliament.

The alliance of the theocrats represents the current period of rule that began in 2004 and lasts to this day. Electoral challenge to the republicans had taken shape in an unlikely political group—the theocratic left faction, which had been mostly absent from formal state politics since the revolution. The legislative turnover in 2004 gave control of the Majles to this group, as represented by the new head of parliament, Gholam-Ali Haddad Adel. And in the following year, the shocking election of President Mahmud Ahmadinejad on the theocratic left over Hashemi Rafsanjani on the republican right represented another turnover, thus largely ending the republican left's prominent position within the republican institutions of the regime once more. Figure 1.5 depicts the current period's theocratic alliance, members of which commonly refer to themselves as principlists (*usulgarayan*), or those committed to the principles of Islam and the revolution. Despite the heavy strains and disagreements within this alliance and the legislative shift to the theocratic right in the 2008 legislative election, placing Ali Larijani as the head of Parliament, the theocratic factions continue to share in the governance of the regime today.

Thus, political power has never been monopolized by a single political faction in the history of the regime. While the factional composition of the state fluctuates, political authority has never been narrowed to the exclusion of all but one group over an extended period. Multiple power centers have composed and shared in the elected institutions of the state. Second, power has never remained even in the hands of a single alliance of factions. Frequent electoral turnover and the checks and balances of the regime disrupt the attempts of any one faction to consolidate their rule. The initial alliance between the theocratic right and

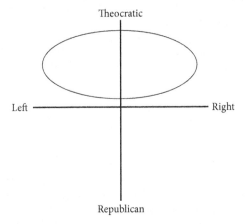

Figure 1.5 Alliance of the theocratic left and the theocratic right from 2004

republican left within the Islamic Republic Party shifted to an alliance of the right (theocratic and republican right) from 1989 to 1996, and then to the republicans (republican left and right) from 1997 to 2003, and finally to the theocrats (theocratic left and right) from 2005 up to the present. These trends highlight the weak capacity of Iranian political parties for eliminating their rivals and seizing control of the state. They further demonstrate the Iranian system's high degree of elite inclusion and power-sharing accommodation within the different veto-playing institutions of the regime, a characteristic that is minimal in dictatorships where hegemonic parties and governing cliques rule in a single-handed fashion over an extended period.

These conditions—strong checks and balances and weak party capacity—reveal two indicators that can be used to determine whether the Iranian regime has qualitatively changed. The first indicator is electoral turnover and divided government, which has been an important element of the hybrid nature of the Iranian political system prior to the 2009 election and indicative of its weak party capacity. Turnover and/or divided government should therefore continue to occur in the post-2009 period to verify that the regime remains a hybrid and that no single faction has monopolized the playing field. The second indicator is the meaningful impact of multiple political factions on the policy-making process of the state, a condition that should reflect the continued importance of the system's strong checks and balances. Policy making should not be a single-handed affair, and the input and contestation of multiple groups must be evident in the formulation of policy. The election of Rouhani in 2013 satisfies the first element, as it signified a major electoral turnover in the executive branch and the prospect for a new center and right-of-center alliance in the Iranian political scene following the collapse of the alliance of the theocrats. In addition, while it may be too early to authoritatively verify the second indicator, the nexus of policy making is likely to shift given the recent election. To illustrate why this should be the case, a thorough discussion of the policy-making process and the larger transformative dynamics of the state, which have led to these shifting factional alliances of power over time, must be presented.

Privatization and the Transformation of Political Order

In order to assess the mechanisms of institutional transformation in Iran (how the regime changes) and to discover its implications for the nature of the Iranian regime (the direction in which it is changing), we need to examine how the Islamic Republic generates internal strategic change. A strategic institutional change is defined as any significant transformation made to the state apparatus in terms of its political, economic, or social institutions that result in a major reorganization and reordering of power relationships in a state. Since the institutional foundation underpinning the elite status quo is fundamentally altered, elite incentives within the political game are significantly altered as well. Such an event consequently disrupts political order and increases uncertainty over the nature of the game and the probability of political survival as an elite in the future—the condition in which Iran finds itself today.

Iran's economic privatization program not only is the most noteworthy case of strategic change since the revolution but—just as importantly for the purposes of this chapter—provides the most effective means for elucidating the intricacies of institutional change under the Islamic Republic. The reason is that, because of the economic nature of the topic, access to information is more readily available, and the prolonged period in which privatization is undertaken also allows for a richer analysis of the slow-moving transformations of elite power relations and the impact of regime institutional design on both elite struggles and political accommodation.

Privatization in Iran not only demonstrates that a move toward dictatorship is unlikely in the foreseeable future but also—counterintuitively—reveals that the growing threat of political hegemony arises from the republican right faction prior to the ascendance of the theocratic left. The republican right's drive for power is a natural consequence of its attempts to expedite economic privatization in an inhospitable veto environment. The restraining institutional mechanisms of the regime, however, disrupt such an outcome and instead produce a discordant and unorthodox privatization scheme that satisfies the interests of a broader spectrum of Iranian elites. In other words, supported by the Supreme Leader, Ahmadinejad acts as a spoiler to the specific privatization plans of Hashemi Rafsanjani while assuring theocratic buy-in into the emerging quasi-privatized economic order. The theocratic left thus restrains the republican right as it comes to be restrained itself by the multifactional regime. This outcome ensures the survival of the theocratic base of power—particularly the position of the Supreme Leader—from perceived political and economic threats without blocking privatization itself. It also unintentionally increases the level of competitiveness among the ruling elite—rather than minimizing it as commonly assumed—because of the destabilizing forces it unleashes against entrenched political networks.

The China Model vs. the Islamic-Iranian Model

At the heart of this elite struggle over the future economic order of the country lie two opposing visions of the state. On one side is the China model of development advocated by the *Kargozaran* on the republican right and spearheaded by Ayatollah Hashemi Rafsanjani. This vision embraces a developmental model on the lines of the World Bank and the International Monetary Fund (IMF) that would construct a modern, privatized, and liberal economy and would more fully integrate Iran into the larger global economy. On the other side is the Islamic-Iranian model of development promoted by the Supreme Leader, Ayatollah Khamenei. It represents an indigenous and culturally "authentic" model that would integrate Iran into the global economy on its own terms as an alternative path to prescribed economic models—particularly when, as will be explained later, Khamenei considers economic liberalism and capitalism ideological threats to the nature of theocracy and, hence, to the survival of his office. The story of privatization in Iran and the ensuing political transformation it launches thus revolves around a slowly unfolding battle between the republican right and theocratic left factions over this vision—a battle that culminates in the 2009 election. This story, even more interestingly, also hinges on the successful manner by which the institutional architecture of the regime reconciles and manages these seemingly irreconcilable forces.

Launching the Campaign

The drive to liberalize and privatize the heavily statist Iranian economy has always been an uphill battle. Entrenched institutional and ideological interests have resisted significant institutional changes to the structure of the economy. The state's domination of the economy was enshrined in the Islamic regime's Constitution within Article 44, giving the state formal control of important organizations, including utilities, banks, industries, mines, and insurance companies. Article 44 therefore underpinned and reinforced the junction of these structural and ideational forces, presenting very significant impediments to the state's economic privatization. Any successful attempt at privatization—and the construction of a capitalist economic order—had to involve constitutional revision.

Yet changing a strong ideationally and structurally rooted institution in the context of many veto players is a formidable task in Iran—a fact made evident by the extended and drawn-out process of its privatization program. Privatization officially began after the end of the Iran-Iraq War with the First Five-Year Economic Development plan of 1989 to 1994 under the Hashemi Rafsanjani administration. The planned liberalization of the Iranian economy, of which privatization was seen as a necessary component, was viewed with suspicion and apprehension by the theocrats—particularly by the Supreme Leader—because he believed that it advanced the plans of the World Bank and the IMF, considered the cornerstones of the imperialistic world economy.

The rift between Khamenei and Hashemi Rafsanjani was thus set in place as their different visions for the development of the country collided. But Khamenei also sensed the political threat that the increasing power and political reach of Rafsanjani began posing as he drove to implement his goals. As a result of these factors, the Supreme Leader advanced and strengthened the theocratic left faction and his own position of power in order to balance the republican right. Khamenei's criticisms of Hashemi Rafsanjani's reconstruction plans following the war and his emphasis on social justice and revolutionary Islamic values were precisely the words that members of the theocratic left faction, such as the Basijis, needed to hear. These ideals would eventually form an important component of the theocratic left discourse and that of the Islamic-Iranian model of development—the language that Ahmadinejad would eventually advance.

Factional Polarization

In order to efficiently legislate and execute its economic plans, the *Kargozaran* would need to limit oppositional voices to its economic agenda within the regime—in short, the republican right had to prevent different veto players from vetoing its policies. Accordingly, this faction would need to either shut out other groups from the main institutions of the state or capture those institutions to push through strategic change—both of which it tried and failed. These efforts— to expand political power in order to implement economic privatization—and the resulting backlash it created from the theocratic left resulted in the polarization of the factional scene by 2004.

Beginning with the 1992 parliamentary election, in the post–cold war context after the collapse of the Soviet Union, the political maneuvering of the republican right was instrumental in the massive disqualification of the republican left from the political scene of the country with the aid of the theocratic right—specifically due to republican left criticisms of the right's economic policies.[11] The new theocratic right parliament that came to power ironically, however, also began to pose a challenge to Rafsanjani's developmentalist economic plans.

Faced with a less than amiable partner, by the mid-1990s, the republican right looked elsewhere for making a new political pact and found the newly stylized republican left faction. Following their disqualification with the 1992 parliamentary elections, the republican left underwent a fundamental rethinking of its socioeconomic and political positions in two areas.[12] The first involved new support for individual civil rights, the development of civil society, and the advancement of democratic forms of rule. The second fundamental change was a shift of belief in a state economy to a market economy. Since the economic policies of the Hashemi Rafsanjani administration were being circumscribed by the theocratic right, the grounds became suitable for the forging of a new political partnership. Accepting liberal economics, in other words, would be the surest way for the republican left to gain the needed institutional support to rejoin the system.

The election of Khatami to office, therefore, while unexpected and reflective of public support for republican left values, ensured the persistence of republican right economic policies in state planning as members of the *Kargozaran* were appointed to the new administration's economic team. Significant advances were accordingly made to the privatization policies of the state under the Khatami administration, particularly under the Third Five-Year Economic Development Plan (2000–2005) when the theocratic right also lost control of Parliament to the republican left in 2000—placing the executive and legislative branches, as well as the Expediency Council, squarely behind the privatization program. The combined sales revenue accruing from the privatization drive in 2003 and 2004 alone, for example, was more than the entire sales revenue gathered between 1991 and 2002.[13]

These shifting dynamics, however, also paved the way for the rise of the theocratic left. While the republican left's move to the right bolstered the position of the republican right in the economic arena, it proved to be a fatal mistake, as the move simultaneously left a vacuum of power on the economic left of the Iranian political scene—a vacuum that the theocratic left would eventually fill. With the support of Ayatollah Khamenei, the theocratic left would transform into a major political force in Iranian politics in the new century, and it would ride the wave of rural uprising, representing the shifting structure of power within Iranian society.[14] According to Samuel Huntington, this phenomenon refers to a stage in the economic development of a country in which the provincial classes rise up against the unequal power and privileges of the elites in the capital city with the help of a section of the capital elite—a reaction against the uneven economic development of capitalist growth in developing countries. The foundational rural uprising in Iran provided the necessary structural support for the empowerment of the theocratic left—especially for a populist such as Ahmadinejad—and the weakening political grip of old-guard republican and theocratic right factions.

Institutional Collision

The Iranian parliamentary election in 2004—which brought the theocratic left to power for the first time since the revolution—thus seemingly produced a sea change in the state's economic development and restructuring policies. It also produced one of the most acute instances of factional in-fighting and institutional stalemate in the history of the Islamic Republic. With the republican left Sixth Majles still in session, the Guardian Council issued a major ruling that would seriously impede the country's privatization plans: it deemed the ceding of state-owned banks and insurance companies to the private sector unconstitutional. And within a few months of starting its formal work, the theocratic left Parliament surprisingly suspended the entire privatization scheme of the country—making any privatization sales by President Khatami illegal. Simultaneously, each case of foreign economic investment was obliged to receive parliamentary approval by a deal-by-deal basis—again limiting the scope of executive discretion. The theocratic left was thus actively using its newfound veto power to stop the republican right's economic plans.

In an unprecedented move, however, Hashemi Rafsanjani, as head of the Expediency Council, entered the political scene to authorize Khatami to ignore Parliament, continue with privatization, and independently ink foreign economic deals without parliamentary review.[15] The Expediency Council also publicly presented a new interpretation of the Constitution—without the approval of the Supreme Leader as necessary—to bolster Khatami's position in executing privatization and legalize the privatization of all major industries and banks.[16] Ironically, the republican right faction attempted to circumvent the main republican institution of the regime—Parliament—in order to execute its economic plans. The Expediency Council, moreover, vetoed the Majles when it was the Guardian Council that was charged with a veto decision.

The privatization policy-making process led to political deadlock, as the Majles and Guardian Council were controlled by the theocrats, and the republicans controlled the presidency and the Expediency Council. With public factional conflict quickly escalating to unprecedented levels, Ayatollah Khamenei intervened to mediate the dispute. He called for a middle approach that supported privatization but also deemed impermissible "any capitalist economic approach" regarding it.[17] While supporting the general process of privatization, as the republican right wanted, Khamenei thus strengthened the position of the theocratic left Parliament—halting privatization and blocking the Expediency Council. His concern was based in part on the weak position of the Iranian private sector in competing with foreign firms but also on foreign purchases of Iranian assets that could have national security implications, such as those involved in the state telecommunications sector. His criticism of a capitalist approach to privatization, however, also sheds light on another of his important concerns over the issue of privatization—that a liberal economic order would be antithetical to Islamic governance and was viewed with suspicion as a step toward regime change or, at a minimum, the weakening of the *velayat-e faqih*.

But how can economic privatization be undertaken without a capitalist approach? What did the Supreme Leader mean? For Khamenei, the answer lay in the Islamic-Iranian model of development—theoretically highlighting why the ideological and cultural position of the theocrats became important at this critical juncture of strategic institutional change. While all political factions now paid lip service to the term "privatization" with the Leader's cue, a common conceptual consensus of the term did not exist between them, thus opening the ideational space for discursive contestation. Within this context, Khamenei

supported the development of an ideological basis to stem the economic and political agenda of the republican factions who were promoting neo-liberal economic orthodoxy and were perceivably threatening theocratic rule. Accordingly,
in 2004, at the height of institutional stalemate over privatization within the regime, Khamenei explained his disdain of the republican right's China model of
development and emphasized the need to develop alternative Islamic models of
development:

> What type of development are we after? This is a critical point in the current
> economic and non-economic discussions underway. Some are after throwing
> out words and detracting the minds of people from critical issues: the China
> model, the Japanese model, the whatever model. The model of development
> in the Islamic Republic accords with the culture, history, heritage and beliefs
> and faith of this people; a completely indigenous model derived from the Ira-
> nian nation itself. One must not copy anyplace; not from the World Bank; not
> from the International Monetary Fund; not from this country on the left, not
> from that country on the right; each place has its own needs. There is a differ-
> ence between using others' experiences and following imposed, dictated and
> mostly outdated models. . . . One must learn from the experiences and knowl-
> edge of others, but the method and model chosen must be completely local.[18]

Article 44 and the Forging of a New Economic Path

Yet, given that an Islamic-Iranian model of development has never been fully
theoretically expounded, privatization moves forward in an ad hoc fashion due
to the intersecting features of the Iranian political landscape. In other words,
the Islamic-Iranian model in its current application is really a standard developmentalist model but only disfigured and revised as it passes through the
system's veto-heavy policy-making channels. Numerous Iranian veto players
create a strong impediment to abrupt, drastic, and unilateral forms of institutional change by incorporating multiple power-wielding partners representative
of eclectic viewpoints in the decision-making process of the state. Competitive
consensus building—rather than single-handed rule—therefore characterizes
the Iranian regime's modus operandi. It is competitive because of the way factions struggle with one another in order to shape the content of policy, leading to
ad hoc and hodge-podge constructions. It is also consensus-based, however, not
because of the manner by which policy is formulated but rather because the final
policy produced is viewed as a consensus by all participating factions despite its
inherent tensions.

With the republican right Expediency Council and the theocratic left Majles at odds over the path of privatization in 2004, only an authoritative revision of Article 44 could open the door to more serious privatization schemes.
Such alteration, however, did not begin at the time of the Expediency Council's

declaratory statements in support of Khatami's economic policy to privatize state banks and insurance companies. Rather, the revision process of Article 44 had begun much earlier in 1998 with the express consent of Ayatollah Khamenei.[19] Hashemi Rafsanjani's direct public support for the privatization process in 2004, however, was unprecedented and contentious not only because there had been no disagreements between the Majles and the Guardian Council to precipitate the Expediency Council's intervention, but, even more importantly, the announcement of the definitive results of the constitutional revision process was premature as it had not yet received Khamenei's formal consent within the policy-making framework established between the two bodies. In fact, earlier on the Leader had explicitly denied approval of the Expediency Council's proposal.

The revision process of Article 44 comprised three rounds of policy drafting between the Supreme Leader and the Expediency Council. More precisely, elite discussions and negotiations took place within the Macroeconomic Commission (*Commission-e Eghtesad-e Kalan*) of the Expediency Council. The commission comprised six individuals in the first round, with four on the republican right (Mohammad Hashemi Rafsanjani [Ayatollah Hashemi Rafsanjani's brother], Expediency Council Secretary Mohsen Rezaei, then oil minister Bijan Namdar Zangeneh, and Central Bank chief Mohsen Nurbakhsh) and two on the theocratic right (Morteza Nabavi and Habibollah Askarowladi). After 2003 in the second and third rounds, the commission was composed of seven individuals: three on the republican right (Mohammad Hashemi Rafsanjani, Mohsen Rezaei, Bijan Namdar Zangeneh), three on the theocratic right (Morteza Nabavi, Habibollah Askarowladi, and Mohammad Javad Iravani), and one on the republican left (Majid Ansari).

Demonstrative of the overall style of elite bargaining and pact making within the regime, a single faction never monopolizes the decision-making process—a condition ensured by the Supreme Leader, who appoints members rather inclusively, bringing a wide variety of elites into the highest organs of the state. The revision of Article 44, as a result, takes place predominantly between the republican right and theocratic right factions on one hand, and between the right factions (the Macroeconomic Commission) and the theocratic left (the Supreme Leader) on the other. As a result, while the plurality and flexibility of elite coalitions create a strong social base of support for the regime, they also generate difficulties in streamlined decision making and efficient management. The process of altering Article 44 of the Constitution took the Expediency Council nine years and sixty-five sessions to complete from 1998 to 2006.[20]

The commission's first policy report was approved by the general session of the Expediency Council in early 2002 and was forwarded to Khamenei for his review. The Supreme Leader delivered his response a year later, in early 2003—denying formal approval and asking the council to rework the plan. For the sake of clarification, it was at this stage of elite negotiations that Hashemi Rafsanjani issued a ruling over privatization in 2004 even though the proposal had not been accepted by the Supreme Leader. Khamenei's main demands consisted of incorporating greater provisions to ensure the sovereignty of the state and emphasizing and augmenting the role of the cooperative sector. The former concerns the protection of sensitive industries and entities from foreign economic control resulting from "unregulated" foreign direct investment—precisely the issue raised by the theocratic left Parliament in 2004 and subsequently opposed by the Expediency Council. The latter point on cooperatives, however, deals with the economic sectors and would become a major point of difference more generally between the theocratic left and the republican and theocratic right. While the state would be obliged to cede its economic companies and financial enterprises as part of the program, the question would devolve not to whether the state should privatize but rather which nonstate sector should be prioritized in the privatization scheme.

The Expediency Council approved and submitted its final revision to Khamenei in December 2004, to which the Leader responded by May 2005—a month before the presidential elections. An analysis of Khamenei's approvals in, additions to, and editing of the general policies of Article 44 reveals that he had agreed to the general privatization policies and framework of the Expediency Council plan. Some of the revisions, however, were significant. He had lent direct institutional support to the strengthening and expansion of the cooperative sector, along with the private sector, in the direction of the new national economy. In fact, more than half of his revisions and additions dealt with the subject of cooperatives, which was addressed in significant detail. These changes did not necessarily mean a lack of support for the private sector, as the policies drafted by the Expediency Council were primarily focused on the latter group. The alterations he made ensured a significant position for cooperatives as a counterweight to the private sector—stipulating that the share of the cooperative sector be increased to 25 percent of the entire economy. One of these policy additions, more importantly, would later pave the way for Ahmadinejad's justice shares program: Clause B-11 called for "the establishment of all-encompassing national cooperatives for covering the first three deciles of society in order to eliminate poverty."[21]

The final policy outcome, therefore, did not reflect a single-handed and narrow interpretation of economic privatization—neither by the left or the right, nor by the republicans or the theocrats. Although some financial institutions and banks were to remain under state control, privatization nevertheless had been approved with the support and inclusion of all factional preferences. Accordingly, because of the broad and multifaceted agreements made by these political institutions within an extended and conflict-ridden policymaking process, the final outcome contained multiple discordant paths and interpretations by which policy could be subsequently implemented.

Delegating Privatization

Forging an economic path and executing privatization would start another round of elite conflict immediately, as the 2005 presidential election occurred on the heels of the revision of Article 44. Whoever won the executive position would be able to steer the specific policy direction of privatization. The direct rivalry between the republican right and the theocratic left manifested itself within the electoral scene for the first time, since the second round of the presidential elections resulted in a run-off between Hashemi Rafsanjani and Ahmadinejad. This event demonstrates the slowly polarizing factional scene between these two camps in the years prior to the election and reflects the divergent viewpoints and tensions within the policy-making process of revising Article 44. Consequently, each figure would bring a different interpretation of the goals and methods of privatization within the same framework of Article 44.

The electoral victory of Ahmadinejad accordingly tilted the regime toward the theocratic left, reemphasizing the slogans of social justice (economic populism) and revolutionary values. It also represented a change of hands over the executive control of the economy after at least sixteen years of republican right rule—foreboding a serious political and economic backlash. Moreover, Ahmadinejad was highly critical of privatization and accordingly stalled on its implementation in his first year in office despite the criticisms he faced.

Eventually, however, the Supreme Leader pushed Ahmadinejad to begin privatization—demonstrating Khamenei's consent to the privatization drive that the republican right wanted but the theocratic left disdained. With the final ratification of Article 44 in the summer of 2006, the Supreme Leader issued an executive order to sell 80 percent of the state's shares in state-owned companies. Immediately after Khamenei's decree, Ahmadinejad formally requested and received the Leader's approval for the distribution of justice shares (*saham-e 'edalat*) to the poorest 30 percent of Iranian society, roughly equivalent to 21 million people—thus setting a unique path for economic privatization.

Between March 2005 and March 2009, the total value of shares ceded by the Ahmadinejad administration was 491,030 billion rials, representing 96.6 percent of the total value of shares ceded between March 1990 and March 2009—indeed, representing a significant undertaking especially for someone who wanted to block the effort.[22] This outcome demonstrates the power of the institutional architecture of the regime for finally incorporating Ahmadinejad and the theocratic left more broadly into the privatization program that they had so adamantly opposed. On the other hand, however, 342,108 billion rials—or 69.7 percent of the total value—were ceded as justice shares to the cooperative sector that was under state control, thus also representing the modifications that the theocratic left would make to the privatization scheme as they bought into the changing economic order.

Naturally, the republican right—and over time, important elements of the theocratic right—were not pleased with this privatization method. One of the primary goals of privatization was to reduce state control of the economy. While Ahmadinejad's privatization scheme transferred a significant amount of state assets to nonstate entities, the role of the state in, for example, choosing and retaining the managers and chairs of newly privatized enterprises was not reduced. Neither the private sector nor the justice share cooperative system that depended on state governance could independently manage and plan the operation of these businesses, as influence remained in state hands.[23] This situation would be even more acute given the selling of state assets—particularly for the repayment of government debt—to quasi-state public entities such as the Social Security Organization and the Retirement Fund. These entities took a 12 percent share of privatization by March 2009.

In the summer of 2007, with his ascension to the head of the Council of Experts, the body charged with monitoring and picking the Supreme Leader, Hashemi Rafsanjani upped the ante by making another contentious move. At the general session of the council, he called on its members to supervise the administration in its implementation of the general economic policies of Article 44.[24] The following evening, he held a private meeting with members of the Council of Experts in his office and again called on them to make the body "more active" in politics.[25] Given that the council had never directly been involved in daily governance and administrative politics, his statement was controversial and instigated heated debate in the country's media outlets. Moreover, a few days earlier, Hashemi Rafsanjani issued a veiled threat to Ahmadinejad that if his economic policies were not corrected, the Expediency Council had the power to interfere, as it was charged with supervising the implementation process. He had not actively intervened thus far because, as he explained, "we are not being serious on the implementation side of Article 44 in order to avoid disputes. Otherwise, there would always be quarrels if we took open positions against the government and the parliament every day for their measures against the policies."[26]

The expanding power of Hashemi Rafsanjani within the Council of Experts and his attempt to politicize the body was threatening to Khamenei, as the Leader interpreted Hashemi Rafsanjani's action not just as a warning signal to Ahmadinejad but to himself, particularly since it was obviously he who had been supporting the president and cushioning him from these pressures. In a meeting with the Council of Experts, Khamenei explained that the body is not "an arena for power [politics]" or "an arena for fighting and [waging] war over power," and that they must be "careful about their words and actions."[27] In a veiled message to Hashemi Rafsanjani, he stated: "I warn them [the enemies] not to come close to the sanctity of the Council of Experts and to take these kinds of games [elsewhere] to other issues."

With the growing personal enmity between Hashemi Rafsanjani and Ahmadinejad, the nature of factional fighting in Iran would become fiercer than ever. The 2009 presidential election, however, would provide the most legitimate avenue for resolving the dispute between the two men and determining the implementation method of privatization. Despite the significant amount of privatization undertaken by Ahmadinejad, it still represented only more than a third of the total value of privatization planned.[28] Privatization, in other words, was far from complete and the stakes of the 2009 presidential election would be the highest in the history of the regime as the presidency offered the last chance for any faction to lead the country's final stage in the state's privatization program.

The Aftershocks of Privatization: Iran in 2009 and Beyond

Today, most analyses of Iran take the 2009 presidential election as a critical frame of reference to evaluate and explain the dynamics of postelection Iranian politics. While there are very attractive reasons for doing this—given that the election produced the most significant mass protests and subsequent state clampdown since the revolution, resulted in the dismantling of reformist left forces from the system, and raised suspicions about the nature of the regime and the political intentions of theocratic hard-liners—I argue that contextualizing Iran with regard to the election of 2009 risks detracting our attention from more fundamental transformative processes unfolding in the country and creating a myopic view of the meaning of elite factional struggles. The presidential election and the contentious politics it produced, in other words, are part of a larger and more important context that tends to be overlooked in the haze of sensational politics. Accordingly, in this concluding section, I discuss the elections in light of the intense power struggle that had taken shape between the republican right and the theocratic left factions over privatization and, thereafter, examining the larger implications these processes hold for the evolution of the Iranian political system in the future.

The 2009 Elections

The Iranian political scene had slowly polarized between the republican right and theocratic left factions beginning in the 1990s—each reflective of the institutional power of its main veto-playing sponsor with Hashemi Rafsanjani and the Supreme Leader. While Khamenei does not belong to any one faction—as he clearly supported the theocratic right in the 1980s—he changed position as part of his larger role of balancing and restraining political factions within the Islamic regime. His support of the theocratic left provided the most effective means of limiting the growing threat of Hashemi Rafsanjani. The republican right—in an attempt to expedite economic privatization—had been weakening the multifactional nature of decision making within the regime in regard to economic policy.

Reflective of the Iranian regime's strong checks and balances and weak party system, the rise of the theocratic left and their gaining control of Parliament in 2004 and the executive in 2005 circumscribed the republican right's economic plans while simultaneously enacting privatization under the mutually revised framework of Article 44. No one faction was able to dictate the terms of policy, and each had to compromise with others. Here, the theocratic left did not end the country's privatization drive as it wanted to at the start of its rule, and the republican right was not able to implement the privatization plan it had envisioned with an unrivaled private sector. Rather, a contradictory and quasi-statist economic order was slowly and painstakingly forged through this unorthodox privatization scheme. More importantly, this process protected the theocratic base of power, and particularly the Supreme Leader, from the perceived threats that a more privatized and liberal economy would pose. In this context, the international sanctions regime over the Iranian nuclear program only furthered the goals of the theocratic left.

The 2009 presidential elections, however, presented the last opportunity to the republican right faction for regaining control of economic policy after its four-year hiatus in rule and for implementing privatization. In fact, one of the main goals outlined by Mussavi in his election campaign was the proper and speedy implementation of privatization[29]—thus assuring the republican right that he would not follow leftist economic policies as he had in the 1980s—and his victory would have most likely resulted in a republican right economic team as had been the case with the Khatami administration. On the other hand, it was also pivotal for the theocratic left to ensure its victory in the election to prevent its economic policies from being undone and to enact the rest of the privatization program. With hindsight, and in this light, the fact that the 2009 election led to the largest social mobilization and street protests since the revolution is not surprising. The economic stakes had never been this high in any other Iranian election. Irrespective of whether electoral fraud had been committed, the incentive structure for the elites and the rising tensions between the two groups because of economic privatization—the most significant strategic change to the structure of the state since the revolution—all but foretold an explosive struggle to capture the executive branch of government in elections.

This conflict—rather than being a struggle of the opposition against the regime, as is sometimes portrayed—was therefore an intraregime conflict that resulted in opposing factions mobilizing the people and protesting against one another. True, the people did not mobilize for economic reasons per se, but the elite were critical in shaping the opportunity structure for the people to mobilize, particularly in the earlier stages of the protests. In other words, the year 2009 saw the most widespread mass protests in the history of the Islamic Republic because the degree of elite contestation over the economy reached its highest levels in the history of the regime just prior to the election, thus creating incentives for the elite to battle over executive control. Indeed, Hashemi Rafsanjani and his family provided important regime support to Mussavi's electoral campaign as well as both pre- and post-election backing to the Green Movement. In his speech on July 17, 2009, weeks after the election, Hashemi Rafsanjani implicitly countered Khamenei's message on the validity of the elections and exclaimed that the country was gripped in a crisis. He also stressed the importance of the people and popular rule determining all of the institutions of the state, even that of the Supreme Leader, and, perhaps as a veiled warning to Khamenei, said that he had spoken with members of the Expediency Council and the Council of Experts for a solution.[30]

Khamenei, on the other hand, was more interested in restraining the economic agenda and political reach of Hashemi Rafsanjani and the republican right than eliminating them. The words of praise and friendship Khamenei bestowed upon Hashemi Rafsanjani in his Friday Prayers speech after the 2009 election was meant as a clear public signal to Hashemi Rafsanjani that he was still a close confidant of the regime and that he would continue to play an important role in formal politics—a gesture saying that Khamenei wanted him in.[31] And he would later explicitly state his desire for "absorbing the maximum and expelling the minimum" number of elites within the regime, again signaling that he had no desire to exclude diverse voices within the regime or change its multifactional nature.[32] Khamenei's reappointment of Hashemi Rafsanjani as head of the Expediency Council in 2012, despite contrary rumors, further supports this reading of events.

At the same time, however, Khamenei's veto of electoral criticism and opposition to Ahmadinejad's reelection victory had to be enforced by the coercive forces of the state; otherwise the position of the Supreme Leader risked drifting into irrelevancy. The minimum guideline—or the "red line"—behind the regime's "authoritarian bargain" to participate in the game is to accept the Supreme Leader's veto power. To reject this veto right would mean to reject the system and thus face expulsion from the regime—as clearly happened to the Green Movement leaders Karrubi and Mussavi but not to Mohsen Rezaei, the third presidential candidate who also questioned election results. Khamenei's gradual strengthening of his Office (*beit-e rahbari*)[33] and expanding the power of the IRGC and the Basij thus paid off, as he was able to enforce his veto decision and ensure his relevancy and survival.

While the enforcement of Khamenei's veto is nothing new for the regime, the amount of energy and resources needed to enforce it has become much higher because of the increased complexity of the system and the changing sociotechnological and media environment. Khamenei will thus constantly need to reinforce and upgrade the infrastructural power of his office just to retain his power and position. His expansion of power, accordingly, does not mean that he has achieved absolute control over all the levers of policy making but rather that he is buttressing his survival capabilities to ensure his position during times of need.

As any rigorous attempt to empirically measure the power of the Supreme Leader in relation to other power centers in Iran over time is largely impractical, two indicators, as discussed earlier, can be used to determine whether the regime has morphed into a personalistic dictatorship since the 2009 election. The first is the actualization of electoral turnover in the executive and legislative branches over several electoral cycles.[34] Since the regime had been witness to turnover in the factions controlling the different branches of power prior to 2009, we should continue to see change in the political makeup of elected office and divided government in the future as well. For example, the 2012 parliamentary election, despite returning the theocratic right to power, still signaled divided government and was an important signal of the theocratic left's failure to capture the Majles and monopolize rule. More importantly, the 2013 presidential election was a defining event that proved that the circle of elite had not been closed with the election of Hassan Rouhani and could still encompass power-sharing across factions. The Supreme Leader, therefore, should not be the primary backer of a single group over an extended period of time that would lead to political hegemony.

The second indicator is the direct input and influence of multiple factions in the policy-making process. If the political maneuverings of different factions can affect the substance of new policy—which can been seen today in the way the theocratic right and republican right factions have moved to curtail the theocratic left in different arenas, the same kind of political dynamics that had characterized the hybrid nature of the political system in the pre-2009 era would have continued in the post-2009 period. While the Supreme Leader can veto legislation and influence the direction of policy, he should not be single-handedly dictating all policy content irrespective of factional dynamics.

The power of the leader is difficult to ascertain independently because Khamenei is most likely not going to use the full extent of his powers under normal circumstances. It will be during periods of intense crises that the Supreme Leader will resort to using his power more expansively to enforce his rule. If the use of the leader's power under normal situations becomes qualitatively different than before, it should reveal itself in the two indicators mentioned earlier so as to mark a shift in regime dynamics.

Implications

Counterintuitively, the relative—and perhaps temporary—weakening of Hashemi Rafsanjani and the elimination of the main leaders and associations of the republican left from the political scene have resulted in heightened competitiveness among the Iranian elite rather than the monopolization of power by a single group. Moreover, the factionalized political scene and the regime's strong checks and balances augment this condition. As the republican right had been a major pole of the regime, its perceived weakening after the 2009 election has led the theocratic right to scramble to fill the void. Consequently, there has been a striking shift of position in some elements of the theocratic right as they moved toward the republican right quadrant—a downward movement on the vertical theocratic-republican axis depicted in figure 1.1. Key individuals such as Ali Motahhari demonstrate this trend as they have taken more critical stances of the regime stressing republicanism and have positioned themselves closer to republican right forces. The regrouping of the republican right over time led to the formation of the Perseverance Front of the Islamic Revolution (*Jebhe-ye Istadegi-ye Enqelab-e Eslami*) for the 2012 parliamentary election that centered on the figure of Mohsen Rezaei and later, with respect to the 2013 presidential election, largely coalesced around the candidacy of Rouhani.

The reasons for this shift are twofold. First, the incentives for joining or allying with the republican right increased for individuals who could strengthen the faction and prevent its power from further diminishing. The republican right needed individuals who were more commonly considered insiders and theocrats who would support its position and voice similar criticisms of the government. Second, the perceived threat of the rising theocratic left, particularly with the 2009 election, raised the level of insecurity and uncertainty of some members of the theocratic right about their future interests and positions within the system. Moving closer to the republican right and forging closer ties between the two factions would thus allow these groups to more forcefully balance the theocratic left.

Prior to the 2013 presidential election, the factional tensions within the regime took shape around two possible coalitions: an alliance of theocrats (both left and right) and an alliance of the right (theocratic and republican). The power triangle thus formed (theocratic left, theocratic right, republican right) represented the factions that constituted the major players of the Islamic Republic at that time, and this unresolved tension, counterintuitively, broadened the range of elites that could simultaneously compete against one another within the system. This institutional condition paved the way for the inclusion of moderate candidates such as Rouhani and Mohammad-Reza Aref in the presidential election and, hence, provided the structural opportunity for broad, cross-factional electoral contestation.

In order to stem this tide and prevent greater defection within the theocratic right toward the republican right, Khamenei also shifted much of his support from the theocratic left to the theocratic right beginning in 2010. He particularly gave greater backing to the Larijani brothers, as heads of the legislative and judicial branches, and he also came to support the theocratic right during its disputes with Ahmadinejad to demonstrate that he can and will constrain Ahmadinejad when necessary.[35] By repositioning himself at the center of this power triangle—the intersection point of the theocratic-based coalition and the right-based coalition—Khamenei indicated that he would not back a single political faction over time and would continue to play his role as balancer. His move signaled that he would guarantee the security and interests of the theocratic right, thereby reducing the incentives for defection. The theocratic right's bolstered position is exemplified organizationally by the United Front of the Principlists (*Jebhe-ye Motahed-e Usulgarayan*), the winners of the 2012 parliamentary election. Khamenei's emphasis on his role as balancer within the regime and above the political fray thus preceded, and hence enabled, a conducive environment for political campaigning in the 2013 presidential election—a necessary condition for the victory of Rouhani.

In contrast, the theocratic left, commonly assumed to be the faction driving the regime toward dictatorship, has ironically been the most fissiparous of all political groupings. The theocratic left has largely split into two different yet overlapping groups despite both benefiting from the rural uprising. The main ideological and political nexus of the faction is best displayed today in the Steadfastness Front of the Islamic Revolution (*Jebhe-ye Payedari-ye Enqelab-e Eslami*) under the spiritual leadership of Ayatollah Mohammad-Taqi Mesbah Yazdi. President Ahmadinejad himself and the network of associates he developed, including individuals like Rahim Mashaei and Hamid Baqaei, best represent the second group, which splintered from the Steadfastness Front. While Ahmadinejad's group is not a fully fledged faction in its own right, it nevertheless was a power to be reckoned with because of the power of the president. A key reason for the split between these groups was the growing shift made by Ahmadinejad toward the republican left quadrant, and that he was less willing to compromise with old-guard political elites compared to the main theocratic left faction—an important point of concern for the Leader. Moreover, members of the Steadfastness Front were displeased with Ahmadinejad trying to forge an independent base of power.

Politically, one of the main goals of the theocratic right today is to constrain the populist forces of the rural uprising and the theocratic left within the institutions of the state—efforts that may succeed in the short term but not in the long run. The provinces, particularly the smaller cities and villages, had felt alienated and ignored by the previous administrations while there was excessive wealth accumulation reflective of uneven development in Tehran. Ahmadinejad and the theocratic left have effectively targeted this base with their economic redistribution policies, including the justice shares programs, ease of access to loans, and extensive state-subsidized housing projects under the Mehr Housing (*Maskan-e Mehr*) program. The rotating provincial cabinet meetings and the funding of development projects enabled by high oil prices bolstered the social standing of the faction in the context of the rural uprising.

The theocratic right attempted to limit the impact of the rural uprising in several ways, a couple of which are evident in the 2012 parliamentary election. Parliament had earlier passed a law requiring a minimum of a master's degree to qualify as a candidate for the elections, demonstrating the growing elitism within the body and indicating elite efforts to limit mass society's access to the legislature. Another example is the vetting undertaken by the Guardian Council against many of Ahmadinejad's supporters, forcing them to run as independents. The calls for a change from a presidential to a parliamentary system, moreover, represent the same theocratic right concerns for limiting the impact of populism on formal regime politics. It is unrelated to the regime moving toward greater dictatorship. In fact, a parliamentary system would be detrimental to the interests of the Supreme Leader. It would unify the republican institutions of the state, thus strengthening civilian officials vis-à-vis the Leader. The current division of the executive and legislative branches into separate veto players under a presidential system allows Khamenei to divide and rule the different factions of the regime more effectively and prevent the monopolization of power by any one group. It also allows him to deflect negative popular sentiments from himself to the president. In light of the structural quality of the rural uprising—rather than a mere political use of populism—a more effective strategy would be to pursue political and fiscal decentralization and to advance local political development. Transferring executive prerogatives and the elections of governors to the people at the provincial level would also reduce the intense systemic stress that presidential elections place on the state.

The regime's currently strong institutional system of checks and balances and its weak political party system, therefore, ensure the incorporation of multiple power centers within the regime and will likely prevent the formation of dictatorship, especially under a conducive international context. Such a fluid and competitive factional scene is suitable for political accommodation and most conducive to the incorporation of a diverse set of political elites—both new and old. The recent election of Rouhani only confirms this condition and further portends the possibility of piecemeal reform within the context of the Islamic

Republic. And just as importantly, now that the main strategic change of privatization has been largely carried out in a manner favorable to the theocrats, the costs of accommodation and compromise between multiple political factions are significantly lower than before.

A critical factor that can make a significant negative impact on the political scene, however, is the international context. External conditions are currently greater impediments to increased political accommodation and moderation of the regime than internal ones. First, the international economic crisis has provided extensive support and psychological cushion for the regime against popular discontent. It has also strengthened the theocratic left's discourse on the evils of capitalism and justified their calls to disregard capitalist economic planning.

And second, the economic sanctions regime will prove to be detrimental to the political trajectory of the Iranian regime. It will reduce policy options that different centers of power can choose to advance and support, thus unifying the policy positions of different factions. For example, it will ensure greater privatization of assets and the awarding of contracts to public and quasi-state entities and the IRGC because of a lack of foreign investment. Sanctions and economic isolation therefore only further entrench and strengthen the position of theocratic hard-liners, supporting their plan for a resistance economy. The same effect is also produced by the increased threats of war and the possible military strikes on Iran's nuclear facilities. In other words, the probability of political accommodation in Iran will decrease because of the current international scene as sanctions work to hasten the consolidation of authoritarian networks.

And lastly, the success and legitimacy of Rouhani's presidency is staked on the international, particularly the US, reaction to his platform of moderation. The more welcoming and accommodating the reaction, the more leverage Rouhani will gain in Iran to pursue his political agenda. In contrast, without a meaningful change in Western and US behavior toward Iran—let alone if sanctions and hostility increase—Rouhani will be discredited at home. The theocrats will use such an opportunity to weaken the republican right faction, to claim the veracity of their ideological position against the West, and to block reform. Instead, however, by incorporating Iran into the international community and the larger global economy, Western states can more productively influence the political opening of the Iranian political system and produce a less conducive environment for the entrenchment of hard-line Iranian forces.

The international community, moreover, can support Iranian political development by aiding the economic development of the country. As Samuel Huntington theorized, the success of the rural uprising is the key to its defeat—as the provincial classes achieve greater economic development, their material interests and political preferences change over time. The current international context, however, only perpetuates the conditions feeding the rural uprising in Iran, thus ensuring that its current success will last for a long time.

Notes

1. For example, Hen-Tov and Gonzalez argue that the contested 2009 election proves that the Iranian regime has transitioned from a semiautocratic hybrid regime to a "post-praetorian" military dictatorship. Elliot Hen-Tov and Nathan Gonzalez, "The Militarization of Post-Khomeini Iran: Praetorianism 2.0." *Washington Quarterly* 34, no. 1 (2011): 45–59.

2. Clinton first made such a public statement on February 15, 2010, and repeated her claims on October 26, 2011.

3. Levitsky and Way demonstrate that state and party capacity are critical elements for determining whether electorally competitive nondemocratic regimes—or hybrids—move toward dictatorship. Steven Levitsky and Lucan Way, *Competitive Authoritarianism: Hybrid Regimes after the Cold War* (Cambridge: Cambridge University Press, 2010).

4. For an overview of this literature, see David Collier and Steven Levitsky, "Democracy with Adjectives: Conceptual Innovation in Comparative Research," *World Politics* 49, no. 3 (1997): 430–451; Larry Diamond, "Thinking about Hybrid Regimes," *Journal of Democracy* 13, no. 2 (2002): 21–35; and Leah Gilbert and Payam Mohseni, "Beyond Authoritarianism: The Conceptualization of Hybrid Regimes," *Studies in Comparative International Development* 46, no. 3 (2011): 270–297.

5. See Gilbert and Mohseni, "Beyond Authoritarianism," for an in-depth discussion of the conceptualization and measurement of hybrid regimes, including a discussion of the Iranian political system.

6. George Tsebelis, *Veto Players: How Political Institutions Work* (Princeton, NJ: Princeton University Press, 2002), 36.

7. Linz provides a thorough discussion on the role of hegemonic political parties in authoritarian and totalitarian political systems. Juan Linz, *Totalitarian and Authoritarian Regimes* (Boulder, CO: Lynne Rienner, 2000 [1975]).

8. For the importance of authoritarian parties in regime politics, see Barbara Geddes, "What Do We Know about Democratization after Twenty Years?" *Annual Review of Political Science* 2 (1999): 115–144; and Jason Brownlee, *Authoritarianism in an Age of Democratization* (New York: Cambridge University Press, 2007).

9. War and social revolution are theoretically considered important causes for the formation and strengthening of ruling political parties. See Samuel Huntington and Clement H. Moore, eds., *Authoritarian Politics in Modern Society: The Dynamics of Established One-Party Systems* (New York: Basic Books, 1970); Theda Skocpol, "Social Revolutions and Mass Military Mobilization," *World Politics* 40 (January 1988): 147–168; and Steven Heydemann, "War, Institutions, and Social Change in the Middle East." In *War, Institutions, and Social Change in the Middle East*, edited by Steven Heydemann (Berkeley: University of California Press, 2000), 1–30.

10. *Salam*, December 29, 1996. For a detailed discussion of the theocratic right's drive to power and the subsequent forging of a republican alliance between *Kargozaran* and the Association of Combatant Clergy to thwart the theocratic right's plans, see Mehdi Moslem, *Factional Politics in Post-Khomeini Iran* (Syracuse, NY: Syracuse University Press, 2002), 240–251.

11. Mohammad Najafi, former head of the Management and Planning Organization (MPO), claims that Hashemi Rafsanjani eliminated the left from the Majles for this reason. See Bahman Ahmadi Amui, *Eqtesad-e siasi-ye jomhuri-ye eslami* (The Political Economy of the Islamic Republic) (Tehran, Iran: Gam-e No, 2003), 393.

12. For an in-depth discussion of the ideological transformation experienced by the republican left faction at this time, see Daniel Brumberg, *Reinventing Khomeini: The Struggle for Reform in Iran* (Chicago: University of Chicago Press, 2001).

13. The data is from the Privatization Organization of Iran.

14. I use the term "rural uprising" here to refer to what Huntington calls the "green uprising." Samuel Huntington, *Political Order in Changing Societies* (New Haven, CT: Yale University Press, 1968).

15. *Islamic Republic News Agency (IRNA)*, September 25, 2004.

16. *IRNA*, October 2, 2004.

17. Information dissemination site of the office of the Leader, October 9, 2004. http://www.leader.ir/langs/fa/index.php?p=content Show&id=2640.

18. Information dissemination site of Ayatollah Khamenei's office, June 16, 2004. http://farsi.khamenei.ir/speech-content?id=3235.

19. *Gozaresh-e commission-e eghtesad-e kalan-e majma'-e tashkhis-e maslahat-e nezam darbareye seir-e tasvib-e siasatha-ye kolli-ye nezam-e piramunn-e asl-e 44-e qanun-e asasi-ye jomhuri-ye eslami-ye iran* (Report of the expediency discernment council of the system's macroeconomic commission on the approval process of the general policies of the system revolving around Article 44 of the Constitution of the Islamic Republic of Iran). Expediency Discernment Council of the System. July 2006.

20. Ibid.

21. Ibid.

22. All the data regarding the value of privatized government assets and percentages claimed by public entities is from the Privatization Organization of Iran.

23. See interview with Mohammad Nahavandian in *Aftab-e Yazd*, October 11, 2007.

24. *Islamic Republic of Iran News Network (IRINN)*, September 4, 2007.

25. *Fars News Agency*, September 7, 2007.

26. *E'temad*, September 1, 2007.

27. Ali Khamenei, "Speech to Members of the Council of Experts." September 6, 2007.

28. *Iran*, September 4, 2008.

29. *Iran*, April 20, 2009.

30. Akbar Hashemi Rafsanjani, Friday Prayers sermon, University of Tehran, Tehran, July 17, 2009.

31. Ali Khamenei, Friday Prayers sermon, University of Tehran, Tehran, June 19, 2009.

32. Ali Khamenei, Friday Prayers sermon, University of Tehran, Tehran, September 11, 2009.

33. See chapter 4.

34. Turnover is an important indicator of electoral competitiveness and demonstrates the integration of multiple centers of power in a political regime. While it is commonly used for the identification of democratic regimes [Samuel P. Huntington, *The Third Wave: Democratization in the Late Twentieth Century*, vol. 4 (Norman: University of Oklahoma Press, 1993); Geddes, "What Do We Know about Democratization after Twenty Years?"; Adam Przeworski et al., *Democracy and Development: Political Institutions and Material Well-Being in the World, 1950–1990* (Cambridge: Cambridge University Press, 2000); Jennifer Gandhi, *Political Institutions under Dictatorship* (Cambridge: Cambridge University Press, 2008)], electoral turnover

is a strong indicator for the broader category of electoral regimes, which encompasses both the democracy and hybrid regime types (Gilbert and Mohseni, "Beyond Authoritarianism"). Using electoral turnover to identify a hybrid regime is a stringent criterion, as some scholars use electoral thresholds instead. Howard and Roessler, for example, use a 70 percent threshold to identify hybrid regimes. Marc Morjé Howard and Philip Roessler, "Liberalizing Electoral Outcomes in Competitive Authoritarian Regimes," *American Journal of Political Science* 50, no. 2 (2006): 365–381.

35. See Naghmeh Sohrabi, "The Power Struggle in Iran: A Centrist Comeback?" *Middle East Brief* 53 (July 2011), for a more thorough analysis of how Khamenei moved to constrain Ahmadinejad in his second term in office.

2 Social Welfare Policies and the Dynamics of Elite and Popular Contention

Kevan Harris

Trying to understand politics in the Islamic Republic of Iran customarily involves ritual poring over of a bewildering list of names, associations, and factions that make up the country's elite. Stories about the exercise of power pit one group against another, or more often, one personality against another. The ups and downs of Iran's politics—its eccentricities, surprises, and impasses—are also said to result from this elite factionalism. Given the paucity of incisive analysis on Iran, this mere recognition of politics is important. Yet there is an obvious problem with such an approach. In developing countries, especially postrevolutionary ones, conflict and rivalry within the political elite is the norm, not an aberration. A full purge of elite competitors in a Stalinist mold costs exorbitant amounts of material and symbolic resources, which is why it occurs so rarely.[1]

The basic question of why intra-elite conflict in Iran exists at all, then, is not very useful. At best, it tells us something we already know about politics in general: elites and their allies want to gain power, or, if not possible, to prevent the loss of power. At worst, it conjures up ill-informed tropes about Iranian cultural exceptionalism, ignoring similar traits in other countries that have different types of politics. Instead, to gain a better grasp of Iran's political dynamics—past, present, and future—we should pay attention to how popular forces and political elites alike struggle over domestic policies in social, economic, and legal arenas. In other words, to get inside elite politics, we need to look outside elite politics where segments of state and society interact, bargain, and contest the status quo. The social compacts that result from these dynamics of contention, in turn, shape the parameters of intra-elite conflict. One such arena is social welfare policy.

Why discuss welfare in an authoritarian state at all? There are two reasons. First, welfare, health, and education policies do not only tell us something about a government's priorities. They also can reveal where a state feels most vulnerable vis-à-vis segments of its population. Historically, no matter the regime type, new social policies often target non-elite groups in the population that exhibit increasing levels of social power. Second, welfare policies can have unintended social consequences, including on chances for democratization. Even in the Middle East, where scholarly and popular accounts portray states sustained from so-called rents and detached from the citizenry, social compacts are arenas of struggle. Who gets in and who is left out is a result of politics, not of petroleum.[2]

In Iran's case, the making and remaking of a social welfare compact has hardly been a top-down method of state control. On the whole, Iran's welfare system appears similar to those in most middle-income countries: a social insurance segment for middle- and upper-income households and an antipoverty segment that attempts to target lower-income households and other disadvantaged groups. Yet a closer look shows how internal pressure from different segments of society repeatedly forced the Islamic Republic to alter its postrevolutionary social compact. By analyzing these episodes of popular contention, we can place Iran's factional rivalries in a broader context of social change, popular mobilization, and claims making from below that constrained and directed the political elite's strategies and capacities.

In this chapter, I point out a set of misconceptions in how we look at both elite politics and welfare organizations in Iran. I then analyze three episodes of contention over social policy. First, I show how the social demands of returning Iran-Iraq War veterans led to an Iranian "GI Bill" in the early 1990s. Second, I illustrate how mass expectations of economic growth and material well-being pushed the government to switch to a proactive family planning program and expansion of higher education. Third, I examine the effect of the 2009 Green Movement on the Ahmadinejad government's decision to partially replace inegalitarian fuel subsidies with a universal cash grant program. In each case, segments of Iranian society constrained the choices of the Iranian state, and fear of internal social pressure and unrest mobilized the political elite to act in a coherently unified, albeit temporary, fashion. External threats to the Iranian elite, conversely, have allowed the state to monopolize a discourse of postrevolutionary nationalism and lessen the need to respond to internal social pressure. I conclude by assessing Iran's probable political futures. Given the historical record, prospects for political accommodation, decompression, or liberalization will be enhanced if and when a reduction in international threats and tensions creates room for revival and intensification of elite conflict spurred on by popular contention. If Iran's conflict with the US and its allies increases, conversely, the likely outcome is a revanchist and autocratic hardening of the state.

Why Elites Get Along (Temporarily)

Judging by the alternating winners and losers of the Islamic Republic's factional struggles over the past thirty years, Iranian politics often look like a seesaw.

Iranian politicians' fortunes have risen and fallen, or vice versa. Judging by the country's domestic policy outcomes, however, Iranian politics often looks like a ratchet. During Mahmud Ahmadinejad's two presidential terms (2005–2013), many of the proposed policies he claimed as his own—such as subsidy liberalization, privatization of state-owned enterprises, and banking and taxation reform—were oddly reminiscent of policies proposed and tried by previous governments. In earlier attempts by presidents Akbar Hashemi Rafsanjani (1989–1997) and Mohammad Khatami (1997–2005), these policies were usually blocked by oppositional factions, which portrayed the proposals as harmful to the revolutionary order. Ahmadinejad and his supporters subsequently presented themselves as authentic revolutionary "principlists" (usulgarayan, *usul* meaning fundamentals or principles). Yet his administration then carried out sweeping changes in the banking, subsidy, housing, and industrial sectors with scant connection to the early postrevolutionary period. This shocked Iran's self-identified reformists, who had wearily spent years trying to shift economic and social policy only to be mired in political deadlock. It also befuddled Iran watchers, who had believed Ahmadinejad's pronouncements of a return to the early days of the Islamic Republic. Instead, in a time-honored tradition, Ahmadinejad criticized his predecessors as inept and then promptly turned around and stole their ideas. By focusing on differing factions' spoken positions, then, we may miss the extent to which intra-elite bargaining or emulation has occurred in policy outcomes.

This was one instance of a recurring problem for analyses of Iranian politics. We cannot understand elite conflict by merely mapping out different ideological positions into a taxonomy. Not only are borderlines between left and right rather porous in the developing world, but Iranian elites are habitually splitting and lumping themselves into new ideological categories and associational networks faster than analysts of Iran can generate the tables and figures to keep up. Taxonomies of this factional playing field are useful as snapshots in time, but they tell us little about how one version changes into another so often and so unpredictably. Instead, we might ask a different question: if intra-elite conflict in the Islamic Republic is the norm, as in nearly all other developing countries, and even more specifically in all competitive authoritarian states, what forces Iran's political elite to come together in effective coalitions, even temporarily?[3] Contrary to popular accounts, institutionalized patronage has not been a source of stable rule in Iran. Fights over state revenue and sinecures tend to exacerbate differences even where elite ideologies look quite similar. The key unifying emotion in elite cohesion is not greed, but fear. Iran's elite factions tend to form coherent political coalitions only when they perceive broad and shared threats to power.[4] This fear can come from outside, via war or foreign pressure, or from inside, via contentious demands in the public sphere. It is during these temporarily coherent coalitions that domestic policy changes are usually pushed through in Iran. These coalitional moments also reconstruct and refashion the ideological and associational networks within which the political elite operates. Eventually, through a reformulated factional field, these coalitions splinter anew into intra-elite conflict.

The source of this pressure matters in determining Iran's prospects for further democratization. External threats tend to generate elite cohesion in Iran, but they also tend to centralize state power in more authoritarian forms. This is because, while perhaps ideologically hollow, nationalism remains a potent force in postrevolutionary states. Nationalism is most easily wielded by state elites in an environment of high external threat, forcing oppositional elites and other social bases of power to back off from serious challenges to the status quo. If external threats can be presented as equally dangerous for all of Iranian society, then the state can even extract compliance from formerly dissenting groups. Internal threats and contention from below, conversely, can force state elites to remake existing social compacts. This is because, after recurring and unmanageable public expressions of discontent, elites begin to perceive the status quo as generating threats to their own continuation in power. These changes in the social compact can be political but have also consisted of shifting who is linked to the state through social and economic policy. In doing so, state elites attempt to incorporate or respond to publicly contentious segments of the population. Unlike external threats, however, these shifts can have unintended consequences that lead to renewed internal demands.[5] In sum, democratization in Iran can be aided by reduction in external threats, as it allows for internal dynamics of contention to force state elites to refashion the postrevolutionary social compact in a politically inclusive direction.

Understanding the difference between external and internal pressure on Iran's political elite is relevant given recent history: conservative victory in the 2009 presidential election, a temporary cross-class mobilization in the Green Movement, increased economic sanctions and military threats by the US and its allies, and the 2013 surprise election of Hassan Rouhani. These incidents compel us to again ask: what are the relations between state and society in the Islamic Republic? The answer has changed over time. In the 1980s, during a renewed global cold war as well as a long "hot" war with Iraq, Iran was commonly portrayed as a totalitarian state that controlled and directed most of its population through a combination of Islamic ideology and coercion.[6] In the 1990s, the appearance of a robust civil society in Iran with its own ideological debates, political identities, and public demands showed that the postrevolutionary trajectory had not produced a totalitarian social order. Instead, it seemed that society was essentially autonomous from a state that ruled from above but was out of touch and disconnected from its population.

After 2009, however, neither totalitarianism nor autonomy described the reality of state-society relations in Iran. The Green Movement had many allies and supporters, but it also had many opponents and skeptics. The 2009 mobilizations could not be sustained partly because of state repression, but also because the movement's coalition of forces rapidly divided among differing visions of reform. There was no continuous broadening of the oppositional coalition as in Egypt in 2011, but rather an upsurge and then narrowing toward a strong but limited oppositional force.[7] The Ahmadinejad government gloated over the 2009 Green Movement's dwindling power but immediately found itself fighting for survival against conservative forces in other branches of the state. Conservative politicians, once seen in accord against their reformist enemies, began to assail each other with internecine attacks. Civil society and the state both appeared internally fragmented, fluidly dynamic, and interlinked. The 2013 election of Rouhani did not negate this dynamic but rather exemplified it. This is not a new, post-2009 phase in the Islamic Republic. Instead, it is the most apt characterization of Iran over the past three decades. Government institutions became embedded deeper in society during the postrevolutionary period than in any previous period of Iranian history, yet various segments of society have likewise constrained and influenced the state's direction and choice of policies.[8] To see this process at work, we can look to Iran's welfare system.

Misconceptions about Iran's Welfare System

Iran is a middle-income country with fewer resources for state spending and weaker capacity to administer programs such as universal health care and generous social insurance offered in some wealthier countries. Nevertheless, like many other low- and middle-income countries, it still possesses social insurance and health care institutions.[9] As the economist Amartya Sen notes, there is a wider and more diverse welfare mix in such countries for both policies and outcomes compared to wealthier countries.[10] In some cases, welfare activities are still provided mostly via household and community networks, with the state absent or incapable of implementing social policy. In other cases, states have made tremendous achievements in health and education through welfare policies even with limited or stagnant macroeconomic growth.

In Iran's case, we do not possess a systematic approach to social and economic policy largely because existing studies focus on the strange and the scary. There is much speculation about the power of the IRGC, the Basij, wealthy merchants (*Bazaaris*), and particularly notorious endowed foundations (*Bonyads*) that own businesses while also providing aid and social support to various status groups such as families of war martyrs.[11] Not all such foundations are religious or linked to the state, but they and the other institutions are disproportionately given a lot of press both inside Iran and in Western accounts. This inordinate emphasis on the strange and scary portrays Iran's welfare policy as solely targeting a narrow segment of the population, often through military or defense-tinged channels, in exchange for quiet consent or active loyalty toward the postrevolutionary government.

These assumptions—that Iran does not have a welfare system like other countries, or that it has a limited system targeted at only those who express loyalty to the regime—are widely off the mark. In fact, most Iranians are connected in some fashion to the Islamic Republic's complex welfare system, even if they do not necessarily see themselves on the receiving end of public policy. In that manner, Iranians are similar to the majority of US citizens who benefit from public sector programs like social security pensions or mortgage tax rebates but do not label themselves as being "on welfare."[12] In a key recent study, Ian Gough and Miriam Sharkh measured variations in welfare inputs (expenditure levels on health and education) and welfare outcomes (improvements in basic health, life expectancy, youth literacy, and female school enrollment) for sixty-five countries across the developing world in 1990 and 2000. They grouped their results into eight clusters based on similar welfare characteristics. Iran falls into their second-highest cluster along with Chile, China, Columbia, South Korea, Malaysia, Mexico, Thailand, and Turkey. All of these countries are categorized as exhibiting relatively good welfare outcomes but lower levels of public spending compared to states in Eastern Europe and wealthier Latin American states like Argentina and Brazil.[13] By these measurements, Iran has a comparatively strong welfare system for its position in the world economy.

Furthermore, parastatal *Bonyads* or military organizations are hardly the core component of Iran's social policy system. The two main welfare organizations as measured by coverage levels—the Social Security Organization (SSO) and the Medical Service Insurance Organization (MSIO)—are state organizations housed under government ministries. Both include contributory health plans in which the individual pays part of the insurance premium in addition to the government and the employer, but they also offer plans for low-income individuals and other special categories in which the government pays almost all of the entire enrollment cost. One reason we rarely hear of the SSO and the MSIO in contemporary accounts of Iranian politics is that these are boring welfare agencies with large bureaucracies, well-trained technocrats, and huge pools of beneficiaries. In other words, they look normal to the outside eye, not strange or scary, and so their impact is ignored. Yet by 2012, these two organizations alone covered more than 75 percent of the population with an array of insurance programs. The largest revolutionary *Bonyad* involved in welfare policy, the anti-poverty Imam Khomeini Relief Committee (IKRC), covers less than 10 percent of the population.

To understand the politics of Iran's welfare system, then, we need a more systematic approach. To start, we can list key welfare policy changes since the 1979 revolution:

- In 1984, the Primary Health Care system was launched, mandating the construction of rural health houses for villages. In the late 1980s, this was enlarged with the construction of urban health posts.
- In 1994, the Comprehensive Welfare and Social Security Law expanded the insurance frameworks of the prerevolutionary 1975 Social Security Law. In addition, the 1986 Self-Employed Insurance Law and the 1990 Labor Law were folded into a Basic Insurance Plan within the 1994 law.
- In 1995, the Public Medical Service Insurance Coverage Act created the Medical Service Insurance Organization (MSIO) to provide health insurance to individuals from various occupational and income groups. MSIO supervises most of the rural health care system.
- In 2000, the Urban Inpatient Insurance Scheme promised inpatient care coverage to the roughly 10 percent of urban residents who were uninsured.
- In 2004, the Ministry of Welfare and Social Security was created, with the SSO and other health insurance organizations placed under its charge. Also passed was the 2004 Family Physician Law, aiming to reform a fragmented tertiary health care system.
- The 2005 Rural Health Insurance Scheme, subsidizing secondary health care for rural households who need services or medical products from urban hospitals.
- In 2011, The Ministry of Welfare and Social Security was merged into the Ministry of Cooperatives, Labor and Social Welfare. In addition, the Basic Insurance Fund was established, merging most of the large health insurance funds into a single entity in an attempt to reach universal coverage.
- In 2014, the Health Transformation Plan increased coverage of inpatient hospital costs, equalized copays for insurance holders, and made a public push to register the uninsured. Hassan Rouhani claimed that eight million individuals had signed up for insurance rolls as a result of the plan.[14]

Over the course of these three decades, Iran's social policies gradually expanded social insurance and welfare programs to reach out to new sections of the population. This process looked starkly different than the oft-stated notion that anyone and everyone who receives something from the Islamic Republic is being bought off, co-opted, or silenced in exchange for handouts. While individuals in any country may decide to support the government because of what the state gives them directly or indirectly, individuals may also use access to state benefits as a source of social power in order to demand new rights and opportunities from that same government. This is why welfare policies, even in authoritarian countries, are never simply mechanisms of co-optation or "buying off the poor." In fact, even when governments design policies with this intention, the outcome rarely proceeds according to plan. Instead, the politics of welfare expansion can have broad unintended consequences. After all, before the 1979 revolution, the Pahlavi monarchy's oil-funded welfare policies most generously targeted workers in the civil service, military, industrial, and oil sectors. Having accrued state benefits during the Pahlavi monarchy, however, individuals in these occupations did not sit out the 1979 revolution. Instead, they were key participants. If welfare—sourced from oil revenue or otherwise—makes for passive and dependent citizens, then the 1979 revolution should never have happened.

The Martyrs Welfare State and Iran's GI Bill

Social revolutions and long wars tend to centralize and expand state power. During the Iran-Iraq War (1980–1988), Iran's state was no exception. Unlike many postrevolutionary states, however, the Islamic Republic did not develop a unified bureaucratic apparatus controlled by a single political party. Instead, dual sets of parallel and overlapping agencies emerged for most state functions, including welfare provision. One side was located in the public sector and state ministries while the other was linked to newly forged revolutionary bodies. This organizational parallelism was not efficient, but it arose for specific reasons. Widespread revolutionary mobilization from below and wartime mobilization from above compelled the political elite to rely on parallel institutions to govern the country. At the war's end in 1988, employment, education, and consumption were salient popular demands. The Islamic Republic attempted to use both halves of this parallel welfare system to deliver on promises made during years of revolutionary élan and wartime sacrifice. New laws and policies broadened the social compact by expanding access to education and social insurance. The process remained uneven and only half realized, but these policies were not the result of any one political faction's ideological stance on welfare policy. Instead, this expansion occurred when a coalition emerged among the political elite to manage the social legacies of revolution and war that threatened the state's long-term survival. A main target was the hundreds of thousands of individuals returning from the war front.

These new state institutions paralleled and competed with state bodies inherited from the Pahlavi monarchy from 1979 onward.[15] In social policy, a wide range of revolutionary organizations were either created or authorized ex post facto. Next to the Planning and Budget Organization with its Pahlavi-trained planning technocrats, an Economic Mobilization Force (*basij-e eqtesadi*) rationed and distributed goods during economic blockade and war. The Construction Crusade (*jihad-e sazandegi*) dispatched thousands of young revolutionaries to work on rural development projects. Private charity funds linked to urban bazaars, which had supported families of jailed militants, were joined up into the Imam Khomeini Relief Committee. The lands and assets of the Shah's Pahlavi Foundation were converted into the Foundation for the Dispossessed, one of several *Bonyads* created in the Islamic Republic's first decade. Such foundations, which included the IKRC, operated independently of the prerevolutionary Social Welfare Organization and Social Security Organization.

This organizational proliferation and parallelism occurred for three reasons. First, the revolutionaries deeply distrusted the previous regime, but the collapse of the Pahlavi monarchy occurred too rapidly for the old bureaucracy to be dismantled. Instead, the bureaucracy was haphazardly purged while newcomers entered in waves. Second, Ayatollah Khomeini loyalists—"followers of the Imam's line"—used parallel institutions to attack, silence, or absorb competing groups from the 1979 revolutionary coalition. Competing Islamic and leftist groups as well as ethnic separatist movements fought against these newly empowered representatives of the state, with a situation of de facto civil war in some areas of the country.[16] The 1980 invasion by Iraq deepened these centrifugal pressures against the Khomeinists, and revolutionary parallel bodies proved to be an effective counterforce.[17]

A third reason for institutional parallelism had little to do with the original intentions of the Islamist political elite. Rather, it was an unplanned method of harnessing popular mobilization. In cities and villages, parallel organizations became avenues for aspirational revolutionaries, clerical and lay alike, to push aside the old guard. Just as Khomeini's closest aides were middle-ranked clergy who deeply resented the quietest tendencies of the highest stratum of the Shi'i establishment, young migrants to urban areas often returned to their villages with intense emotional energy garnered from street demonstrations, new expectations for increased status within their local milieus, and heightened senses of empowerment that led them to attempt to upend elite networks.[18] This form of mobilizational power uses personal, face-to-face horizontal networks to subdue existing local elites and their traditional authority. Yet, as in any social movement, this power is "difficult to sustain and requires draining commitments of personal time and energy."[19] As everyday politics normalizes and exhausts the emotional energy of revolutionary upsurges and social movements, mobilizational power either dissipates or is channeled into organizations.[20] As the urban poor, the war-wounded, rural farmers, or upwardly mobile members of the younger revolutionaries added their demands onto the state's agenda, parallel organizations such as the Construction Crusade, the IKRC, and the IRGC absorbed this popular mobilization.

In other words, Iran's institutional parallelism cannot be solely attributed to Khomeini's charismatic leadership. Neither did it directly result from a Hobbesian state consolidation whereby segments of the revolutionary coalition—left, liberal, Islamist—competed for power. The motivations and participation of millions in their country's history also mattered. As Asef Bayat noted about this early postrevolutionary period, "the rhetoric used by the Islamist authorities reflected the intense competition between them and secular leftist forces over who could mobilize the poor politically. The poor took advantage of this discursive opportunity to advance their claims—without, however, lending much allegiance to either side."[21] According to one estimate, one in six Iranians over age fifteen became members of state revolutionary bodies within the first three years.[22]

Khomeini loyalists assumed full command over the state by the early 1980s. As soon as their rivals were subdued, however, this new political elite began to internally divide. These emergent factions scarcely agreed on issues of social and economic policy. A statist faction argued for eliminating wide inequalities between classes, preventing wealth concentration, supplying basic needs for all citizens, and crafting a "mixed" economy that limited excessive capital accumulation through taxation and regulation. A mercantilist faction demanded the strict interpretation of Shi'i jurisprudence on economic matters. They emphasized the naturalness of class inequality, the legitimacy of private property, and the harmfulness of state intervention in domestic commercial matters other than usury prohibition. For this mercantilist faction, private solutions for poverty and inequality could be found in the Islamic texts. Clerics outside the state would raise religious taxes to administer welfare funds and foundations.[23]

Neither side imagined the wartime growth of a state-linked parallel welfare system. Nevertheless, the hybrid qualities of these new revolutionary welfare organizations appealed to both factions. The statist faction favored them over existing Pahlavi bureaucracies because of these organizations' perceived zealous cadres, their engagement in transforming the social order, and their numerous endorsements by Khomeini. The mercantilists saw these organizations' parastatal or parallel position as legitimating the status of Shi'i clergy as rightful political guides while they also limited the concentration of power by the state apparatus itself. The welfare system developing by the late 1980s was not forged from either faction's blueprints, but it sufficed to fit their politics.

While revolutionary mobilization from below was being absorbed via state formation, the government increasingly needed to provide incentives from above for mobilization in the Iran-Iraq War. The procurement of war volunteers through the Islamic Republic's ideological exhortation has been greatly exaggerated—partly by the Iranian state itself. Tales of martyrs and wartime agitprop should not be taken at face value simply because religion played a role. A reinvigorated nationalism that fused a distinct sense of territorial and cultural identity with Shi'i symbols of sacrifice was no doubt important. As Farideh Farhi noted, during early campaigns, infantry volunteers were not hard to obtain.[24] The Islamic Republic increased its public calls for war support as the 1980s wore on. The louder the volume, though, the more these calls signified the state's weakened ability to recruit through such entreaties alone. Cheering tales of Basiji sacrifice and Islamist internationalism aside, in reality material incentives from the state multiplied. By doing so, the state shifted status and prestige toward participants in revolutionary organizations, whether on or off the war front.

War and welfare are often historically linked. Mass participation in war engenders an egalitarian sense of social justice, and war exigencies create new state organizations.[25] Government efforts to secure participation and support of workers and citizens often lead to expansions of social compacts at or after war's end.[26] In Iran, the growing links between warfare and welfare designated the notion of "martyr" as a political category far more than a religious one. By the end of the 1980s, Iran had developed a "martyrs welfare state," wherein the state created new policies toward individuals perceived to have sacrificed or committed energy to the cause of the revolution.[27] Such a rhetorical turn is hardly unique to Iranian or Islamic contexts—martyrs have been political currency from the French Revolution to the Spanish Civil War and the Italian fascists.

As I learned from interviewing Iranians who lived through the war, many different groups and individuals lobbied for their inclusion into status categories that designated them as eligible for newly created social rights and benefits. Women's organizations asked for income support, including employment opportunities, for individuals whose husbands or sons were fighting. Fuel, rice, and water shortages led to protests demanding increased rations and price controls in several cities including Tehran during the mid-1980s. War refugees fleeing from border zones requested housing and employment. Missile and bomb attacks destroyed houses not just near the front but in over fifty cities including Tehran, leading to evacuation drills and emergency response demands. Those who did have jobs, especially in the civil service sector, saw their incomes eaten away by inflation. Many Iranians who had either volunteered or been drafted into the armed forces were concerned about the state of their households upon return. Would they still have a job? Who would pay their rent?[28] As the criticisms piled up and the war dragged on, the state responded with more material incentives even as its resources dwindled.

These policies took a variety of forms on both sides of the parallel state welfare system. While many private businesses shuttered their doors, government employment expanded from 19 percent of the labor force in 1976 (1.6 million) to over 31 percent by 1986 (3.5 million).[29] If we exclude military and security employees, total state employment still rose from around 800,000 in 1977 to 2 million by the early 1990s.[30] The enlargement of the public sector was not a direct result of the state's dependence on oil. In most low- and middle-income countries, there is a social insurance motive for expansion of government jobs. Public employment is not the most efficient way of providing social insurance, but for states with low capacity it is the easiest and most direct method.[31] In Iran, boosting public employment provided access to social welfare benefits for millions of individuals who had been excluded from state programs before 1979.

Conscription remained in place, but the state promised much in return for military enrollment and made these promises tangible via the parallel government institutions of the martyrs welfare state.[32] The Martyrs Foundation began to deliver monthly stipends to widows and parents of war casualties. The IKRC sent aid for tens of thousands of soldiers' families. The War Refugees Foundation paid for housing costs of families who had lost or evacuated their dwellings. The Foundation for the Dispossessed handled veterans' affairs up until 1988 when a separate organization was created for the task, providing health care and therapy to returning soldiers who had suffered major injury including chemical weapons exposure. All of these activities not only justified the existence of such parallel bodies of welfare policy but also expanded the government's reliance on them.

This newly formed martyrs welfare state went beyond basic alleviation of hardship. It transformed the social compact between the state and society. This was not a natural outcome of populist ideologies of the 1979 revolution. The requirements of war mobilization were a crucial factor. As observers noted at the time, compared to Iraq's "capital-intensive" technologically advanced army, Iran was forced to maintain a "labor-intensive" military strategy.[33] This meant greater resources and status had to be conferred onto soldiers and volunteers. A key mechanism of this status conferral was through access to education. In the 1982 nationwide test (*Konkur*) for entry into the country's reopened university system, slots were allocated to "martyr" categories—families of war casualties and military participants were a key target. Yet this "revolutionary quota" also included people not fighting in the war at all, but rather serving the "cause of the revolution" in other parallel organizations. As the war continued, the revolutionary quota rose from 15 to 35 percent of public university slots.[34]

Expanding the social contract provided leverage for segments of the political elite to compete against rivals in ministries, Parliament, and unelected bodies. It also increased the political costs of the war itself. In 1989, Prime Minister Mir-Hossein Mussavi scored points against critics by hailing this welfare expansion: "Over the past few years, a great deal of effort has been made towards social justice and towards the protection of the deprived. At times the government was on the verge of being called apostate by certain factions . . . [but] thanks to the repeated emphasis made by the leader [Khomeini], the protection of the deprived has become a principle and an unalterable course of action in our system."[35] By the late 1980s, Iran's political elite realized that further continuation of the war would deplete most of the remaining resources for social expenditure.

As Planning Organization head Masud Roghani Zanjani later noted, this would "maximize the discontent of the population" and call into question "the legitimacy of the system."[36] While segments of the Islamic Republic's political elite expanded the social contract in order to win the war, pressures emanating from this expanded social contract in turn pushed the state to bring the conflict to a resolution.

Just after war's end, a temporary coalition of political elites cemented into law elements of the martyrs welfare state. Members of the statist faction as well as a nascent "pragmatic" segment associated with newly elected president Hashemi Rafsanjani placed the revolutionary quota into the Law to Facilitate Handicapped and Volunteer Veterans to Enter Universities and Higher Educational Institutions. The law stated that, if available, 40 percent of public university slots would be reserved for veterans and their families. It was the GI Bill of the Islamic Republic.

This may seem a strange analogy, but Iran's experience has much in common with the political context for the original GI Bill in the United States. US veterans' benefits after World War I were viewed as miserly by soldiers, often tied to local patronage systems, and unevenly distributed. The New Deal actually reduced targeted benefits for veterans in the 1930s even as Franklin Roosevelt expanded aid for workers and unemployed citizens. During World War II, the Roosevelt administration and the armed forces chief of staff planned postwar educational grants and loans for a relatively limited quota of 100,000 former service members. The expansive and generous postwar education benefits of the GI Bill were due not to Roosevelt's progressive vision but to the conservative American Legion. During the war, the organization lobbied the US Congress heavily and alerted public media to the paltry benefits that still existed for World War I veterans. The American Legion's efforts helped force Roosevelt to eventually sign the more extensive GI Bill in 1944. Returning veterans would be eligible for policies that specifically tied social rights to individuals' military-civic service, not national citizenship. While stewarded by a conservative coalition and targeted toward soldiers, the GI Bill subsequently delivered unintended political consequences: many African American veterans who went to college under the bill's provisions later became activists in the civil rights movement.[37]

Wartime mobilization, in sum, made both the US and Iran susceptible to pressure to expand the social contract in unplanned ways. In addition to the university quota system, between 1989 and 1994, Iran's government also passed new labor, social security, and health insurance legislation. This expanded social compact looked generous on paper but remained unevenly implemented over the next decade. Nevertheless, its enactment illustrated the depth of the bargain the postrevolutionary elite had to make in order to generate badly needed legitimacy in the short-term. This postwar social compact created a new framework of rights and expectations upon which the political elite, soon divided again into three competing factions, were compelled to consider.

Iran's Fertility Revolution and Expansion of the Middle Class

As Hashemi Rafsanjani's first economy and finance minister, Mohsen Nurbakhsh, recalled, "with the war's end we did not have the excuse anymore to tell people not to consume."[38] In the 1990s, intra-elite political conflict revolved around how to grow the Iranian economy. Hearing of success stories to the east—for example, Taiwan and South Korea—many Iranian politicians reconsidered the role of the state in economic and social policy. Economic growth, members of the pragmatist faction believed, could lessen internal pressure from newly empowered social groups. Grow the economic pie for all, they argued, instead of redistributing it to some.

However, no supra-institutional force existed—certainly not the new Leader and Supreme Guide, Ayatollah Ali Khamenei—that could permanently solve the collective action problem of elite conflict. Major policy shifts would be difficult to push forward. Competing ideological arguments partly stemmed from each faction's supporters and social bases, but battles over social policy change were also shrewdly instrumental. Members of the political elite used nationalist appeals and antirevolutionary accusations in order to justify their respective positions. Given how rare agreement occurred, we should examine those policies around which an elite consensus took shape and were actually carried through. In social policy, this took place within two broad areas: universal primary health care coupled with family planning, and mass secondary and tertiary educational expansion. These policy shifts occurred because Iran's political elite feared challenges toward political stability and believed these policies would secure it. These policies were both far more successful than anyone imagined. However, both policy shifts also contributed to unintended social transformations that led to subsequent public challenges directed at the political elite, including the 2009 Green Movement.

The shifts were initiated with an eye toward the East Asian economic "miracle" of the late 1980s by a group of politicians and intellectuals that began to coalesce around Hashemi Rafsanjani and his advisors in the Planning and Budget Organization (PBO). These self-described pragmatists believed that foreign investment, export-oriented manufacturing, and the shrinking of the public sector should be implemented in order to transform Iran's economic structure. Once president, Hashemi Rafsanjani attempted to politically frame such policies in a manner similar to Deng Xiaoping in socialist China, whereby rapid economic growth could be the instrument for the achievement of the goals of the revolution itself. The journalist Mohammad Quchani sardonically branded this approach as "white-collar hezbollahi."[39] For the new pragmatists, market forces would accomplish for the revolution what the state could not. With employment and prosperity, the Islamic Republic could foster a loyal middle class whose members saw their livelihoods as intertwined with the post-1979 order. These politicians also realized, however, that the East Asian economic "miracle" rested on two social welfare foundations that only the state could implement: lower population growth and an educated workforce.[40]

Statist political elites, mostly housed in the Iranian Parliament by the late 1980s, opposed the market-friendly policies of Hashemi Rafsanjani's First Five-Year Development Plan (1989–1994). Mercantilist elites, however, embraced economic liberalization in its initial stages and joined with Hashemi Rafsanjani to outflank their factional opponents. After a decade of war, popular sentiment sided against the statists as well. The alliance of mercantile elites and market-friendly technocrats did not last long, however. As segments of the First Five-Year Plan were implemented—privatizing state-owned companies, lifting price controls, inviting foreign investment, and obtaining loans from international agencies and wealthy countries—the mercantile faction began to criticize Hashemi Rafsanjani along lines quite similar to those of the statists. Economic growth could be achieved domestically, they announced, without subjecting Iran's revolutionary achievements to the whims of foreign powers. Underlying the denunciations were also material concerns. Many Iranian businessmen had become wealthy during the 1980s in areas where the state selectively permitted the domestic private sector to function. Opening up these sectors to competition, especially from abroad, would challenge preferential access to economic activities that domestic business enjoyed.[41]

Aside from these elite disagreements, Hashemi Rafsanjani's liberalization project seriously floundered because of internal social pressure. As Economy and Finance Minister Nurbakhsh realized, postwar demand for higher consumption could not be easily suppressed. While Iran's exports went up after 1989, imports went up even higher. Luxury goods, construction and building materials, factory machines, and consumer durables all flooded into an increasingly open economy. Hashemi Rafsanjani's advisors planned to pay for the imbalance with future oil revenues and new loans from foreign governments. Unfortunately for the technocrats' elegant economic models, geopolitics intervened. Oil prices plummeted after the 1991 US-Iraq Gulf War. The US pressured other states to forestall new loans to the Islamic Republic. Though it still had access to a few high-interest loans from European and Asian sources, Iran strained to finance its import imbalance. As before, Iran's Central Bank engaged in measures of last resort: printing money to fill the revenue gap. Demand for imported foreign goods, coupled with increased money supply, hurt less competitive domestic producers and drove up prices. The shift was an economic form of blowback due to a rapid realignment in the political elite. While in 1986, the Islamic Republic had proudly declared itself free of all entangling foreign debt, by 1993–1994 it was on the precipice of a foreign debt crisis.

Annual inflation leapt to 50 percent by 1994. Bloody protests broke out in poor urban neighborhoods, particularly in Mashhad and Tehran.[42] Critics of Hashemi Rafsanjani's administration—mercantile and statist elites alike— pointed to the protests as evidence of malfeasance and corruption. Stung by the accusation, Hashemi Rafsanjani tempered his goals, and economic policy became deadlocked. Iran's 1993–1994 economic crisis thus revealed more than the simple presence of intra-elite conflict. It showed that state attempts to address middle-class demands for higher consumption could lead to unrest from poorer citizens whom the state also claimed to represent. The social schism broke apart a temporary elite coalition. Public contention had forced Iran's politics to realign.

Though policies aimed at rapidly transforming Iran's economic structure backfired, this was not the case in the sphere of health policy. In 1984, the government began to construct a network of "health houses" in Iran's rural areas, indirectly based on Cuban and Chinese models of primary health care (PHC). Though a few experiments existed before the revolution, young officials in the Ministry of Health pushed for it to become national policy in the 1980s. Many of them, including Health Minister Alireza Marandi, had trained at US universities. Health houses are staffed by skilled clinicians, are located close to villages, and provide free health services. The project was enormous in scope, yet the state provided the resources for this massive expansion of the social contract. By 2010, PHC clinics were available for more than 95 percent of Iran's rural population.

Iran's PHC clinics did not initially promote family planning measures. Some revolutionary elites—though not all—distrusted population control policies introduced in the Pahlavi era. In the early 1980s, Iran's total fertility rate averaged around six births per woman. Yet by 1989, the government backed a huge push to promote family planning, including free contraception and a public relations effort to reduce family size. This happened for at least two reasons. First, women's organizations in Iran lobbied the state to provide resources for family planning. Clerical elites who opposed contraception came under criticism. Tools for population control, women's organizations proclaimed in public media and newspapers, should be in the hands of the people and involve their active participation. This social pressure from below was a continuation of the mobilizational legacies of the revolution, which made a place for women in the public sphere as long as they could represent their aims as pious.[43]

Second, the 1986 census calculated annual population growth at the alarming level of 3.5 percent, doubling the population in twenty years. Public health professionals and PBO technocrats warned the government that Iran's high birth rate would make increasing per capita income nearly impossible in the postwar economy. Out-of-control population growth, they told the clergy, would lower overall health rates, hurt agricultural production, and bring about an unemployed generation of youth—all of which, PBO head Roghani Zanjani stated, would create "conflict with the [political] system." Once a group of the political elite came on board, including Hashemi Rafsanjani, Ayatollah Khomeini was asked for support. Iran's leader issued a religious ruling allowing for family planning methods to be promoted by the state, which Roghani Zanjani later recalled as "one of the master feats of the Imam [Khomeini]." The strategy was clear: "None of the clergy could resist this policy . . . and only God knows if he had not done this what situation we would have been in."[44] The First Five-Year Plan estimated in 1989 that, even with significant reduction in the birth rate, Iran's population would still double to 100 million by 2011. This turned out to be too modest by far. The population in 2012 instead reached 75 million. The decline was more rapid than anyone had expected, and by 2000 the birth rate had crossed below the replacement ratio of just above two births per woman. The reasons for this demographic shift are complex, but a large body of evidence points to the expansion of health houses as a major factor, given that most of the birth rate reduction occurred in rural households.[45]

While visiting health houses in 2009–2010, I asked clinicians why such a stark decline occurred and heard two key answers. First, health houses did not insist on changes in family size during the war years, when villagers often first encountered and utilized the clinic's health services. Second, most clinic workers were given resources and prestige in order to keep them in their positions. Indeed, many health house workers I met had been in their posts for over twenty years. Both policies established the face-to-face relationships that made subsequent implementation of contraceptive use, birth spacing, and other family planning measures effective. In addition, public health workers told me that an "active" policy of monitoring households and communicating contraceptive options to rural households was crucial for their acceptance. In urban areas, though clinics were available, a "passive" policy remained where contraception and health information was simply made available to interested couples. Overall, the successful rollout of rural health care did not occur by top-down fiat or by clerical fatwa. Instead, popular contention made an early impact on policy struggles among a divided political elite, which then coalesced around an ideological consensus that small families were good for economic development.

A similar process can be seen in the expansion of education. In 1976–1977, after a half century of Pahlavi modernization, 3.8 percent of university-age Iranians were enrolled in higher education. By 2012, 55 percent of near-university-age Iranians were enrolled in higher education.[46] This growth, which mostly took place after the Iran-Iraq War, was no natural process. The Islamic Republic actively expanded higher education in both public and private forms. In nearly every middle-sized town today, for example, branches of semiprivate university systems provide easy access to college. A few clerics in Qom may decry universities as immoral sites where gender mixing and moral impurity flourishes. This has not stopped their construction or halted the popular demand for educational accreditation. In 2010, over 1.2 million high school students took the university entrance exam; 60 percent were female.[47] During the 1980s and 1990s, women's groups pushed for the removal of restrictions on female enrollment in particular education fields. One result today is that in fields such as medicine, there are far more female students than men.[48]

Just as political elites viewed population stabilization as key to economic success, many in the Islamic Republic also believed that an expanded social contract would produce the necessary educated cadres for the public and private sectors' planned development goals.[49] Extensions of primary education into rural areas and secondary education into urban zones spurred a virtuous circle of declining fertility and rising educational attainment. This welfare expansion deeply affected the country's social structure. Whereas about 5 to 6 percent of Iran's labor force worked in professional and technical occupations in 1976, by 2006 this figure stood around 12 to 13 percent—about 2.5 million individuals.[50] This figure underrepresents Iran's self-identified middle class, since one can include other members in the household, current university students, or younger sons and daughters in working-class households who may move upward in status via educational attainment.

Overall, the Islamic Republic's educational push resulted in a reversal of the revolutionary status order. Whereas in the early 1980s, commitment to the revolution was valued and rewarded, by the 1990s prestige and status were increasingly associated with technical expertise. The rising emphasis on educational credentials was linked with the growing relative size of Iran's middle class and its concomitant increased social power to make demands and protest in the household, university, workplace, and public sphere.[51] We read much about the Iranian middle class, but few ask where this widening social stratum actually came from. Middle classes have shrunk in other developing countries after military or economic crises. Such a class was not automatically produced in Iran. In reality, the growth in Iran's middle classes after the 1979 revolution is rooted in the state's pursuit of economic modernization. This should not imply that middle-class individuals are therefore "bought off" through social policy. In fact, the opposite consequence is more accurate: social transformations linked to this expanding middle class in Iran affected and reshaped ideologies and alignments within the country's political elite.

In the wake of 2009's Green Movement, former president Hashemi Rafsanjani publicly alluded to the relationship between postelection protests and social policies implemented from the 1990s onward: "It is presently impossible to rule society by suppressing it, the very society that comprises 3–4 million students and millions of educated people. Women, who were staying at home and were deprived of an arena for resistance, today are seated in most of the university positions. Those who entered the university, resist more easily and freely."[52] As the most powerful social mobilization in Iran since 1979, the Green movement pressured the political elite in numerous ways, including on conservative-engineered plans for social policy.

The Green Challenge to Subsidy Liberalization

While the Pahlavi monarchy also implemented price controls, Iran's subsidy system is largely a legacy of the Iran-Iraq War. In the 1980s, the state capped prices and controlled distribution for basic foodstuffs, fuels, and public utilities. The first attempt to partially liberalize subsidies occurred under President Hashemi Rafsanjani. When the government switched from planned rationing to a more market-oriented subsidization of commodities in 1990–1991, prices of some goods were allowed to float. As Iranians recall today, eggs and chicken both notably became costlier after the war. However, a core basket of fuel and staple foods, along with health services and pharmaceuticals, remained fixed at state-determined prices. The government paid the price difference between subsidized consumption and the cost of production or import. As a universal set of transfers, poor families in Iran benefited from this consumption basket in absolute terms, but wealthier families spent on and consumed more subsidized goods.

With oil prices relatively low in the 1990s, Iran's political elite largely regarded subsidization of fuel and electricity as useful economic inputs for domestic producers. Many state-owned enterprises took advantage of lower energy costs to maintain high profits without much industrial upgrading. While a few economists in the Hashemi Rafsanjani and Khatami administrations argued for price liberalization, there was no consensus for a policy shift. As oil prices starkly rose in the 2000s, however, elite calculations changed. By 2008–2009, the government was spending between 30 and 40 percent of its budget on gasoline subsidies.[53] Fuel consumption in Iran—not to mention traffic jams—increased at alarming annual rates. International financial bodies such as the World Bank and the International Monetary Fund (IMF) had long recommended reforming subsidies for economic reasons.[54] Given US threats to embargo Iran's gasoline imports by the late 2000s, some conservative elites also saw the subsidy system as a security threat for the Islamic Republic. An elite consensus formed to overhaul the subsidy system in order to reduce state expenditure and lower petrol consumption. Ahmadinejad heralded the forthcoming policy as a cure for the country's economic woes. The sudden popular upsurge in 2009, however, forced a change in Ahmadinejad's liberalization plan away from a targeted cash grant toward a universally available stipend. By looking to this process, we can see how the effects of the Green Movement went beyond a brief upsurge in street protests. In fact, the events of 2009 shaped a major realignment of Iran's political elite by splintering its conservative side. Without the Green Movement, there is little chance Hassan Rouhani would have been elected four years later.

When newly elected in 2005, President Ahmadinejad seemingly held economic and social policies contrary to his predecessors. The market was out; the state was back in. After two years, however, Ahmadinejad began to promote policies that sounded similar to Hashemi Rafsanjani and Khatami-era plans: merging ministries, reforming taxes, privatizing banking, boosting non-oil exports, and liberalizing increasingly costly fuel subsidies. In fact, subsidy reform became the centerpiece of Ahmadinejad's attempt to brand his administration as more competent, expert-led, and talented than his reformist opponents.

Short-term reasons for subsidy liberalization were clear enough, as climbing global oil prices widened the gap between costs of fuel production and consumption. Iranian gasoline prices were so low compared to those of neighboring countries that border crossings with Turkey, Iraq, Pakistan, and Afghanistan teemed with smugglers and petty traders who lived off the arbitrage opportunities. Yet the logic of "getting the prices right" for fuel and staple goods in Iran went beyond crisis management and budgetary pressures. The IMF advocated for removing price subsidies in developing countries, and they found an unlikely supporter in the right-wing Iranian president. Compared to the "committed" climate of the early postrevolutionary era and its general distrust of foreign institutions and expertise, Ahmadinejad's embrace of the IMF was the ultimate sign of technocratic respectability. By using management-speak and portraying his domestic economic and social policies as expertly crafted, the engineer-cum-president attempted to revamp the conservative brand as well as compete with the popular resonance of reformist political discourse. He did largely this by borrowing policy ideas proffered by technocratic pragmatists in the 1990s and taking credit for them. Ahmadinejad may have not implemented them as promised (few politicians do), but the unintended consequence of Iran's right-wing shift toward a politics of technocratic expertise was an overall convergence on social and economic policy after two decades of elite disagreement.

On welfare policy, the convergence was quite visible. There is now general acceptance among Iran's political elite of a mixed public/private social insurance model with poverty alleviation programs for the poorest Iranians, comparable to Brazil, Turkey, or Malaysia. Politicians argue over the degree to which welfare laws stipulated in the 1990s and 2000s have been fulfilled and funded, rather than overturn bills associated with reformists in the 1990s. Samadollah Firuzi, social affairs director of the Welfare and Social Security Ministry in 2011, stated that the Ahmadinejad government's intentions were to fully execute Hashemi

Rafsanjani's Basic Social Insurance Plan passed in the 1990s.[55] Reformist politicians advocated consolidating parallel welfare organizations into a single agency during the 1990s, but conservatives blocked the measures. Under Ahmadinejad, however, these forms of state centralization were no longer perceived as politically threatening. In fact, the Welfare and Social Security Ministry further extended social insurance to new groups of the population, such as construction workers, transport workers, and rural manufacturing labor, all of which had been proposed by the previous Khatami government. This process, which could be labeled "reformism without reformists," cannot be understood by using previous factional taxonomies of the 1990s. Once conservatives had assumed power in the executive branch, their success in the short term led to emulation of reformist strategy in the long term. Subsidy liberalization was to be the key shift in this process.

As Ahmadinejad began in 2008 to widely promote the idea, however, conservative elites in Iran's parliament worried about the gamble. The conservative-mercantilist elite that supported Ahmadinejad in 2005 had fractured into various divisions, some of which were increasingly critical of the polarizing president and wary of his revamping of the right. The president hinted that revenue saved from subsidy liberalization would then be "targeted" toward lower-income households. Parliament continued to block changes through spring 2009, arguing that the plan was either too radical or not radical enough, that it would create an inflationary spiral or a group of "dependent poor." Even with the reformists sidelined after the 2005 presidential elections, elite cohesion among the conservatives was absent.

The 2009 postelection protests presented a stark challenge to Iran's conservative elite. Though the demonstrations consisted of people from multiple social classes and occupations, the Green Movement's main social base was Iran's growing middle class.[56] If not apparent beforehand, the events of 2009 proved that conservative elites could not afford to ignore middle-class aspirations if they wanted to stay in power with any expectations of stability. No matter the actual election results, the Green protests pressured this elite in two important ways. First, as they were occurring, the street protests united the conservatives and convinced them to push through their own version of reformists' economic policies including subsidy reforms. Second, as Iran's economy deteriorated from 2010 onward, schisms among conservatives reopened and deepened as various conservative elites sought to capitalize on public anger by presenting their own platforms as the technocratic solution to Ahmadinejad's mistaken efforts. The election of the centrist liberal Hassan Rouhani amid a fragmented conservative field in 2013 should be understood in this light.

After the size and frequency of Green protests declined in late 2009, Ahmadinejad resuscitated the idea of subsidy reform. The president proposed to cut subsidies over a five-year period and target the cash saved to lower-income households, sagging industry, and the health care system. Parliament passed a version of the bill in January 2010. In spring of 2010, Leader Khamenei stated that economic revitalization should be the government's priority and backed the effort. The president announced, with the certitude of an engineer, that freeing up prices would jump-start production efficiency and be accompanied by a larger batch of market-friendly reforms, including a value-added tax (VAT), a revamping of the overburdened banking sector, and privatization of Iran's large public enterprises. This package was nearly identical to liberal-technocratic plans made in the 1990s but ferociously opposed by conservative-mercantilist elites. Threatened by public contention and oppositional critique in 2009, the remaining political elite of the Islamic Republic attempted to reap legitimacy through performance execution of new policies—no matter their origin. This elite unity did not last long, however.

In early 2010, the Ahmadinejad government informed Iranians that they would be categorized by income cluster to determine eligibility for income transfers after subsidy liberalization had begun. There were only three clusters, labeled with Persian letters: A (the wealthiest), B, and P. Any person could send their national ID number to the newly created Subsidy Reform Organization from a mobile phone and receive their assigned cluster's letter via a text message. Despite years of high oil revenues and economic growth from 2005–2010, many felt their own life chances had been blocked by the state's heavy hand. Absolute poverty is not high in Iran, but inequality is glaringly apparent. When recent entrants into Iran's newly educated middle classes received their SMS-displayed cluster and saw that they were placed in the wealthiest category, they stared at their phones in disbelief. So soon after the 2009 protests, it seemed to many Iranians, as a journalist recounted to me in Tehran, that the entire middle class was being punished for public defiance and shamed for their own upward mobility.

The vocal resentment was palpable. Parliament members began to go public about receiving complaints from constituents. Memories of riots and demonstrations were fresh. Thus when the president finally launched the Targeted Subsidies Reform Plan in December 2010—nine months late—the low-income cash transfer scheme had surprisingly been transformed into a universal cash transfer to all Iranians of 450,000 rials per month. The bill's name turned out to be a misnomer, since there was no targeting of cash to poorer households at all. The usually stingy IMF applauded the move, holding that such a "simple compensatory scheme could win a broad-based social support for even massive price increase[s]." In fact, the IMF essentially endorsed the notion that the state needed to win over the middle class or face renewed public contention: "Denying support for the upper income groups risked triggering public discontent among the group of biggest energy users."[57]

As with many middle-income countries, Iran lacked the administrative capacity in 2010 to accurately measure and verify individual household incomes on a national scale. It was technically easier to give all citizens a cash transfer, but this was still far more expensive than means-testing recipient households. The social threat of internal contention and renewed protest was a more pressing concern. As a result, an unintended consequence of contention arising from the 2009 unrest was to convert a pro-market scheme into a new universal social policy for all citizens. In welfare systems, it is generally more difficult to cut or retrench a universal policy than a narrowly targeted one. After a few years, high inflation had eaten away some portion of the transfer, but as of 2015, the Rouhani administration has still not been able to remove a significant segment of households from the grant rolls. Such a cut may be likely, but as with any new social policy, Iran's income grant is now one more site of social bargaining that did not previously exist.

Protracted Nationalism and Three Future Paths

In the wake of 2009's postelection unrest, Iran's ideological spectrum at the elite level seemed to have irrevocably narrowed to a small conservative faction. Yet in 2013, the competitive side of this competitive authoritarian regime returned in force. Instead of seeing the events of 2009 as a break in the Islamic Republic's political development—one in which the system was fundamentally transformed into a unified authoritarian state—we should look back on the Green demonstrations as having prompted a restoration in intra-elite competition. The widespread resonance of Green Movement slogans and demands forced conservative political elites to scramble and respond with their own counterproposals of change and renewal.

This should not imply, however, that Iranian politics are trapped in a cyclical return to a "golden mean" of intra-elite conflict somewhere between one-party authoritarianism and parliamentary democracy. Instead, there are three possible trajectories over the next several decades, depending on the balance of external and internal threats and pressure on the Islamic Republic's political elite.

High External Threat: Authoritarian Consolidation

In Steven Levitsky and Lucan Way's study of democratization after the cold war, the authors argue that Western linkages of various sorts—economic, political, civil society—were key drivers. Latin American and Eastern European countries historically contained denser ties and flows with the US and Western Europe. As a result, they were more prone to democratization than parts of Africa, Asia, and the former Soviet Union. In other cases, as in Benin or Mali, Western leverage in poorer states where Western links exist can lead to democratization.

The Islamic Republic of Iran does not fall into either of these categories. Instead, postrevolutionary states in China, Cuba, Eritrea, Vietnam, Zimbabwe, and Iran, all emerging out of revolutionary or liberation struggles, have survived decades of international pressure and economic crisis well into the present.[58] Even under such duress, however, these states exhibit levels of intra-elite factionalism comparable to other developing countries. What keeps these regimes together is a protracted nationalism flexed by state elites in times of high external threat. Like it or not, nationalism can be more easily and effectively wielded by states which came to power via popular revolution as opposed to counter-revolutionary putsch, colonial implant, or military takeover.

As Dan Slater points out, legitimately perceived external threats against states that have recent experiences of Western intervention or domination tend to generate high status anxiety among elites, even among the opposition. These individuals are less afraid of international ostracism and isolation than of status deflation and domestic vulnerability. In situations of high and increasing external threat, hard-line elites tend to thrive while moderate elites are forced to back down. This is because believable external threats allow authoritarian rulers to extract compliance and resources from different elite groups depending on the country, whether in the military, industry, the middle class, or communal/ethnic leaders. In such moments, regimes can construct far more durable ruling pacts than in times of normal intra-elite conflict. During the latter, the state must expend material and symbolic resources to maintain a semblance of cohesion, while in the former, elites will willingly sacrifice narrow interests and hand over resources to the state because their own power feels wholly threatened. Slater's logic here is utterly Hobbesian. Imminent threats tend to force elites together more than unreliable promises of shared material gain. This is why patronage systems with corrupt client networks are not sufficient to keep regimes in power indefinitely.[59]

After the 1979 revolution, external threats of war and counterrevolutionary putsch cemented elite cohesion in the early years of the Islamic Republic. It is often claimed that the war allowed Khomeini to take control of the revolution, but do we ever consider the alternative that, without the war, there would be no Iranian state at all today? Certainly this possibility preoccupied those factions that reluctantly turned subservient to Khomeinist elites. However, elite cohesion generated in revolution and war tends to fragment as soon as the external threat subsides. Moreover, after war's end, the reliance of the state on popular mobilization led to the creation of an expansive social compact in response to internal demands. It is more difficult, therefore, to present popular mobilization at home as a legitimate internal threat, given that Iran's image of itself is one of revolutionary mobilization. This legacy can be seen in both the annual demonstrations of the state and the more spontaneous demonstrations of the Green Movement. It is why the state expends so much political energy on the institutionalization of mobilizational power which, to those on the outside, seems like hollow and routinized public acts.

Given these dynamics, the most likely path to authoritarian consolidation within the currently factionalized Iranian elite is via a legitimate, endemic threat from the US or other powerful foreign actors. This is what oppositional Green Movement leaders warned from 2009 to 2013, and what reformist dissidents argued beforehand. This path could take the shape of a military-run regime, if elite solidarity in the IRGC can be believed; a further replacement of elected bodies by unelected ones, such as the Leader's office; or a unified single party or association that usurps all state organs.[60] Economic threats and sanctions, too, are not irrelevant, as they can reverse processes of middle-class formation that will lead to the erosion of this segment's social power. Sanctions will not overturn or democratize the Iranian regime, just as they had little positive impact in Cuba. The longevity of twentieth-century postrevolutionary states in hostile environments tells us that in the presence of persistent and legitimate external threats, state elites can monopolize a protracted nationalism and wield it over internal challengers to consolidate their rule.

Pressure from Everywhere: Status Quo Ante

This chapter contends that intra-elite conflict in Iran cannot be understood through its own ideological pronouncements and temporary rivalries. Instead, intra-elite positioning emerges as much from outside pressure as from conflict within the elite. This is why, over the past three decades, a seemingly static persistence of Iranian factionalism has operated concurrently with frequent electoral and policy surprises. It is a balancing act, but one that rests neither on totalitarian methods of rule nor an isolated state autonomous from Iran's rapidly changing society. On the contrary, civil society and state elites are both fragmented and interlinked with each other.

If external threats intermittently continue, but do not escalate into persistently dangerous and believable ones, then internal pressure from various segments of Iranian society will once again force state elites to refashion ideologies and policies in order to alter Iran's social compact. This is because, after recurring and unmanageable internal expressions of contention and discontent, the political elite comes to perceive the status quo as a threat to its own continuation in power. The existing social compact loses legitimacy over time, resembling a "protection racket" for elites and generating inclusionary claims from below. Changes to the social compact sometimes benefit poorer Iranians, as with the martyrs welfare state, and sometimes aid and expand the middle classes, as in the 1990s push for economic development via educational credentialing. These differences within and between social classes are important, as cross-class solidarity is never automatically produced, but there has been a cumulative increase of social power over the past thirty years. The Green Movement was an expression of this power, not a sign of disempowerment.

Nevertheless, a political shift toward a more democratic and competitive state in the persistence of external threat is unlikely. This is because powerful state elites fear the consequences of such a transition, whether it ends in political exile, human rights trials, or worse fates. Oppositional elites may promise "pacts" of political transition, but they are not credible as long as external threats are real. Therefore, if continued external and internal pressure occurs in the next several decades—"pressure from everywhere"—a continued seesaw of conflict, negotiation, policy shift, and renewed conflict in the political elite is likely. This does not mean that the disempowerment of existing elites or the emergence of new elites is impossible; on the contrary, it is integral to the process.

Contention from Below: Political Opportunities for Democratization

The idea that welfare policy in an authoritarian state is primarily a mechanism of co-optation and quiescence is a poor reading of politics and history. Nearly all successful social movements in middle-income countries are so broad that they encompass individuals from multiple social classes. Do we really believe that these cross-class popular movements, such as the Green Movement at its height, are disconnected from social policy organizations? This is implausible. Rather, the opposite seems more likely. In competitive authoritarian states like Iran, where there is little support from outside the country, elites are forced to create and re-create social compacts with the population in order to ward off, channel, cleave, or acquiesce to contention from below.

Iran seems a prime candidate for successful cross-class democratic mobilization. It is an increasingly educated middle-income country, it lacks a history of divisive sectarian or communal strife, and it has a pedigree of rebellion from which to create new and inspired nationalist myths to challenge the protracted nationalism of the state. Even its internal religious networks are divided, with numerous members of the clergy outwardly critical of the state. In other words, there likely will be plenty of future opportunities for mobilization. Just as with the Green Movement itself or other examples in the Middle East, these opportunities cannot be predicted in advance, nor can they be sparked intentionally from outside. A "pacted transition" model of democratization, whereby existing elites receive credible assurances that they will not be severely punished in exchange for relinquishing power—for example, South Africa—can only be negotiated when cross-class mobilizational movements and dissident elite leaders can credibly present this option as a viable outcome to recalcitrant members of the state leadership.

The Islamic Republic contains few Western links of the types Levitsky and Way identified, but there is precedent on which to expand. Actually, pride gained through international recognition and exchange is the obverse of the status anxiety that Iran's political elite exhibits when faced with images of Western domination and intervention. If Western policy makers better recognized these underlying tendencies, including the influence of how their own actions are perceived by Iran's political elite, then more linkages could be created. These actions could induce the Islamic Republic to create stable and rule-based institutions that can be platforms for future democratic challenge.

Openings and engagements may not immediately lead to internal change, but one of the most misguided readings of Iranian history over the past three decades has been the assumption that internal change—within both state and society—was not already happening. Outside of a disastrous state collapse, which would not be replaced with anything democratic and Western-friendly, the only path to political change is to shift the balance of external and internal pressure so that those who wield the latter can better exploit future opportunities, which will assuredly come at moments we cannot predict.

Notes

1. See the coda in Stephen Kotkin, *Stalin: Volume I: Paradoxes of Power, 1878-1928* (New York: Penguin, 2014).

2. Steffen Hertog, "Defying the Resource Curse: Explaining Successful State-Owned Enterprises in Rentier States," *World Politics* 62, no. 2 (2010): 261–301.

3. Steven Levitsky and Lucan Way define "competitive authoritarianism" as "civilian regimes in which formal democratic institutions exist and are widely viewed as the primary means of gaining power, but in which incumbents' abuse of the state places them at a significant advantage vis-à-vis their opponents." Steven Levitsky and Lucan Way, *Competitive Authoritarianism: Hybrid Regimes after the Cold War* (Cambridge: Cambridge University Press, 2010), 5. The authors exclude Iran from this category, instead classifying it as a "tutelary" regime where elected bodies are constrained by nonelected (religious) bodies. In my reading, Iran still fits well in their main definition: "regimes in which opposition forces use democratic institutions to contest seriously for executive power" (16).

4. Dan Slater addresses the puzzle of why elite cohesion rarely occurs in authoritarian regimes in *Ordering Power: Contentious Politics and Authoritarian Leviathans in Southeast Asia* (Cambridge: Cambridge University Press, 2010). Slater finds that states such as Malaysia and Singapore that faced continuous revolutionary threats from below were most likely to result in enduring authoritarian pacts constructed by a factionalized elite. In Iran, such "protection pacts" have been far more temporary.

5. Slater argues that countries that faced the most threatening cross-class challenges from below at the time of state formation produced the most enduring authoritarian regimes. Unlike revolutionary states such as Iran, however, Slater's cases mostly existed in a favorable external environment with US support during the cold war. Here I bring in external threats as an additional cause of elite cohesion.

6. See the analysis in Daniel Brumberg, *Reinventing Khomeini: The Struggle for Reform in Iran* (Chicago: University of Chicago Press, 2001), 10–20.

7. Two differences between Iran and Egypt's mobilizational waves stand out: Egypt's unrest was broader in class composition, whereas Iran's cross-class demonstrations quickly splintered into a middle-class oppositional rump; Egypt's demonstrations spread much wider across the country in both urban and rural locales, whereas Iran's unrest was primarily located in the capital of Tehran. See Kevan Harris, "The Brokered Exuberance of the Middle Class: An Ethnographic Analysis of Iran's 2009 Green Movement," *Mobilization: An International Quarterly* 17, no. 4 (2012): 435–455.

8. As Joel Migdal notes, "[State] authority involves demanding obedience from the population and loyalty means gaining support, often voluntary support, from that population. The state is at once dominator and supplicant." Joel Migdal, "Researching the State." In *Comparative Politics: Rationality, Culture, and Structure*, edited by Mark Lichbach and Alan Zuckerman, 2nd ed. (Cambridge: Cambridge University Press, 2009), 167.

9. See Ian Gough and Geof Wood, eds., *Insecurity and Welfare Regimes in Asia, Africa and Latin America: Social Policy in Development Contexts* (Cambridge: Cambridge University Press, 2004); Stephan Haggard and Robert Kaufman, *Development, Democracy, and Welfare States: Latin America, East Asia, and Eastern Europe* (Princeton, NJ: Princeton University Press, 2008).

10. Amartya Sen, "Mortality as an Indicator of Economic Success and Failure," *Economic Journal* 108, no. 446 (1998): 1–25.

11. See Suzanne Maloney, "Islamism and Iran's Postrevolutionary Economy: The Case of the Bonyads," in *Gods, Guns, and Globalization: Religious Radicalism and International Political Economy*, edited by Mary Ann Tetreault and Robert Denemark (Boulder, CO: Lynne Rienner, 2004), 191–218; the RAND reports of Frederic Wehrey et al., *The Rise of the Pasdaran: Assessing the Domestic Roles of Iran's Islamic Revolutionary Guards Corps* (Santa Monica, CA: Rand, 2009); and David Thaler et al., *Mullahs, Guards, and Bonyads: An Exploration of Iranian Leadership Dynamics* (Santa Monica, CA: Rand, 2010). The RAND reports are not necessarily incorrect and contain useful factual content, but they do not provide systematic accounts of Iran's economy and its welfare system.

12. See Suzanne Mettler, *The Submerged State: How Invisible Government Policies Undermine American Democracy* (Chicago: University of Chicago Press, 2011). Mettler's surveys reveal that while most US citizens will broadly claim that they do not receive help from the US government, when asked about individual programs they will identify themselves as beneficiaries. Although no such surveys exist in Iran, I have observed similar perceptions among Iran's middle- and upper-income strata.

13. Miriam Abu Sharkh and Ian Gough, "Global Welfare Regimes," *Global Social Policy* 10, no. 1 (2010): 27–58.

14. Compiled from Hossein Ibrahimipour, Mohammad-Reza Maleki, Richard Brown, Mohammadreza Gohari, Iraj Karimi, and Reza Dehnavieh, "A Qualitative Study of the Difficulties in Reaching Sustainable Universal Health Insurance Coverage in Iran," *Health Policy and Planning* 26 (2011): 485–495; Mohammad Hajizadeh and Luke Connelly, "Equity of Health Care Financing in Iran: The Effect of Extending Health Insurance to the Uninsured," *Oxford Development Studies* 38, no. 4 (2010): 461–476.

15. Mehdi Moslem, *Factional Politics in Post-Khomeini Iran* (Syracuse, NY: Syracuse University Press, 2002), Ch. 1; Ali Gheissari and Vali Nasr, *Democracy in Iran: History and the Quest for Liberty* (Oxford: Oxford University Press, 2006), 89.

16. See the recollections of sociologist Hamid-Reza Jalaeipur in Salname-ye Noruz, E'temad, 1394/2015, 209–215.

17. Bahman Ahmadi-Amui, *Eqtesad-e siasi-ye jomhuri-ye eslami* (The political economy of the Islamic Republic) (Tehran: Gam-e No, 1382/2003), chap. 1.

18. Shaul Bakhash, *The Reign of the Ayatollahs: Iran and the Islamic Revolution* (New York: Basic Books, 1986): chap. 6; Kaveh Ehsani, "Islam, Modernity, and National Identity," *Middle East Insight* 9, no. 5 (1995): 48–53.

19. Jeffrey Winters, *Oligarchy* (Cambridge: Cambridge University Press, 2011), 16–17.

20. Randall Collins, "Social Movements and the Focus of Emotional Attention." In *Passionate Politics: Emotions and Social Movements*, edited by Jeff Goodwin, James Jasper, and Francesca Polletta (Chicago: University of Chicago Press, 2001), 27–44.

21. Asef Bayat, "Tehran: Paradox City," *New Left Review* 2, no. 66 (2010): 106.

22. Kaveh Ehsani, "The Urban Provincial Periphery in Iran: Revolution and War in Ramhormoz." In *Contemporary Iran: Economy, Society, Politics*, edited by Ali Gheissari (Oxford: Oxford University Press, 2009), 27; also see UNIDO, *Non-Farm Employment for Rural Poverty Alleviation: A Report on the Regional Seminar, Pilot Projects, and Country Papers* (Vienna: United Nations Industrial Development Organization, 1995).

23. Instead of left vs. right or modern vs. traditional, I use here the characterization of elite factions developed by Eva Leila Pesaran, *Iran's Struggle for Economic Independence: Reform and Counter-Reform in the Post-Revolutionary Era* (London: Routledge, 2011).

24. Farideh Farhi, "The Antinomies of Iran's War Generation." In *Iran, Iraq, and the Legacies of War*, edited by Lawrence Potter and Gary Sick (New York: Palgrave Macmillan, 2004), 101–120; also see Ezzatollah Sahabi and Hoda Saber, "Forsat-e an do sal va tavan-e an shish sal" ("The opportunity of those two years and the damage of those six years,") *Iran-e Farda*, no. 58 (1999), 23–26.

25. Iranians tend not to link the war period with later social policy initiatives, just as Europeans and Americans do not do so in their own historical memories. As one young Iranian scholar remarked to me, "For most of us, the war always seemed a hindrance to development and progress . . . which later got started again during reconstruction." This is because, as historian Bruce Porter notes, liberal activists and social reformers usually "cannot accept that the welfare institutions which they regard as hallmarks of human progress could possibly have been derived in part from anything so horrendous as war." Bruce Porter, *War and the Rise of the State: The Military Foundations of Modern Politics* (New York: Simon and Schuster, 1994), 193. Yet the timing of most Western welfare initiatives correlates rather neatly with the two world wars; see Andrew Abbott and Stanley DeViney, "The Welfare State as Transnational Event: Evidence from Sequences of Policy Adoption," *Social Science History* 16, no. 2 (1992): 245–274.

26. See John Markoff, *Waves of Democracy: Social Movements and Political Change* (Thousand Oaks, CA: Pine Forge, 1996); Beverly Silver, *Forces of Labor: Workers' Movements and Globalization since 1870* (Cambridge: Cambridge University Press, 2003).

27. The term "martyrs welfare state" comes from Ervand Abrahamian's *The Iranian Mojahedin* (New Haven, CT: Yale University Press, 1989), 70. Incidentally, the Iraqi state—a secular Ba'athist regime—also labeled its casualties as "martyrs." For Persian vocabulary used to define war participants, see Farhi, "The Antinomies of Iran's War Generation," 115–116.

28. These contentious demands, from interviews conducted in 2009–2011, were brought up by Iranians who lived near the war front in Khuzestan as well as those in Tehran during the 1980s. Also see Nader Nazemi, "War and State-Making in Revolutionary Iran" (Ph.D. diss., University of Washington, 1994).

29. Sohrab Behdad and Farhad Nomani, "What a Revolution! Thirty Years of Social Class Reshuffling in Iran," *Comparative Studies of South Asia, Africa and the Middle East* 29, no. 1 (2009): 89.

30. Kaveh Ehsani, "'Tilt but Don't Spill': Iran's Development and Reconstruction Dilemma," *Middle East Report* 191 (1994): 21. Nazemi, "War and State-Making in Revolutionary

Iran," claims that the number of civil bureaucrats jumped from 630,000 before the revolution to over 1.5 million by 1985.

31. Dani Rodrik, "What Drives Public Employment in Developing Countries?" *Review of Development Economics* 4, no. 3 (2000): 229–243.

32. The material incentives for participation in the Iran-Iraq War were comically portrayed in the 1996 Kamal Tabrizi film *Leili Is with Me*, in which a photographer volunteers for the war in order to get a housing loan.

33. Dilip Hiro, *The Longest War: The Iran-Iraq Military Conflict* (New York: Routledge, 1991), 112.

34. Nader Habibi, "Allocation of Educational and Occupational Opportunities in the Islamic Republic of Iran: A Case Study in the Political Screening of Human Capital," *Iranian Studies* 22, no. 4 (1989): 19–46; Keiko Sakurai, "University Entrance Examination and the Making of an Islamic Society in Iran: A Study of the Post-Revolutionary Iranian Approach to 'Konkur,'" *Iranian Studies* 37, no. 3 (2004): 385–406.

35. Spoken on January 1, 1989, p. 52 in *Daily Report, Near East & South Asia*, FBIS-NES-89-001, January 3, 1989.

36. Ahmadi-Amui, *Eqtesad-e siasi-ye jomhuri-ye eslami*, 170.

37. Suzanne Mettler, *Soldiers to Citizens: The G.I. Bill and the Making of the Greatest Generation* (New York: Oxford University Press, 2007), 20–22.

38. Ahmadi-Amui, *Eqtesad-e siasi-ye jomhuri-ye eslami*, 103.

39. Mohammad Quchani, *Yaqeh sefidha* (The White-Collars) (Tehran: Naqsh-o-Negar, 2000). While Rafsanjani and his allies were attacked as antirevolutionary in the press, especially by self-proclaimed radicals from the 1980s statist faction, their arguments tracked the broad ideological shift in the third world during the late 1980s and 1990s; see Philip McMichael, *Development and Social Change: A Global Perspective*, 5th ed. (Thousand Oaks, CA: Sage, 2011).

40. See Gough and Wood, *Insecurity and Welfare Regimes*, for productivist welfare policies in East Asia.

41. For example, initial support of public sector privatization by Habibollah Askarowladi in 1989, a key representative of Iran's mercantile class, soon turned into opposition once it was realized that bazaar-linked merchants would not be the main recipients of plum state-owned enterprises. Pesaran, *Iran's Struggle for Economic Independence*, 100–101.

42. Ehsani, "'Tilt but Don't Spill': Iran's Development and Reconstruction Dilemma"; Asef Bayat, *Street Politics: Poor People's Movements in Iran* (New York: Columbia University Press, 1997), 98.

43. Homa Hoodfar, "Bargaining with Fundamentalism: Women and the Politics of Population Control in Iran," *Reproductive Health Matters* 4, no. 8 (1996): 30–40; Homa Hoodfar and Samad Assadpour, "The Politics of Population Policy in the Islamic Republic of Iran," *Studies in Family Planning* 31, no. 1 (2000): 19–34. Many accounts inaccurately report that birth rates increased throughout the war because of state exhortation to produce large families. The birth rate actually leveled off as early as 1981, and the slight revolutionary uptick mostly came because of a rise in marriages during 1979–1980. As with most revolutions, Iranians had high expectations after the fall of the Shah. Many of them therefore got married and had children soon afterward, but at the same rate as before the revolution. Nevertheless, whatever the exact rate, it was high enough to create alarm among public health professionals. See Mohammad Abbasi-Shavazi, Peter McDonald, and Meimanat Hosseini-Chavoshi, *The Fertility Transition in Iran: Revolution and Reproduction* (New York: Springer, 2009).

44. Ahmadi-Amui, *Eqtesad-e siasi-ye jomhuri-ye eslami*, 189–190.

45. Agnes Loeffler and Erika Friedl, "Cultural Parameters of a 'Miraculous' Birth Rate Drop," *Anthropology News* (March 2009): 13–15; Djavad Salehi-Isfahani, Mohammad Jalal Abbasi-Shavazi, and Meimanat Hosseini-Chavoshi, "Family Planning and Fertility Decline in Rural Iran: The Impact of Rural Health Clinics," *Health Economics* 19, no. S1 (2010): 159–180.

46. Ahmad Ashraf, "Education VII: General Survey of Modern Education," *Encyclopedia Iranica* online edition, 2011; UNESCO Education Statistics, 2014. The latter number is the UNESCO "gross enrollment ratio," which calculates a ratio of all student enrollees, no matter their age, divided by the number of potential students in the university-age cohort. It thus includes older enrollees, which is instructive for our purposes as a measure of social demand for higher education.

47. *Mehr News*, August 1, 2010.

48. Goli Rezai-Rashti, "Exploring Women's Experience of Higher Education and the Changing Nature of Gender Relations in Iran." In *Gender in Contemporary Iran: Pushing the Boundaries*, edited by Roksana Bahramitash and Eric Hooglund (London: Routledge, 2011), 46–61.

49. Ahmadi-Amui, *Eqtesad-e siasi-ye jomhuri-ye eslami*, 258.

50. Behdad and Nomani, "What a Revolution!" 89.

51. See Eric Hooglund, "Changing Attitudes among Women in Rural Iran." In *Gender in Contemporary Iran: Pushing the Boundaries*, edited by Roksana Bahramitash and Eric Hooglund (London: Routledge, 2011), 120–135.

52. *Mehr News*, December 15, 2009.

53. See Kevan Harris, "The Politics of Subsidy Reform in Iran," *Middle East Report* 254 (2010): 36–39.

54. For example, see Farrukh Iqbal, *Sustaining Gains in Poverty Reduction and Human Development in the Middle East and North Africa* (Washington, DC: World Bank, 2006).

55. *Jam-e Jam*, January 19, 2011.

56. See the ethnographic and statistical evidence in Harris, "Brokered Exuberance."

57. Dominique Guillaume, Roman Zytek, and Mohammad Reza Farzin, *Iran—The Chronicles of the Subsidy Reform*, IMF working paper (Washington, DC: International Monetary Fund, 2011), 8, 14.

58. Indeed, Levitsky and Way argue, "policies of sustained isolation—as in the case of U.S. policy toward Burma, Cuba, and Iran—may undermine the prospects for democratization by reducing linkage." Levitsky and Way, *Competitive Authoritarianism*, 353.

59. Slater, *Ordering Power*, 276–277; Dan Slater, "Review of Competitive Authoritarianism: Hybrid Regimes after the Cold War," *Perspectives on Politics* 9, no. 2 (2011): 385–388.

60. To claim that Iran is becoming a militarized state, as some in US policy circles do, and then in turn threaten that state with external war or separatist conflict, is to create a self-fulfilling prophecy. In cases such as Indonesia, Russia, Turkey, or Sri Lanka, violent conflict tended to bring the military further into power.

3 Education as Public Good or Private Resource

Accommodation and Demobilization in Iran's University System

Shervin Malekzadeh

Pupils have never credited teachers for most of their learning. Bright and dull alike have always relied on rote, reading, and wit to pass their exams, motivated by the stick or by the carrot of a desired career.

—Ivan Illich, *Deschooling Society*

In the play a young man meets the long-awaited Hidden Imam, who informs him that he has been selected to help bring justice and order to the world. The young man balks. He has college entrance exams the next day, he tells the imam. He has studied obsessively, he explains, and cannot afford to miss them. He then turns to the imam and asks: "Can't we save the world next week?"

—Afshin Molavi, *The Soul of Iran: A Nation's Journey to Freedom*

Acts of intimidation and formal warning filled the month of June as authorities in Iran scrambled to contain the unexpected mobilization of millions of young people during the buildup to the 2009 presidential elections in Iran. For weeks, the streets of Tehran and other major cities had been filled with spontaneous but unauthorized rallies by partisans of all political stripes, proclaiming the virtues of their candidates. By June 12, what had been at best a guarded tolerance to these gatherings quickly gave way to force and violent crackdown as Iran tumbled into what would become the largest political and social crisis since the 1979 revolution. With the validity of the elections called into question, millions of Iranians took to the streets to demand, "Where is my vote?"[1]

For the more than 1.3 million students preparing to take the university entrance exam, political turmoil could not have come at a more inauspicious time. On a national calendar filled with religious holidays and commemorations, few events were as sacred as the annual ritual of the *Konkur.* The test was sanctified by the sacrifices of children and their families; months, even years, of preparation had gone into preparation for a test that would determine whether students would be accepted into college as well as their major course of study. The ongoing chaos in the streets raised the specter of cancellation, of breaking with ritual, pushing the exam back into the next year. Frayed nerves were made worse by an anonymous text message warning test takers that anyone found to have participated in the marches before or after the presidential election would automatically fail. Beleaguered officials quickly denounced the message as false and issued a reassuring statement that some ten thousand additional security officers would be on hand to secure the test sites.[2]

As it turned out, the extra security was not needed. The day of the *Konkur* passed without incident, producing in the summer of 2009 the first major break in nearly two weeks of regular protest and repression. For students and their families, the choice to prioritize participation in the exams over the uncertain promise of a still-unfolding political crisis was hardly a choice at all. The risks were too high, the costs too certain, the benefits far too uncertain.

This chapter explores the ways in which universities have increasingly become part of the state's strategy for securing the quiescence of Iranian youth. Ordinary Iranians have over the past three decades appropriated the country's secondary and postsecondary school systems for themselves, repurposing an ideological apparatus whose principal aim is to produce Islamic citizens loyal to the regime. Even as the appropriation of the educational system by ordinary Iranians for personal economic gain undermines the state's political and social agenda, the transformation of schooling from a public good into a coveted private resource presents an opportunity for the state to consolidate its authority over members of society.

This thesis challenges the widely held belief that the survival of the Islamic Republic of Iran (IRI) depends on the placation of Iran's youthful population through political mechanisms. It is commonly assumed that university education, and in particular the education of women, has produced a mortal threat to the IRI, a million ticking time bombs wired by the pedagogical state and inadvertently set against the revolution's foundations. Absent a "natural process of democratization" to contain and gradually release the collected energies of the student population, Iran's unhappy youth are sure to explode "as soon as they find an outlet for discharge."[3] I explore the possibility that not only is such a democratic process unnecessary, but it may be counterproductive for producing a long-lasting, durable, and above all, peaceful accommodation between the state and university students. Future accommodations will emerge not because an entrenched but vulnerable state apparatus is shouted down by an ever-emboldened student movement, but as a result of the banal interactions of ordinary Iranian families with a modernizing, developmentalist state whose legitimacy is increasingly secured through the distribution of academic credentials and merits, the educational "goodies" seen as essential to future economic and social success.

This chapter asks the reader to let go of assumptions they may have about the emancipatory effects that schooling has on young minds. Rather than looking to the university campus as the locus of transformative politics from above, democratic change is likely to be produced by ordinary members of society from below—by citizens, not subalterns, former students, not student movements—who, disciplined by the state and by choice, can take advantage of the institutional spaces made available to them by a state in formation.[4]

The correlation between schooling and student activism is particularly confused in the case of Iran, where popular and academic accounts of schooling's effects oscillate between a K–12 population easily molded by their teachers into loyal Islamic citizens and rebellious university students who actively reject Islam and the sacred values of the revolution in favor of the profane pursuit of freedom and fun.[5] Young Iranians, according to this convention, are naturally susceptible to the state's message—until they turn eighteen or go to college.[6]

To be clear, careerism does not preclude oppositional activism against the state. Indeed, significant segments of the student population consistently put their own futures at risk in spite of the extraordinary sacrifices that they and their families have made to be accepted into the university system. It is not uncommon to find student leaders drawn from the best students (*daneshjuyan-e nabegheh*) enrolled in the country's most prestigious departments and universities, by definition those who have the most to lose by their protests and the most to gain through their quiescence. Nothing in this chapter denies the virtue of their actions or the righteousness of their cause.

Rather than explain why the few are willing to risk it all, I choose instead to explore why the many agree to participate. Two dynamics do much of the work here: an increase in the perceived value of accreditation and a concomitant cost of student activism have transformed postrevolutionary schooling in Iran from a project of moral reform into a transactional relationship between Iran's educational system and a population more concerned with acquiring the distinctions and opportunities of "getting the paper" than becoming proper Islamic citizens.[7] In return for conceding the ideological character of the school system, state authorities have secured the cooperation of families and the withdrawal of their children from oppositional activities.

An emphasis on producing a meritocracy based on standardized testing and clear benchmarks for progress beginning in the late 1980s has also undermined state efforts to inculcate political Islam. Rather than internalize the state's message, standardization trains students and teachers to identify the material that will get students "past the test" and on to the next level. Internalizing the official ideology has little to no bearing on the central purpose of schooling for Iranian families and their young children, which is to get the grade, get the degree, get the job. The meritocracy thus becomes a trap for the ideological state, as revolutionary knowledge has become another measurable, an obstacle to be overcome on the path to college.

Reconstruction and the turn away from ideology in favor of the fostering of "technocratic talents," though a persistent source of contentious politics between conservatives and moderates in the government, has nonetheless been met with the tacit approval of state authorities willing to accommodate the population's desire for an equitable path for academic success. The consequences for state penetration have been tremendous. Fueled by a modernizing state determined to secure its borders, its revolution, and its legitimacy through the provision of educational goods, the rapid expansion of secondary, postsecondary, and graduate education since the 1990s has been enthusiastically embraced from below.

After analyzing the historical development of postsecondary schooling since 1979, I turn to a more narrow focus on the changing relationship of student movement organizations (SMOs) with liberal politics. Despite their present reputation as paragons of resistance to an authoritarian state, student groups in Iran were late to the democratic game. SMOs throughout the 1980s and early 1990s aligned with radical left elements in the government, enthusiastically embracing the enforcement, sometimes brutally, of the official line on campus, a role analogous with today's Student Basij Organization (SBO). It was only after the expulsion of their patrons from positions of authority and power in the early 1990s that the leadership of the Iranian student movement began the turn to democracy. Caught up in the cycle of what Bahman Bakhtiari has described as the politics of exclusion, the development of the student movement in Iran from dutiful appendage of the Islamic state to a democratic force at the forefront of Iran's nascent civil society was less teleology than the contingent outcome of brute politics.[8]

SMOs are unlikely to be a significant part of democracy's future. Starting in the late 1990s, state authorities began the systematic replacement of independent student movement organizations with official, state-funded student groups, quietly abandoning long-standing efforts to produce a broad-based university population of loyal, Islamic citizens in favor of a narrower but more ideologically certain group of students. This includes the Student Basij Organization, which I describe as the latest manifestation of the politics of exclusion as well as its endgame.

Official efforts to preserve student activism, ebullient but under the strict control of the state, are unlikely to work. Composed of a rigid organizational structure dependent on the state, the SBO provides its members an exclusive array of material benefits, including preferred standing in the university admissions process as well as an intangible sense of belonging. Taken together, this bundle of incentives dampens the ideological fervor of the SBO and renders members' relationship with the authorities transactional in nature.

I conclude by drawing upon Asef Bayat's concept of the social nonmovement to provide a preliminary sketch of how the private appropriation of the university system by ordinary Iranians has created some of the necessary conditions for the consolidation of democracy. Not unlike how Benedict Anderson describes the impact of the printing press, the establishment of universities in every corner of the country has produced a binding generational experience never before seen in modern Iranian history.[9] By eradicating long-standing hierarchies between the educated few and the unlettered many, making normal what was once exceptional, university education has fostered an ordinary sameness among the country's citizens that will prove to be propitious for democratic accommodation in Iran.

Names and Numbers: Iran's University System, 1979–2010

Iran's modern university system began with a single campus, the University of Tehran, founded in early 1935. Between 1935 and the 1979 revolution, the university system grew to include 341 institutions of higher education serving some 180,000 students. Today, more than thirty years after the founding of the IRI, entering students can choose from a wide range of options: 2,390 nationwide universities and higher education centers, divided between state and nonstate sectors.[10]

At the core of the state system are what is known alternatively as the *daneshgah-e sarasari, daneshgah-e dolati,* or *daneshgah-e ʿomumi,* 119 nationwide public universities that operate under the administration of the Ministry of Science, Research, and Technology (MSRT).[11] Considered the most prestigious of Iran's universities, *sarasari* schools provide tuition-free university education and operate daytime courses taught between September and June on a two-semester academic calendar, not unlike universities in the United States and Europe.

Educational planners established the distance learning university *Payam-e nur* in 1988 as a way of enhancing the capacity and reach of the university system into underserved and remote areas. *Payam-e nur* universities, or "Message of Light," operate through 550 learning centers across the country. In 1992, the Applied Science and Technology university, or *daneshgah-e jameʿ ʿelmi karbordi,* was founded to provide technical and vocational education for those interested in working in the industrial, agricultural, or service sectors of the economy. More than two decades later, *Payam-e nur* and Applied Science and Technology systems combine to include more than half of all of Iran's centers of learning, with 1,289 locations.

More than three hundred state universities operate under the purview of government ministries other than the MSRT, including Foreign Affairs; Post,

Telegraph, and Telephone; Roads and Transportation; and most notably, the Ministry of Education, which operates the largest share, some 274 universities.[12] These universities act as in-house centers of learning and provide pre-service and in-service courses for current and prospective ministry employees, generally in exchange for a commitment of service.

Fiscal and demographic pressures during the first decade of IRI prompted state leaders to allow the establishment of private universities and learning institutes, referred to as *gheir-e dolati*, or nonstate schools. Islamic Azad became the first private university to be sanctioned by the postrevolutionary regime. Founded in 1982, for many years Islamic Azad universities operated on what might best be described as a shoestring budget. Classes took place in public buildings or laboratories, often on loan from the then much larger public university system. Admissions to Islamic Azad was much easier than the more onerous *sarasari* schools, reflective of what was then its mission to provide education to nontraditional and older learners, individuals who were not necessarily interested in obtaining a formal credential or degree.

Islamic Azad is now one of the largest university systems in the world, with 385 campuses across Iran and in neighboring countries. Though it is technically a nonprofit organization, its $200 billion in claimed assets puts the Islamic Azad in a category well above even the most well-endowed universities in the United States, including Harvard at nearly $44 billion.[13] Until very recently, students and their families viewed Islamic Azad universities as little more than diploma mills or "safety" schools for students unable to gain access to the more prestigious public university system. Although *sarasari* universities remain the preferred choice for many young Iranians and their families, today private universities no longer operate under the perception that they are "second choice" or fallback options.[14]

A select group of universities remain uniquely insulated from the dynamic of merit and demobilization described here. Though small in number, they are significant because of their unique relationship to the Islamic system, or *nezam*. The universities of Imam Khomeini, Imam Baqer, and Imam Sadeq serve as centers for the selection and training of future cadres. Graduates are funneled directly into positions of leadership in various organs of the state, based on a loose division of labor between the universities. While all three institutions stress religious training as part of their curricula, Imam Khomeini is the most connected to the seminary system, or *howzeh*, in Qom and therefore tends to produce graduates who go on to work for the Office of the Supreme Leader. Imam Baqer operates under the authority of the Ministry of Information, its graduates channeled directly into the intelligence agency.

Imam Sadeq is perhaps the most significant of these three institutions in terms of its role in shaping and staffing the various branches of the government. Imam Sadeq was established in 1982 and continued to operate as one of the few universities allowed to remain open during the Cultural Revolution.[15] Imam Sadeq is highly selective and granted an unusual amount of autonomy; in addition to the required *Konkur*, it administers its own system of selection for students and teaching staff, as well as its own curricular materials. Classes are strictly gender-segregated and deal exclusively with subjects in the humanities and social sciences, or *'olum-e ensani*. It serves a role much like that of the Institut d'Etudes Politiques de Paris; graduates go on to work in relevant agencies and ministries, in particular the Ministry of Foreign Affairs and *Seda va Sima*, or National Radio and Television.[16]

Students who attend Imam Sadeq tend to be self-selecting, with a deep commitment to the Islamic *nezam*, or system. Complicating, perhaps even corrupting, this ideological fidelity is the near certainty that a degree from Imam Sadeq will lead to a future career in the state sector, a highly prized outcome for most university students. Despite Imam Sadeq's status as a *khas* or special university in service to the public authority, it, like all universities in Iran, is not immune to appropriation by ordinary Iranians for personal ends.

The Role of Universities

From the beginning, the leadership of postrevolutionary Iran has viewed the country's universities as an instrument for securing national independence and self-sufficiency, as well as validating the superiority of the Islamic system of government. Iranian universities were to be distinguished by their righteous character:

> Of course we should use knowledge as a means to help humanity achieve salvation. This is the difference between the Islamic view of knowledge and the materialistic view. We want to acquire knowledge in order to help humanity achieve salvation, growth, self-actualization, and justice. We want to acquire knowledge in order to help humanity realize its old dreams.[17]

Monica Ringer describes as the "modernization dilemma" the effort to adopt Western technology and political institutions while preserving local cultures and "authentic" selves.[18] While the modernization dilemma has a long pedigree in Iran, with origins in the educational debates of the nineteenth century, the IRI stakes its legitimacy on being the first to do it right. A common refrain by leaders is that the blind importation and aping of foreign concepts and technology under the Shah had been detrimental to the independence of Iran. Only through the indigenization of knowledge can Iranian universities ensure that science and technology will be put to righteous use:

> One important pillar of this resistance is knowledge. It is knowledge that has given us self-confidence. If we were dependent on foreign companies to

extract and refine oil for us, if we were dependent on foreign companies to build pipelines for our natural gas, if we were dependent on European experts to run our health system, if we were dependent on foreigners to provide us with food, if we were dependent on the Israelis to manage our agriculture and industry, if we were dependent on France, Germany and others to run our nuclear industry, we would not have this self-confidence today.[19]

The pursuit of knowledge requires an Islamic (i.e., Iranian) foundation of learning to receive the imprimatur of legitimacy. Education must be, in other words, a strictly local affair, designed by and for Iranians:

> The meaning of the Islamicization of universities is that they become independent. The meaning of the Islamicization of universities is that they become independent and separate themselves from the west or dependent on the east. We want to have an independent country, an independent university, and an independent culture.[20]

This does not mean that the research, science, and technology of foreign countries are to be ignored. Rather than develop from scratch an Islamic body of knowledge in the arts and sciences, Iran's leadership has since the revolution embarked on an old and familiar effort to draw from foreign sources the knowledge necessary for the further development and progress of Iran. Leaders extol the virtues of taking what is necessary from the foreigners but do so with the expectation that Iran will one day produce all of this material on its own:

> We are not embarrassed to learn from the westerners . . . we are not at all ashamed and we shall not be hesitant, we will go pursue [their knowledge] as their students. However, this apprenticeship comes with two conditions, conditions that unfortunately the Pahlavi regime did not abide. The previous regime closed its eyes and opened its arms wide and whoever came, with whatever they gave, the Pahlavis took. One of the two conditions is that whatever we take in, we shall first assess to see if it is of benefit to us or not. If the knowledge is one-hundred percent beneficial, then we shall accept it one-hundred percent. . . . The second condition is that this relationship of "master and student" must not last forever . . . one must not be a student forever. We must make ourselves professors.[21]

There is no religious prohibition on using foreign know-how, and tradition mandates that the true Muslim "seek to gain knowledge even in China."[22] However, foreign knowledge must never be accepted as whole cloth but must be tailored to the body, as it were, of Iran:

> We are not against the process of getting raw materials from them. It should not be assumed that we reject the products of western culture and its scientific advance that are sometimes miraculous. Such dogmatism is not in line

with Islamic views at all and we never follow this trend. We should design the building and it is not important where the raw, needed materials are procured. *However, these materials should fit the design* (emphasis added).[23]

If universities protect the country from threats from abroad, state leaders have also deployed postsecondary schooling as a means to secure tranquillity and legitimacy at home. Iran's new leaders following the revolution embarked on a program to extend the university system into underprivileged and underserved parts of the country, including remote rural areas as well as the neighborhoods of the urban poor, both as a way to achieve social justice through a more balanced geographic distribution of cultural capital, particularly to the principal constituents of the new regime, the *mostaz'afin* or dispossessed, and to reaffirm populist bona fides.[24]

State universities have led the way, penetrating into every province and nearly every major city.[25] Most of the growth occurred during the postwar period and outside the major metropolitan areas of Tehran, Tabriz, Isfahan, and Shiraz, where state universities had long been established, and was instead concentrated in underdeveloped *ostans* (provinces) such as Ilam, Bushehr, and Lorestan.[26]

The construction of provincial universities coincided with an aggressive strategy of localization. State planners established an elaborate quota system in the 1980s to encourage the enrollment of underrepresented students from provincial areas in the university system. These quotas also proved effective in halting the migration of student populations from rural areas to Iran's urban centers, particularly to Tehran.

Localization policies were so effective that they produced an unexpected reversal in the usual flow of students throughout most of the twentieth century from the provinces to the capital. Today, Tehran residents who fail to gain entry into local universities find themselves pulled toward outlying provinces. Tehran remains the center of the student population in Iran, as a ratio of the entire population, and many attend nonstate private universities in provinces adjacent to the capital. Iran's university population remains somewhat centralized, with the five provinces of Tehran, Isfahan, Khorasan Razavi, Fars, and Khuzestan comprising 45.8 percent of the total student population, but this concentration of students is less impressive in historical context. According to figures published for the 1990–1991 school year, Tehran alone had 40 percent of all students.[27]

Students seek schooling because they seek jobs. Markets in turn have responded to the demand. It is not by coincidence that Tehran's neighboring provinces of Qazvin, Mazandaran, and Markazi are among the small handful of provinces with a majority of private schools. Private schooling provides a market solution for students who want to stay near their families in Tehran but could not get into Tehran universities. One need only make the short trip from the capital to the town of Damavand. Located in a bucolic setting just thirty-six miles east of Tehran, Damavand ranks as the city with the greatest concentration of university students. Out of a population of over thirty-six thousand, approximately 40 percent are university students.[28] This is hardly by coincidence or because Damavand is a particularly important center of learning. Damavand's most notable quality is that it is close to the capital. The concentration of students there is the direct consequence of market forces responding to the demand for accessible alternatives to study in Tehran, where competition for entry into the university system is much more fierce.

The Appropriation from Below

Following his election in 1989, just weeks after Khomeini's death, President Akbar Hashemi Rafsanjani made it clear that his administration's top priority would be the restoration of Iran's war-devastated economy.[29] Development and reconstruction became the new watchwords as, for now, the incoming administration set aside the goal of expanding the revolution in favor of a more pragmatic social and political agenda.[30]

The introduction of meritocracy and specialization as the principal criteria for employment in the public, and to a lesser extent, private sectors set the stage for the rapid growth of the university system during the 1990s. This expansion came at a fortuitous time as Iran's postrevolutionary baby boomers were beginning to come of age. An expanded university system gave the state a means for absorbing the coming deluge, averting in the short term what threatened to be a demographic crisis of young people seeking to enter the workforce. This tactic of using universities as a form of crisis management would be repeated by subsequent administrations.

Ordinary Iranians, exhausted by years of austerity and constant mobilization and coming out of an almost unbroken decade of revolution and war, responded enthusiastically to the new educational opportunities provided by the postrevolutionary state. Soon the new meritocracy gave rise to its lesser cousin, credentialism or *madrak-garaei*. Being competent became interchangeable with being credentialed, particularly in the public sector, where the most desirable jobs were located.[31]

Economist Djavad Salehi-Isfahani argues that Iran's rigid labor market is the primary reason that families place so much value on the university degree. In an atavism of the revolution's leftist sensibility and commitment to social justice, the regime passed a measure in 1993 making it very difficult for a business or state agency to dismiss employees for cause. As a result of this law, hiring became risky business for both public and private employers. In a normal labor market, employers are free to dismiss employees that are ill-suited to the work that they were hired for. In the Iranian economy, a restricted labor market effectively forces employers to be stuck with their employees once the latter are on the job; competence has little bearing on job survival. As a consequence, employers look for ex ante signals of worker competence and productivity. All things being equal, the *Konkur* has effectively become this signal as it offers a reliable and universal measure of skill, albeit a rarefied set of abilities relevant only perhaps to the *Konkur* itself:

> Imagine a young student watching the behavior of her most likely employer: virtually all new public jobs require a university degree, once employed she will be paid according to the level of her formal schooling, and promotion and layoff are not directly related to her productivity. The signal is loud and clear: learn and study what you will but above all get a university degree![32]

A quick look at hiring practices in the public sector industries between 1992 and 2001 illustrates this point; in this period, the explosive growth of university education began. In Iran, as in most developing countries, a position in the state bureaucracy is prized over public sector work for its job security and relatively flexible work hours. For men without a university degree, public sector work remained relatively within reach a decade after the era of reconstruction began. Male employees with only a high school diploma remained steady in the period between 1992 and 2001, at employment rates of 23.12 percent to 25.14 percent, respectively. Employment rates for university-educated males, by contrast, more than doubled, going from a little more than 14 percent of the workforce in 1992 to over 32 percent in 2001.[33]

Employment rates for female employees show a more conclusive connection between university education and hiring practices in the public sector. In 1992, approximately 43 percent of all female state workers only had a high school education. That figure dropped by 9 points in 2001, to 34 percent. In the same period, the percentage of state workers with a university degree climbed by more than 20 points, from just under 40 percent to over 61 percent. These figures indicate that in contrast to their male peers, more university-educated women were applying for public sector work, and that state agencies were responding with more discretion in their hiring practices. For families with young daughters, the message was clear: without a degree, their child was unlikely to be hired.

But what happens when there are no jobs to be had? Official figures today show that 45 percent of all of Iran's unemployed workers hold at least a college degree. Recent graduates face an unemployment rate of 15.6 percent, which is higher than the national average.[34] For women the prospects are even especially dire. Most students complete their university education without securing a job or an obvious career path. More than 21 percent of all young people *with* a college degree were unemployed according to 2013 state figures, more than double the official national average.[35] An astounding 43 percent of college-educated women are without work. Young, overqualified, and unemployed, most of Iran's college graduates continue to live at home and toil away at jobs unrelated to their degrees and majors, a state of adolescent suspension that political scientist Diane Singerman has memorably labeled "waithood." They are unlikely to be hired even with a university degree, and certain not to be hired without it; thus, these figures call into question the utility of going to college in the first place.

While a college degree still offers on average greater social and economic opportunities than those available to non–degree holders, there is mounting evidence that the long-term benefits of going to university are approaching balance with its social and economic costs, seen most dramatically in the phenomenon of "waithood," the delayed entry of youth into the labor and marriage markets, and by extension, adulthood.[36] With unemployment rates for young college-educated Iranians greater than the average for the entire country, increasing numbers of youth are living at home with their parents while they await work.[37] One is reminded of the famous joke popular among Soviet workers during the worst years of the Brezhnev era when economic and social malaise were particularly acute: "We pretend to work, they pretend to pay us." Updated for today's Iran, this same joke might be formulated as follows: "In Islamic Iran they pretend to educate us, and we pretend to get jobs."

For now, pressure from below for access to a university education has not included a demand for jobs. Unlike in the US, where current debates reflect a growing sense that young people who played by the rules but now face diminished prospects in the job market have been sold a bill of goods, young people in Iran appear to be doubling down on the promise of higher education.[38] The evidence is most dramatic at the top of the educational system, where bottlenecks that once existed at the undergraduate level are steadily being pushed upward to the graduate level. Of the approximately 900,000 students who apply each year for a master's degree, only 60,000 are accepted, some 6 percent. The figures for a Ph.D. are even worse. Only 4 percent of those seeking a doctorate make it through, a meager 6,000 students out of 127,000 applicants.[39]

There is an alternative explanation for the persistence of students in the post-revolutionary school system, one unconcerned with neoliberal links between schooling and wage employment. More difficult to measure but no less significant as a factor fueling the educational boom of the past quarter century is the desire for dignity, to feel fully human. Sending a son or daughter to school, praying for him or her to be accepted at a university, became a form of justice. The provision of university education in rural and poor urban areas was for many segments of Iranian society the first time that they felt that someone cared about their plight. Attention brought a measure of dignity and self-worth to these long-neglected groups. It is a feeling captured by the expression *adam hesab shodand*, literally "being counted as human":

> Although the Shah's reform program had given peasants land and thereby increased their wealth and income, coming from above, it did not provide them with a new identity to go with the land. The newly liberated *ra'iyat* class [sharecroppers, literally "subjects"] still knew who they were and did not consider themselves full citizens. Even the many landless rural residents who migrated to the cities in the 1970s could not easily shed their identity. While no longer *ra'iyats*, they remained *dehatis* (villagers), a pejorative term still used in Iran to refer to people with poor manners or crude taste.[40]

Beyond the utility of education there is the feeling that under this regime, Iran's subalterns were able to (finally) claim their place in society as *citizens*, Islamic or otherwise.

Changes in enrollment patterns have been significant. The Pahlavi school system enrolled around 9 million students at its peak and had a coverage rate that never surpassed 60 percent, most of it concentrated in the primary level. Most students attended only elementary school, dropping out around the third grade; girls, after the second grade. In a country where, within living memory, the accomplishment of a sixth-grade diploma is remembered as an outstanding achievement, current gross enrollment rates of eighteen-to-twenty-four-year-olds in universities are on pace to make going to college a shared generational experience for most young Iranians.[41] The implications of this solidarity will prove crucial for the fate of democracy in Iran.

The State, Constrained by Its Own Success

While universities provide an important opportunity for the IRI to reproduce its legitimacy, the conciliation of a restless population is hardly its official function. The university system provides a cornerstone of the IRI's strategy to preserve the territorial integrity of Iran by providing for the country's economic and technological self-sufficiency, as well as acting as bulwarks against the ceaseless "cultural war" waged by the United States and her European allies against the youth of Iran.

The problem is that the bulwarks are being managed for the most part by humanities majors. Following the election of Mahmoud Ahmadinejad in 2005, conservative political, religious, and social leaders have relentlessly inveighed against the pernicious influence of "Western" philosophy and literature, and they raise the specter of a humanities literature that promotes skepticism and doubt in religious principles and beliefs. The shrillness of these voices only grew in the wake of the 2009 presidential crisis. "Many of our universities are under the influence of the humanities," proclaimed conservative newspaper editor Morteza Nabavi a year after the election, "the same humanities in which God is dead. In their . . . books they say openly 'God is dead and has no place in the political sphere, only humans are central [to such affairs].'"[42]

It is unclear what, if anything, can be done to remove the humanities or to "restore" God into the curriculum. The humanities, or *reshtehaye 'olum-e ensani*, have provided a major point of entry for students into the university system.[43] Of the nearly 3.8 million students enrolled in universities across Iran during 2009–2010, more than 1.6 million were enrolled in humanities departments, representing some 45 percent of the total student population. Whereas Iran's university population saw a seventeen-fold increase between 1978 and 2007, in that same period the number of humanities students increased by a factor of twenty-five.[44] Cheaper to organize and support than the sciences, the humanities have provided the leaders of the Islamic Republic with a quick and dirty way of bringing social and educational justice to remote villages and traditionally underserved urban populations.

State planners seeking to retrench the humanities thus face a thorny challenge. Anxiety over the pernicious effects of the humanities conflicts with efforts to secure state legitimacy at home. Purging the country's humanities departments of its "subversive elements" is likely to come at the cost of diminished participation rates, an unacceptable outcome from the perspective of an expansionist state. Complicating matters even further is the correlation between the humanities and the female student population. During the 2009–2010 school year, approximately 650,000 women were enrolled as humanities majors, some 65 percent of all humanities students.[45] The drive to place limiting quotas on the number of students accepted into humanities departments—the official policy is to have it down to 14 percent by 2015—risks undermining hard-fought gains of the past thirty years. The authorities simply cannot have it both ways. The salvation of Islamic schooling through the removal of so-called subversive elements will necessarily undermine the state's capacity to deliver on its promise to provide education for all Iranians.

Demobilized by Benchmarks and Testing

Postrevolutionary education *by its nature* demobilizes students and creates an environment in which politics and religion are for the most part external to the educational process. The culture of test taking that permeates Iran's educational system—with the *Konkur* at its apex—is largely to blame. Multiple-choice testing emerged in the late 1980s as an equitable response to the state struggle to process Iran's postrevolutionary "youth bulge" through the school system. The practical effect was the entrenchment of what was an already rigid and traditional pedagogy inherited from the previous regime, one rooted in methods of rote learning based on materials drawn exclusively from textbook content.

Iran, like many other countries where only a long memory-based and multiple-choice examination is used to determine admission to university, has seen its schools turn into "factories for exam cramming."[46] The memorization of easily forgotten facts in order to do well on the "big test" appears to work against efforts to inculcate Islamic and revolutionary values.[47] Teachers and students avoid political discussions about current affairs unrelated to the material found in textbooks, as these are seen as having the potential for unwanted and highly contentious confrontations in the classroom. Politics is an unwanted distraction from what is the primary task at hand, namely getting a grade, passing the test, and moving on to the next level:

> During the various stages of education, from elementary school to junior high, from high school and even until university, today's education means that the instructor makes four important points and the students takes these same four points and memorizes them, then later repeats this information on a test so that he or she can ultimately acquire a certificate (*madrak*).[48]

Rather than engage in open and contentious debate in the classroom, students are more likely to be subtly subversive, with disruptive behavior focused on "grade grubbing" or convincing teachers to reveal answers. Teachers know better than to try to resist these efforts:

> Right now in our society a good teacher is one that only teaches [facts]. It's not important if she behaves badly, she only has to teach well. Parents and students will tolerate bad language (*bad-dahani*) or rudeness (*raftarha-ye gheir-e tarbiati*), so long as the teacher teaches well. Why? Because of the promise of the *konkur*![49]

Iran's school system has managed to produce an efficient, transparent, and for the most part, objective system of measure of student achievement. Testing offers refuge from the corruption of access and personal connections (*parti bazi*) that plagues Iran's social spheres. The gauntlet of standardized tests that children must overcome in order to enter the university of their dreams provides families with a clear pathway to success.

Years of investment in children's education, made in a growing market in private schools and test preparation courses, means that students are more likely to be socialized to be academic strivers than loyal Islamic citizens *or* political protestors.[50] Paola Rivetti recently noted that scholars must be careful to not reflexively assume that students are naturally inclined to engage in opposition and protests. She writes that while it may be the case that universities are "the locus of dissent *par excellence*," they are also "the crucible where a sense of patriotism is instilled in students and the future political elite is educated and socialized into politics."[51]

Neither scenario may be true. Students who managed to avoid the educational system at age six or fourteen are unlikely to be seduced by the various state-sponsored activities and associations found on the university campus, including the SBO. The same logic of careerism that compels millions of young people to reach for the brass ring of a college degree is unlikely to abate once that goal is within sight.

Student Movements and the Politics of Exclusion

A persistent source of tension in the state's relationship with its university population stems from leaders' official desire to have "dynamic" and politically aware youth, but whose participation in political activities are restrained by state planning. Student movements are an indelible part of the regime's identity as well as the collective memory of revolution, having played a critical role in the overthrow of the Pahlavi regime as well as the subsequent consolidation of power by forces aligned with Khomeini. Enthusiasm for politically active students tends to be coupled with deep ambivalence. The old anxieties linger, left over from the chaos and tumult of the days and months leading up to the Cultural Revolution. Leaders hedge, sometimes with unhidden alarm, as in the following address by Ayatollah Khamenei:

> The spirit of political activities should be kept alive in universities because it can fill the youth with dynamism. We need dynamic youth. A university that is not involved in politics and is totally indifferent to political issues will be devoid of enthusiasm and dynamism. It will also become an appropriate place for the growth of dangerous intellectual and behavioral microbes.[52]

Khamenei commends the university environment even as he pathologizes entire segments of the student population ("dangerous intellectual and behavioral microbes"), suggesting the need for quarantine. He claims that authorities are responsible for preventing the "pathogens" from infecting the body social:

> But the meaning of political activities in universities should not be misinterpreted. Participation of universities in political activities does not mean that universities should become a place that can be abused by political movements, groups, and elements to further their political goals . . . Political activities have to be planned.[53]

The contradictory desire for "planned" spontaneity is a lingering effect of the tumultuous early days of the IRI when, in the wake of the overthrow of the Shah, previously allied leftist, liberal, and Islamic student associations turned against each other, transforming the country's universities into virtual battle-grounds with marches, demonstrations, and physical confrontations occurring daily.

Gaining control over the universities became an immediate priority for the new authorities. Responding to months of turmoil and conflict between student groups on the country's university campuses, and fully cognizant of the important role that the universities had played in ending the Shah's reign—and therefore, their potential for ending reign of the current regime—on June 12, 1980, Ayatollah Khomeini established the Headquarters for the Cultural Revolution (*Setad-e enqelab-e farhangi*), formally launching what came to be known as the Cultural Revolution (1980–1983). Although the formal purpose of the Cultural Revolution was to extricate the corrupt influence of foreign powers "east and west" from university campuses, the closure of Iran's campuses was a play by the ruling authorities to consolidate their own power on campus. Once the universities reopened in the fall of 1983, only state-sanctioned Islamic Student Association (ISA) groups and their umbrella group, the *Daftar-e tahkim-e vahdat-e howzeh va daneshgah*, Office for the Consolidation of Unity between the Islamic Seminaries and the Universities—known more commonly as the *Daftar-e Tahkim-e Vahdat*, or Office for the Consolidation of Unity (OCU)—were allowed to have a presence on campus.

The old anxieties from those initial days of conflict persist to this day. Akbar Mahdi observes that the IRI has had difficulty in balancing this traumatic past with its future. Students, after all, were critical in the movement that led to the end of the monarchy, and therefore they cannot easily be expunged from either the official narrative of the past or the present: "The regime wants to have it both ways. It wants to claim that students are free to organize and be politically active, but only if they are Muslim and supporters of the IRI. It wants to have an active body, but only if its activities support the causes of the regime."[54]

"Regime" may be too big a word. For the most part, the loyalty of student movement organizations to the revolution has not been an issue. Ruptures between authorities and students have for the most part been along partisan lines. Like all of Iran's postrevolutionary institutions, SMOs are deeply affected by factional rivalries, closely mirroring at the local level what Bakhtiari calls the national "politics of exclusion."[55] According to Bakhtiari, Iran's political system achieves stability through the exclusionary policies of one faction or coalition toward its factional rivals. The politics of exclusion persists because no single faction is ever fully in charge or able to achieve a decisive consolidation of power. Groups shut out from the center regularly cycle back into power, in a pattern that wreaks havoc on the capacity of the IRI to govern but nonetheless produces a political equilibrium that sustains the system.[56]

What was a once vibrant, diverse, and independent student movement dissolved completely into the ruling structure, or *nezam*, following the establishment of the Headquarters for the Cultural Revolution, now known as the Supreme Council for the Cultural Revolution. Although today the ISA and OCU are associated with the reform and opposition movements in Iran, in their first incarnation during the 1980s these two groups operated as an appendage of the state, then under the control of what is now known as the Islamic left.[57] ISA members acted as the state's eyes and "muscle" on campus, creating a repressive environment for most of the student population. Many nonmembers responded with alienation and fear to student organizations that were given a free hand to act, often physically, against classmates deemed to insufficiently "Islamic" or supportive of the regime.

The death of Khomeini and the election of Hashemi Rafsanjani to the presidency in the summer of 1989, along with the dissolution of the position of prime minister, held throughout the decade by Mir-Hossein Mussavi, saw the departure of the Islamic left from the government. With their patrons cast into the political wilderness, members of the ISA and OCU experienced a decline in their influence on the government. Rather than seek new sponsorship or alliances with the Hashemi Rafsanjani administration, student activists maintained close ties with men like former prime minister Mussavi, then culture minister Mohammad Khatami, and above all, source of emulation Grand Ayatollah Hossein-Ali Montazeri. The symbiotic relationship of students and political leaders continued outside the corridors of power, as both groups embarked on a long process of study and introspection that led to the Iranian reform movement, culminating in the surprise election of Khatami to the presidency in 1997.

For the political forces on the right of the political spectrum, the absence of student allies on university campuses was a cause for concern. They responded by establishing three major student associations to act as their campus proxies, in a top-down fashion that would become characteristic of the right's relationship with the student movement. By far the most important of these right-aligned student groups was the SBO, whose sole allegiance was to the Office of the Supreme Leader and the figure of Ayatollah Khamenei.[58]

The election of Khatami to the presidency in 1997 saw a restoration of the religious left, as well as the return of the ISA and the OCU as a political and social force. Khatami's surprise victory was due in no small measure to the mass mobilization of friends and families by university students, a phenomenon that his political rivals on the right viewed with great alarm. Unable to compete with the popularity of the reformists among university students, conservative forces stepped up their efforts to strengthen the SBO as a proxy force for containing the ISA and the OCU.

Victory at the ballot box in the late 1990s and early 2000s lead to increased tensions between officials and their student allies. Although the OCU gained a seat at the table as a player in the Khatami administration, the two had very different agendas and ambitions. Student groups came to view the Khatami administration as too conservative in its dealings with the Supreme Leader and other conservative elements of the regime. They pressed Khatami to use his authority and the mandate of "twenty million votes" to produce democratic changes to the Constitution and structure of the Islamic Republic. The government in turn increasingly viewed the student movement as unnecessarily making the lives of administration difficult, undermining the reform movement with their demands.

Events came to a head in July 1999, when peaceful protests of University of Tehran students in support of the recently closed reformist paper *Salam* was met with violent action by state forces, including members of the SBO. Six days of protests ensued in what came to be known as the 18th of Tir, or *Kuye daneshgah* (University Street), at the time the most widespread and violent clashes between state and society since the 1979 revolution.

The incident prompted a final rupture between reformists and student activists and led to the fracturing of the OCU. Although the Khatami administration quickly came to the defense of student protesters in order to prevent further bloodshed, behind the scenes government officials working in tacit agreement with the student leadership drew distinctions between activists who were "*khodis*," "in-group" forces deemed loyal to the revolution, and "*gheir-e khodis*," "out-group" members deemed to be anti-regime.

This action proved fatal to the unity of the OCU leadership. Disenchantment with the Khatami administration and growing frustration with the inability of the student movement to gain greater traction led many to reconsider the utility of the factional alliance with the reformists. Irreconcilable divisions emerged between those who wished to push the student movement into a more broad-based civil society movement and those who believed that the preservation of the *nezam* was tantamount, more important than the promotion of one faction over another. The social movement and pro-*nezam* wings of the OCU formally separated in 2002 into the 'Allameh and Shiraz factions, respectively. Shortly thereafter, ultraconservative students took full control of the Shiraz faction, declaring it to be the only "true" version of the OCU, effectively marking its demise.

For conservative forces, the lesson of July 1999 was that the use of force, combined with the forced isolation and exclusion of political opponents, works. Authorities doubled down on their relationship with the SBO, most notably by approving a law ensuring that 40 percent of admissions to all universities would be active Basij members.[59] Four official student groups are operating with state permission on university campuses, all of them aligned with conservative forces.[60]

Without question, the most significant of these is the SBO in terms of numbers, financial resources, and above all, affiliation with the Office of the Supreme Leader. Official figures place the number of SBO members in 2010 at 600,000, with seven hundred offices in different academic departments throughout the country.[61]

The End of Exclusion and the Rise of the Social Nonmovement

The politics of exclusion that have characterized Iran's postrevolutionary student movement for so long is today rendered irrelevant because there is no one left to exclude. Although lip service is given to the importance of maintaining an "aware" student population (*daneshjuyan-e agah*), in the wake of the 2009 protests state leaders have set out to systematically sanitize the country's university campuses, to "keep out the microbes" as it were. Inoculation has meant the prohibition of oppositional SMOs, replaced by state-sponsored organizations such as the SBO.[62] Though the election of Ahmadinejad sparked a brief rejuvenation of oppositional activity, the period since 2005 has been one of intensifying pressure on autonomous student groups, and in particular on the ISA and 'Allameh faction of the OCU, who maintain a presence on university campuses despite their official designation as illegal groups.

So far, the state's carrot-and-stick approach to its "student problem" has proven successful. Many students reject activism out of an abundance of caution for the damage that protests brings to their economic and social futures, as well as a growing and reasoned skepticism that protests will produce tangible results. One former student wrote about the brief flourishing of student activism during the Green Movement:

> On one level, it seems necessary for the greater democratic movement in Iran. On another, I think it is in the best interests of the students themselves to focus on their schoolwork, and not have to pay such a hefty price. Having worked closely with the Muslim Students Association at my school, I know that the students themselves and their families face this dilemma every single day even when the environment was less lethal: do we become more politically active and risk everything? Or mind our own business and just get on with our lives?[63]

There appears to be a growing recognition that the student movement and young people in Iran cannot achieve their goals outside a broader social context of change:

> "I'm against protests because I don't think they work," Marjan, a design student in her 20s who voted for Karroubi in 2009, told me. "People just get hurt.... Iranians are scared, and they *should* be scared. Sometimes people say,

'Even if I'm dead, something good will happen after that.' But what if you get killed for nothing? I'd rather have slow change than a revolution."[64]

A *Los Angeles Times* profile of Babak Zamanian, a former engineering student turned student leader, offers a sobering account of sacrifices seemingly made "for nothing." The profile was written well before the rise and fall of the Green Movement; Zamanian went from being one of Iran's most outspoken students to "one of its walking dead":

> Zamanian, 22, now doubts that it was worth it. Maybe he should have kept quiet and stuck to his studies at Tehran's Amir Kabir University of Technology, he says. He could have become a mining engineer, like his dad wanted, raised a family and read books and newspapers to sate his passion for politics.[65]

Zamanian's story is hardly unique, and reading his mournful tale raises painful questions about the ethics of looking to the young to produce change, to say nothing of their ability to see it through in isolation from the rest of society.

Faith in the irrepressibility of youth continues unabated, however, with many analysts holding on to the expectation that the next political crisis in Iran will begin with the students. There are even suggestions that hard-line members of the SBO will eventually defect from their sanctioned role, following the historical precedent established by the ISA and OCU. Mohammad Sahimi deems such an outcome inevitable:

> And was the primary goal, of taming the universities, achieved? The answer is an emphatic no. By the time Rafsanjani began his second term as president in 1993, the same [ISA] and OCU that had played important roles in the "cultural revolution" had become critics of his government. They played an important role in the landslide victory of Mohammad Khatami in the 1997 election. The July 1999 uprising in the dormitories of the University of Tehran that shook the nation demonstrated that the universities can never be a tool in the hands of the hardliners and reactionaries, at least not in the long run.[66]

Few could have anticipated that the ISA and OCU, which were so dogmatic throughout the 1980s, would break with the state in pursuit of liberal democracy. Might the SBO follow a similar path?

Such a scenario is highly unlikely. Even at the height of their collaboration with the state during the 1980s, both groups were characterized by their grassroots and autonomous nature. The ISA and OCU were, and remain, fully organic operations, unfunded and unorganized by the state. The SBO, by contrast, is completely "state" in its origins, funding, organization, and purpose. It neither is independent nor seeks to be, and it is without any real self-identity other than its function as the servants of the Supreme Leader.

This does not mean that the SBO is a sure ally for Iran's conservatives. Basij members emerge from the same meritocratic system as their non-Basij peers and are not immune to the economic and social pressures described earlier in this chapter. Formal studies by the Basij confirm that most Iranians (62 percent), Basij and non-Basij, perceive material benefits to be the motivating factor for membership in the SBO.[67] These survey results were reaffirmed by a 2006–2007 survey of SBO members. Sociologist Saeid Golkar found that 66.3 percent of respondents reported that their fellow members had joined the organization in order to receive incentives such as university admissions privileges, future employment and promotion opportunities, and welfare services. This somewhat cynical assessment of the SBO membership did not apply to the respondents themselves. When asked why they had joined, 96.7 percent listed "ideology" as the most important reason.[68]

That we continue to think of universities "as centers of dissent and opposition to repressive ruling elites"[69] speaks to the significant legacy of student activism during the middle of the twentieth century in Iran, as well as a more generalized notion that universities are constitutionally inclined toward political and social activism. Democratic breakthroughs are unlikely to begin with university students or the university campus. The combination of consent and coercion is simply too much, the allure of material incentives too strong, the logic of the meritocracy with all of its norming attributes too powerful. It is not lost on the IRI that the last Shah of Iran met his end largely because of the activism of university students. It is a lesson internalized, and a mistake that Iran's current leaders are determined not to repeat.

Quietude should not be confused with quiescence, however. The comprehensive expansion and normalization of university education has already produced the most educated generation in Iranian history. Without being oriented toward a particular ideology or political project, this cohort represents a political force just by virtue of its presence. This generation of students constitutes what Asef Bayat describes as a social nonmovement, "the collective actions of noncollective actors [who] embody shared practices of large numbers of ordinary people whose fragmented but similar activities trigger much social change" that is unguided by leadership from above.[70] Dispersed, atomized, and divided, a growing share of Iranians have nonetheless formed collective identities through their participation in postsecondary institutions, "linked to one another passively and spontaneously through 'passive networks.'"[71] Their unspoken solidarity produces a "a politics of redress through direct action."[72]

Faced with the weight of numbers, states have little choice but to accommodate the piecemeal demands of millions of young adults and their families. Under repression and constant surveillance, the desire to go to college poses the greatest risk for the authoritarian state because of the "consequential effect on norms and rules in society of many people simultaneously doing similar, though contentious things."[73] Of course, in the Iranian context, being similar is not contentious; by attending college citizens are doing precisely what the state wants. Quietude is a condition and an outcome for participation in the educational system. Yet participation makes it possible to affect social norms and rules. Students not only do "similar things," they become more similar by doing, by being in the university classroom together.

Bayat cautions that this unfocused pressure from below should not be confused as the "harbinger of democratic transformation."[74] "Youth may become agents of democratic change," he writes, "only when they act and think politically; otherwise, their own narrow youthful claims may bear little impetus for engaging in broader social concerns."[75] There has to be a critical moment of self-awareness, a cultivation of consciousness through praxis prior to the assault on the authoritarian state. The quiet, hidden encroachments of nonmovement subalterns will be fully transformative only *after* the pivot to the visible and noisy politics of social movements engaged with state authority.[76]

Bayat unexpectedly adheres to a conventional understanding of how "real" political change occurs with this move. Having criticized resistance authors for the tendency "to confuse an awareness about oppression with acts of resistance against it," Bayat sneaks intentionality back into his analysis. The effect, no doubt unintended given Bayat's normative commitments, is to affirm the indispensability of the enlightened few who, having fused cognition with practice, reach out to the state on behalf of a general population assumed to be incapable of doing the same on its own.

If the value of the concept of the nonmovement is to recover the presence and the power of the hidden subaltern by drawing our attention to alternative, *potential* forms of politics taking place outside the state's view and without intention, then it remains unclear why students need to abandon their "narrow" selves for broader change to occur. Perhaps social and political transformation is not a matter of obtaining consciousness in the minds of the young. After all, the near-ubiquity of sending a son or daughter to college, or of knowing a family member who has already graduated with a degree, means that campus life and the world outside the university can no longer be conceived as distinct realms in Iran, one in need of saving by the other, but as parts of an intermeshed social reality that share the same fate. What might a truly ordinary movement on behalf of democracy look like, a politics in which, rather than one group acting on behalf of others, the two become one and the same, made similar by their shared experiences? What if the ordinariness of students' habitus becomes indistinguishable from the mundane practices of society at large?

The lives of students may play a significant role in securing democratic futures, no matter how oblivious or carefree those lives may appear to the outside observer. Universities, by contributing to the erosion of long-standing divisions between the learned few and the unlettered many, have created conditions in Iran in which democracy is *already being consolidated*. Being an ambitious student while in college, and participating in the routine of a mundane life afterward, is a type of prefigurative politics, a moral and social reform that produces the necessary conditions for democracy's consolidation, if not its initial spark.

From Extraordinary Experiences Comes an Ordinary Breakthrough

The principal aim of this essay has been to push back against the perception that Iran's university and youth populations are, either by their nature or by their functional role as students, drawn to oppositional activity against the state and regime. Analysts regularly assume that this is a regime forever put at risk by the demographic time bomb of educated and restless youth, the 70 percent of the country's population under age thirty. They claim that the IRI has effectively defused the "youth threat" by conceding the ideological character of the school system to families in exchange for the withdrawal of their children from oppositional activities.

The growth of university education in Iran, rather than instilling enthusiasm for political Islam, promotes the demobilization and depoliticization of the student body. Rather than occupy themselves with uncertain political movements, students pursue academic credentials that will, presumably, hopefully, secure their economic and social futures. Despite considerable outrage in the media and among the general public about the inability of Iran's educational system to funnel graduates into the workforce, the demand for college among ordinary Iranians remains insatiable and unlikely to diminish in the near term.

Finally, the historical development of the student movement since 1979 toward democracy has been more contingent than functional, the result of changes in factional alliances. An independent student movement only emerged in the postrevolutionary period after the once-dominant Islamic left was shut out of power in the late 1980s. By the time student leaders made their move to head the democratic movement in Iran, it was too late. Curtailed by a repressive state and burdened by the growing perception that student issues and advocacy were irrelevant to the lives of ordinary Iranians, SMOs found themselves increasingly marginalized both on and off campus.

Old obligations die hard, however. Intellectuals have played an outsized role in the social and political development of modern Iran, a legacy that many student leaders are keen to preserve. In a 2007 interview, student activist Abdollah Momeni explains that the student movement views itself as a social vanguard whose privilege is to have access to the truths needed for political reform.

This knowledge makes the university student uniquely qualified to intervene on behalf of the larger population.

> Since the true capital of the student movement lies in its intellectual power and capacity for analysis, it is qualified to critically observe and to assess the limits and consequences of the government's actions without aspiring to gain power itself.

Momeni goes on to describe the particular work that student movements provide:

> The student movement is the collective consciousness of the people, which with the aid of its constant evaluation of the various power relations at work, promotes freedom and democracy and reduces the gap between the dominant politics and the interests of the people.[77]

Tragically, the relevant gap was between student activists and the population that they aspired to represent, rather than between the state and the people.[78] In every major protest movement since the 1990s, including the 1999, 2003, and 2009–2010 Green Movement protests, student groups have proved unable to expand or sustain their message or leadership beyond the university campus in a durable way.

Part of the reason, of course, is that the guidance of students is no longer needed nor desired. The ongoing expansion of the university student population, both in raw numbers and in social background, is on track to make the label of "student leader" a distinction without a difference. Although Iran's 3.7 million students constitute only 5 percent of the country's total population, more than 30 percent of youth ages eighteen to twenty-four are enrolled in some form of higher education, well on pace to reach the state's formal goal of 60 percent by 2025, a remarkable achievement if we consider that in 1996 less than half of fifteen- to eighteen-year-old Iranians were enrolled in high school, much less interested in going to college.[79] With the expansion of education and the arrival of an intellectual in every village and city neighborhood, the presence and importance of the intellectual has diminished considerably. Why be led by someone else's vision when I can come up with my own? The leveling of Iran's educated society means that in the future, rather than university students leading mass protests, demonstrations are more likely to feature protesters who happen to be students.[80]

Alexis de Tocqueville observed many years ago that the democratic age leads to the loss of distinction, the irrevocable erosion of the authority of our "betters." Citizens "do not recognize any signs of incontestable greatness or superiority in any of their fellows, [and] are continually brought back to their own judgment as the most apparent and accessible test of truth."[81] For those living in the age of equality, "confidence in any particular man . . . is destroyed" and "a general distaste for accepting any man's word as proof of anything" becomes one's default mode.[82]

Postsecondary education, designed to identify and affirm what is exceptional about Iran, has made men and women ordinary. Attending university was once an extraordinary experience, the exclusive purview of wealthy and well-connected elites. While the meritocracy produces its own set of hierarchies based on the accumulation of cultural capital, as access to college becomes more commonplace, an expectation instead of an exception, the possession of a university degree has become less relevant to authority or citizenship.

Paradoxically, by producing conditions of "ordinary sameness," universities fuel the present mania for degrees—recall the demand for advanced degrees, for the Ph.D. and the M.A.—which in turn accelerates the demand for even more universities to be constructed and made available to the population. Agonies about being ordinary, of not having the proper distinction, or any distinction at all—a distinction that once was readily available simply by passing the big test or getting into the right school—fuel the ceaseless pursuit of credits and merits. This too was anticipated by Tocqueville: "a multitude of artificial and arbitrary classifications are established to protect each man from the danger of being swept along in spite of himself with the crowd."[83] Restless and increasingly alike, Iranian citizens seek to secure their "special worth" through the losing struggle to accumulate more degrees that then enable them to purchase the material goods that will separate them from the crowd, including more university degrees!

Universities have made men and women ordinary in Iran. This may turn out to be the most important work that they do. In a country long governed by rigid social hierarchies premised on wealth and on education, the erosion of unearned distinction may not necessarily lead to the outbreak of democracy, but it will surely matter when the next democratic breakthrough comes. Democracy is more likely to survive because the hard work of producing the leveled social and political expectations that distinguish the democratic soul from the feudal, the present from the past, will have already happened. Democratic transformation is surely already taking place in Iran, an extraordinary and so far unnoticed change produced by the accumulation of ordinary, educated lives.

Notes

1. Shervin Malekzadeh [as "Anonymous"],"Dispatch from Tehran: Blood and Defiance in Azadi Square," *Salon*, June 16, 2009. http://www.salon.com/2009/06/16/tehran_three.

2. "Iran Tightens Security amid University Exams," *Press TV*, June 25, 2009. http://edition.presstv.ir/detail/99019.html.

3. Ali Akbar Mahdi, "The Student Movement in the Islamic Republic of Iran," *Journal of Iranian Research and Analysis* 15, no. 2 (November 1999): 5–32.

4. The empirical claims in this chapter are in line with a theoretical literature that rejects the binary of resistance-domination in order to examine agency in terms of existing

structures. Here I am strongly influenced by Afsaneh Najmabadi's observation that the "disciplinary techniques and emancipatory promises" of schooling are simultaneous and mutually enabling. See Afsaneh Najmabadi, "Crafting an Educated Housewife in Iran." In *Remaking Women*, edited by Lila Abu-Lughod (Princeton, NJ: Princeton University Press, 1998), 91–125. Saba Mahmood makes a similar claim with her insight that we ought to view "agency not as a synonym for resistance to relations of domination, but as a capacity for action that historically specific relations of subordination enable and create." Saba Mahmood, "Feminist Theory, Embodiment, and the Docile Agent: Some Reflections on the Egyptian Islamic Revival," *Cultural Anthropology* 16, no. 2 (May 2001): 203.

5. Arnon Groiss, *Iranian Textbooks: Preparing Iran's Children for Global Jihad* (Mevaseret-Zion, Israel: Center for Monitoring the Impact of Peace, 2007); Saeed Paivandi, *Discrimination and Intolerance in Iran's Textbooks* (Washington, DC: Freedom House, 2008). http://www.rdfi .org/pdf/textbook.pdf; Hossein Aryan, "Commentary: How Schoolchildren Are Brainwashed in Iran," *Radio Free Europe/Radio Liberty*, May 27, 2010. http://www.rferl.org/content /Commentary_How_Schoolchildren_Are_Brainwashed_In_Iran/2054304.html. It is not just Western observers who see failure. "These were children who had been nurtured by the Islamic Republic. Suddenly [one day] we opened our eyes and saw that they were soldiers in the anti-religious [Green] Movement, willing to take on all manner of risk." As reported in *Sedaye sabz-e azadi*, June 5, 2010. http://www.irangreenvoice.com/article/2010/may/06/3086.

6. A veritable cottage industry has emerged since the 1990s as journalists and academics pursue Iran's elusive youth population for evidence of democratic breakthroughs. Some recent examples include Nazila Fathi, "An 'Iranian Spring': How Iran's Youth Are Seeking Reform in a New Way," *Huffington Post*, February 23, 2015, http://www.huffingtonpost.com/nazila-fathi /iranian-spring-irans-youth_b_6664786.html; Matt McCann, "Youth in Iran: Inside and Out," *New York Times*, January 26, 2014, Lens.blogs.nytimes.com/2014/01/16/youth-in-iran-inside -and-out/?_r=0; Nicholas Kristof, "In Iran, They Want Fun, Fun, Fun," *New York Times*, June 20, 2012, http://nyti.ms/1EyCo9R; "Young Iranians 'Claustrophobic' as Culture Is Forced Online but Accessed in Private," *The Guardian*, June 3, 2014, http://www.theguardian.com /world/iran-blog/2014/jun/03/iran-youth-internet-restrictions-claustrophobia. For an academic approach, see Roxanne Varzi, *Warring Souls: Youth, Media, and Martyrdom in Post-Revolution Iran*, (Durham, NC: Duke University Press, 2000).

7. "Learn and study what you will," writes one longtime observer of Iran's educational system, "but above all get the university degree!" Djavad Salehi-Isfahani, "Human Resources in Iran: Potentials and Challenges," *Iranian Studies* 38, no. 1 (March 2005): 133.

8. Bahman Bakhtiari, *Parliamentary Politics in Revolutionary Iran* (Gainesville: University of Florida Press, 1996).

9. Benedict Anderson, *Imagined Communities: Reflections on the Origin and Spread of Nationalism* (London: Verso, 1983).

10. "*Amar-e daqiq te'dad-e daneshgahha-ye iran*" ("Precise statistics of Iran's universities"), *Mehr News*, May 13, 2011.

11. On March 8, 1979, less than one month after the overthrow of the monarchy, the first formal legislative action of the new regime and revolutionary government was to establish the Ministry of Culture and Higher Education. Parliament established a separate Ministry of Health and Medical Education in 1985 to oversee medical training of doctors and physicians. The ministry overseeing the university system received its current name of Ministry of Science, Research, and Technology in 2000 as part of the Third Economic, Social, and Cultural Development Plan.

12. The Ministry of Education is responsible for the pre-university school system.

13. Hamid Farokhnia, "Azad University: A Schooling in Power Politics," *Tehran Bureau*, July 8, 2010. http://www.pbs.org/wgbh/pages/frontline/tehranbureau/2010/07/a-schooling-in-power-politics.html.

14. Azad universities, for example, have their own, equally rigorous version of the *Konkur*.

15. The formation of the Headquarters of the Cultural Revolution marked the beginning of what came to be known as the Cultural Revolution (1980–1983). Authorities shuttered universities ostensibly to "Islamicize" the curricula and to purge "West-struck" students and professors from campuses. Ideological motivations obscured the primary political purpose of the Cultural Revolution, which was to provide cover for the consolidation of power of Khomeini and his adherents on college campuses, then racked with constant turmoil. With leftist, liberal, and Islamic groups facing off against each other daily, universities were transformed into ideological, and even physical, battlegrounds. Gaining control over the universities was the immediate priority, and only when this was accomplished did the state begin reopening campuses in the fall of 1982.

16. "Imam Sadeqis" tend to take care of their own when it comes to hiring new personnel and staffing decisions.

17. "Supreme Leader's Speech in University of Tehran," February 2, 2010. http://english .khamenei.ir//index.php?option=com_content&task=view&id=1314&Itemid=4.

18. Monica Ringer, *Education, Religion, and the Discourse of Cultural Reform in Qajar Iran* (Costa Mesa, CA: Mazda, 2001).

19. Khamenei's Speech to University Professors," August 25, 2011. http://english.khamenei .ir/index.php?option=com_content&task=view&id=1520&Itemid=4.

20. Ruhollah Khomeini, "The Meaning of Cultural Revolution: Address to Iranian Students in Tehran, April 26, 1980." In *Islam and Revolution*, edited and translated by Hamid Algar (London: Mizan, 1981), 297. Passages such as the ones cited lend credence to what Farideh Farhi has called the "almost pathological" Iranian yearning for independence. Farideh Farhi, "The Revolutionary Legacy: A Contested and Insecure Polity." In *Viewpoints Special Edition: The Iranian Revolution at 30* (Washington, DC: Middle East Institute, 2009), 29–31.

21. *"Shagerdi bas ast!"* ("Enough with being a student!"). Khamenei speaking to a group of teachers in Fars, April 21, 2008, cited in Seyyed Ali Khamenei, *"Ta che tasviram konand"* ("Reflections on how we can . . . selected remarks by the Leader about education"). http://farsi .khamenei.ir/speech-content?id=8118.

22. Seyyed Ali Khamenei, speech made on the occasion of the first anniversary of the establishment of the Supreme Council of Cultural Revolution, December 25, 1985. http://www .iranculture.org/en/about/rahbar/mrahbar/b01-02.php.

23. Ibid.

24. The *mostaz'afin*'s role in the revolution is complicated, to say the least. This group may have become the symbol of the revolution after the Shah's overthrow, but their actual participation during the revolution was limited—in the case of the rural poor, nonexistent—and came only in the revolution's final stages. In some cases, the poor were even hostile to the revolutionaries. For an excellent discussion, see Charles Kurzman, *The Unthinkable Revolution in Iran* (Cambridge, MA: Harvard University Press, 2004), 100–101. Kurzman bases his analysis on ethnographies carried out by researchers before and during the revolution. See also Farhad Kazemi, *Poverty and Revolution in Iran* (New York: New York University Press, 1980); and Janet Bauer, "Poor Women and Social Consciousness in Revolutionary Iran." In *Women and Revolution in Iran*, edited by Guity Nashat (Boulder, CO: Westview, 1983), 141–169.

25. Out of 367 metropolitan areas, 347 have at least one public or private university.

26. After the 1934 establishment of Iran's first university in Tehran by Reza Pahlavi, subsequent universities were established in Tabriz, Isfahan, and Shiraz in 1946. For growth figures,

see Keiko Sakurai, "University Entrance Examination and the Making of an Islamic Society in Iran: A Study of the Post-Revolutionary Iranian Approach to '*Konkoor*,'" *Iranian Studies* 37, no. 3 (September 2004): 385–406.

27. "*Joz'iat-e amar-e atlas-e melli-ye amuzesh-e keshvar*" ("Details of the statistics of the national atlas on education in the country"), *Hamshari*, January 3, 2011. Further diluting the impression that students are concentrated in a single part of Iran is the fact that the ratio of students to the total of these five provinces more or less matches the ratio in the population (approximately 46 percent). In other words, proportionally there is not much difference between the student population and the overall population of these territories.

28. "*Joz'iat-e amar-e atlas-e melli-ye amuzesh-e keshvar.*"

29. Nick B. Williams Jr., "90% of Iranian Votes are Cast for Rafsanjani," *Los Angeles Times*, July 30, 1989.

30. Market liberalization faltered well before the end of Hashemi Rafsanjani's second term. For a good overview of how politics, and Rafsanjani himself, undermined free-market reforms, see Laura Secor, "The Rationalist," *New Yorker*, February 2, 2009.

31. Although public sector salaries were modest, they offered job security and a dependable wage.

32. Salehi-Isfahani, "Human Resources in Iran," 133.

33. Ibid., 132.

34. "*Afzaesh-e zarfiat-e daneshgahha, afzaesh-e faregh-ol-tahsilan-e bikar*" ("Increase in the universities' capacity, increase in unemployed graduates"), *Hamshari*, July 26, 2009.

35. *Mehr News*, May 28, 2014. http://www.mehrnews.com/news/2299004/5-6-.

36. Diane Singerman, "The Economic Imperatives of Marriage: Emerging Practices and Identities among Youth in the Middle East," working paper no. 6, Wolfensohn Center for Development at Brookings Dubai School of Government, The Middle East Youth Initiative (September 2007). Singerman paraphrases the economic phenomenon of "wait unemployment," meaning long periods of unemployment, endured by educated young people in countries with large public sectors in the hopes of securing a well-paying and likely permanent state job.

37. Salehi-Isfahani notes that the transition to adulthood for educated youth is often more difficult than for less educated youth. Salehi-Isfahani addresses the relationship of education and employment to the Third Development Plan of the postrevolutionary period in "Iran's Third Development Plan: A Reappraisal," working paper e06-4, Virginia Polytechnic Institute and State University, Department of Economics (2006): 14. For a more recent analysis that reinforces earlier findings on the crisis of transition, see Salehi-Isfahani, "Iranian Youth in Times of Economic Crisis," Dubai Initiative, Dubai School of Government and the Harvard Kennedy School, September 2010.

38. For recent examples from the US experience, see the discussion in the *New York Times*, December 3, 2013. http://www.nytimes.com/roomfordebate/2012/03/01/should-college-be-for-everyone/college-graduates-pay-is-slipping-but-still-outpaces-others; or *CBS News*, December 5, 2013. http://www.cbsnews.com/8301-18563_162-57336409/6m-young-u.s-adults-live-with-their-parents/.

39. "Olaviat-e Baznegari-ye olum-e ensani" ("Priority of reviewing the human sciences"), *Mehr News*, March 11, 2011, http://www.mehrnews.com/fa/NewsPrint.aspx?NewsID=1271488.

40. Djavad Salehi-Isfahani, "The Revolution and the Rural Poor," *Radical History Review*, no. 105 (Fall 2009): 140–141.

41. According to the World Bank (using data provided by the Statistical Center of Iran), enrollment rates of eighteen-to-twenty-four-year-olds are well over half or 58 percent (2013). See http://data.worldbank.org/indicator/SE.TER.ENRR.

42. Reported in *Sedaye sabz-e azadi*, June 5, 2010. http://www.irangreenvoice.com/arti cle/2010/may/06/3086.

43. The category of *'olum-e ensani* translates literally as "human sciences." Although I use the term "humanities" in this article, in Iran *reshtehaye 'olum-e ensani* also includes studies in the social sciences.

44. Azam Khatam, "Iranian Paradox: The Inverted Relation of University and Society," *Universities in Crisis: Blog of the International Sociological Association (ISA)*, May 26, 2010. http://www.isa-sociology.org/universities-in-crisis/?p=480.

45. Reza Noruzzadeh and Mojgan Mehrparvar, *Gozaresheh melli-ye amuzesh-e 'ali, tahqiatq, va fanavari 1389-90 (A national report of higher education, research, and technology 2010-11)* (Tehran: Institute for Research and Planning in Higher Education, 1391/2012). Engineering, by contrast, came in a distant second, with 176,303 students.

46. Shahrzad Kamyab, "The University Entrance Exam: Crisis in Iran," *International Higher Education* no. 51 (Spring 2008): 22-23.

47. Zahra Karimimobian, "*Yadgiri be jaye hafezeh mehvari*" ("Learning instead of superficial memorization"), *Hamshari*, October 5, 2007.

48. In interviews with high school students, Mohammad Rezaei found that some of his respondents did not know what the concept of "political system" (*nezam-e siasi*) signified. In general, students were unversed in even the most basic facts regarding how their government functioned or its history, much less in possession of any heartfelt commitment to the values of the revolution and political Islam. Direct resistance seemed to be less of a problem than a generalized apathy toward politics, if not a willful ignorance of the formal ideology and history of the revolution. Mohammad Rezaei, *Tahlili az zendegi-ye ruzmareh-ye danesh amuzeshi: Naresaeiha-ye gofteman-e madreseh (An analysis of the daily lives of schoolchildren: The failures of school discourse)* (Tehran: Society and Culture, 2008), 221.

49. Hamid Babavand, "*Ma ra az nazdik bebinid*" ("Look at us from up close"), *Moallem* (September-October 2007): 6.

50. Some 217 students who were active socially and politically in universities during their undergraduate studies were banned entrance to graduate-level study for political reasons between 2005 and 2010. This figure suggests that the scale of active participation in student movement activity on campus is rather small. See "Punishing Stars: Systematic Denial of Higher Education in Iran," International Campaign for Human Rights in Iran (ICHRI), 2011. http://www.iranhumanrights.org/wp-content/uploads/punishing-stars-english-final.pdf.

51. Paola Rivetti, "Student Movements in the Islamic Republic: Shaping Iran's Politics through the Campus." In *Iran: A Revolutionary Republic in Transition*, edited by Rouzbeh Parsi (Paris: Institute for Security Studies, 2012), 81-99.

52. Khamenei's speech at the University of Tehran, February 2, 2010. http://english .khamenei.ir//index.php?option=com_content&task=view&id=1314&Itemid=4.

53. Ibid.

54. Mahdi, "The Student Movement in the Islamic Republic of Iran," 26.

55. Bakhtiari, *Parliamentary Politics in Revolutionary Iran*.

56. Of the four parliaments voted into office in the period 1980-1992, each had a radically different composition in terms of political faction. A different coalition controlled each Parliament. Only 4 percent of the Majles deputies survived all four elections; over twelve years and four uninterrupted elections, the turnover ratio for elected officials was an incredible 60 percent. In the 1992 parliamentary elections alone, there was a mere 30 percent reelection rate. Bahman Bakhtiari, "Parliamentary Elections in Iran," *Iranian Studies* 26, no. 3/4 (1993): 375-388.

57. See Mahdi, "The Student Movement in the Islamic Republic of Iran."

58. In a speech delivered to the University of Tehran's Basij students on January 31, 1998, Khamenei signaled that they must begin to take a more aggressive and active political stance on campus. For an excellent overview of the development of the Student Basij Organization since 1990, see Saeid Golkar, "The Reign of Hard-Line Students in Iran's Universities," *Middle East Quarterly* (Summer 2010): 21–29.

59. Although the law mandates that state and nonstate universities apply this quota, state universities did not implement the requirement during Khatami's tenure.

60. These are the *jame'eh eslami*, the SBO, the Shirazi branch of the OCU, and the *anjoman-e eslami mostaqel-e daneshjui* or Independent Islamic Student Association.

61. By comparison, the pro-regime Shirazi faction of the OCU is estimated to have no more than two thousand members. Interview with Saeid Golkar, September 13, 2011.

62. It does not appear that this will be a short-term strategy. Starting in the 2011–2012 school year, ideological-political training became a requirement for all members of the SBO, an action that represents a complete abandonment of mass mobilization in favor of cadre building.

63. Muhammad Sahimi, "'Cultural Revolution' Redux," *Tehran Bureau*, May 11, 2010. http://www.pbs.org/wgbh/pages/frontline/tehranbureau/2010/05/cultural-revolution-redux.html.

64. Roland Elliott Brown, "Notes from the Underground," *Foreign Policy*, August 31, 2011, http://www.foreignpolicy.com/articles/2011/08/31/notes_from_the_underground?page=full.

65. Borzou Daragahi, "Broken by Prison, for a Cause All but Lost," *Los Angeles Times*, December 23, 2007. http://www.latimes.com/la-fg-zamanianarchive23dec23-story.html.

66. Sahimi, "'Cultural Revolution' Redux."

67. Davud Parchami, "*Sanjesh-e gerayesh-e mardom be basij*" ("Examination of the public's predisposition to the basij"), *Basij Studies Quarterly* 18–19 (2003): 45–90.

68. Saeid Golkar, *Captive Society: The Basij Militia and Social Control in Post-Revolutionary Iran* (New York: Columbia University Press/Woodrow Wilson, 2015), 185.

69. Sahimi, "'Cultural Revolution' Redux."

70. Asef Bayat, *Life as Politics* (Stanford, CA: Stanford University Press, 2010), 14.

71. Ibid., 18–19.

72. Ibid.

73. Ibid., 20.

74. Ibid., 19.

75. Ibid.

76. Writing in another context, Bayat argues that "decentered" notions of power, in which power "circulates" without authorship, underestimates state power. "Like it or not," he writes, "the state does matter," and must be earnestly engaged if the lives of the subaltern are to be improved. Asef Bayat, *Street Politics: Poor People's Movements in Iran* (New York: Columbia University Press, 1997), 164.

77. Mohammad Tahavori, "*Esteqrar-e demokrasi va hoquq-e bashar, shart-e sekut-e jonbesh-e daneshjui: Goftegu ba Abdollah Momeni*" ("Establishment of democracy and human rights is the condition for silence of the student movement: A conversation with Abdollah Momeni"), *Gozaar*, July 1, 2007. http://www.gozaar.org/persian/interview-fa/3608.html/. Since the true capital of the student movement lies in its intellectual power and capacity for analysis, it is qualified to critically observe and to assess the limits and consequences of the government's actions without aspiring to gain power itself.

78. Momeni, a longtime member of the *Advar-e tahkim-e vahdat* and a veteran of the 1999 student protest, was arrested in the early days of the Green Movement.

79. *"85 darsad-e daneshjuyan-e keshvar dar 20 reshteh!"* ("85 percent of the country's university students in 20 fields!"), *Mehr News*, May 13, 2011. http://www.javanemrooz.com/news/newsreader/mehrnews/show-598186.aspx.

80. We have already seen an example of this dynamic during the Green Movement. Thanks to Mohammad Ayatollahi Tabaar for this phrasing.

81. Alexis de Tocqueville, *Democracy in America*, translated by George Lawrence (New York: Perennial Classics, 2000), 430.

82. Ibid.

83. Ibid., 605.

PART II

INSTITUTIONAL EVOLUTION

4 The Office of the Supreme Leader

Epicenter of a Theocracy

Mehrzad Boroujerdi and
Kourosh Rahimkhani

As a theocratic state born through a popular revolution, the Islamic Republic of Iran (IRI) has exhibited both democratic and authoritarian features since its inception. The Supreme Leader is considered the epicenter of Iran's theocratic authority structure and the ultimate arbiter of Iranian politics. Ayatollah Seyyed Ali Khamenei has managed to mold the Iranian regime to his liking through both his talent and his fortunate institutional position. He has exhibited deft political skills and is the accidental beneficiary of a theocratic system that decided to deal with the challenges of its postcharismatic leader phase, after Grand Ayatollah Seyyed Ruhollah Khomeini's demise, by concentrating more power in individual hands. Whereas Khomeini used his charisma to consolidate the office of the Supreme Leader, Khamenei strengthened this office through bureaucratic aggrandizement, reliance on security forces, and informal politics. Thanks to his long administrative career, hypersecurity outlook, and micromanager disposition, Khamenei has incrementally subdued his political and clerical opponents and amassed a great deal of power in the Office of the Supreme Leader. This position represents a parallel government that is powerful, not transparent, and unaccountable. Any discussion of the political evolution of the Islamic Republic needs to grapple with the hefty position of the Office of the Supreme Leader and the formidable assets at its disposal.

Agreeing with Niall Ferguson that the "power of any individual ruler is a function of the network of economic, social, and political relations over which s/he presides," this chapter presents an "institutional" approach by arguing that Khamenei's religious and charismatic liabilities forced him to rely more and more on "power institutions."[1] In particular, we address the following five major questions: How has the institutional/constitutional setup of the Office of the Supreme Leader evolved since the 1979 revolution? To what extent does the hardline direction of the Office emerge because of the person who occupies it rather than an institutional/constitutional setup that determines this orientation? What institutional assets and informal leverage does the Supreme Leader enjoy and how well can he bypass democratic rules, torpedo pacts, and restore factional balance? How does the Office of the Supreme Leader function? Finally, how has the Supreme Leader handled attempts by clerical rivals, reformist politicians, and the hard-line faction to curtail his power, and what conclusions can be drawn about any future transitional process?

Passing of the Torch

On June 3, 1989, the charismatic leader of the Iranian revolution, Grand Ayatollah Ruhollah Khomeini (1902–1989), passed away. A day later the members of the first Assembly of Experts met in a special session to decide whether a "Leadership Council" or a single leader should succeed him. Four Ayatollahs—Ali-Akbar Meshkini (1921–2007), Seyyed Abdolkarim Mussavi Ardebili (1926–), Mohammad Fazel Lankarani (1931–2007), and Abdollah Javadi Amoli (1933–)—and three Hojjatoleslams—Khamenei (1939–), Akbar Hashemi Rafsanjani (1934–), and Seyyed Ahmad Khomeini (1946–1995)—were proposed as possible members of the alternative "Leadership Council." At the end, the vote was 45 to 23 in favor of electing a sole Supreme Leader.[2] In a second-round vote, the members of the Assembly of Experts voted 60 to 14 to elect Khamenei as the new Supreme Leader, while a minority pushed to elect Grand Ayatollah Mohammad-Reza Golpayegani (1899–1993).[3] The election of a man who was of a modest clerical rank; was younger than all those mentioned, with the exception of Khomeini's own son; and did not possess any political charisma was met with raised eyebrows in many Iranian households.[4]

Khamenei's election was technically unconstitutional since at the time of his election he was not a *marja'-e taqlid* (source of emulation) as required by Articles 107 and 109 of the 1979 Constitution, which was still in effect when he became the Supreme Leader.[5] To somehow get around the problem, the ninety-five-year-old Ayatollah Mohammad-Ali Araki (1894–1994) was recognized as the new *marja'* while Khamenei worked to consolidate himself as the new Supreme Leader and build up his religious credentials. His standing in the clerical pecking order improved through the successive deaths of Grand Ayatollahs Shahabeddin Mar'ashi Najafi (1897–1990), Abolqasem Khoei (1899–1992), Hashem Amoli (1903–1993), Golpayegani, and finally Araki himself. With the demise of each of these clerical heavyweights, Khamenei's lieutenants pushed for his recognition as the next *marja'* by asking the followers of the deceased ayatollahs to transfer their loyalty as well as charitable contributions to Khamenei as the supreme authority in charge of the welfare of Shi'is.[6] Yet all these efforts failed because of the opposition of the Shi'ite hierocracy both inside and outside Iran.

Even though Khamenei had received all of Khomeini's constitutional powers and had inherited his organizational network, the clerical establishment was not yet willing to coronate him as the new source of emulation. In 1994 upon Araki's death, the influential Society of Qom Seminary Teachers (*Jame'eh Modarresin-e Howzeh-ye Elmiyyeh-ye Qom*) put forward the names of the following seven ayatollahs as suitable candidates for becoming the *marja'*: Mohammad-Taqi Behjat (1915–2009), Fazel Lankarani, Khamenei, Nasser Makarem Shirazi (1926–), Seyyed Musa Shobeiri Zanjani (1927–), Mirza Javad Tabrizi (1926–2006), and Hossein Vahid Khorasani (1921–).[7] Meanwhile, the Society of Combatant Clergy (*Jame'eh-ye Rohaniyat-e Mobarez*) endorsed only three of these names: Fazel Lankarani, Tabrizi, and Khamenei.[8] For political reasons, the two organizations had glossed over Grand Ayatollah Ali Sistani (the *marja'* of Najaf) and three reformist ayatollahs inside Iran who were at odds with the regime: Ayatollahs Hossein-Ali Montazeri (1922–2009), Mussavi Ardebili, and Yusef Sane'i (1937–). Two weeks after Araki's death, Khamenei, who still faced the criticism of the Shi'ite hierocracy, ended his procrastination and declared on December 14, 1994, that because of his heavy responsibilities as the Supreme Leader he had no intention of becoming a *marja'* inside Iran. Yet he added: "but for the *marja'iyyat* for outside of the country, it is a totally different case. I accept this responsibility because doing otherwise will be harmful."[9]

So how did Khamenei, who encountered such challenges initially, position himself at the fulcrum of Iranian politics so that all other offices of the state revolve around him? Surely much of his success can be attributed to his personality. A leading political psychologist who studied the leadership profiles of two hundred world leaders describes Khamenei in this manner: "Khamenei's scores (low in belief that he can control what happens and high in need for power) suggest that he will challenge constraints but do so in an indirect, behind-the-scenes manner. And, indeed, although Khamenei does have ultimate authority in the Iranian political system, he prefers to maintain control and maneuverability by not being 'out in front.'"[10]

Khamenei compensated for his lack of charismatic qualities and religious credentials by being a consummate micromanager with an intimate knowledge of the Iranian political machinery. Born into a clerical family in Mashhad, he attended seminary training in Mashhad and Qom and was imprisoned under the Shah for his political activities. Since the 1979 revolution, he has held a series of important positions including Tehran's Friday Prayer Leader (1980), member of the Revolutionary Council (1979–1980), Deputy Minister of Defense (1979–1980), supervisor of the Revolutionary Guards (1980), Deputy of the First Parliament (1980–1981), member of the First Assembly of Experts (1983–1989), president (1981–1989), member of the First Expediency Council (1988–1989), and Supreme Leader since 1989. In many of these positions he experienced episodes that could only be construed as affronts. He was not an original member of the Revolutionary Council but was brought in later. While Khamenei was the first cleric to serve as president, Khomeini made it known that he was a staunch supporter of the lay Prime Minister, Mir-Hossein Mussavi. Although before becoming the wartime president Khamenei had served as Deputy Minister of Defense and supervisor of the Islamic Revolution's Guard Corps (IRGC), Khomeini did not delegate the title of Commander in Chief to him as he had done with the first president, Seyyed Abolhassan Banisadr.[11] In 1988, Khomeini publicly admonished Khamenei for not understanding the principle of "the absolute mandate of jurist" (*velayat-e motlaqeh-ye faqih*). Khamenei became the Supreme Leader only after Montazeri, who had served as the officially designated Deputy Supreme Leader from 1985 to 1989, had been ousted by Khomeini.[12] Even as Supreme Leader, he has had to share the stage with four presidents (Hashemi Rafsanjani, Khatami, Ahmadinejad, and Rouhani) who have tried to outshine him.

Constitutional Augmentation of Power

The year 1989 proved to be monumentally important in the history of the Islamic Republic. The eight-year war with neighboring Iraq had ended the year before, and now Khomeini and his lieutenants were eager to ensure a smooth transition of power and to address some of the exigent problems of statecraft (i.e., factionalism, overlap of authority) that the revolutionary state had faced in its first decade of existence.[13] The year, however, began with an international controversy after Khomeini issued a fatwa against Salman Rushdie on February 14, 1989. While the fatwa against the author of *The Satanic Verses* was dominating international headlines, things on the domestic front were about to change in important ways. On March 28, Khomeini ousted his designated successor Montazeri, the most prestigious of his pupils. The dismissal reopened the question of succession. Aware of his own impending death, Khomeini ordered the revision of the 1979 Constitution.[14] On April 24, he wrote a letter to President Khamenei informing him that he had appointed a twenty-member Council for the Revision of the Constitution (plus five deputies to be chosen by Parliament). The main duty of this council was to solve the inherent contradictions of the 1979 Constitution. These included the competing prerogatives of the Supreme Jurist and the *marja'-e taqlid*, the tension between the president and the prime minister, and the conflict between the Guardian Council and the Parliament. The council, which had to finish its deliberations in less than two months, went to work immediately and amended 46 of the 175 original articles of the Constitution (26 percent) and added two more of its own.[15] Khomeini, however, died on June 3 and did not live to see these results, which were approved in a referendum held on July 28 (the same day Hashemi Rafsanjani was elected president).

Perhaps the most consequential change in the amended Constitution was to concentrate even more power in the hands of the Supreme Leader than the framers of the original document were willing to do.[16] On January 6, 1988, Khomeini had issued a fatwa in which he stated in no uncertain terms that the Supreme Leader not only is the ultimate arbiter within the Iranian political system but can also—based on the interests of the state—even suspend religious rules such as praying, fasting, or pilgrimage. By this ruling, Khomeini had articulated what became known as the principle of "the absolute mandate of jurist" (*velayat-e motlaqeh-ye faqih*). Yet it was clear that no standing cleric could match both Khomeini's religious pedigree and political credence. The solution was to decouple the mandate of the Supreme Leader (*velayat*) from the position of *marja'iyyat*. A mere five days after he had appointed the Council for the Revision of the Constitution, Khomeini responded publicly to a query from the chair of the Assembly of Experts, Ayatollah Ali-Akbar Meshkini, by stating: "From the beginning I believed and I had insisted that the condition *marja'iyyat* is not necessary. A *mojtahed-e adel* (a just jurist) who is confirmed by the respected [members of the Assembly of] Experts from across the country is sufficient." Armed with this quotation, the council dropped all explicit references to the *marja'iyyat* requirement in the amended Constitution. "The 1979 stipulation (Article 5) that the Supreme Leader be 'recognized and accepted' by 'the majority of the people' (a requirement for the *marja'iyyat*) was also dropped. Thus, while the level of religious scholarship required for leadership was lowered, political experience was given greater weight."[17]

Furthermore, the amended Constitution dramatically extended the constitutional powers of the Supreme Leader. It transferred the responsibility for resolving the conflict between the three branches of powers (Article 113) from the president to the Supreme Leader (Article 110).[18] The five-member Supreme Judicial Council (established in 1980) was dissolved in favor of a single "Head of the Judiciary" to be appointed by the Supreme Leader (Article 157). Moreover, the Supreme Leader assumed the power to appoint and dismiss the head of the Islamic Republic of Iran Broadcasting (Article 175). The Supreme Leader was also given the power to appoint two personal representatives to the newly created Supreme National Security Council (Article 176). The size and power of the Council for the Discernment of the Expediency of State Interest (hereafter referred to as the Expediency Council), which had been created by Khomeini in February 1988, was expanded so that it not only arbitrates between Parliament and the Guardian Council (Article 112) but also advises the Supreme Leader on "determination of the general policies" of the Islamic Republic of Iran (Article 110). The status of the Guardian Council was also enhanced, as it was empowered to supervise elections for the Assembly of Experts (Article 99).[19] This, however, created a circuitous path since the Supreme Leader appoints half (six clerics) of the sitting members of the Guardian Council, who in turn were to approve the qualifications of the same people who are supposed to oversee the performance of the Supreme Leader.[20]

These changes led many Iranian scholars like Anoushiravan Ehteshami to conclude that "constitutionally and practically the (Supreme) Leader's position remains the locus of power in the republic, around which are spun the other offices of the state."[21] This assessment is graphically demonstrated in figure 4.1.

According to the amended Constitution, the Supreme Leader came to enjoy the following formal powers:

Delineation of the general policies of the Islamic Republic of Iran after consultation with the Expediency Council.

- Supervision over the proper execution of the general policies of the state.
- Issuing decrees for national referenda.
- Signing the decree formalizing the election of the president of the Republic by the people. The suitability of candidates for the presidency, with respect to the qualifications specified in the Constitution, must be confirmed by the Guardian Council before elections take place, and, in the case of the first term of a president, by the Leadership.
- Dismissal of the President of the Republic, with due regard for the interests of the country, after the Supreme Court holds him guilty of the violation of his constitutional duties, or after a vote of Parliament testifying to his incompetence on the basis of Article 89.
- The power to appoint and dismiss the Head of the Judiciary; the six clerical members of the powerful Guardian Council; the Chief of the Joint Staff; the commanders of the three branches of the Armed Forces; the Commander of the Revolutionary Guards; and the Director of Islamic Republic of Iran Broadcasting (national TV and radio).
- The power to appoint and dismiss personal representatives to a wide range of civil organizations, foundations, and corporate bodies such as the Supreme National Security Council.
- The power, as the Supreme Commander of the Armed Forces, to make declarations of war and peace and order the mobilization of the Armed Forces.
- Establishing new institutions and bodies based on the powers granted to him by Article 110 of the Constitution.
- Pardoning or mitigating the sentences of convicts, within the framework of Islamic criteria, on a recommendation from the Head of the Judiciary.

The constitutional amendments of 1989 heavily stacked the deck in favor of the Supreme Leader. Legally entrusted with these enhanced powers, Khamenei decided to effectuate them in practice. However, his lack of religious credentials and still-diminutive influence in the overall political system forced him initially to share power with the newly elected and empowered President Hashemi Rafsanjani.[22] Khomeini's political power had been divided between his two closest lieutenants, Khamenei and Hashemi Rafsanjani. "Dual leadership seemed

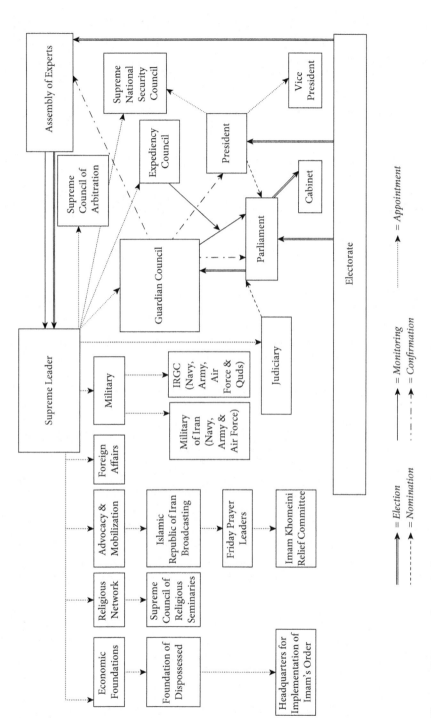

Figure 4.1 Structure of power in Iran

Legend:

⟹ = Election
- - -▷ = Nomination
——▶ = Appointment
······▷ = Monitoring
—·—·▷ = Confirmation

quite appropriate for the emergent system of post-charismatic, collective clerical rule."[23] According to Saïd Amir Arjomand, "Khamenei had begun as the weaker partner of the post-Khomeini diarchy."[24] Whereas Khomeini's charismatic qualities had enabled him to amass a great deal of power and yet present himself as an "arbiter" among warring factions, Khamenei was unable to achieve the same results. As Asghar Schirazi has put it, "After his election, Khamenei made every effort to emulate his predecessor's role as an authority positioned above all branches of the government which could balance among the rival camps. However, the more he failed in this attempt, the more pressure he came under to seek support from forces which shared his attitudes, had been successful in the struggle for a share of power and, because of their position in the religious academies, were able to guarantee support for him in those circles."[25]

Subduing the Clerical Fiefdom

With his apprenticeship as the Supreme Leader over, Khamenei realized that he needed to dilute the power of rival Shi'ite *ulama* to bolster his own standing. One way to marginalize the Shi'ite hierocracy was to extend his bureaucratic and financial control over the religious institutions. The deaths of Grand Ayatollahs Mar'ashi Najafi and Golpayegani, who had fought to keep the clerical establishment independent from the state, paved the way for Khamenei to reorganize the clerical fiefdom.[26] As early as 1991, Khamenei had recommended the creation of the Supreme Council of Religious Seminaries of Qom (*Showra-ye 'Ali-ye Howzeh-ye Elmiyyeh-ye Qom*; SCRSQ), which was finally established in 1995.[27] The SCRSQ is responsible for all the administrative, educational, and financial affairs of the Qom seminaries.[28] This body also helped to standardize the content of the curricula and modernize the administrative system by digitizing library holdings and setting up a new computerized system of stipend disbursement to ensure how much each seminary student was receiving.[29] Today, most of the 228 to 270 residential seminaries (*madresehs*) in Iran follow the educational curriculum set up by SCRSQ.[30] According to Article 6 of the Charter, the members of SCRSQ are appointed based on the recommendations of the *Jame'eh-ye Modarresin-e Howzeh-ye Elmiyyeh-ye Qom* (Society of Qom Seminary Teachers), and approval of the Supreme Leader and the *marja'* of Qom.[31] However, as a testimony to Khamenei's power within this body, most of the current nine conservative ayatollahs on the council have served as his personal representatives to various state bodies.

Another institution created by the Supreme Leader in 1991 is the Theological Seminaries Center for Services (*Markaz-e Khadamat-e Howzeha-ye Elmiyyeh*), which according to its former director provided social welfare services (insurance, housing, marriage loans, etc.) to over 160,000 clerics.[32] The Leader appoints the members of the central council of this center.[33]

Yet another important undertaking during Khamenei's tenure as Supreme Leader was the bureaucratization of the Friday Prayer institution. In 1984, Khomeini had appointed a seven-member committee named *Dabirkhaneh-ye Markazi-ye A'emmeh-ye Jom'eh* [Central Headquarters of Friday Prayer Leaders] to deal with the various issues facing Prayer Leaders.[34] According to Hashemi Rafsanjani's memoirs, the members of this body had differences with Khamenei, who was serving as president at that time.[35] In 1993, as Supreme Leader, Khamenei reconstituted this body as *Showra-ye Siyasatgozari-ye A'emmeh-e Jom'eh* (the Friday Prayer Policymaking Council—FPPC) by keeping only three of the original members and expanding the size to nine. He also ordered that the headquarters of FPPC move from Qom to Tehran in order to be closer to him.[36] The FPPC is in charge of the appointment, dismissal, and evaluation of all Friday Prayer Leaders throughout the country except for those dispatched to the provincial capitals, handpicked by Khamenei himself.[37] FPPC also coordinates the content of *khotbehs* (Friday Prayer speeches), publishes weekly bulletins containing the talking points for the imams, and sends them to over 830 preachers performing Friday prayers across the country. An army of thirty-two thousand functionaries are actively involved in the machinery that has been set up specifically for organizing weekly Friday prayers.[38] According to the FPPC's secretary, Mohammad-Reza Taqavi, no political party in Iran can match the FPPC's organizational muscle and outreach. Taqavi has further maintained that the Friday Prayer imams they seek to hire are relatively young (between ages thirty-five and forty-five) and are typically appointed to a three-year probationary term, after which they will be evaluated to see if they deserve an additional five-year term.[39] In order to enhance their chances of being picked by FPPC, young seminary students who aspire to become Friday Prayer Leaders gravitate toward studying with officially sanctioned clerical mentors. Their loyalty can pay off, as 43 percent of the members of the Fourth Assembly of Experts are Friday Prayer Leaders.[40]

In addition to the Friday Prayer Leaders, the Supreme Leader also appoints personal representatives to each of Iran's thirty-one provinces. Most of these commissars lead the Friday prayer congregations, but their main duty is to represent the Supreme Leader in the provinces and manage the affairs of their constituencies above and beyond the government. Khamenei's personal provincial representatives often outflank the governors dispatched by the Minister of Interior. The Supreme Leader also has personal representatives to special constituencies (i.e., representatives in the Sunni minority community) as well as a number of foreign countries (Iraq, Pakistan, Syria, the United Arab Emirates, and the United Kingdom). Khamenei even enjoys the protection of a military unit comprising clerics named "Imam Sadeq's 83 Brigade" (Qom), which was formed during the course of the Iran-Iraq War.

Unlike other clerics who had to rely mainly on the religious alms taxes (*khoms va zakat*) paid by the pious, the Supreme Leader has had access to substantial governmental and special funds. Many of the organizations that he and his clerical allies set up either had an official line item in the state budget or were free from any taxation or oversight by organs of the state such as the National General Inspectorate. Furthermore, parastatal institutions such as the Foundation for the Dispossessed (*Bonyad-e Mostaz'afan*) were able to set up businesses, publishing houses, and educational academies that didn't fall under the supervision of other *marja'* besides Khamenei.[41] The Supreme Leader also had the added advantage of finding employment for his pupils within either the vast state bureaucracy or the colossal machinery that is run out of his *Beyt*.[42] This helps channel students toward him despite the fact that he may not have the religious standing of some of his peers in the *howzehs*.[43]

Over the years Khamenei has also extended his bureaucratic tentacles over the seventy thousand mosques operating throughout the country by gaining control of organizations like the Islamic Propaganda Organization (IPO)[44] or establishing new ones such as *Markaz-e Residegi be Omur-e Masajed* (Center for Supervision of Mosques' Affairs).[45] In addition, the Ministry of Culture's *Setad-e 'Ali-ye Kanunha-ye Farhangi Honari-ye Masajed* (Supreme Headquarters of Cultural and Art Centers of Mosques) claims to work with over 13,400 such cultural and art centers throughout Iran.[46] The main duty of these institutions is to monitor activities in the mosques and appoint and train imams for leading them. Finally, another means through which the Supreme Leader monitors events taking place in various mosques is by having allowed the paramilitary Basij forces to establish operational bases in the mosques. The cumulative impact of these activities has turned the mosques into the most significant players in every neighborhood from the urban centers to the faraway villages.

Use of Formal and Informal Powers

If the powers of the purse and persuasion were not enough to make the clerical caste acquiescent, Khamenei, like his predecessor Khomeini, has not been reticent about punishing dissident clerics.[47] The organ of retribution was often the Special Court of Clergy (SCC), which is under the jurisdiction of the Supreme Leader and operates outside the Iranian judiciary.[48] Mirjam Künkler, who has studied the SCC, writes: "When Khamenei succeeded Khomeini as the *Rahbar* [Leader], he significantly expanded the SCC. While the courts had hitherto functioned on the basis of no specific code, Khamenei commissioned an extraordinary ordinance of 47 articles, which was expanded in 2005.[49] Khamenei also expanded the court, originally only extant in Tehran, to ten other branches in the country (Ahvaz, Esfahan, Hamedan, Kerman, Mashhad, Qom, Rasht, Sari,

Shiraz, and Tabriz) and commissioned the creation of a separate prison network to serve the SCC."[50] Clergymen such as Ahmad-Reza Ahmadpur, Assadollah Bayat Zanjani (1941–), Azimi Qadimi, Hossein Hashemiyan, Mohsen Kadivar (1959–), Seyyed Hossein Kazemeini Borujerdi, Abolfazl Mussavian, Seyyed Mohammad Musavi Khoeiniha (1941–), Mojtaba Lotfi, Hadi Qabel, Abdollah Nuri (1950–), and Hassan Yusefi Eshkevari (1949–) have been subjected to trials at the hands of SCC for what could only be described as "political offenses."[51]

The Supreme Leader has not hesitated to invoke the official powers entrusted to him to reverse outcomes not to his liking. In 2000, he vetoed a less draconian Press Law being pushed by reformist members of Parliament (MPs). In 2005, he reversed the decision of the Guardian Council, which had disqualified the reformist presidential candidate Mostafa Mo'in. In 2009, he put an end to all the demands for recounting or canceling the results of the contested presidential elections by declaring them accurate and legitimate. Similarly, when supporters of President Khatami during his eight-year presidency were invoking the notion of "dual sovereignty" to emphasize his popular mandate, and when Ahmadinejad resorted to the authority of the Hidden Imam to bolster his version of "dual sovereignty," Khamenei made it clear that he was not amused by either.

There are other ways in which the Supreme Leader can short circuit and dilute the democratic features of the Constitution. Consider, for example, the manner in which many deputies of the Assembly of Experts—Iran's equivalent of the College of Cardinals—are elected. Khamenei dispatches his personal representatives to various provinces. These representatives, who as mentioned earlier often outrank local officials, get to know the local power brokers and solidify their networking ties. Then when the time comes for election to the Assembly of Experts, they run for office and often are easily elected. In the fourth round of the Assembly of Experts, 21 percent of the deputies have backgrounds as Leader's Representatives. Having owed their careers to the Supreme Leader in the first place, they are quite unlikely to vote against him in the Assembly.[52]

However, it is not possible to appreciate the full weight of the powers of the Supreme Leader unless one takes into account his informal leverage as well. Khamenei employs a vast repertoire of measures and techniques—not often sanctified by the Constitution—to influence politics. Some of the ways in which he influences outcomes are by forming ad hoc committees[53] and kitchen cabinets; holding consultation sessions with key personalities; and offering nonbinding advice to presidents about policies or the performance of ministers, to MPs about legislative issues before Parliament, and to rival blocs about coalition building.[54] When the situation calls for it he simply drops a hint about his preferences only for his protégés to invoke those words as the "wishes and commands of the Supreme Leader."[55] For example, in 2009 Khamenei criticized the content of social science and humanities curricula in Iranian universities. Subsequently, the

High Council of Cultural Revolution commissioned the Institute for Human Sciences to reevaluate the content of 38 different academic fields of study.[56] Khamenei was not content with revising the pedagogical content of the soft sciences in Iranian universities but had expressed a concern that 2 million out of 3.5 million university students in Iran were majoring in social science and humanities while there were not enough faculty members committed to Islamic ideology to train them.[57] He has even objected to such mundane issues as the brand name of a car being built by Iranian engineers.

Finally, the Supreme Leader has exercised informal leverage through the expansion of the Basij organization, the employment of panegyrists (*maddah*), and perhaps even the organizing of plainclothesmen ruffians (*lebas shakhsiha*) who serve as unofficial storm troopers.[58]

Economic Muscle of the Supreme Leader

As partially shown in figure 4.2, the Supreme Leader has numerous economic foundations and advocacy organizations that fall within his jurisdiction. What is often ignored is how economically powerful these institutions are. Based on the Budget Law of 2011 (see table 4.1)—approved by Parliament and the Guardian Council and implemented by the president—the combined budget of four important formal institutions (Headquarters of the Armed Forces' General Command, Expediency Council, Guardian Council, and the Islamic Republic of Iran Broadcasting) is less than half of the budget of one single social welfare organization, the Imam Khomeini Relief Committee (IKRC).[59]

Table 4.2 provides insights into how Iran's vast religious machinery is oiled and how the provision of social welfare programs can serve as "an important instrument of social control."[60] As one of us has written elsewhere:

> Any discussion of Iran's informal economy should make mention of the role of myriad quasi-private foundations and religious endowments called *bonyads* that manage state-owned enterprises. These large state-affiliated conglomerates, which are often run by clerics and their lay allies, have a firm grip on Iran's economy through their monopolistic and rent-seeking transactions. Vast amounts of property expropriated from the Shah's family and other members of the old elite passed to state-run foundations and *bonyads*, which are charged with aiding the poor. These foundations became a key patronage mechanism, locking in the clergy's leverage over large sectors of the economy.[61]

What is remarkable about the plethora of parastatal organizations that mushroomed after the revolution is that they receive large subsidies, often are exempted from taxation, and are not subject to parliamentary supervision—and that they do not fall under Iran's General Accounting Laws to be subjected to financial audits. Because of lack of transparency, it is difficult to gauge their real

Economic Foundations	Advocacy & Mobilization	Foreign Affairs	Military and Law Enforcement	Clerical Affairs
Supervision and Audit Office	Islamic Republic of Iran Broadcasting	Islamic Culture & Communication Organization	Armed Forces' General Command HQ	Special Court of Clergy
Foundation for Dispossessed	Imam Khomeini Relief Committee	World Assembly for the People of the House of Prophet	IRGC (Navy, Army & Air Force, Quds Force)	Imam Sadeq's 83rd Brigade (Qom)
Imam Reza Foundation	Disenfranchised Foundation of the Islamic Revolution	Society for Reconciliation among Islamic Sects	Mobilization Organization (Basij)	Al-Mostafa International Seminary
Headquarters for Implementation of Imam's Order	Newspapers (*Kayhan, Ettela'at, Jomhuri-ye Eslami*)	Supreme Leader's Representative in Foreign Countries	The Military of Islamic Republic of Iran (Navy, Army & Air Force)	Supreme Council of Religious Seminaries
IRGC Cooperative Foundation	Islamic Propaganda Organization		Law Enforcement Forces	Islamic Propaganda Office of Qom Seminary
Pious Endowments Organization (*Owqaf*)	Center for Supervision of Mosques' Affairs			Al-Zahra Society (Women Seminary)
Fifteenth of Khordad Foundation	Supreme Leader's Representatives in Sunni Minortiy Community			Qom's Seminaries Center for Services
Abdolazim Shrine Foundation	The Friday Prayer Policymaking Council			Imam Khomeini Education and Research Institute
Ma'sumeh Shrine Qom	Headquarters for Performance of Prayers			Hajj and Pilgrimage (*Bes'he Rahbari*)
	Organization for Propagation of Virtue and Prohibition of Vice			
	Supreme Leader's Representatives in All Universities			

Figure 4.2 Institutional tentacles of the Supreme Leader

Table 4.1 Budget of formal institutions in fiscal year 2011–2012

Institution	Budget
IRGC (Navy, Army, Air Force, and Quds Force)	$9,457,750,000
Law Enforcement Forces	$2,629,840,000
The Military of Islamic Republic of Iran (Army, Navy, and Air Force)	$2,572,910,000
Islamic Republic of Iran Broadcasting	$658,679,000
Headquarter of the Armed Forces' General Command	$80,986,700
Guardian Council	$34,991,500
Expediency Council	$26,920,500

Table 4.2 Budget of corporate bodies in fiscal year 2011–2012

Institution	Budget
Imam Khomeini Relief Committee	$1,952,270,000
Mobilization (Basij) Organization	$510,709,000
Qom's Seminaries Center for Services	$151,204,000
Supreme Council of Religious Seminaries	$131,191,000
Al-Mostafa International Seminary Qom	$116,096,000
Islamic Propaganda Organization	$94,234,700
Islamic Propaganda Office of Qom Seminary	$51,077,700
Supreme Leader's Representatives in Universities	$47,364,800
Pious Endowments Organization (*Owqaf*)	$44,271,600
Friday Prayer Leaders	$21,765,900
World Assembly for the People of the House of Prophet	$20,862,700
Supreme Council of Cultural Revolution	$18,265,100
Center for Supervision of Mosques' Affairs	$13,603,700
Special Court of Clergy	$12,680,100
Society for Reconciliation among Islamic Sects	$12,080,300
Coordination Council of Islamic Propaganda	$10,898,600
Al-Zahra Society (Women Seminary-Qom)	$9,631,880
Headquarter for Performance of Prayers	$6,348,400
Sadra Wisdom Foundation	$4,988,030
Organization for Propagation of Virtue and Prohibition of Vice	$4,262,500

economic power within Iran's economy. However, experts estimate that "*bonyads* own some 20 percent of the asset base of the Iranian economy and contribute 10 percent to the country's GDP."[62]

Of one such *Bonyad*, the Disenfranchised Foundation of the Islamic Revolution (DFIR), Suzanne Maloney writes: "A conservative estimate would number its subsidiaries as at least 800 (although figures as large as 1,500 are regularly cited), employing up to 700,000 workers (or as much as 5 per cent of the male labor force), with a total value in the $10 to $12 billion range. The Bonyad's contribution to the national income is significant, although here too estimates vary (anywhere from 1.5 to 8–10 percent of GDP)."[63] With such economic muscle we can appreciate that *Bonyads* play an important social mobility function: they facilitate social mobility by supporting poor people in rural areas and members of the lower middle class. For example, the IKRC reportedly assists more than four million Iranians with services. This includes 24 percent (1.5 million) of all the elderly and 60 percent (1.5 million) of all women-headed households.[64] All in all, 59 percent of its aid recipients live in rural areas, and women account for 65 percent of its constituency.[65]

In the postrevolutionary era, the Supreme Leader became the beneficiary of some important religious injunctions, such as collecting the alms tax and the administration of *Owqaf* (the Pious Endowments Organization), which was entrusted to a ministry under the Shah's regime. Perhaps the most important charitable foundation, which has been under the control of a representative of the Supreme Leader, is the Imam Reza Foundation (IRF) (*Astan-e Qods-e Razavi*). IRF is reported to have "an annual budget of $2 billion, mostly from the alms given by pilgrims."[66] According to Mohammad Gholami, *Owqaf*'s Deputy of the Shrines, in addition to IRF which operates the Imam Reza shrine, more than ten thousand other shrines across Iran draw millions of pilgrims each year.[67]

Another important institution operating under the supervision of the Supreme Leader (according to Article 49 of the Constitution) is the Headquarters for Implementation of Imam's Order (HIIO) (*Setad Ejrayi-e Farman-e Emam*), which was formed in 1989. HIIO was entrusted with receiving the confiscated assets and properties of high-ranking officials of the old regime, representatives of American and Israeli companies, people who left the country, members of opposition groups, and all unclaimed properties, inheritances as well as money confiscated from criminals and drug traffickers. A reformist Iranian website puts the assets of HIIO at $40 billion and considers it the second largest economic cartel in Iran after IRGC.[68] In September 2009, *E'temad-e Mobin*, a joint consortium of HIIO and IRGC, bought a 51 percent share in Iran's telecommunication company, minutes after it was privatized.[69] Worth almost $8 billion, this purchase was hailed as Iran's largest-ever business transaction.[70]

Yet another important foundation that answers only to the Supreme Leader is the Fifteenth of Khordad Foundation (FKF). FKF was established by Ayatollah Khomeini in 1981 as a charitable foundation to help solve the economic problems caused by the revolution and the Iran-Iraq War. According to Iranian newspapers, FKF has a number of production companies, cooperatives, and goods distribution outfits and uses the revenues generated from these activities to advance its goals.[71] A clear example of how these foundations can impact the domestic and even foreign policy of Iran and become an instrument of factional politics came in November 1992. More than three years after Khomeini's fatwa against Salman Rushdie and in the midst of President Hashemi Rafsanjani's efforts to improve Iran's ties with the outside world, FKF increased its bounty for hunting down Rushdie to more than $2 million. Interestingly enough, Khamenei, who at the outset of the Rushdie affair in February 1989 as Iran's president had suggested that Rushdie could be granted a pardon if he repented (i.e., uttered the *towbeh*) for his offensive novel, did not condemn FKF in his new position as the Supreme Leader. These examples, which represent just the tip of the iceberg, help demonstrate how formidable economic machinery available at the disposal of the Supreme Leader can represent an entrenched obstacle to reformist politics in Iran.

Role of the Office of the Supreme Leader

The organ that is directly responsible for the dissemination of the wishes of the Supreme Leader is his office, referred to as *Beyt-e Rahbari* (the Office of the Supreme Leader). Even though there is no mention of the office in the Iranian Constitution, there is no doubt that this office is Khamenei's executive arm. It is a customary practice among the *marja'* to have an office that collects religious taxes, responds to the inquiries and needs of their constituency, and deals with the affairs of theology students who study with them. These offices are often small and rely on a traditional bureaucratic style of operation. After the revolution, the requirements of dealing with these functions in addition to the day-to-day politics of the country led Khomeini to create an office in which his son Seyyed Ahmad Khomeini and Ayatollah Mohammad-Reza Tavassoli [Mahallati] (1930–2008) played crucial roles. Since becoming the Supreme Leader, Khamenei has substantially expanded the role, size, and power of the *Beyt-e Rahbari*. The office is now much more opulent than traditional offices of *marja'* (including Khomeini's) and is a mixture of traditional clerical organization and modern bureaucracy. The ever-increasing power vested in the *Beyt* has come at the expense of such institutions as religious seminaries, the judiciary, the presidency, and Parliament as well as of other sources of emulation. Presumably the Assembly of Experts is designed to oversee the actions of the Supreme Leader (and by extension his lieutenants), but so far it has been reticent to challenge the Supreme

Leader even in a single instance. The same holds true for the Expediency Council, which has not demonstrated any proclivity to second-guess policies articulated by the Supreme Leader. Indeed, it is hard to think of any institution external to the Office of the Supreme Leader (besides the IRGC) that can potentially check its actions.

In addition to performing normal constituency services, the personnel of the office perform such functions as lobbying MPs and cabinet ministers (often behind the scenes); convey the wishes of the Supreme Leader to interested parties; serve as troubleshooters and go-betweens with political, military, and intelligence officials; conduct sociological studies of citizenry's needs and grievances; and supervise the colossal social and economic institutions operating under the umbrella of the Supreme Leader. Since the Iranian government does not have the right to monitor or tax the institutions that operate under the command of the Supreme Leader, the office has its own Supervision and Audit Bureau, headed by the former Speaker of Parliament Hojjatoleslam Ali-Akbar Nateq Nuri. In addition, the office has other bureaus including Clerical Affairs, Cultural Affairs, Foreign Relations, Military Affairs, Public Affairs, and Security-Political Affairs.

Khamenei rewards loyalty and puts his trust in longtime acquaintances. Many of those who are close to him either hail from his province of birth (Khorasan) or served with him when he was deputy defense minister or president in the early days of the Islamic Republic.[72]

While none of those who currently serve in the *Beyt-e Rahbari* have the stature to emerge as a future Supreme Leader, this group's collectivity will still affect a potential succession process. Since the issue of succession will likely be intertwined—just as it was in 1989—with internal struggles over the role, power, and authority of various individuals and governing institutions, one should not underestimate the ability of those sitting closest to the center of power in shaping the eventual outcome.

Dealing with the Rising Power of IRGC

Since the end of the Iran-Iraq War in 1988, the leverage of the IRGC has consistently been increasing in such institutions as the Expediency Council, the Assembly of Experts, Parliament, and the cabinet. In many ways this is a natural process as clerics have increasingly retreated from electoral positions toward nonelected offices and as the IRGC alumni of the Iran-Iraq War have come to enjoy political success thanks to their service in the war, name recognition, and the networks of economic and social privilege that they have come to enjoy.[73] The rising political fortune of the IRGC has led some commentators to conclude that it is monopolizing power and making the Supreme Leader and the clerical class ever more ephemeral and marginal. We find this alarmist argument suspect on a number of conceptual and factual planes. The relationship between the IRGC and the clerical establishment during the past three decades has been both fluid and multifaceted. During the first decade of the revolution, the IRGC was a political factor but not a major political player independent of the clerical establishment. The entry of IRGC officials into the political realm started as soon as the war ended, as former IRGC officials entered the editorial boards of newspapers, national radio and TV, and the Ministry of Culture and Islamic Guidance. A decade later, many guardsmen had exchanged their military uniforms for civilian careers as cabinet ministers or deputy ministers, members of Parliament, judiciary officials, provincial governors, mayors, ambassadors, cultural attachés, politicians, government employees, university administrators, directors of think tanks and foundations, business leaders, and chief executive officers of industrial companies.

According to the Iranian Constitution, the Supreme Leader is the commander in chief of the armed forces and appoints and promotes the commanders of the regular army as well as the IRGC (commander, deputy commander, and other top-level posts).[74] In addition to appointing its top brass, the Supreme Leader also appoints a personal representative to the IRGC who sits on its Command Council.[75] In contradistinction to regular armies where officers advance based on the principle of meritocracy, the personal relationship of the IRGC commanders with the Supreme Leader determines who gets the top post.[76] Hence the Supreme Leader has the power to replace IRGC commanders in a game of musical chairs so as to preclude any one individual from becoming too powerful. Another layer of protection for the Supreme Leader is an army of twelve thousand clerics who are employed as "moral guides" for the IRGC's rank and file but also serve as the eyes and ears of the Leader to guard the Guards. The guardsmen recognize that (a) thanks to the patronage of the Supreme Leader, the IRGC has remained autonomous from the government, political parties, and clerical circles and acquire lucrative (often no-bid) contracts; and (b) the protection umbrella of the Supreme Leader inhibits any other organ from investigating what goes on within the IRGC or its front organizations.

It is fair to say that the IRGC might wish to take advantage of a Supreme Leader who is old and frail or to play the role of a spoiler who can wield a veto power. After all, considering the tense nature of Iran's domestic and international politics, one can see the IRGC acquiring more agenda-setting power in the future. But Khamenei already shares many of the hard-line views of the IRGC because of the following lived experiences. First, it is reasonable to speculate that the assassination attempt that left him paralyzed in one hand in 1981 has contributed to his security-minded outlook and his distrust of others' intentions. Second, his first important position after the revolution was deputy minister of defense, where he supervised the IRGC during its period of infancy. Thus,

Khamenei knows the institutional culture and the leadership personnel of IRGC extremely well. Third, he was a wartime president for seven of his eight years in office, and this experience has left an indelible mark on his worldview. Finally, he receives daily intelligence reports and is aware of the plots against him both internally and externally. Hence, to maintain that such a shrewd political operator as Khamenei is cuckolded by the IRGC or is passively beholden to them is not convincing. Khamenei recognizes that under the present Constitution, no position is more secure than his. He recognizes that a good number of senior clergy are rather skeptical about the IRGC's rising status, and he can use this fact as leverage against the guardsmen. Finally, we should remember that his political cost-and-effect calculations are not the same as those of the Revolutionary Guards. For example, Khamenei did not succumb to the recommendation of the IRGC's top brass to punish Mir-Hossein Mussavi and Mehdi Karrubi more seriously after the 2009 Green Movement.

Sultanism or Praetorianism

The disputed June 12, 2009, presidential election, which brought forth the largest mass demonstrations against the ruling regime, was one of the most significant turning points in the history of the Islamic Republic of Iran. The Iranian government brutally crushed the protest movement, imprisoned reformist leaders, and sidelined some of the Supreme Leader's chief rivals and critics. These events gave rise to the question of whether the post-2009 structure of political power in Iran was qualitatively different from the one preceding it. Two competing theories, Sultanism and praetorianism, came to the fore in this regard.[77] The first view, as articulated by some Iranian reformist thinkers, maintains that a new Sultanistic regime has emerged whereby Khamenei acts more and more like a sultan who is not responsive to anyone.[78] They maintain that the postelection uprising forced the Supreme Leader to become more reliant on the IRGC and "oppression" became the Iranian regime's "principal means of sustaining Sultanism." On the other hand, some scholars assert that the 2009 postelection repression testifies to the systemic intervention in politics by the Revolutionary Guards, who have emerged as the preeminent power brokers within Iran's bona fide "praetorian state."[79]

We believe that while the Iranian state may have some of the characteristics of both Sultanism and praetorianism, it is still premature to label it as either. Max Weber defined Sultanism as an "extreme case" of patrimonialism and maintained that it arises "whenever traditional domination develops an administration and a military force which are purely instruments of the master."[80] Following Weber, several scholars have elaborated on the notion of Sultanism as a type of personalistic domination in which the sultan rules based on his own discretion and through coercion and fear. For example, Juan Linz and Alfred Stepan define a Sultanistic regime as one in which "the private and the public are fused, there is a strong tendency toward familial power and dynastic succession, there is no distinction between a state career and personal service to the ruler, there is a lack of rationalized impersonal ideology, economic success depends on a personal relationship to the ruler, and, most of all, the ruler acts only according to his own personal unchecked discretion, with no larger, impersonal goal."[81] In a subsequent work, H. E. Chehabi and Linz further refine the notion of a Sultanistic regime by maintaining that "it is based on personal rulership, but loyalty to the ruler is motivated not by his embodying or articulating an ideology, nor by unique personal mission, nor by any charismatic qualities, but by a mixture of fear and rewards to his collaborators. The ruler exercises his power without restraint, at his own discretion and above all unencumbered by rules or by any commitment to an ideology or value system. The binding norms and relations of bureaucratic administration are constantly subverted by arbitrary personal decisions of the ruler, which he does not feel constrained to justify in ideological terms."[82]

We believe that some of the key features of Sultanism are absent in today's Iran. The fate of the regime is not closely bound up with the fate of the ruler, and the legal and symbolic institutions of the regime are not a simple façade.[83] We don't see any strong tendency toward familial power and dynastic succession.[84] The Supreme Leader's preferences don't always carry the day.[85] Moreover, he does not act only according to his own personal unchecked discretion but rather exercises the powers granted to him by the Constitution. Furthermore, even during his more than two decades as the Supreme Leader, he has been challenged by three presidents who have tried to emasculate him by emphasizing their popular mandates. Finally, the Supreme Leader has not been immune from the incessant factional infighting that has come to characterize the Islamic Republic.[86] Even after members of the reformist wing were effectively removed from the ruling power centers after 2005, the system remains pulsating and factionalized. The conservative camp—known as the principlists (*usulgarayan*)—is not a homogenous group; to consolidate his power, Khamenei needs their assistance, and this perpetuates their interdependency.

The alternative theory of praetorianism also suffers from a number of shortcomings. According to Amos Perlmutter and Valerie Plave Bennett's definition cited earlier, one of the classical institutional features of praetorianism is the military's systemic intervention in politics. Yet it is hard to conceive of the IRGC's interventions in Iranian politics as "systematic." For much of the last three decades, the power of the clerical oligarchy has dwarfed that of the military establishment. There have not been any hard or soft coups d'état by the military or a decapitating of the clerical establishment. Nor can we consider the IRGC as an ideological force, since, commensurable with rising political and economic interests, its praxis as a rational actor trying to protect institutional interests has grown. While those who formerly wore the epaulettes of the Revolutionary Guards have made their forceful debut on Iran's political scene, it is an exaggeration to consider them the sole power broker in Iran.[87] In *Political Order in Changing Societies*, Samuel Huntington identified the "absence of effective political institutions" and unmediated group political action as hallmarks of a praetorian state.[88] The new elite who came to power in Iran in 1979 have developed institutions and made the state more muscular. They have also adopted the language of public goods (national defense), volunteerism, and public-mindedness to move beyond private interests and to contain political chaos in a country that has experienced an "integrative revolution," that is, "an explosion of political mobilization and participation."[89]

The popular protests that erupted after the June 12, 2009, presidential elections demonstrate why the Islamic Republic can't adequately be captured by such narrow terms as "Sultanism" or "praetorianism." Yet the events of June 2009 also demonstrated the central role of the Supreme Leader in shaping the political outcomes of the country. His hands-on involvement demonstrated that the Supreme Leader is the crucial player within the ecology of authoritarianism in Iran. His unambiguous endorsement of the declared results, forewarning to opponents, and unwillingness to compromise showcased the leviathan proclivities of the Supreme Leader. The lesson was not lost on anyone that there was a zero-sum quality to the increasing assertiveness of the Supreme Leader as far as other political institutions were concerned. Yet Khamenei also came to pay a heavy political price at this time of mass political mobilization. More than three decades after the revolution, Iranians were witnessing a spontaneous movement—not led by clerics—capable of drawing millions of people into the streets. The way the regime handled the popular protests elevated the rifts and cleavages within the political hierarchy to a new level. Perhaps most importantly, the legitimacy accumulated by some thirty elections held previously was forfeited by the suspiciously lopsided vote for the sitting president Ahmadinejad. In this ambiance, Khamenei lost a great deal of his legitimacy as the disgruntled public held him accountable for all that transpired. His hold on power was now more firm than ever, yet the accompanying price tag was not at all negligible. He had alienated the supporters of the Green Movement and lost the allegiance of many reformist politicians and technocrats who were sitting on the fence.

In short, despite what may appear as an impressive list of victories and prerogatives, one should not underestimate the price that the regime in general and the Supreme Leader in particular have paid along the way. In the immediate aftermath of the 2009 election, intra-elite factionalism reached unprecedented levels as many former comrades-in-arms walked off the political stage.[90] Despite the considerable efforts of his enthusiasts to promote a cult of personality around him, the Supreme Leader paid a heavy political price as he became the target of both fury and jokes after the 2009 contested elections.[91] While Khamenei's supporters consider him an almost infallible guide, his detractors consider him the man most responsible for the regime's long list of shortcomings. Moreover, a new season of open criticism of the Supreme Leader himself began as former and present conservative members of Parliament objected to the legitimacy of the Supreme Leader's decision-making authority and political interventions.[92]

After 2009, the bickering within the ranks of the conservative establishment intensified as Khamenei's behind-the-scenes urging for unity fell on deaf ears. In the lead-up to the 2012 parliamentary elections, in an unusual move for the Supreme Leader, Khamenei entrusted Ali-Akbar Velayati (one of his leading advisors) and Ayatollah Mohammad-Reza Mahdavi Kani (then chair of the Assembly of Experts) to unify a number of conservative factions, but the effort failed as each faction issued its own separate list of candidates. The sharp disagreements between conservative elites continued into the 2013 presidential elections as conservative candidates failed to reach consensus once again. At the end, four of the six candidates on the ballot belonged to the conservative camp, and together they failed to garner more than 44 percent of the votes, enabling Hassan Rouhani to come to power with the endorsement and support of the reformist camp.

As a further testimony to Khamenei's less-than-mighty ability to put his imprint on things, consider the following two telling episodes. The man who was the foremost beneficiary of Khamenei's blessing of the 2009 elections became the first sitting president to openly challenge him. In a Friday Prayer sermon delivered on June 19, 2009, Khamenei openly stated that his views were closer to those of President Ahmadinejad than to his longtime companion Hashemi Rafsanjani. However, a month later a public confrontation between the Supreme Leader and the president surfaced as Khamenei ordered Ahmadinejad to dismiss Esfandiar-Rahim Mashaei as his first vice president. In a telling case of resistance, Ahmadinejad ignored the Supreme Leader's request for a week, and when a number of his own ministers sided with Khamenei, he dismissed them and appointed Mashaei, his son's father-in-law, as his chief of staff. Less than two years later, another major rift between the two men emerged in public. Ahmadinejad dismissed intelligence minister Heydar Moslehi, who had previously served as the Supreme Leader's representative in the IRGC's air and ground forces. Khamenei asked Ahmadinejad to reinstate Moslehi, but to demonstrate his displeasure, Ahmadinejad did not show up in the presidential palace for eleven days, nor did he reappoint Moslehi to his post. In a break with previous protocol, Khamenei felt compelled to intervene by overruling the president's decision on April 19, 2011, and asking Moslehi to continue serving as the intelligence minister.

These two cases, which are emblematic of the contradictory trends discernible in Iranian politics, simultaneously illustrate the growing discretionary power of the Supreme Leader and the ensuing insubordination of his underlings. Loyalty to the Supreme Leader has become a prerequisite for career advancement, but a new generation of front-line bureaucrats who have been empowered by the revolution and war are not willing to be mere docile functionaries. Khamenei's lack of charisma has ensured that the cacophony within the system will not end anytime soon.

Conclusion

As we look into possible scenarios for Iran's political future, three competing pictures present themselves. The first is the continuity scenario, in which the Supreme Leader maintains the status quo, controls factional infighting, and keeps in check the power of any potential rival. In this scenario, nonelected institutions (such as the IRGC, cleric-dominated bodies, and the Office of the Supreme Leader) will be further boosted while the power of elected institutions will be diminished.[93] This scenario is most probable, since serious alteration to an institutional arrangement becomes more costly over time because of path dependency, bureaucratic inertia, and the opposition of front-line bureaucrats. In this scenario, the possibility of domestic political reconciliation or accommodation between competing political blocs becomes less likely. A despondent reformist camp may hang on to the hope that it is still possible to insist on a democratic reading of the Constitution, but the praxis of the Supreme Leader is making that ever more impossible. It is highly unlikely that, even with the handover of power to a new Supreme Leader, we will witness any lessening of the role of this office through constitutional amendments, short of a monumental political crisis. Khamenei has already been in power for more than two decades,[94] and since he is in his midseventies it is logical to expect that he has carefully planned his succession both to maintain his legacy and to ensure the least amount of dissonance in a factionalized polity. If he were to depart from the scene in a normal and gradual manner, his office could ensure a smooth succession by summoning the Assembly of Experts, controlling the news flow, and other means.

There are also a good number of ancillary factors that lead us to believe that the current order of things will continue. The Iranian state is less dependent on oil as a percentage of total government revenues than in prior decades. In addition to the diversification of revenue sources, the overall demographic composition of the country has also improved as the population growth rate hovers around 1.2 percent (circa 2014). If the present rate is maintained, the country's youth bulge will largely dissipate as this decade unfolds. The country is not burdened by heavy foreign debts or a serious shortage of goods. There are no powerful unions that can paralyze the economy and no serious labor unrest that the government cannot handle with a mixture of rewards and brute force.[95] The citizenry may be living under the oppression of the state, but the fear of a chaotic future (à la post–Arab Spring) is not necessarily appealing. Resolving the nuclear dispute with the United States and other Western countries could also help to further perpetuate the current status quo.[96] The second and third scenarios are what could disrupt the continuity picture.

The second scenario is the revival of popular protests in a country that has been quite revolutionary in its modern history. Considering that the level of dissatisfaction among most social groups in the country is already high, there is always the possibility that an event could trigger an uprising. Over the last two decades, the Iranian state has faced two important shocks to its system: in 1997 when Khatami was elected president with more than twenty million votes, and in 2009 with the Green Movement. In both instances a social movement emerged at a time when there were deep cleavages among the ruling elite. While such a small number of cases does not allow for articulating any causal relationship, it can hint at the dormant potential of another round of mass protests considering the incessant factional fighting and worsening economic conditions.

Yet one has to remember that the 2009 protests dissipated because of the following set of factors: (a) lack of a coherent ideology on the part of the opposition; (b) absence of any major defections within the military establishment or the clerical caste; (c) inability of the opposition to paralyze the economy—since they didn't have much leverage over the country's domestic trade or credit system, nor did they enjoy an independent economic base of their own; (d) inability of a mainly Tehran-based opposition movement to galvanize the disenfranchised sections of the citizenry (i.e., urban poor, labor movements, ethnic and religious minorities, and women); and (e) the state's recourse to brute force. Indeed, the regime felt confident enough that eighteen months after the June 2009 presidential elections it removed decades-old subsidies for food and energy and held parliamentary and presidential elections in 2012 and 2013, respectively. Furthermore, by adopting a business-as-usual approach, the state managed to convince most reformists that instead of staying on the sidelines they should once again take part in electoral competition, which they did in 2013.[97] While Khamenei's track record over the last two decades demonstrates that he is not willing to concede any space to oppositional elites, he has demonstrated enough political acumen to prevent situations from spinning out of control. The approach that he adopted in the course of the 2013 presidential elections—which enabled a centrist candidate to emerge victorious—was widely different from the stand he took leading to the distressing experience of the 2009 election. In light of these factors, we consider the chances for the emergence of a viable social movement capable of mass mobilization to be rather slim.

The third scenario is one in which the Supreme Leader dies unexpectedly (of natural or unnatural causes) either without having left a will (highly unlikely) or with his wishes ignored by institutions like the Revolutionary Guards or the Assembly of Experts, leading to a new agenda based on the notion of the expediency of the state and national crisis. Here again one probable contingency must be entertained. Could the IRGC overrule the "unfavorable" choice of the next Supreme Leader by the Assembly of Experts and intimidate them into accepting its own choice?

It seems that at this point in time one can only offer conjectures in answering the preceding question. As demonstrated by the literature on transition to democracy, further securitization of the political ambiance, restriction of electoral participation and competition, heavy-handed treatment of adversaries and rivals, or tinkering with the current institutional setup could each ignite yet another popular protest more vociferous in its calls for the removal of the Supreme Leader. As far as the role of the Supreme Leader is concerned, some lingering questions will have to be answered. Did Khamenei feel compelled to walk down this hard-line path in the first place, and is he cognizant of the path dependency problem that state leaders like him have to deal with?[98] Does he have the requisite conceptual complexity and good sense of political timing to handle the moment of transition? Will he have the requisite brokerage ability to co-opt and cajole the behemoth bureaucracy and entrenched elites that have spun around him? What types of major institutional adjustments or bargains is he willing to entertain as the price for staying in power?

Notes

1. Niall Ferguson, "Complexity and Collapse: Empires on the Edge of Chaos," *Foreign Affairs* 89, no. 2 (2010): 26. Eva Bellin has argued that three key features of an institutionalized organization are being "rule governed, predictable, and meritocratic." See Eva Bellin, "Coercive Institutions and Coercive Leaders." In *Authoritarianism in the Middle East: Regimes and Resistance*, edited by Marsha Pripstein Posusney and Michele Penner Angrist (Boulder, CO: Lynne Rienner, 2005), 28. Each of these characteristics needs to be a bit amended to account for the peculiar nature of politics in the Islamic Republic of Iran.

2. http://www.siasi.porsemani.ir/node/1373.

3. This vote tally is confirmed by Ayatollah Hashemi Rafsanjani in his memoirs. See http://www.khabaronline.ir/detail/217914/politics/parties.

4. This was compounded by the fact that in November 1985, Khomeini had endorsed the appointment of Grand Ayatollah Hossein-Ali Montazeri as his successor by the Assembly of Experts but disqualified him in 1989 when the latter objected to human rights violations in the country.

5. The amended Constitution—which removed the requirement of the Supreme Leader being a *marjaʿ*—was officially approved in a referendum on July 28, 1989. For the full text of

the amended Constitution, see http://www.princeton.edu/irandataportal/laws/constitutions /Constitution-English-1368.pdf.

6. For one example, see Shaul Bakhash, "Iran: The Crisis of Legitimacy." In *Middle Eastern Lectures: Number One*, edited by Martin Kramer (Tel Aviv: Moshe Dayan Center for Middle Eastern and African Studies, 1995), 111.

7. http://jameehmodarresin.org/index.php/etelaiyeh/40——1373/330-252.

8. "Grand Ayatollah Khamenei as Marja' of Shi'ite Muslims," *Keyhan Havai* (December 7, 1994/16 Azar 1373), no. 1110.

9. *Iranian State News Agency* (IRNA), December 14, 1994.

10. Margaret G. Hermann, "Content Analysis." In *Qualitative Methods in International Relations: A Pluralist Guide*, edited by Audie Klotz and Deepa Prakash (New York: Palgrave, 2008), 161.

11. The title of Commander of Armed Forces was instead bestowed upon the Speaker of the Parliament, Hashemi Rafsanjani.

12. It fell upon Khamenei to keep Montazeri under pressure and/or house arrest from 1989 to 2009, but this only helped to augment the latter's popular support.

13. In June 1987 Khomeini had agreed that the Islamic Republican Party be dissolved because of intense factional infighting.

14. Khomeini had handed over his will to the government for safekeeping in December 1987.

15. http://tarikhirani.ir/fa/events/3/EventsList?Page=&Lang=fa&EventsId=149&Action =EventsDetail.

16. The principle of *velayat-e faqih* had been approved by the Constitutional Assembly of Experts in 1979 by a vote of 58 for, 8 against, and 4 abstentions. See the newspaper *Iran* (September 16, 2002/25 Shahrivar 1381), appendix. For a review of the entire proceedings, see Majles-e Showra-ye Eslami, *Majles-e barrasi-e nahayi-ye qanun-e asasi-ye jomhuri-ye eslami-ye Iran, surat-e mashruh-e mozakerat-e majles-e barrasi-e nahayi-ye qanun-e asasi-ye jomhuri-ye eslami-ye Iran*, 4 vols. (Tehran: Edareh-e Kol-e Omur-e Farhangi va Ravabet-e Omumi-e Majles-e Showra-ye Eslami, 1985–1989).

17. David Menashri, *Post-Revolution Politics in Iran: Religion, Society, and Power* (London: Frank Cass, 2001), 17.

18. The eight-year war with Iraq, which was the largest example of mass mobilization in modern Iranian history, had forced the Iranian state to develop new administrative capacities. The question of how these capacities were to be channeled and supervised in the postwar era was causing endless friction among the various centers of power in Tehran.

19. It already had the power to supervise the presidential and parliamentary elections.

20. The tangible impact of this change was felt a year later in 1990, when elections were held for the second session of the Assembly of Experts. Armed with its newly bestowed powers, the Guardian Council set new qualifications for clerics running for the Assembly of Experts. To block the entry of radical clerics, the qualification criteria were changed and many of the candidates were rejected or forced to withdraw as they saw it demeaning to subject themselves to a religious knowledge test (see Ayatollah Asadollah Bayat's interview on the 1990 Assembly of Experts election in *E'temad Melli*, March 4, 2009). All in all, 42 percent of registered candidates (77 out of 183) were either rejected or forced to withdraw (*Ettela'at*, October 27, 1998). This trend continued in all future elections as well.

21. Anoushiravan Ehteshami, *After Khomeini: The Iranian Second Republic* (London: Routledge, 1995), 49.

22. Since the aim of the 1989 amended Constitution was to concentrate power in fewer hands, it had also created a stronger presidency by abolishing the office of the Prime Minster.

23. Saïd Amir Arjomand, *After Khomeini: Iran under His Successors* (New York: Oxford University Press, 2009), 37.

24. Ibid., 179.

25. Asghar Schirazi, *The Constitution of Iran: Politics and the State in the Islamic Republic* (London: Tauris, 1997), 78.

26. The subsequent departures of Ayatollahs Behjat, Fazel Lankarani, and Tabrizi further eased Khamenei's reshaping of the seminary system.

27. http://farsi.khamenei.ir/others-note?id=10312.

28. The charter of SCRSQ can be seen at http://www.princeton.edu/irandataportal/laws /charter-supreme-council-s/.

29. In early 1997, SCRSQ established the Islamic Seminaries Management Center for Ladies. See http://www.hawzah.net/fa/MarkazView.html?MarkazID=12219.

30. http://farsi.khamenei.ir/others-note?id=10312. The number of seminaries does not include those in Esfahan or Khorasan provinces (Northern, Southern and Razavi). See *Shahrvand-e Emrooz*, no. 67 (October 2008/Mehr 1387): 62–63.

31. http://www.princeton.edu/irandataportal/laws/charter-supreme-council-s/.

32. http://hawzahnews.com/TextVersionDetail/237542 (May 27, 2010).

33. http://www.csis.ir/NSite/FullStory/News/?Id=130.

34. *Sahifeh-e emam*, vol. 19. http://en.imam-khomeini.ir/en/c5_3203/Book/English /SAHIFEH-YE_IMAM_Volume_19_.

35. Akbar Hashemi Rafsanjani, *Be su-ye sarnevesht: Khaterat-e Hashemi Rafsanjani sal-e 1363* (Tehran: Daftar Nashr-e Maaref Enqelab, 2006), 47.

36. *E'temad-e Melli* (July 26, 2009/4 Mordad 1388).

37. Ibid.

38. *Fars News Agency*, (July 25, 2015/3 Mordad 1394). http://www.farsnews.com/newstext .php?nn=13940503000340.

39. The age factor is important here as these young preachers (a) have almost no history of political activism before the revolution and (b) have the stamina to serve as the vigilant eyes and ears of the clerical establishment in the four corners of the country.

40. Kourosh Rahimkhani, "The Institutionalization of the Clerical Establishment in Post-Revolutionary Iran: The Case of the Friday Prayer Leaders," paper presented at the biannual conference of the International Society for Iranian Studies, Los Angeles, CA, 2010.

41. In addition to Khamenei, the Society of Qom Seminary Teachers recognizes Ayatollahs Vahid Khorasani, Shobeiri Zanjani, Makarem Shirazi, Safi [Golpayegani] and Sistani as the other *marja'*. See http://www.jameehmodarresin.org/index.php/2014-01-23-07-32-22/599-495.

42. The patronage network of the Supreme Leader also extends to foreign students from the Muslim world (primarily from Arab countries, Central Asia, the Far East, and South Asia) who come to Al-Mostafa International Seminary in Qom to study Islamic jurisprudence. Al-Mostafa International Seminary also has branches in several other countries.

43. By most accounts the highest-learned present Grand Ayatollah in Iran is Ayatollah Hossein Vahid Khorasani (1921–). Born in Mashhad, he attained the status of *ijtehad* in 1948 (when Khamenei was merely nine years old) and underwent further training in Najaf. Vahid Khorasani has not accepted any important political position in the postrevolutionary period.

44. http://www.rasanews.ir/NSite/FullStory/?id=128706. IPO was founded in 1981, but Khamenei expanded its mandate in 2001 and gets to appoint its director. Its mandate is to promote religious literature (http://www.ido.ir/myhtml/sazman/sazman.aspx). One important subunit of IPO is *Setad Eqameh-ye Namaz* [Headquarters for Performance of Prayers] that coordinates prayer ceremonies throughout the country by training preachers, holding workshops and exhibitions, evaluating prayer rooms and facilities in schools and offices, and so

on. This headquarters was established on the orders of Ayatollah Khamenei (see http://center
.namaz.ir/page.php?page=showarticles&cat=32&id=1&office=center).

45. This center was established in 1989 on Khamenei's orders (see http://www.masjed.ir/fa
/aboutus/history).

46. http://www.rasanews.ir/NSite/FullStory/?id=128912.

47. A prominent group of clerics, including Grant Ayatollahs Seyyed Kazem Shari'atmadari
(1903–1986), Hossein-Ali Montazeri (1922–2009), Seyyed Hassan Tabatabai Qomi (1907–2007),
Ahmad Azari Qomi (1925–1999), Seyyed Mohammad Shirazi (1926–2001), Mohammad-Taher
Shobeir Khaqani (1909–1985), and Mohammad-Sadeq Rouhani (1926), were put under house
arrest under Khomeini and Khamenei.

48. The full name of this organization is *Dadsaraha va Dadgahha-ye Vizheh-ye Rohaniyat*
(Special Prosecutor's Offices and Courts of the Clergy). It was established in 1987 by the personal order of Ayatollah Khomeini even though it had not been mentioned in the Constitution.
The mandate of SCC, which is functionally independent of the regular judicial framework,
is to investigate transgressions of the clerics (murder, rape, stealing), and defrock them if
necessary.

49. The articles were first approved by Khamenei in 1990. The originals and the amended
articles can be read at http://www.princeton.edu/irandataportal/laws/scc/ and http://www
.princeton.edu/irandataportal/laws/scc-amendments/.

50. Mirjam Künkler: "The Special Court of the Clergy (*dādgāh-e vizheh·ye ruhaniyāt*) and
the Repression of Dissident Clergy in Iran." In *Constitutionalism, the Rule of Law and the Politics of Administration in Egypt and Iran*, edited by Said Amir Arjomand and Nathan Brown
(Albany: SUNY Press, 2012), 90–139.

51. Khamenei has also been equally tough on his lay detractors. Almost anyone who has
written a critically worded open letter to him has faced mistreatment, imprisonment, exile, or
death.

52. Because the clerical members of the Guardian Council, whom Khamenei appoints, are
also responsible for approving the credentials of Assembly of Experts candidates, he can keep
out noncompliant personalities. Khamenei can also ensure an outcome agreeable to him by
discouraging too many candidates running from the same province.

53. For example, he appointed a committee to investigate the outcome of the 2009 elections, and in the lead-up to the 2012 Majles elections he appointed a personal representative to
try to unify the conservative bloc so that they would not publish multiple lists of candidates
(the effort failed). One such ad hoc body is the Supreme Board of Arbitration and Adjustment
of Relations among the Three Branches of Government (SBAARATBG), which the Supreme
Leader created in July 2011. While it has not been hugely active yet, this body can potentially
usurp some of the functions of the Expediency Council. It is not clear whether SBAARATBG,
which has not been sanctioned by the Constitution, is a temporary or permanent council.

54. For example, Khamenei made clear his objections to Hashemi Rafsanjani's economic
reconstruction plans and to the Khatami administration's cultural policies.

55. One notorious interpreter and advocate for the wishes of Khamenei is Hossein
Shari'atmadari (b. 1947), the Supreme Leader's representative at the newspaper *Keyhan*.

56. By November 2011, the director of the Institute for Human Sciences reported that
they had completed revising the content of 555 university courses. See http://www.bbc.co.uk
/persian/iran/2011/11/111126_l44_universities_humanitie.shtml.

57. The Supreme Leader has a personal representative in most important Iranian universities, and the power of these individuals can rival that of the university president.

58. http://www.dw.de/dw/article/0,,4521706,00.html.

59. IKRC was established on March 5, 1979, with the prime objective of providing services and relief (pensions, loans, and grants) to the poor and those in need. See http://www.emdad .ir/en/history.asp.

60. Mahmood Messkoub, "Social Policy in Iran in the Twentieth Century," *Iranian Studies* 39, no. 2 (2006): 251.

61. Mehrzad Boroujerdi, "Iran." In *The Middle East*, 13th ed., edited by Ellen Lust (Washington, DC: CQ Press, 2014), 501.

62. Arang Keshavarzian, *Bazaar and State in Iran: Politics of the Tehran Marketplace* (Cambridge, UK: Cambridge University Press, 2007).

63. Suzanne Maloney, "Agents or Obstacles? Parastatal Foundations and Challenges for Iranian Development." In *The Economy of Iran: Dilemmas of an Islamic State*, edited by Parvin Alizadeh (London: Tauris, 2000), 155. According to the official website of DFIR, in 2002 it employed more than fifty-six thousand workers.

64. http://faryabnews.ir/press/index.php/1392-01-19-05-38-02/8083.html (February 24, 2015). For a more comprehensive account of the activities of the Imam Khomeini Relief Committee, see http://www.emdad.ir/upload/nashriat/nashriyeh/No13.pdf.

65. http://old.ana.ir/Home/Single/3748 (January 1, 2013).

66. See Ali A. Saeidi, "The Accountability of Para-governmental Organizations (Bonyads): The Case of Iranian Foundations," *Iranian Studies* 37, no. 3 (2004): 483.

67. *ISNA* news agency, March 14, 2011. Some of the more well-known shrines in Iran are Ma'sumeh Shrine, Abddolazim Shrine, and Shah Cheragh Shrine, which have their own foundations.

68. http://www.rahesabz.net/story/20436/.

69. In 2009, this company served twenty-five million landline subscribers and thirty-one million mobile subscribers. *Fars News Agency*, August 29, 2009.

70. The director of HIIO, Mohammad Mokhber, was placed on the European Union's sanction list on July 26, 2010.

71. *Ettela'at* (August 12, 1981/21 Mordad 1360), and *Jomhuri-e Eslami* (February 10, 1994/21 Bahman 1372).

72. Khamenei has appointed many of those who served as ministers in either one of his two cabinets as his advisors or members of the Expediency Council. Among these are Gholam-Reza Aqazadeh, Habibollah Askarowladi, Javad Ejei, Hassan Habibi, Mohammad Javad Iravani, Alireza Marandi, Bijan Namdar Zangeneh, Mohammad Reyshahri, Ahmad Tavakkoli, and Ali-Akbar Velayati.

73. At the outset of the Iran-Iraq War, the IRGC was a force of no more than 20,000 to 30,000. Today educated estimates put the number of the Guards between 120,000 to 150,000 with some 50,000 retirees. See Rand Corporation, *The Rise of the Pasdaran: Assessing the Domestic Roles of Iran's Islamic Revolutionary Guards Corps* (Santa Monica, CA: Rand, 2009), 8; and Alireza Nader, "The Revolutionary Guards," *Iran Primer*, http://iranprimer.usip.org /resource/revolutionary-guards.

74. Khomeini delegated the position of commander in chief of the armed forces first to President Banisadr and then to Speaker of Parliament Rafsanjani, whereas Khamenei has decided not to delegate any portion of his military mandate.

75. Khomeini was represented by such individuals as Hassan Lahuti Eshkevari (1927–1981), Fazlollah Mahallati, Seyyed Hassan Taheri Khorramabadi (b. 1938), Mohammad-Reza Faker (1945–2010), and Abdollah Nuri (b. 1950). Khamenei was represented by Ayatollah Mahmud Mohammadi Araqi (b. 1952), Ayatollah Mohammad-Ali Movahhedi Kermani (b. 1931), and Hojjatoleslam Ali Sa'idi.

76. For example, Mohsen Rezaei was tapped at the young age of twenty-seven to lead the IRGC for sixteen years (1981–1997) because of his involvement in armed struggle before the revolution and his having served in the committee providing security for Khomeini upon his return from exile.

77. Praetorianism has been defined as "a situation where the military class of a given society exercises independent political power within it by virtue of an actual or threatened use of military force." Amos Perlmutter and Valerie Plave Bennett, eds., *The Political Influence of the Military: A Comparative Reader* (New Haven, CT: Yale University Press, 1980), 199.

78. See Akbar Ganji, "Rise of the Sultans," *Foreign Affairs* (June 2009).

79. See Elliot Hen-Tov and Nathan Gonzalez, "The Militarization of Post-Khomeini Iran: Praetorianism 2.0," *Washington Quarterly* 34, no. 1 (2011): 45–59; and Ali Alfoneh, *Iran Unveiled: How the Revolutionary Guards Is Turning Theocracy into Military Dictatorship* (Washington, DC: American Enterprise Institute, 2013).

80. Max Weber, *Economy and Society: An Outline of Interpretive Sociology*, edited by Guenther Roth and Claus Wittich (Berkeley: University of California Press, 1987), 231.

81. Juan J. Linz and Alfred Stepan, *Problems of Democratic Transition and Consolidation* (Baltimore: Johns Hopkins University Press, 1996), 52.

82. H. E. Chehabi and Juan J. Linz, *Sultanic Regimes* (Baltimore: Johns Hopkins University Press, 1998), 7.

83. It is also important to remember that whereas the Supreme Leader does not have the authority to dissolve Parliament or the Assembly of Experts, the latter can theoretically dismiss him.

84. Khamenei's older brother, Seyyed Mohammad Hosseini Khamenei (b. 1935), retired from Parliament in 1988 and now heads both the Sadra Philosophical Foundation and the Iranology Foundation, whereas his younger brother, Seyyed Hadi Hosseini Khamenei (b. 1947), left Parliament in 2004, and the two reformist newspapers he founded were banned by the judiciary on the charge of castigating political leaders. Khamenei's second son, Mojtaba (b. 1969), is reputed to be a powerful behind-the-scenes player in his father's operations, but he does not hold any official positions.

85. For example, during the 1997 presidential election it became obvious that Ali-Akbar Nateq Nuri was Khamenei's favorite candidate, but he lost the election to Mohammad Khatami by a 44 percent margin.

86. Political disagreements have reached such a threshold that at least four members—Abdollah Nuri, Karrubi, Mussavi, and Mussavi Khoeiniha—of such a stately body as the Expediency Council have been tried or put under house arrest.

87. Mehrzad Boroujerdi and Kourosh Rahimkhani, "Revolutionary Guards Soar in Parliament," *Iran Primer.* http://iranprimer.usip.org/blog/2011/sep/19/revolutionary-guards-soar-parliament.

88. He writes: "in all stages of praetorianism social forces interact directly with each other and make little or no effort to relate their private interest to a public good." Samuel P. Huntington, *Political Order in Changing Societies* (New Haven, CT: Yale University Press, 1968), 196, 197.

89. Amir Arjomand, *After Khomeini*, 112.

90. Unlike his predecessor, Khamenei did not play an impartial role in preventing the tilting of the balance of power in favor of one faction.

91. As the saying goes, the greatest enemy of authority is contempt.

92. In January 2012, in a live controversial television interview in the state media, Emad Afrugh (b. 1957), a former conservative MP, maintained that even the Supreme Leader can be

subjected to impeachment. In 2012, one outspoken and prominent Majlis deputy, Ali Motah-hari (b. 1957), publicly complained that Parliament had become a de facto unit of the Office of the Supreme Leader. Furthermore, in 2014 Motahhari also publicly opposed the continuing house arrest of Mussavi and Karrubi.

93. The facts that the Eight Majles (2008–2012) voted to deprive itself of the right to monitor institutions under the umbrella of the Supreme Leader and that Khamenei told the leadership of the Assembly of Experts in 2012 that they can't question him about the details of his choices point to this direction. Furthermore, in the area of sensitive foreign policy issues (nuclear negotiations, Iraq, and Syria), the Supreme Leader is the ultimate arbiter.

94. With the exception of Mohammad-Reza Shah, Khamenei's tenure as ruler exceeds that of any other person ruling Iran since 1900.

95. Only 20 percent of Iran's workers are employed in workplaces that have more than thirty-five employees. Most labor protests in Iran revolve around unpaid wages and short-term employment contracts and don't galvanize the working public. Furthermore, according to the Iran Statistical Center, 80 percent of the 1.4 million Iranians with higher-education degrees are public sector wage and salary earners. This means they can be cowed by the power of the purse.

96. While it can be argued that a "grand bargain" can undercut one of the key ideological props of the Supreme Leader's power, history shows us that such a radical reversal is not neces-sarily hard to justify for the regime. After all, the Iranian state had promised to rid Iraqi people from the tyranny of the Ba'athist regime but ended up signing a cease-fire agreement with it in 1988.

97. For the reformists, the surprising election of Rouhani as president once again dem-onstrated that in Iran's fluid political scene, "defeat is by no means total, victory is in no way unqualified, [and] grief not at all permanent." See Mehrzad Boroujerdi, "The Reformist Move-ment in Iran." In *Oil in the Gulf: Obstacles to Democracy and Development*, edited by Daniel Heradstveit and Helge Hveem (Aldershot, UK: Ashgate, 2004), 66–67.

98. See Mehran Kamrava, "Preserving Non-Democracies: Leaders and State Institutions in the Middle East," *Middle Eastern Studies* 46, no. 2 (2010): 251–270.

5 Electoral Politics, Power, and Prospects for Reform

Yasmin Alem

In the year commemorating its thirtieth anniversary, the Islamic Republic faced its most imperiling political crisis. Elections, often referred to as one of the pillars of the system by its leadership, nearly became the cause of its undoing with the disputed reelection of incumbent president Mahmud Ahmadinejad bringing about eight months of protests. Turmoil on the streets spilled over into the political arena, further exacerbating the level of polarization among an increasingly fractured revolutionary elite. Above all, the inherent contradictions in Iran's hybrid political system, which blends the democratic notion of popular sovereignty with the Islamic principle of *velayat-e faqih*—guardianship of the jurisprudent—came to surface during the tumultuous months that followed the disputed 2009 election. Consequently, Iran's leadership was confronted with two equally unpalatable options: address the electoral demands of a disgruntled segment of the population or pursue a crackdown on dissent. It chose repression and weathered the storm. But the fate of the electoral system was left uncertain. The 2012 parliamentary election, a contest limited to a group of conservative loyalists, suggested that moving forward the exclusionary function of electoral politics in the Islamic Republic would dwarf its ability to serve as a medium to aggregate interests and bring about legitimacy. The surprise election of Hassan Rouhani, an outspoken critic of the status quo, in the 2013 presidential election, however, demonstrated a shift in the opposite direction. Thus, the pendulum continues to swing between diverse functions of elections in a complex system, which itself is in constant flux.

Regularly held elections have been one of the most salient features of the Islamic Republic. Four tiers of popularly elected institutions—stipulated in the Constitution—are considered important arenas for intra-elite competition and the management of factional conflicts. Although Iran is not a Western-style liberal democracy, elections for the legislature, the presidency, local councils, and the Assembly of Experts provide the Iranian electorate with a platform to exercise political participation. In fact, Iranian citizens have used the electoral process to effect meaningful change in the country's political course. The upset election of Mohammad Khatami in 1997 is a case in point, when high turnout resulted in the victory of an underdog candidate, despite the ruling establishment's preference for his rival. Three years later, in 2000, Iranian voters stormed polling stations and elected a reformist-dominated Parliament.

Nevertheless, the degree to which elections in the Islamic Republic can be considered democratic is a matter of debate. On one hand, elections have not been trivial staged events, in the sense that preselected candidates are ushered into elected positions. On the other hand, electoral contests have been subjected to state intervention and fall short from qualifying as genuine contests between all contending political forces in the Iranian political system. Yet even within a constrained and controlled structure, the electoral process has had meaningful and palpable implications for the social and economic policy direction of the country and the evolution of the political system.

This chapter highlights the features and evolving patterns of electoral politics in the Islamic Republic of Iran. Its goal is to assess whether, in the aftermath of the 2009 election debacle, the Iranian electoral system could serve as a platform for meaningful contestation of power. The 2009 purge of reformist factions, an important segment of the postrevolutionary elite, will provide a case in point to determine whether the Iranian polity is shifting from a factionalized and divided structure of power to one that is becoming increasingly centralized and monopolized by a single bloc. The issue at the crux of this chapter is the role that electoral politics has played in shaping the structure of power in the Islamic Republic.

To evaluate these questions, this chapter defines the purpose and significance of elections within the Iranian political system, examines the state's electoral policies and practices, and assesses the evolution of the electoral system in the past three decades. We focus on legislative elections, since the process of elite jockeying and circulation occurs at the lower levels of the Iranian political pyramid, of which the parliamentary level is the most significant. By the same token, the state has devoted substantial effort over the past three decades to regulating the electoral laws governing parliamentary elections. Traditionally setting the trend for presidential contests, parliamentary elections have served as a barometer to determine the direction of the institution of elections in Iran.

Elections under the Islamic Republic

Although elections in the Islamic Republic have always fallen short from qualifying as free and fair, based on internationally recognized standards, they do matter for at least three main reasons.

First, the image of popular support has been quintessential for the ethos of a regime born out of a popular revolution. In the decade following the 1979 revolution, elections reinforced the regime's legitimacy by highlighting its popu-list and republican features. The importance of this function increased over time, as revolutionary fatigue and disillusionment set in and obliged the state to pro-actively marshal high participation to showcase its broad base of support to both domestic opponents and foreign foes.

Second, elections have served as a vehicle for managing intra-elite competi-tion and preventing factional rivalries from turning into a destabilizing force. Regularly held national elections have shaped the political landscape of the Islamic Republic by providing a well-structured environment for elite enthrone-ment and circulation. For instance, many members of the political elite have served in Parliament or made their bid to enter it. Iran's current Supreme Leader, Ayatollah Seyyed Ali Khamenei, was elected to Parliament in 1980; he then went on to serve two consecutive terms as president from 1981 to 1989. Former presi-dents Akbar Hashemi Rafsanjani and Mohammad Khatami were both members of Parliament (MPs) in the 1980s.[1] At least one third of cabinet members under Prime Minister Mir-Hossein Mussavi and former presidents Hashemi Rafsan-jani and Khatami served in the legislature as well. More importantly, the rise and fall of political currents in the Islamic republic have been closely linked to the electoral process. Shortly before the 1988 parliamentary elections, a schism in the Society of Combatant Clergy (*Jame'eh-ye Rohaniyat-e Mobarez*, JRM) led to the formation of the left-leaning Association of Combatant Clergy (*Majma'-e Rohaniyun-e Mobarez*, MRM).[2] This fissure led to the emergence of two opposing currents, the conservative and reformist factions, which came to define Iran's po-litical landscape for the following two decades. Similarly, the 1996 parliamentary elections provided the platform for the rise of a new political party, the Servants of Construction (*Kargozaran-e Sazandegi*). A dispute between then president Hashemi Rafsanjani and the leadership of the JRM over the 1996 election lists motivated a group of pragmatic technocrats close to Rafsanjani to establish the Servants of Construction Party. Their electoral success harbingered the rise of the reformists in the 1997 presidential election.[3] Less than a decade later, the elec-toral victory of conservatives in the 2004 parliamentary elections heralded the ascension of a new radical class of conservative forces, known as the principlists, to power.[4]

Third, elections have played an important role in the Iranian electorate's po-litical socialization and interest aggregation, by providing a medium through which citizens have registered their grievances with the government, expressed their interests and, at times, challenged the status quo. Between 1997 and 2001, Iranian citizens registered their discontent with the establishment by voting in reformist candidates against regime-endorsed conservative contenders in presi-dential, parliamentary, and local council elections. In the 2003 local council elections, however, the public's frustration with the slow pace of reform led to increased voter apathy and a notable decline in participation rates. With only 49 percent of eligible voters casting ballots nationwide, in contrast to the 64 percent who had participated in the 1999 local council elections, low voter turnout facilitated the electoral victory of conservative forces.[5]

The limited degree of political and ideological pluralism countenanced in elected institutions has had meaningful impact on the social, economic, and political course of the country. For instance, the Islamic Republic's economic policies under President Hashemi Rafsanjani (1989–1997) concentrated on economic liberalization and postwar reconstruction, whereas under President Ahmadinejad, Iran's economic policies centered on social justice and the distribution of wealth.[6] In the sociocultural arena, while President Khatami (1997–2005) and the Sixth Majles (2000–2004) emphasized on the rule of law, the creation and strengthening of civil society, and the relaxation of press censorship, President Ahmadinejad (2005–2013) and the Seventh Majles (2004–2008) imposed heavy restrictions on the media and fought against "Western cultural invasion."[7]

Although elections have played an important role in the political evolution of the Islamic Republic, they have also been the drivers of contentious politics. For this reason, unelected institutions have gradually developed a number of electoral strategies to curb their clout. Over the past three decades, the rules and parameters of the electoral process have been carefully amended to prevent unpredictable election outcomes, establish an uneven playing field in the electoral arena, and cement the hold of unelected institutions on power. The manipulation of rules goes beyond fine-tuning candidate eligibility criteria. It includes the establishment of a political parties law that strictly inhibits opposition parties from functioning freely and has prevented the emergence of any political bloc capable of posing a serious threat to the ruling apparatus. Coercive media policies have also limited the functioning of independent media and made it daunting for journalists and newspapers to work without the fear of arrest or closure. In short, the state has developed a set of policies, laws, and practices that can be described as guided competition, limited contestation, and controlled mobilization. Learning from political setbacks such as Khatami's and the subsequent rise of reformists, the ruling establishment has gradually moved to close the loopholes in the electoral process to preempt the rise of competing forces.

Guided Competition

Elections in the Islamic Republic have invariably been conducted in the framework of guided competition. In essence, Iran's two election management bodies, the Guardian Council and the Ministry of Interior, have played a prominent role in managing and controlling the electoral process. The Guardian Council (GC), a twelve-member body composed of six theologians and six lay Muslim jurists, is in charge of overseeing the electoral process. Provided with a broad mandate by the Constitution, the Guardian Council has for most of its history acted as the political watchdog of the *nezam*, a term that means "order" and refers to the governing system of the Islamic Republic.

Considered one of Iran's most powerful institutions, the Guardian Council has been dominated by conservative forces since its inception in 1979.[8] Beyond validating the credentials of candidates, the Guardian Council has significant supervisory powers, including approving the date of elections, receiving complaints and adjudicating electoral disputes, annulling elections in an electoral district or halting the election process, approving amendments to and revisions of all electoral laws, and certifying election results.[9]

The council has traditionally used its powers to enforce exclusionary practices. By exercising its supervisory rights, it has tightly controlled the nature of competition. Employing its right to interpret the Constitution, the council has established electoral policies and stifled reform initiatives with its legislative jurisdiction. For instance, in 1991, it interpreted Article 99 of the Constitution to assert, "The Guardian Council's supervision of elections is approbatory and applies to all stages of the electoral process, including the approval and rejection of candidates," thus modifying its authority from one that supervised the electoral process to one that sanctioned it. Despite the assertion by former council spokesperson Ayatollah Mohammad Emami Kashani that the blade of "unequivocal supervision" of the Guardian Council is the blade of due process of law,[10] the council's vetting rights has become one of the most important obstacles to genuinely contested elections by all political forces in the Islamic Republic.

However, the council has not always employed this discretionary mechanism to limit electoral competition. For example, under pressure from Khatami's reformist government, it approved the credentials of over 90 percent of registered candidates in the 2000 parliamentary elections, many with reformist affiliations.[11] Since 2004, however, it has increasingly implemented its approbatory authority to debar candidates from rival political affiliations, namely the reformists, and other recalcitrant political forces from entering the political arena. Using its extensive legal jurisdiction, the council has also repressed electoral reform initiatives. In 2003, it rejected a proposed amendment to the election law that aimed at curtailing the council's powers by removing its right to vet the nomination of candidates—on the grounds that it contradicted the Constitution on 39 counts and Islamic law on 7 counts.[12]

Exercising its supervisory powers, the Guardian Council has altered undesired electoral outcomes. At times, the council has used its authority to annul election results to produce outcomes that favor the ruling establishment. In the six parliamentary elections conducted between 1980 and 2000, the results of thirty, twelve, fifteen, three, sixteen, and ten districts were altered, purportedly based on politically motivated reasons.[13] For instance, during the parliamentary elections of 1980, citing technical violations and insufficient security, the council nullified the election results of several districts in the province of Kurdistan. It was no coincidence that most of the annulled seats were won by supporters of the Kurdish Democratic Party, which was engaged in a bitter conflict with the central government over the rights of Kurdish ethnic minorities.[14]

After annulling the results of sixteen districts in the 1996 parliamentary elections, Ahmad Jannati, then Secretary of the Guardian Council, justified the decision by accusing the winners of those seats of providing false promises to their constituencies and buying votes. Though the nullification was described as an effort to "safeguard the real votes of the people,"[15] it had significant implications for the political composition of the new Parliament. In effect, it tilted the balance of power in favor of conservative forces and facilitated their seizure of key leadership positions in the Fifth Majles (1996–2000). Similarly, in the 2000 parliamentary elections, the council annulled a staggering 25 percent of all votes cast in Tehran.[16] This alternation allowed two establishment candidates, Hashemi Rafsanjani[17] and Gholam-Ali Haddad Adel, who had fought a losing battle before the nullification of the results, to each gain a seat in the Sixth Majles.[18]

Although Article 26 of the Constitution guarantees freedom of association, this right is heavily restricted in practice.[19] The Law on the Activities of Political Parties, Trade Societies, and Islamic and Recognized Religious Minority Associations passed by the Majles in 1981 provides a detailed legal base for the Ministry of Interior to restrict the free functioning of political parties. According to the parties' law, all political groups, associations, and parties must apply for an operating permit with a commission in the Ministry of Interior, titled the Commission on Article 10. This supervisory organ has a wide mandate, which includes licensing parties and monitoring their activities and finances, among other functions. It also has the power to suspend the licenses of political groups and refer them to the judiciary, who in turn can revoke their license permanently. In the aftermath of the 2009 disputed election, the commission recommended that the operating license of two leading reformist organizations, Islamic Iran's Participation Front (*Hezb-e Mosharekat Iran-e Eslami*) and the Mojahedin of Islamic Revolution (*Mojahedin-e Enqelab-e Eslami*), be revoked and that they be dissolved.[20]

In 2011, Parliament initiated a revision to the party law. The Parties and Association Law Reform Plan, currently under review by members of Parliament, contains key provisions such as strict licensing requirements; a description of persons banned from membership in political parties and associations; the process for holding demonstrations by political parties;[21] and narrow and vaguely defined violations under which parties can lose their legal license. The proposed amendments also subject electoral coalitions and fronts—formed during election cycles—in addition to political parties and organizations, to government-issued licensing. If the proposed amendments were to pass in Parliament, the added layer of restriction would allow the government to further exert control on electoral competition, curtail the activities of regime critics, and politically disenfranchise segments of the population whose loyalty to the regime is deemed questionable by authorities.

Limited Contestation

The Islamic Republic has created a Manichean binary structure for electoral contestation. An insider-outsider dichotomy has served as a potent tool for electoral containment, maintained through hand-tailored legal instruments. Numerous amendments to the election law, particularly the alteration of rules governing candidate eligibility, have created entry barriers for regime outsiders, critics as well as opponents. With each revision to the Majles election law, candidate eligibility criteria have become more rigid and citizens' choices more constricted.

In 1980, to stand for parliamentary elections a candidate—in addition to age, citizenship, and education requirements—had to believe in the values of the Islamic Revolution. By 1984, amendments to the election law made "faith in Islam, practical obligation to Islamic tenets, faith and practical obligation to the Islamic revolution, and demonstrated loyalty to the Constitution" mandatory requirements for eligibility. A decade later, in 1995, the most stringent candidacy eligibility criteria were instituted, requiring candidates to "demonstrate loyalty to the principle of the absolute rule of the jurisprudent."[22] These opaque criteria have provided the ruling conservative establishment with the legal justification to separate insiders (*khodi*) from outsiders (*gheir-e khodi*) in the electoral arena. Maintained through a two-level system of candidate screenings conducted by the Ministry of Interior and the Guardian Council, the wide-scale disqualification of candidates has noticeably reduced the circle of regime insiders and transformed their composition over the past three decades. In 1980, 12 percent of registered candidates were deemed unfit to run for Parliament; by 1996 this number increased to 39 percent.[23] Preelection candidate screenings in 2000, 2004, 2008, and 2012 barred 8 percent, 24 percent, 29 percent,[24] and 31 percent[25] of registered candidates from competing in parliamentary elections, respectively.[26]

Although regime insiders are politically enfranchised, they are not guaranteed immunity. Political borders between insiders and outsiders are nebulous and subject to change over time, based on political realities on the ground. Regular elections have provided the system with an avenue to redefine boundaries between those with unimpeachable loyalty and those with questionable fealty. Between 1984 and 2012, many incumbents—former members of Parliament and previously vetted candidates—were declared unfit to compete in parliamentary elections. In 1992, the Guardian Council rejected the credentials of 41 incumbents. In 1996, out of the 1,892 disqualified candidates, 310 had been deemed fit by the council to run in previous polls.[27] In 2004, in an unprecedented move, the Guardian Council rejected the credentials of 80 sitting members of Parliament. Most of these deputies were from the ranks of the pro-reformist political groups such as Islamic Iran's Participation Front and the Mojahedin of Islamic Revolution, who were also prevented from fielding candidates in the 2008 parliamentary elections.[28] In 2012, of the 262 sitting members of Parliament seeking re-election, 43 had their credentials rejected.[29] These regular demarcations not only have helped keep the elite in line but have filtered out candidates whose loyalty to the system has become dubious. At least three sets of noteworthy demarcations have redrawn political boundaries in the Islamic Republic.

Overall, the state has pursued two types of demarcations. In the 1980s, as the Islamic forces close to Ayatollah Khomeini were attempting to consolidate their power, the state implemented a stringent and irreversible demarcation policy toward groups and individuals whose loyalty to the revolution had become questionable. This is exemplified in the state's electoral policies toward the Iran Liberation Movement (ILM, *Nehzat-e Azadi-ye Iran*), a political organization that was part of the incongruous revolutionary coalition that overthrew the monarchy. Though founding members of the ILM were elected to Parliament in 1980, they were politically sidelined after objecting to the policies of the Islamic forces loyal to Ayatollah Khomeini. After boycotting the 1984 parliamentary elections, some members of the ILM decided to register their candidacy for the 1988 legislative elections. Ali-Akbar Mohtashamipur, then Minister of Interior, wrote a letter to Ayatollah Khomeini asking about the eligibility of ILM members to participate in the poll. In response, Ayatollah Khomeini stated that members of the ILM were not qualified to serve in any executive or legislative capacity and accused them of being agents of the United States, lacking political acumen as well as a general understanding of Islamic precepts and tenets.[30] This response became the basis for the Guardian Council's systematic rejection of the credentials of ILM members, affiliates, and supporters from competing in electoral processes, including but not limited to the 1985 presidential and 2000 parliamentary elections.[31] In 2004, the Ministry of Interior, under Mohammad Khatami, approved the candidacy of seven applicants who were distantly associated with the ILM in the first stage of candidate screenings. The Guardian Council, however, reversed this decision in the second stage of vetting and disqualified all registered applicants.[32]

In some cases, however, the state has employed a flexible demarcation policy. For instance, in the 1992 parliamentary elections, the conservative-dominated Guardian Council excluded left-leaning Islamic groups, who were part of the revolutionary coalition, from the electoral process. Mass disqualification coupled with negative campaigning against these groups in media outlets resulted in 141 MPs losing their seats in the elections for the Fourth Majles (1992–1996), including incumbent Mehdi Karrubi, who had served as the speaker of Parliament in the previous session.[33] These groups, however, subsequently rebranded their political identity and, in contrast to the liberals who were purged in 1984, staged a comeback under the banner of reformists in the 2000 parliamentary elections. The establishment's leniency, however, proved ephemeral. In 2004, the reformists confronted a new set of institutional barriers in the electoral arena. Not only were a significant number of sitting members of Parliament barred from seeking reelection, but two thousand individuals aligned with reformist groups had their credentials rejected by the Guardian Council.[34] The same policy was applied in the 2008 parliamentary elections. The Guardian Council along with the conservative-controlled Ministry of Interior denied reformist forces access to the legislature. At least forty-eight parliamentarians aligned with the reformist coalition in the Seventh Majles were debarred from running as candidates in 2008. Mostafa Tajzadeh, a prominent member of Islamic Iran's Participation Front, argued that the mass disqualifications amounted to preelection engineering and determined the fate of 160 out of the parliament's 290 seats even before elections had commenced.[35]

Following the disputed 2009 presidential election, political demarcations have become increasingly irreversible. The 2012 parliamentary elections, in which twenty reformists from second- and third-tier political groups won seats in the Majles,[36] demonstrated that *nezam* has a limited appetite for allowing threatening or expelled political actors and groups from reentering the political arena. The redrawing of political boundaries persisted in the 2013 presidential election. The disqualification of Esfandiar-Rahim Mashaei, President Ahmadinejad's preferred candidate and former chief of staff, seemed to suggest another round of— permanent or temporary—political demarcations. Ahmadinejad and his allies in fact joined a group of former insiders who were also barred from the race, including former president Hashemi Rafsanjani,[37] as well as the dozens of reformist candidates who were blocked from participating in the 2013 local council elections.[38]

Controlled Mobilization

Despite its exclusionary policies toward political actors, the Islamic Republic has traditionally sought and encouraged mass participation of the populace in electoral processes. This is partly due to the regime's identity as the product of a referendum and popular uprising. Equating voter participation with the Islamic concept of *bay'at*, the state has employed a blend of religious and revolutionary rhetoric to depict elections as the populations' renewal of allegiance with their rulers.[39] The target audience for the projection of popular support has consisted of foreign foes, domestic opponents, and their supporters.

Foreign Foes

Threatened by outside enemies who have questioned its legitimacy since its inception, the Islamic Republic has used high voter turnout to prove its popularity. The mobilization of citizens is not exclusive to electoral competitions. In fact, this strategy has been applied to other politically significant arenas including weekly Friday prayers, street parades, and national and religious holidays. Moreover, unlike "façade" electoral regimes, such as Egypt under Hosni Mubarak or Syria under Bashar Al Assad, the Islamic Republic has been reluctant to resort to farce or trumped-up participation rates. In the nine parliamentary elections held between 1980 and 2012, participation rates have oscillated between a low of 51 percent (in 2004) and a high of 71 percent (in 1996). For presidential elections, turnout rates have fluctuated at a slightly higher rate during the same period. The lowest participation rate for presidential elections occurred in 1993 with 51 percent turnout, whereas the participation of 85 percent of the electorate in the 2009 election was a record high.[40]

Domestic Opponents

Internal critics and opponents of the state have always contended that their exclusion from the political arena will emasculate the pluralistic nature of the Islamic Republic and dishearten its supporters. Calls for boycotting the elections have been a constant feature of elections during the last two decades. Still, electoral boycotts lack a successful record in achieving their goals of undermining the legitimacy of the regime. For instance, members of two prominent left-leaning political groups, the Association of Combatant Clergy and the Office for the Consolidation of Unity, abstained from participating in the 1996 parliamentary elections. Yet despite their boycott, the turnout rate reached a record high of 71 percent. A similar phenomenon occurred in 1997, when in spite of the ILM's call for boycott, 79 percent of eligible voters participated in the heated presidential election of that year.[41] According to official statistics, on average 60 percent of the electorate have participated in parliamentary elections and 65 percent in presidential elections between 1980 and 2012, which is more than average turnout in many Western democracies. High participation rates have allowed the political establishment to portray its domestic opponents as irrelevant, while touting its broad base of support.

Regime Supporters

Disillusionment is the nemesis of revolutions. The Islamic Republic has used mass participation in elections as a tool for preserving revolutionary by depicting high turnout as a tribute to its broad support and credibility, especially for its main constituents. Interestingly, for the establishment, images of epic participation in national elections trump the real numbers.[42] Images of mass participation are continuously fed to supporters and enemies alike using circular propaganda to ensure that they believe that support for the state is broad and its legitimacy beyond doubt.

Though mandatory voting laws do not exist in the Islamic Republic, the elections stamp that is registered in citizens' identity cards after voting is considered a quasi-requirement for opening the doors of state bureaucracy in Iran, including access to government subsidies and benefits as well as facilitating registration at academic institutions. Thus, government employees, members of the armed forces, some students, and the segment of the population that has a client-patron relationship with the state participate in elections in order to maintain their benefits.

In addition to courting these voters, the regime has employed tactics to encourage participation of the remainder of the electorate. These include easing of social liberties in the months leading up to elections, providing more space for debate in the press, and permitting limited or targeted criticism of government policies. Between 1992 and 2000, the ruling establishment countenanced a politically vibrant atmosphere prior to the elections to portray itself as an electoral democracy. Yet immediately after the elections, it reinstated the previous status quo by tightening control over the media and cracking down on journalists who had been critical of the ruling establishment during the election season. Since the 2000 parliamentary elections, the state has progressively reversed this tactic despite occasionally providing the media with carte blanche to denigrate its political rivals prior to the elections. For example, in the months leading up to the 2004 parliamentary elections, while pursuing a widespread crackdown on the media and the imprisonment of dozens of journalists, the state allowed conservative-aligned press outlets to harshly criticize reformist members of Parliament who had organized a sit-in to protest the Guardian Council's disqualification of incumbent MPs.[43]

In addition to the ruling establishment, political groups have also pursued mass mobilization strategies ahead of elections. The reformists have regularly used grassroots electoral campaigns to encourage high voter turnout to help improve their fortunes in the face of restrictive electoral policies and institutional biases. While this policy proved successful in the 1997 presidential election and the 2000 parliamentary elections, it failed to deliver the desired outcome in the 2003 local council elections. The inability of reformist politicians to effect real change and increased disgruntlement among their supporters led an important segment of their base to abstain from voting, thus enabling the conservative political establishment to regain the electoral territory that it had lost to the reformists.

The ruling establishment's policy toward high turnout rates has also not been static over time. Although mass participation has allowed the *nezam* to showcase its legitimacy, it has also been the source of instability. In fact, exceptionally high turnouts have heralded an eruption of collective demands for change in the status quo. For instance, high participation rates in the 1997 and 2009 presidential elections (79 percent and 85 percent, respectively) occurred at the height of popular discontent with the country's political trajectory and posed a dilemma for the Islamic Republic's leadership: to heed the call for change, as they did in 1997 with the election of President Khatami, and grudgingly share power, or to resist popular demands and suppress protests as they did in 2009 following the disputed reelection of President Ahmadinejad. Experience demonstrates that both strategies are costly.

An alternative understanding of mass participation appears to have emerged among the ruling elite: while lackluster electoral events could cast a shadow on the Islamic Republic's legitimacy, zealot participation could pose a threat by catapulting unwelcomed forces into the inner-power circle or creating unrest. As a consequence, the state appears increasingly more in favor of controlled mobilization, which allows the establishment to reap the benefits of a relatively acceptable turnout (anything above 50 percent) but helps it avoid turmoil and instability.

The Ninth Parliamentary Elections

Three decades of electoral experience, with all its complexities and contradictions, came to the fore in the 2012 parliamentary elections. As the first set of elections since Iran's strongest political earthquake—the disputed 2009 presidential vote and its tumultuous aftermath—the parliamentary poll was a litmus test for the future of electoral politics in Iran. The use of enhanced exclusionary mechanisms, the perennial insider-outsider dichotomy, the struggle for political survival and superiority, and evolved mobilization strategies were all indicative of both continuity and change in the Iranian theocracy's electoral system.

The 2012 elections were not merely an electoral contest among the remaining political groups in the Islamic Republic's inner circle over Parliament's 290 seats. More importantly, they were a showdown between two of Iran's most powerful political figures, Supreme Leader Khamenei and President Ahmadinejad— a two-dimensional electoral competition occurring both at the top of Iran's political pyramid and among its elites.

After his public rift with Khamenei in April 2011, Ahmadinejad and his lieutenants came under unprecedented pressure from the ruling apparatus.[44] Political boundaries shifted overnight, pushing Ahmadinejad and his associates to the circle of outsiders. They were dubbed the "deviant current," accused of corruption, and charged with holding anti-clerical views. Several of the president's aides became targets of judicial investigation, some were arrested, and a few were handed prison sentences by the judiciary. Ahmadinejad fought back by seeking to retain a base of support in the next Parliament. Even a minority presence in the legislature could have potentially deterred his foes from sidelining him or prosecuting his allies after his term ended in 2013.

The president's team therefore devised an array of electoral tactics to increase its chance of bypassing the obstacles of guided competition and limited contestation. They pursued the so-called *cheragh khamush* (lights off) strategy and fielded candidates from small constituencies, meanwhile maintaining a low profile in big cities to evade disqualification by the Guardian Council. The president's supporters also used economic incentives to tilt the balance in their favor. Promises to distribute state resources were carefully timed to marshal the support of lower-income constituencies.[45] Above all, the president and his allies hoped to affect the electoral results through their control over the Ministry of Interior, which is responsible for the first stage of the two-stage candidate screenings as well as the administration of elections.

Notwithstanding these machinations, Khamenei and the state-institutions allied with him were well positioned to thwart Ahmadinejad's plans. First the Guardian Council reinstated the credentials of candidates who were critical of Ahmadinejad and had been disqualified by provincial executive committees (assembled by local governors appointed by Ahmadinejad).[46] Next, allies and supporters of the president who had passed the provincial-level vetting had their credentials rejected by the council's supervisory committees.[47] A number of sitting MPs who were alleged to have close ties to the president were also barred from standing for reelection. Official estimates suggested that 30 percent of registered candidates had their credentials rejected, which was slightly higher than in the 2004 and 2008 parliamentary elections but did not significantly deviate from the average 27 percent disqualification rate.

The ruling conservative establishment also applied its stringent exclusionary practices to outsider groups, forcing some out and others to self-exclude from the electoral process. For example, leading reformist groups and politicians, led by former president Khatami, had preemptively announced a set of conditions for their participation in the elections. The conditions included the release of all political prisoners; freedom for all political parties and groups and the removal of all restrictions on their activities; adherence of all, particularly government officials, to the principles of the Constitution and the execution of all of its articles, especially its true spirit—meaning those articles that respect the rights of the people; and the holding of free and fair elections.

As major reformist parties remained proscribed and their main political leaders stayed under house arrest or marginalized, the Coordinating Council of Reformists Coalition, comprising eighteen reformist groups, released a statement in November 2011 declaring that it would not present a candidate list for the ninth parliamentary elections.[48] Green Movement leaders Mir-Hossein Mussavi and Mehdi Karrubi shared the position of the Coordinating Council of Reformists Coalition and told their supporters to refrain from participating in the vote.[49]

Notwithstanding these boycotts and in order to depict a pluralistic image in the elections, the regime cajoled second- and third-rank reformist groups and actors including the Democracy Party (*Hezb-e Mardomsalari*) and House of Workers (*Khane-ye Kargar*) to enter the contest. According to official sources, more than seven hundred reformist candidates participated in the elections. Mansur Hosseini, the Secretary General of the Followers of the Path of Imam (the Eighth Parliament's Reformist Caucus), refuted these claims and said that reformists were not able to field a single candidate in many provinces. He added that out of the forty reformist-aligned incumbent MPs, only twenty took part in the 2012 parliamentary elections.[50] In the end, only nineteen individuals affiliated with reformist groups secured seats in the new Parliament.

The same façade was erected to portray voter participation as epic, while in reality the ruling establishment tightly controlled participation, lest it became a security threat. This was achieved by simultaneously intimidating domestic opponents to deter them from participating, while cajoling traditional voters to produce a satisfactory participation rate. Before the March elections, Mohammad Dehghan, a member of the Eighth Majles's executive board, warned that the "seditionists"—a term used to describe supporters of the Green Movement—and "deviants" were attempting to use the elections to undermine the security of the Islamic regime.[51]

Against this backdrop, the 2012 vote was conducted under a highly securitized environment. Before the elections, several journalists and bloggers were arrested, pressure on civil society increased, and access to the Internet was restricted.[52] Relying on the images of long lines at the polling stations to restore the legitimacy tarnished by the 2009 elections, the establishment adopted a three-pronged strategy to coax traditional voters to participate in the parliamentary elections:

Patriotic Sentiments

Iran's state-controlled media (IRIB) continuously streamed patriotic programming and jingoistic messages to encourage the electorate to vote. These messages equated voting with the most important national and religious duty, highlighted the people's power in determining the country's political trajectory, and depicted Iran's political system as the freest and most advanced in the world. On Election Day, the IRIB devoted five of its national channels, all of its provincial broadcast, and its English-language Press TV to live election coverage. With nationalistic music playing in the background, commentators regularly urged the electorate to vote for the sake of the country's future. Moreover, for the first time in the history of legislative elections, television debates were organized between prominent candidates from different conservative factions.

Religious Convictions

Employing religion as a tool of statecraft is not a new phenomenon in the Islamic Republic. Ever since the 1979 referendum that established the Islamic Republic, Iranian leaders have characterized participation in the election as a religious duty. In the lead-up to the 2012 poll, Khamenei compared voting to the mandatory five times of prayer prescribed in the Muslim faith.[53] Grand Ayatollah Nasser Makarem Shirazi, an ultraconservative cleric and a source of emulation for Shi'ites, issued a religious fatwa, describing abstention as a "grave sin."[54]

Specter of War

External threats were also used to encourage participation in the elections. Bellicose rhetoric, saber rattling, and escalating tensions between Iran, Israel, and the United States over Tehran's disputed nuclear program created a climate of fear that the ruling apparatus exploited to persuade the electorate to participate in the elections. Billboards warning citizens of the dire consequences of boycotting the elections for national security were put up in major cities. For instance, one billboard in the capital city of Tehran stated, "If the participation in the parliamentary elections is less than 50 percent, the United States will launch a military strike against Iran." Voters were urged to prevent an attack by the US or Israel by voting, which would show their support for the Islamic Republic and become a "slap in the face of arrogant powers."[55]

On Election Day, the *nezam* brought its extensive electoral experience and population control prowess to bear. According to Iranian officials, 64 percent of eligible voters participated in the elections. The events that transpired on March 2, 2012, were a double win for the political establishment. On one hand, by masterminding and orchestrating a grand electoral spectacle, the state arguably redeemed itself from the 2009 electoral debacle. On the other hand, the political establishment sent a strong message to its recalcitrant opponents that it is very much in control and still enjoys the support of a broad base of the population.

With the conclusion of the second round of voting on May 4, 2012, the fate of 286 of the Majles' 290 seats were determined.[56] The results revealed that the United Principlist Front (UPF),[57] closely linked to the Supreme Leader, won a majority by receiving 86 parliamentary seats (30 percent) across the country. Despite its extensive campaigning, the Steadfast Front secured only 35 seats (7 percent) nationally.[58] Some 45 (16 percent) of elected candidates appeared on both lists. Independent deputies had a strong showing in the vote and won 106 seats (37 percent). Candidates who ran on a pro-reform platform (mostly affiliated with second- and third-tier reformists) won only 19 seats (6 percent), bringing the reformists' presence in Parliament to its lowest ebb (in 2008 they won 40 seats).[59] The remaining 9 parliamentary seats (4 percent) went to smaller conservative-aligned coalitions.

The high number of so-called independent delegates in the Ninth Majles does not undermine the previously described impermeability of the circle of power in Iran. Instead it can be partially explained by the exclusionary mechanisms embedded in the Iranian electoral system. Candidate registration data from five elections between 1992 and 2008 reveal that a significant number of incumbents have had their credentials rejected by the Guardian Council, which has provided newcomers with the opportunity to contest their seats. Despite their independent status, these newcomers are not complete outsiders. In the words of Ahmad Tavakoli, conservative deputy from Tehran, "The independents are not unknown personalities to us. Even if we haven't worked with them in the past, we are familiar with their political affiliations and associations."[60] Tavakoli's remarks highlighted the closed nature of Iran's power structure, to which outsiders have limited access.

In fact, the Guardian Council, with its intrusive background checks and vetting mechanisms, impedes independent candidates from access to the Majles. Second, such representation of independent newcomers is one of the elements of continuity in Iran's postrevolutionary electoral history. The first and fifth Parliaments were composed of a similar percentage of independents. While in the First Majles the independent delegates coalesced around the Islamic Coalition, which was the dominant parliamentary faction, in the Fifth Majles they formed a coalition called the Independent Deputies (*Namayandeg an Mostaqel*) of Hezbollah.

Yet, although the successful and incident-free 2012 elections demonstrated that the political establishment had learned from its mistakes and can weed out undesirable candidates and orchestrate acceptable participation, Iran's political system is far from becoming a monolithic or single-party authoritarian system. In the absence of prominent reformist groups, the electoral field became the undisputed dominion of the conservatives. But instead of highlighting the harmony in the conservative camp, the elections brought its dissonance to the surface and exacerbated splits. Whereas in 2008, heterogeneous conservative factions directed their negative campaigning efforts against the reformists, in 2012 they turned against each other. From launching attacks through online and print media outlets to wide-scale SMS campaigns, competing conservatives attempted to create negative biases against their rivals in the court of public opinion. Given the blurred boundaries between professional and personal realms in Iranian politics, personal attacks quickly rendered a bitter competition into an acerbic foray. Attempts to bring the various conservative factions under the umbrella of a single electoral coalition, to present a unified list of candidates throughout the country, came to naught as differences between conservative factions proved to be unbridgeable. More than sixty coalitions and fronts mushroomed around the country to compete for the 290 seats in Parliament.[61]

Since its inception, factionalism has constituted an integral part of electoral politics in the Islamic Republic. In the absence of political parties, amorphous and fractured groups form ephemeral coalitions that often disappear as rapidly as they had formed.

In the first parliamentary elections held in March 1980, two dominant political forces competed in the electoral arena. The first group, called the Grand Coalition, consisted of Islamic organizations glued together by their loyalty to the leadership of Ayatollah Khomeini and included groups such as the Islamic Republic Party, the Society of Combatant Clergy of Tehran, and the Mojahedin of Islamic Revolution and presented candidates in most constituencies. The second group consisted of forces with mostly secular and moderate Islamic orientations and included groups such as the ILM. Running under the list of Eponym (*Hamnam*), they presented a list of thirty candidates in Tehran and endorsed a handful of candidates in six provincial districts.[62] While candidates did not run on mutually exclusive lists, by most accounts, of the 234 seats in Parliament, the Grand Coalition secured 130 seats, while the secular and moderate forces claimed 50 seats, with the remaining seats won by independent candidates.[63]

Having secured a majority in Parliament and control of its leadership, the Islamic forces began to marginalize the voices of their rivals in the legislature. At the same time, the state embarked on a systematic purge and violent suppression of its political opponents. Between 1980 and 1984, organizations such as the National Democratic Front, the People's Mojahedin Organization, the People's Fadayian Guerrilla Organizations, and the Tudeh Party were either formally or effectively proscribed. By the second parliamentary elections, held in 1984, the activities of the ILM were severely restricted, and as a consequence ILM members decided to boycott the elections. The liquidation of the ILM from Parliament set the Islamic Republic on a political trajectory defined by the hegemony of Islamist political groups in the electoral arena.

Between the second and third parliamentary elections, new schisms emerged among Islamist groups with differences in ideology and policy preferences (in the economic, foreign policy, and sociocultural arenas) creating deep divisions among them. In the end, the dissolution of the Islamic Republic Party in 1987 and a fissure in the Society of Combatant Clergy in 1988 produced two political currents: the Islamic right (or conservatives) and the Islamic left (or reformists). With the marginalization of the reformists in the Seventh Majles, rifts began to appear in the conservative ranks. In the 2005 presidential election, the conservative camp failed to coalesce around a single presidential candidate, and instead five conservative personalities threw their hat in the race. In the 2008 parliamentary elections, a bid to create a grand conservative coalition (between traditional, moderate, hard-line, and pro-Ahmadinejad factions) proved unsuccessful.[64] Again in 2012 the conservatives failed to unite under one coalition and splintered into several competing groups.

Today, intraconservative differences are increasingly defined not by ideology, as was the case in the early years of the revolution, but by political and economic interests. While on the surface, ideology and revolutionary values construct the lexicon of political groups and actors, real competition today is over political power and control of state resources. These two interrelated issues have come to define electoral competition in the Islamic Republic since 2005. In July 2006, the Supreme Leader issued a decree ordering the acceleration of the country's privatization act (embedded in the Constitution's Article 44) and called for the transfer of 80 percent of state-owned assets to the private sector.[65] Using the Supreme Leader's decree, President Ahmadinejad embarked on an ambitious program to privatize Iran's state-run economy.

This controlled privatization consisted of issuing lucrative licenses to a small network of trusted individuals, cooperatives, and IRGC-affiliated companies. According to a report by the Parliament Research Center, the composition of the economy as a result of Ahmadinejad's "privatization" policies has undergone a strong shift away from the government toward the semigovernmental sector. This pseudo-privatization coupled with unprecedented oil revenues amounting to more than twelve times the total of oil export earnings since 1979 has intensified competition among various factions as each vies to increase its clout and enhance its base of power.[66]

Because of this, economic interests have been pushed to the forefront of the political bickering. In the transition from state-owned to semi-state-owned economy, more control over the levers of political power directly translates to greater access to limited economic resources. In a rare admission, Ahmadinejad acknowledged the relation between political power and economic opportunities in Iran when he said, "It is amazing how much money the candidates are spending to become a lawmaker—it seems as if they get more than just the salary of an MP."[67] In this new environment, holding political office is now tantamount to having access to economic privileges and as such a coveted commodity.

Prospects of Institutional Change in Iran

With every election, inherent contradictions of the Islamic Republic's Constitution, which combines popular with divine sovereignty, come to the surface. At times, however, this dichotomy has proven destabilizing for the *nezam*. Given that the elimination of a century-old institution of elections in Iran is inconceivable, all contemporary Iranian rulers have tried instead to neutralize it. By closing legal loopholes, eliminating outsiders, and controlling mobilization, the Islamic Republic's political establishment has used the electoral process to consolidate its power. Despite this achievement, taming Iran's convoluted and polarized political system appears elusive, without neutralizing other rival power centers and institutions.

In October 2011, Supreme Leader Khamenei floated the idea that the country's political system could undergo fundamental change. "The current political system of the country is presidential, and the president is elected directly by the people. This is a good and effective system," he said. He then surprised many by adding, "But if one day, possibly in the distant future, it is felt that a parliamentary system is more suited for electing those responsible for the executive branch, then there would be no problems in making changes to the system."[68]

Despite the low probability of such a change, the political system established in 1979 offers both the flexibility and the precedent for such a transformation. In 1988, the father of the revolution, Ayatollah Khomeini, initiated an extensive institutional transformation. The Office of the Prime Minster was abolished and its responsibilities were divided between the Office of the Supreme Leader and the popularly elected president. The constitutional change not only further empowered the president but also augmented the authority of the Leader. Putting the judiciary and the state-media's leadership into the hands of individuals appointed by the Leader instead of governing councils and creating the Expediency Council were among other significant institutional changes brought about by amending forty articles of the 1979 Constitution.[69]

Ayatollah Khamenei, who was president at that time, was closely involved in the revision process. After being appointed as Iran's new Supreme Leader, he approved the drafted amendments and ordered a national referendum, pegged to the 1989 presidential elections, to approve the new Constitution. According to official figures 97 percent of voters approved the amended Constitution, even though only 55 percent of eligible voters participated in the simultaneously held referendum and presidential election.[70]

While a similar change is not imminent—at least not in the short run—it is not an entirely inconceivable notion. An institutional change that abolishes the presidency and replaces it with an appointed prime minister could resolve the two-decade-long tension at the pinnacle of Iran's polity. From an institutional perspective, the dysfunctional bifurcate structure of power has been problematic under Iran's second Leader, Ayatollah Khamenei. Article 110 of the Constitution provides the Office of the Leader with extensive political power, including "the power to determine the general policies of the state," and designates him as the commander-in-chief of the armed forces. The Leader also has the power to appoint or dismiss the director of official state media, the head of the judiciary, and members of the Guardian Council. Although the president's position is subordinate to that of the Leader, he is the head of the government and is constitutionally endowed with jurisdiction over budgetary issues and the authority to command the day-to-day affairs of running the country. He also has the power to appoint members of the cabinet, ambassadors, and governors[71] and is vested with limited power over matters of foreign policy, national security, and policy coordination as the chair of the Supreme National Security Council.[72] If the Office of the President were abolished, the Leader would be eliminating the most serious rival power center and resolving a dual leadership structure that has repeatedly stymied his power consolidation.[73]

From a personal perspective, Iran's current Supreme Leader has had an acrimonious rapport with all three presidents who have served under him. The relationship between the Leader and his first president, Hashemi Rafsanjani, a once-cordial relationship rooted in decades of friendship, turned into an acerbic rivalry in Hashemi Rafsanjani's second presidential term (1993–1997). The visions of the two main architects of the Islamic Republic began to diverge as the pragmatic Hashemi Rafsanjani embarked on a program of economic liberalization to reconstruct Iran's war-torn infrastructure. Blaming Hashemi Rafsanjani's liberal policies as the cause of rampant corruption in the country, Khamenei began to side with factions opposing the president.[74] In 1997, Hahsemi Rafsanjani's two-term presidency came to an end. His former Minister of Culture and Islamic Guidance, Mohammad Khatami, a moderate cleric who was a member of the revolutionary elite, succeeded him. Between 1997 and 2005, the Leader and his second president engaged in an intense power struggle. Khatami's programs for political liberalization and his new political discourse on strengthening civil society, upholding the rule of law, promoting political pluralism, and furthering freedom of press were considered anathema to the custodian of the Iranian theocracy.

After sixteen years of enduring noncompliant presidents, Khamenei ostensibly handpicked Ahmadinejad to play the role of the pliant president. Despite sharing the Leader's strategic vision on social justice and enmity with the West, Ahmadinejad's submission to the Supreme Leader was an ephemeral affair. Like his predecessors, he too defied the authority of the Supreme Leader. He stepped into the Leader's traditional turf by dismissing several key ministers, including Foreign Minister Manuchehr Mottaki and Minister of Intelligence Heydar Moslehi. Ahmadinejad went as far as refusing to attend government functions and sequestering himself at his residence for eleven days following the Leader's reinstatement of Moslehi in his position; glorifying Iran's pre-Islamic past; and refusing to disassociate himself from his controversial chief of staff, Esfandiar-Rahim Mashaei. If the past is a prelude to the future, the Leader is likely to experience another taxing relationship with his next president. By replacing the popularly elected president with an executive appointed by a docile parliament, Iran's Supreme Leader would be able to dismiss and appoint the head of the government at will.

An institutional change that abolishes the presidency could also resolve a practical predicament: the holding of presidential elections and the potential security threats associated with them. As previously discussed, emotional national campaigns, high voter turnout, and unexpected electoral outcomes have at times been a destabilizing force for the *nezam*.

If the presidency were eliminated, then the legislative and executive powers could be merged into one institution. But that does not mean the empowerment of the Majles or the shift to a more democratic system. Historically, the Majles has provided a well-structured arena for the management and arbitration of factional politics in the Islamic Republic. Yet Parliament's role and independence have gradually decreased over the years as it become a more subservient entity overshadowed by the Office of the Leader. The Leader's interventions in Parliament's affairs through his legal powers and extraconstitutional prerogatives have become more frequent. Examples of such interventions abound. In 2000, Ayatollah Khamenei issued a state fiat (*hokm-e hokumati*) to block the reformist-dominated Sixth Majles (2000–2004) from liberalizing the Press Law. In 2009, he staged another intervention by advising members of Parliament to approve the ministers proposed by President Ahmadinejad.[75] In 2011, Ayatollah Khamenei instructed Parliament to increase the allocations for the judiciary and the military in the 2011–2012 budget. Ali Motahhari, a conservative MP and son of one of the revolution's founding fathers, Ayatollah Motahhari, recently called Parliament "an extension of the Leader's abode."[76] Sa'id Abutaleb, another conservative MP, in 2006, described the constraints to the independence of the Majles:

> The Majles is neither governed by its rules of procedure nor by constitutional law. Even the voting of MPs and their consensus on an issue has nothing to do with the functioning of the Majles. On several occasions, I have personally witnessed a bill approved by a parliamentary vote only to have the Majles approve a contradictory bill several months after it. It is a secret network that governs the Majles.[77]

Moreover, the legislature's powers are capped by the Guardian Council. Article 94 of the Constitution vests the council with the authority to review all legislation passed in the Majles and the power to approve or reject a bill on the basis of its adherence with Islamic precepts and constitutional law. Estimates suggest that between 1980 and 1996, the council rejected between 27 percent and 40 percent of the legislation passed in Parliament.[78] Between 2000 and 2004, the Guardian Council used its veto power to block 111 of 295 progressive pieces of legislation passed by the sixth session of Parliament, acting as the single most important obstacle to Parliament's legislative jurisdiction.[79]

Moreover, although Article 86 of the Constitution stipulates that "Majles deputies are free to express their views, and shall not be prosecuted or arrested for giving their views in the Majles," at the recommendation of Ayatollah Khamenei the Majles passed a bill to amend Article 4 of its Rules of Procedure.[80] In early 2012, the Parliamentary Supervision over Members of Parliament bill amended Article 4 of its Rules of Procedure that defines parliamentarians' offenses in vague terms such as "acting against national security and other security-related crimes" and "committing behavior that undermines the dignity of elected office." Running in contradiction to Article 86 of the Constitution, which provides MPs with parliamentary immunity, the new parliamentary supervision will further curtail the lawmakers by constantly holding a sword of Damocles over their heads.

Since 1979, the Islamic Republic has conducted thirty-four elections. Although these elections have been neither entirely free nor fair, they have been contested. They have provided an arena for the elite to negotiate their differences or settle political claims, albeit at times acrimoniously. In parallel, they have provided the state with a potent tool for managing inter-elite conflicts to maintain a complex and often fragile political equilibrium. Over time, however, Islamic conservative factions have taken control of unelected institutions and closed electoral loopholes that could allow rivals to challenge their grip on power or induce transformative change in the political system. Most significant of these institutions is the Guardian Council, which is judge, jury, and prosecutor on all matters related to elections. Its presence is ubiquitous and its powers are unbounded, guiding the competition into a narrow channel in which only desired candidates are permitted to participate.

Despite occurring inside a closed and constantly shrinking circle of regime insiders, the electoral process has had a palpable and meaningful impact on the social, political, and economic evolution of the regime. At times, polls have produced unexpected outcomes that have challenged the status quo or posed a threat to the regime's stability. Traumatized by electoral results of the past fifteen years that empowered rival power centers—Khatami's 1997 upset victory and the reformists' takeover of Parliament in 2000, or the 2009 disputed presidential elections and its ensuing uprising, which brought protestors to the streets—the *nezam* inaugurated its fourth decade in power with a dramatic narrowing of the electoral arena. The purge of a segment of the revolutionary elite following the 2009 presidential election persisted in the 2012 parliamentary elections.

Despite tight control over all of their aspects, elections are far from becoming irrelevant in the Islamic Republic. Given endemic factionalism, Iran is likely to remain a divided polity. Political factions will continue to change, evolve, and splinter. The political establishment is likely to continue using the electoral system to control the fissures among its loyalists, prevent factional clashes from becoming an existential threats, and dim prospects of collective action against the state. Given existing legal and structural mechanisms, the framework under which elections are conducted will likely persist. The two polls that ensued after the disputed 2009 elections have followed this pattern. Both the 2012 parliamentary elections and the 2013 presidential poll were marked by exclusionary practices, which forged a guided competition amid controlled mobilization of the electorate. Yet as the degree of the state's electoral policies, the goals pursued, and the electorate's response differed, the two polls produced fundamentally different results. In 2012 a combination of voter apathy and the application of strict exclusionary electoral rules facilitated the election of a pliant Parliament filled with conservatives, whereas in 2013 the limited degree of competition tolerated by the state encouraged high turnout and brought into office a pragmatic president who, despite being a consummate insider, was a critic of the country's trajectory.

Absent structural reforms, the electoral system's mechanisms of guided competition, limited contestation, and controlled mobilization will stymie efforts by opposition forces to make the electoral arena a focal point for systemic transformation. But while the core of the electoral system and its exclusionary nature remains intact, its boundaries will likely remain in constant flux.

Notes

1. Coincidentally, Ahmadinejad also ran an unsuccessful election bid in the 2000 parliamentary elections.

2. For more information on this, see Mehdi Moslem, *Factional Politics in Post-Khomeini Iran* (Syracuse, NY: Syracuse University Press, 2003), 69–70.

3. The Servants of Construction Party won eighty seats in the 1996 parliamentary elections and forged an alliance with the Mojahedin of Islamic Revolution in the fifth Parliament (1996–2000) under the parliamentary faction called the Hezbollah Association of the Majles. The alliance between the pragmatic conservatives of the Servants of Construction Party and their support for Mohammad Khatami in the 1997 presidential election was instrumental in his election victory. For more, see Said Amir Arjomand, *After Khomeini: Iran under His Successors* (Oxford: Oxford University Press, 2009), 62–71.

4. For a detailed account on the rise of hard-line conservative forces, see Anoushiravan Ehteshami and Mahjoob Zweiri, *Iran and the Rise of Its Neoconservatives: The Politics of Tehran's Silent Revolution* (London: Tauris, 2007).

5. The turnout rate was significantly lower in major cities. For instance, in Tehran only 12 percent of eligible voters cast a ballot in the capital. For an overview of voter participation rates, see Yasmin Alem, *Duality by Design: The Iranian Electoral System* (Washington, DC: International Foundation for Electoral Systems, 2011).

6. For an overview on President Rafsanjani's economic policies and Iran's First Five-Year Plan, see Moslem, *Factional Politics*, 164-167. For a comparison between Hashemi Rafsanjani

and Ahmadinejad's economic policies, see Evaleila Pesaran, "Challenges Facing the Iranian Economy in Iran." In *A Revolutionary Republic in Transition*, edited by Rouzbeh Parsi (Paris: Institute for Security Studies, 2012), 41–59.

7. Amir Arjomand, *After Khomeini*, 92–95, 159–160.

8. The idea for establishing the Guardian Council was borrowed from Iran's 1906 Constitution, which envisaged a body composed of senior clerics overseeing legislation passed in the Majles with the objective of preventing the enactment of laws in conflict with the Islamic code. Article 2 of the Supplementary Fundamental Laws of October 1907 stipulated the composition of a council with a minimum of five devout theologians elected by the members of the National Consultative Assembly from a list presented by the *ulama*. The formation of such a council, however, did not transpire under the monarchy, and it was only after the 1979 revolution that the Guardian Council convened for the first time.

9. For details on the rules governing the elections of the Majles, see "The Law for the Elections of the Islamic Consultative Assembly" and "The Law on the Guardian Council's Supervision of the Elections of the Islamic Consultative Assembly." http://www.princeton .edu/irandataportal/elections/electoral-laws/.

10. Moslem, *Factional Politics*, 239.

11. Alem, *Duality by Design*, 35.

12. "A Review of the Twin Bill Fiasco," *Iran Cultural Media Center*, March 23, 2003.

13. Asghar Schirazi, *The Constitution of Iran: Politics and the State in the Islamic Republic*, translated by John O'Kane (London: Tauris, 1997), 91–94.

14. Bahman Bakhtiari, *Parliamentary Politics in Revolutionary Iran: The Institutionalization of Factional Politics* (Gainesville: University Press of Florida, 1996), 68.

15. Moslem, *Factional Politics*, 241.

16. The GC declared that 534 ballot boxes in the district of Tehran, totaling 726,266 votes, were invalid.

17. Amid accusations of electoral fraud, Hashemi Rafsanjani resigned from the Tehran delegation on May 25, 2000. *"Besyari bayad rad salahiyat mishodand: Gozareshi-e az khaneye mellat"* ("Many had to be disqualified: A report from the house of people"), *Cheshm Andaz Iran* 8 (2001): 25.

18. Meir Litvak, "Iran: Jomhuri-i Islami-i Iran," *Middle East Contemporary Survey* 24 (2000): 213–218.

19. Article 26 of the Constitution states, "The formation of parties, societies, political or professional associations, and Islamic or other religious societies of the recognized minorities is permitted, provided they do not violate the principles of independence, freedom, national unity, Islamic standards and essentials of the Islamic Republic."

20. Michael Theodolou, "Iran Bans Two Leading Reformist Political Parties," *The National*, September 29, 2012. http://www.thenational.ae/news/world/middle-east/iran-bans-two -leading-reformist-political-parties.

21. Article 27 of the Constitution guarantees the right to assembly. If the amendments to the party law are approved in its current iteration, individuals and groups who want to hold demonstrations would need to register with and receive approval from the Ministry of Interior. This would undermine the freedom of assembly guaranteed by Article 27 of the Constitution.

22. Majid Saili Kurdahih, *Sayr-e tahavol qavanin-e majles dar Iran* (Evolution of parliament's laws in Iran) (Tehran: Markaz-e Asnad-e Enqelab-e Eslami, 1999), 429–431.

23. *Ettela'at*, April 11, 1992.

24. Kaveh-Cyrus Sanandaji, "The Eighth Parliamentary Elections in the Islamic Republic of Iran: A Division in Conservative Ranks and the Politics of Moderation," *Iranian Studies* 42, no. 4 (September 2009): 621–648.

25. "More than 3000 Registered Applicants Are Approved by the Guardian Council," *Mehr News*, February 22, 2012. http://mehrnews.com/fa/newsdetail.aspx?NewsID=1539730.

26. Alem, *Duality by Design*, 21. The disqualification rates for the 2012 parliamentary elections are based on statistics released by a spokesperson of the Guardian Council.

27. Seyed-Javad Qadimi Zaker, *Nezarat-e estesvabi dar dorehaye mokhtalef-e entekhabat-e majles-e shoraye eslami* (Supervisory approval in various Islamic consultative assembly elections) (Tehran: Ravabet-e Daftar-e Tahkim-i Vahdat, 1378/1999), 223-224.

28. Sanandaji, "The Eighth Parliamentary Elections," 628.

29. The Parliament's Deputy Speaker Comments on the Disqualification of Incumbent MPs. *Khabar Online*, March 24, 2012, http://khabaronline.ir/detail/204996/politics /parliament.

30. Bahman Esma'ili, *Entekhabat-e majles haftom* (The seventh parliamentary elections) (Tehran: Markaz-e Asnad-e Enqelab-e Eslami, 1384/2005), 200–202.

31. In the 1985 presidential election, the Guardian Council rejected the credentials of forty-six out of fifty individuals who had registered for the race. Among those barred from contesting the election was Mehdi Bazargan, who had served as prime minister following the 1979 revolution.

32. Esma'ili, *Entekhabat-e majles haftom*, 486–500.

33. Masoumeh Sotoudeh, "*Az oj-e hemayat to haziz-e hazf*" ("From zenith of support to nadir of elimination"), *Nasim Bidari* (May 2011): 70–73.

34. Alem, *Duality by Design*, 35.

35. Sanandaji, "The Eighth Parliamentary Elections," 629.

36. The calculation of reformist representation in the 2012 Ninth Majles is based on the author's compilation of candidates' affiliations and biographies. For the list of the names of Parliament's reformist candidates, see http://khabaronline.ir/detail/202185.

37. Farideh Farhi, "Rafsanjani Shut Out of Iran's Presidential Race," *IPS News*, May 22, 2013. http://ipsnews.net/2013/05/rafsanjani-shut-out-of-irans-presidential-race.

38. "Reformists Are Barred from Taking Part in the Local Council Elections," *Bahar*, May 10, 2012.

39. For more on the propaganda significance of participation rates in the Islamic Republic, see Hosein Ghazian, "*Entekhabat-e majles va natayeji ke kesi ra khoshnud nemikonad*" ("The implications of the parliamentary elections: An outcome that satisfies no one"), *BBC Persian*, May 3, 2012. http://www.bbc.co.uk/persian/iran/2012/05/120503_l13_iran_majlis_election .shtml.

40. For participation rates, see the Iran Data Portal, http://www.princeton.edu/irandata portal/elections/parl/, and http://www.princeton.edu/irandataportal/elections/pres.

41. For the efficacy of election boycotts in the Islamic Republic, see Mohammad Quchani, "Tahlil-e entekhabat majles nohom" ("Analysis of the ninth parliamentary election"), *Aseman Weekly*, April 15, 2012.

42. Hosein Ghazian, "The Ninth Parliamentary Elections in Iran: Challenges and Perspectives," Heinrich Boll Stiftung Foundation, February 21, 2012. http://www.boell.de/downloads /worldwide/Ghazian_The_Ninth_Parliamentary_Elections_in_Iran.pdf.

43. The information in this section is the result of interviews with several Iranian journalists including Nikahang Kowsar, Alireza Eshraghi, Vahid Pourostad, and others who wished to remain anonymous.

44. The quarrel between the Supreme Leader and the president was over the forced resignation of Minister of Intelligence Heydar Moslehi. Moslehi stepped down from his position in April 2011, only to be reinstated by the Supreme Leader a day after. In protest, the president

refused to appear at work for eleven days. Following this public rift, Ahmadinejad came under unprecedented pressure from Parliament. Many parliamentarians called for his impeachment for disobeying the Leader. In the end, he was summoned to the Majles in March 2012 to explain his disobedience of the Leader. For more, see Saeed Kamali Dehghan, "Iran's President and Supreme Leader in Rift over Minister's Reinstatement," *The Guardian*, April 27, 2011. http:// guardian.co.uk/world/2011/apr/27/iran-president-supreme-leader-rift; and Marcus George, "Ahmadinejad Grilled by Hostile Iran Parliament," *Reuters*, March 14, 2012. http://reuters .com/article/2012/03/14/us-iran-ahmadinejad-parliament-idUSBRE82DoNK20120314.

45. Although not implemented despite the promise, the government announced its plans to increase the amount of cash grants and distribute another round just days before the election.

46. Thirty-two sitting MPs who were outspoken critics of the president were barred from seeking reelection in the first stage of candidate screenings.

47. In the words of an official, the Guardian Council was able to spot and weed out 45 percent of Ahmadinejad's supporters. Parisa Hafezi, "Analysis: Ahmadinejad Seen Big Loser in Iran Election," *Reuters*, February 17, 2012. http://reuters.com/article/2012/02/17/us-iran -politics-idUSTRE81GoMK20120217.

48. *"Mose'ye shoraye hamahangi-ye jebhe-ye eslahat dar entekhabat 'elam shod"* ("The coordinating council of reformist front announced its position on the parliamentary elections"), *Aftab News*, December 21, 2011. http://aftabnews.ir/vdcbo8b88rhba8p.uiur.html.

49. Mehdi Karrubi was quoted as characterizing the March 2012 vote as a "sham election" on the official website of his party, the National Trust Party (*Hezb-e E'temad-e Melli*). For the full statement, see http://sahamnews.net/1390/10/141272. Kaleme, Mussavi's official website, quoted him as saying, "Given the current circumstances, it is impossible to remain hopeful about the elections and participation in them." http://kaleme.com/1390/12/12/klm-93150.

50. *Khabar Online*, February 13, 2012. http://khabaronline.ir/detail/198830/politics/election.

51. *Khabar Online*, January 23, 2012. http://khabaronline.ir/detail/195283/politics/election.

52. Amnesty International, "We Are Ordered to Crush You: Expanding Repression of Dissent in Iran," February 28, 2012. http://amnestyusa.org/sites/default/files/mde13002012en .pdf.

53. *Rooz Online*, March 3, 2012, http://roozonline.com/persian/news/newsitem/archive /2012/march/03/article/-23fc72a7bc.html.

54. *Resalat*, February 23, 2012. http://resalat-news.com/Fa/?code=93412.

55. Parisa Hafezi and Zahra Hosseinian, "Iran Parliament Vote Seen Bolstering Supreme Leader," *Reuters*, March 2, 2012. http://reuters.com/article/2012/03/02/us-iran-election-id USTRE82109P20120302.

56. The 290 seats represent a mix of single- and multi-member constituencies. Over 65 percent of representatives are elected from single-member constituencies with small populations. The other seats are allocated to representatives from Iran's major cities. The city of Tehran, with thirty parliamentary seats, is the largest and most politically significant district in Iran. Five parliamentary seats are reserved for religious minorities. Citing electoral irregularities, the Guardian Council annulled the election results of four districts. The elections for the voided districts were held later.

57. The United Principlist Front (*Jebhe-ye Motahed-e Usulgarayan*), headed by Ayatollahs Mohammad-Reza Mahdavi-Kani and Mohammad Yazdi, consisted of conservative ranks from moderate, traditional, and hard-line factions. Although these groups were juxtaposed together under the banner of the United Principlist Front, fierce rivalry persisted between them. Their aim was to marginalize and exclude their principal opponents, especially reformists and supporters of President Ahmadinejad.

58. The Steadfastness Front (*Jebhe-ye Payedari-ye*) brought together hard-line influential forces that came to power with Ahmadinejad's 2005 electoral victory. Its membership also included individuals who served in cabinet positions in Ahmadinejad's first administration.

59. Mohammad-Reza Tabesh, who was the speaker of Parliament's minority faction from 2008 to 2012, announced that the reformists would not be forming a caucus in the Ninth Majles. *Aftab News*, June 8, 2012. http://aftabnews.ir/vdcbswb8zrhbswp.uiur.html.

60. *E'temad*, March 13, 2012.

61. *Khabar Online*, February 20, 2012. http://khabaronline.ir/detail/199762/politics/election.

62. Houchang Chehabi, *Iranian Politics and Religious Modernism: The Liberation Movement of Iran under the Shah and Khomeini* (London: Tauris, 1990), 283.

63. Hossein Bashiriyeh, *Jame'eh shenasi-e iran: Doreh-ye jomhuri-ye eslami-ye Iran* (A sociological study of Iran: The Islamic Republic era) (Tehran: Ney, 1384/2005), 78.

64. Sanandaji, "The Eighth Parliamentary Elections," 621–648.

65. For a more elaborate discussion of the politics surrounding privatization, see Chapter 1.

66. "*Gozaresh-e daramad hay-e nafti-ye 33 sal-e*" ("A report on 33 years of oil revenue"), *Iranvij*, January 17, 2012. http://www.iranvij.ir/339028.

67. *Entekhab*, February 15, 2012. http://entekhab.ir/fa/news/52645.

68. Shaul Bakhash, "No Elected President for Iran?" *Iran Primer*, October 31, 2011. http://iranprimer.usip.org/blog/2011/oct/31/no-elected-president-iran.

69. Amir Arjomand, *After Khomeini*, 37–39.

70. Alem, *Duality by Design*, 65.

71. Articles 122 to 128 of the Constitution.

72. Article 176 of the Constitution.

73. From a legal point of view, if the Constitution is amended and the post of president is eliminated, its powers will need to be divided between the Leader, Parliament, and the prime minister. An amendment would provide the Leader with the opportunity to appropriate more power by allocating more of the presidential authorities to his office, since he would have to approve the revisions to the Constitution before it is put to a referendum.

74. Moslem, *Factional Politics*, 200–202.

75. In August 2009 Mohammad Reza Bahonar, the Deputy Speaker of Parliament, told members of the Islamic Society of Engineers that had it not been for the recommendations of the Supreme Leader, more than eight or nine of the ministers recommended by the president to Parliament would have failed to receive an approval. *BBC Persian*, September 4, 2009. http://bbc.co.uk/persian/iran/2009/09/090904_he_ir88_bahonar_khamenei.shtml.

76. "*Majles sho'bei az daftar rahbari shodeh ast*" ("The Parliament has become an extension of the Leader's office"), *Deutsche Welle*, October 28, 2011. http://dw.de/a-15493448.

77. *Iranian Labor News Agency (ILNA)*, March 23, 2006.

78. Schirazi, *The Constitution*, 91.

79. Kaveh Ehsani, "Round 12 for Iran's Reformists," *MERIP Online*, January 29, 2004. http://merip.org/mero/mero012904.

80. In a speech delivered to a delegation from Parliament, Khamenei said, "The Parliament has the right to supervise members of its own body, and determine the fate of individual representatives." *Islamic Consultative Assembly News Agency (ICANA)*, January 18, 2012. http://www.icana.ir/newspage.aspx?Newsid=188172.

PART III

POLITICAL AND IDEOLOGICAL CHALLENGES

6 The Rule of Law and Conflict in the Reform Era

Mehrangiz Kar and Azadeh Pourzand

THE INSPIRATION FOR THIS CHAPTER comes from a personal experience with the Iranian judicial system. One of us—Mehrangiz Kar—was arrested in 2000 upon her return to Iran after attending a conference in Berlin on the future of reform in Iran. She was taken to the third branch of the Islamic Revolutionary Court in Tehran. The Islamic Revolutionary Court is a special court that was created shortly after the revolution to render judgment against prerevolutionary officials. It has since found permanent standing and deals with what is identified as crimes against the Islamic revolution. The typical charges include action against national security, disruption of public peace of mind, and slander against the Leader. This court has no constitutional standing. Kar's interrogation, lasting several hours, was interrupted at times by phone calls to the questioning judge. Each time, a masculine and authoritative voice on the other side of the line could be overheard, giving instructions to her interrogator *and* judge to speed up the process. And each time the judge would respond by saying, "Yes sir. Absolutely! I will do as you wish. Just let me make the process legal."

It took Kar a while to realize that the judge was asking the person at the other end of the line for more time only to give the essentially illegal detention a semblance of legality by granting the option to appeal the case to a higher court. Kar decided not to play this game and refused to proceed with a request to appeal a case that was without merit from the start. When Kar told the judge that she had no request for an appeal, the surprised judge said that it was very strange for an accused person to refrain from appealing the court order. Kar responded by saying that she was an attorney and had made both a professional and a personal decision not to appeal.

After several minutes of the judge insisting on an appeal and Kar refusing, something strange happened. The judge closed the door, stood in front of Kar, and, in a desperate tone, said, "I request this of you: I plead with you to file a request for an appeal. If your appeal does not appear on the order, my professional and judicial position will be at risk." Throughout her career as a lawyer, Kar had never faced such a truly unexpected and complex situation, and yet now she was facing it as an accused. A judge of the Islamic Revolutionary Court was making a plea to a politically accused woman! Slowly, she began to pity him. She asked, "How would my refusal to appeal threaten your judicial position?" With a fragile voice that was breaking in his throat, the judge said, "The country has become respectful of the rule of law. It is no longer like how it was before. We have to protect our positions more than ever."

She asked him again, "But aren't you saying that it is unlikely for higher judicial authorities and courts to null your orders? So then what legal value would my objection or appeal hold?" He responded, "You are indeed correct. But without your appeal attached to this order, there could be suspicion that politics has impacted this case rather than the law. Then it would be highly probable that you and the reformists will make a case against me for not having obeyed the law in my judicial decision making. You might also claim that I have restrained you from your legal right to appeal, in which case I stand to lose in this game." The situation was quickly descending into a tragic comedy. Kar wrote down her request for appeal with haste, affixed her signature to the document, and walked into the waiting room so that she could be taken to prison.

This encounter brings many questions to mind. Was the judge's desperate expression an indication that the election of the reformist president Mohammad Khatami in 1997 and his emphasis on rule of law had instilled fear among the authorities of the Islamic Republic? Yet although the judge seemed concerned about maintaining the appearance of due process, his superior on the other side of the phone was not. Was the rule of law being used as an instrument of authoritarian rule, or was the emphasis on the rule of law instead, opening a door for forces interested in due process?

From our point of view, these questions go to the heart of the debate that persists both inside Iran and within the opposition outside Iran over whether it is possible to reform the Islamic republic through reliance on the principles that are embedded in the Constitution of the Islamic republic. The cause for the persistence of this debate, even after the 2009 contested presidential election, and furthermore the reason that the notion of "rule of law" occupies such an important place in this debate are first historical and second based on experience. They are historical because since the Constitutional Revolution of 1906, the notion of rule of law or accountability to laws by all people and institutions as well as legal and procedural transparency as a check on arbitrary rule has been at the center of Iran's public discourse. They are also experiential because implementation of the laws in the books—irrespective of whether they are progressive or reactionary laws—has been a serious problem in Iran.

For reformers who are interested in both accountability and respect for citizens' rights, the problem poses itself on two fronts, at times working against each other. On one front, there is a serious desire for laws to be changed to adapt to the needs of a rapidly changing society. But on the other front there is the question of whether insistence on the implementation of laws that are on the books—even bad laws—is necessary for the eventual movement away from arbitrary rule.

For the conservatives who are in full control of Iran's unelected institutions, the question of rule of law poses itself in a different way. As Kar's experience with the revolutionary court judge suggests, the notion of rule of law also has double-edged implications for them. On one hand, law and order or rule *by* law is a useful instrument of control and claim to legitimacy. On the other hand, rule *of* law threatens their political position if citizens' rights are given their due standing in everyday life and institutional conduct. Hence, conservatives are also faced with a constant task of interpreting laws in such a way that counters the reformist interpretation in order to present their decisions in a variety of arenas as rule by law. But many times when this strategy fails to work or appease, they also engage in undercutting, even violating, laws that are on the books or rule *of* law.

This is why in Iran the constitutional and practical questions regarding the rule of law became one of the focal points of tension between the reformists and conservatives during Khatami's presidency (1997–2005), particularly during the period when the reformists also won in the parliamentary elections and took control of the sixth session of the postrevolution Parliament (2000–2004). In some important ways, rule of law continues to be a source of competing interpretations even among the conservatives today. Given these dynamics, it is important to understand what the reformist politicians tried to do, what means and principles they relied on to build their case, where and when they were successful, and in which ways and on the basis of which principles their efforts were blocked in both theory and practice.

The usual definition given regarding the rule of law in which "all persons, institutions and entities, public and private, including the State itself, are accountable to laws"[1] is highly abstract and ideal. Other criteria that make implementation of rule of law possible, such as "judicial independence, consistency with international human rights standards, equality, and equal enforcement, separation of powers, and participation in decision making, legal certainty, avoidance of arbitrariness and procedural and legal transparency"[2] require prerequisites that do not exist in a political system like the Islamic Republic of Iran (IRI). For this reason, in this chapter we take a more contextual approach in line with the history and current developments of the country. In doing so, we introduce instances of internal conflict within the IRI during the reform era that are rooted in both ideological disagreements and political disparities. Overall, this chapter illustrates positive or constructive qualities embedded in the IRI's body of laws that, if practiced, could strengthen the democratic elements of the current political system. Although laws alone do not entirely establish ground for democratic governance, certain elements in the Islamic Republic's laws can facilitate the transition away from both authoritarian and arbitrary rule. Furthermore, through the study of three cases, we will elaborate how the reformists used these elements to make an argument for a more law-abiding and democratic system and how a different interpretation of the Constitution, relying on Islamic principles and expediency or interest of the system (*maslahat-e nezam*), operated as key counterarguments to the reformist interpretation. The overarching principle of *maslahat* is so vague and so exclusively situated in the highest offices of the land—the office of the Leader and its advisory body, the Expediency Discernment Council of the System (*Shoraye tashkhis-e maslahat-e nezam* (generally translated as Expediency Council)—that it has the potential of being used arbitrarily and without any explanation to override the decisions made by every other institution of the Islamic Republic, including the legislature, which is identified as the main source of laws in the Constitution. The same principle has been used to counter and then abandon anachronistic laws touted by very conservative clerics, but, operating within no legal guidelines, it may also become the main source of arbitrary rule. Before moving to the analysis of some of the key capacities and limitations of Iran's laws regarding the rule of law in theory and in practice, however, a brief history of the evolution of the concept in Iran is needed.

Evolution of the Rule of Law in Iran

The IRI was established in February 1979; its founders, in essence, erected a framework based on a modern legal system to legitimize their ideology rooted in an interpretation of Shi'i Islam. In other words, the Islamic Republic's founders introduced their government as one that was respectful of the rule of law based upon the principles and directives of Shi'ism. The 1979 Constitution prescribes that these principles are to be interpreted and protected by the Guardian Council.[3] Furthermore, the Constitution declares that judges are obliged to consider Islamic opinions and interpretations (*nazarieh-ye fiqhi*) of competent Islamic scholars (*mojtahedin*) whenever the law is vague or silent about a particular topic.[4] A brief review of the concept of rule of law as it has developed in Iran helps explain this formulation.

The history of modern legislature in Iran began with the Constitutional Revolution, which gave birth to Iran's first Constitution. For the first time, a parliamentary system, comprising the representatives of the people, was established. The all-male Parliament (Majles) would review and evaluate bills before turning them into laws. The absolute power of the monarch became limited and the Majles was granted the responsibility to check his power. Facing and fighting many challenges, Iran entered the era of constitutional law for the first time in its history. The most important objective of this transition was described in the slogan "The monarch should not rule but reign."

This ideal, however, remained limited in practice. The monarchs of both the Qajar and Pahlavi dynasties often violated the Constitution. An example of this violation was evident in the election of Majles representatives. According to the 1906 Constitution, parliamentary elections were to be free without the interference or control of the monarch. However, during the rule of Mohammad-Reza Shah Pahlavi, all candidates for Majles were essentially vetted indirectly by SAVAK, the intelligence service of the Pahlavi regime. The continuous violation of constitutional law by both Pahlavi kings resulted in escalating dissatisfaction among those who valued the rule of law. Mohammad-Reza Shah's disregard for freedom of expression, press, and independent political parties, all of which were protected by the 1906 Constitution, was significant in mobilizing secular opposition to him in the name of rule of law. Moreover, the Pahlavi dynasty's disregard for Islamic law catalyzed the mobilization of the religious opposition. A historic example of the king's violation of rule of law that antagonized the proponents of Islamic law was Reza Shah's royal decree to ban the Islamic veil in 1936. The fact that it came by a royal decree and was imposed by force made it quite arbitrary and violated the constitutional provision that gave a role to Islamic scholars in preventing legislations deemed contrary to Islamic law. Ultimately, the disregard of Islamic law and principles deepened the opposition of religious groups against the Pahlavi dynasty and helped shape the effort to re-Islamicize the postrevolutionary Constitution.

The 1979 Constitution—amended in 1989—also delineated limitations on state power. It emphasized the right of the people and the necessity of the rule of law. This emphasis was conditional upon the accordance of laws with "Islamic principles." But even agreement with Islamic principles did not prevent authorities from disregarding the initial emphasis on the rule of law. For instance, the authorities created barriers in delivering the premises of the third chapter of the Constitution (The Rights of the People) and held unfair trials without the presence of a jury in violation of Article 168 of the Constitution.[5] So after eighteen years of lack of respect for its own laws and constitutional principles, the Iranian electorate welcomed Khatami's promises of reform. During his presidential campaign, he initiated a discourse about reform within the boundaries of the IRI with a strong emphasis on the rule of law (*hokumat-e qanun*). Khatami's slogan of rule of law was groundbreaking even though it did not dispute clerical supremacy, which was also embedded in the Constitution. It triggered a popular discourse on the rule of law, a discourse that was previously overshadowed by Islam and Islamic rule (*hokumat-e eslami*).[6] In May 1997, in his first campaign speech, emphasizing the importance of the rule of law, Khatami stated, "Religion has been the element calling people to establish and consolidate civil society . . . a society in which the government belongs to the people and is the servant of the people, not their master." To further highlight the importance of laws, he stated that for various cultural and historical reasons, "neglecting order and disregarding the law have become a habit in our society." He then stated, "We must strive in every way to ensure that the law forms the basis of order and that we have a society which is lawful in every respect."[7]

During his presidency, Khatami sought to use the theoretical capacity of IRI's body of laws to bring about reforms. He insisted on the need for everyone to submit to the rule of law even if particular laws were not necessarily consistent with democratic principles. His aim was to prioritize the consistent implementation of existing laws in order to minimize arbitrary and politically driven decisions superseding the law.

But based on which historical and theoretical principle did Khatami place the rule of law at the core of his agenda? Did he believe that in IRI's political system there were sufficient legal opportunities and capacities to facilitate a degree of reform? Did he believe that these reforms would pave the path toward betterment in arenas such as the rights of the people, the economy, foreign affairs, and civil society? On which principle or factor had Khatami relied to push for reforms, and why did he take the risk of bringing up the topic of reform?

Undoubtedly, Khatami was aware of at least some of the challenges that he faced in putting forth his agenda. However, as an ardent supporter of the Islamic Republic and its founding principles, he thought that reforms aimed at strengthening the rule of law within the limitations posed by the IRI were possible during his presidency and beneficial to the regime as a whole. Even though he was aware of the conservative tendencies of the Leader, Ayatollah Seyyed Ali Khamenei, Khatami must have believed that he would receive some support from him and other key figures and institutions in proceeding with his agenda of reforms. Above all, Khatami believed that the Islamic Republic would not be able to maintain its legitimacy without responding to the demands of the people for reform and the rule of law. In fact, in a speech in 1999, he stated, "The stability of the revolution is only possible with the rule of law."[8] Similarly, in March 2002, he noted, "Defending the revolution is defending the Constitution."[9]

In his attempt to persuade officials to embrace existing opportunities for reform without violating IRI's principles, Khatami based his arguments on the possibilities in the Iranian body of laws and the Constitution. Along with his supporters, Khatami believed that the theoretical capacity of the Islamic Republic's Constitution was not fully implemented and/or was disregarded in practice. He believed that the rule of law would gain strength if authorities took a consistent and strict approach in delivering the full capacity of the existing laws in practice. All in all, Khatami was aware of the opportunities that could facilitate reform. For instance, he was aware that the principle of *ijtihad*, which is emphasized in the Constitution, has the capacity to make the reform of laws possible as well as strengthen the rule of law itself. Moreover, he had understood the power of the press in initiating and promoting discourses of reform and in reflecting the demands of the people. However, Khatami and his followers faced numerous complex barriers in their attempts to use opportunities for reform within the confines of the Islamic Republic.

Constitutional Debates and the Potential for Reforming Laws

From the onset of the reformist era, the opposing reformist and conservative camps confronted one another. Each camp offered alternative and often opposing takes on the Islamic Republic's capacities for democratic governance. The hard-line conservative camp was often quick to react to the attempts by reformists to identify and use constitutional capacities for reform. On one hand, the reformists highlighted such capacities in an attempt to persist on the relevance of reform. On the other hand, without ever denying the rule of law in theory, the conservatives produced alternative interpretations of the same capacities that effectively blocked the path to reform. This continuous interpretive clash is critical in understanding the political dynamics of the reform era and beyond.

The reformists claimed that the democratic capacities of the Constitution were not being used to their full potential. In emphasizing constitutional capacities for accommodating the rule of law, they repeatedly referred to several articles of the Constitution that protect the rights of the people. The conversation generated did not remain within the confines of the Islamic Republic's upper echelon. Because of the multiplicity and diversity of newspapers and publications during the reform era, these discussions about different aspects of the Constitution as well as its specific articles were reproduced in the press, raised popular awareness, and become a part of people's daily conversations.

Republicanism versus Islamism

At the most general level the conversation focused on which aspect of the Constitution carried more weight. Emphasizing the republican aspect of the Islamic *Republic*, the reformists, whose quest had gained legitimacy with high voter turnouts in both the 1997 presidential election and the 2000 parliamentary election, demanded that the three branches of the government (executive, legislative, and judiciary) respect one another's independence and responsibilities as prescribed by the Constitution. On numerous occasions, Khatami spoke about the importance of respect for the republican aspect of the Constitution while also acknowledging the merits of the Islamism embedded in it. Speaking in an interview with Iranian television, Khatami said, "In the same way that those who do not approve of Islamism are not worthy of respect, those who do not approve of the Islamic Republic or the republican nature of the state are not worthy of respect either." He continued, "When we talk about the Islamic Republic, we mean the Islam that the Imam [Ayatollah Khomeini] had presented. It was the Islam that he expressed and it was an Islam which officially recognized the people's right to define their own destiny."[10] Similarly, other reformist figures stressed the republicanism of the IRI to further advance the discourse of rule of law during the reform era. For instance, a reformist parliamentarian, Mohsen Armin, highlighted the importance of republicanism at a Majles session in 2001 and said, "Unfortunately, in the revolution's second decade many efforts have been made to weaken the republicanism of the system, which is one of the most important achievements of Iranian history." He further noted, "To weaken one aspect [republicanism] will cause the other's [Islamism's] enfeeblement."[11]

Reacting, the conservative opponents of the reform began to highlight the Islamist aspect of the Constitution. Without explicitly rejecting the rule of law and republicanism, the clerics of the conservative camp declared Islamism the most important basis for Iran's republic. Essentially, the conservative rhetoric focused on the primacy of Islamism over republicanism. For instance, Ayatollah Mohammad-Taqi Mesbah Yazdi, a prominent conservative opponent of the reform movement, said:

> There are those who, unfortunately because of weakness of their religious faith or the influence of infidel culture, think that the concept of the Islamic Republic is composed of two parts: Republic and Islam and today; we hear such words from those whom we never expected to utter such a view. . . . Some have become so impudent as to say that if the Islamic part runs against the Republican part, the latter takes precedence! . . . The choosing of the term "republic" was to reject the monarchic system and not the kind of republic which is currently [in existence] in the West, the type of democracy in which everything depends on the will and whim of the people. Our republic is one whose aim is Islam, not that we have a republic next to Islam and as a separate objective, because this would constitute infidelity. The term republic is just the frame which, in this present age, has been chosen for the realization of the rule of Islam, and has no essence [of its own].[12]

Without rejecting the rule of law in theory, the conservative camp insisted on Islamic rule as the basis for its republican elements, hence rejecting the reformist attempt to highlight the rule of law as an inextricable element of republicanism.

The Debate over Key Constitutional Principles

Articles 4 and 72 of the Constitution state that the only source of legislation is the shari'a law.[13] However, the Constitution also includes elements of contemporary norms and human rights principles. The third chapter of the Constitution, which addresses the right of the people, includes Articles 24–27. These four articles—which deal with freedom of the press and expression, right to privacy, and freedom of association and assembly—are essentially the foundation for reform. At the same time, they all come with the caveat that their implementation should not undermine Islamic principles and values. Accordingly, in the eight years of Khatami's presidency, these articles turned into contest arenas and sources of tension among various governmental institutions. While relying on the support of influential power centers such as the Guardian Council and the judiciary, the hard-line conservatives interpreted and implemented these four foundational constitutional articles in an opposite fashion to the way the reformists interpreted them. Further, they used the conservative interpretation and implementation to gradually weaken the reformists. As a result, reformist-controlled institutions such as the Ministry of Culture and Islamic Guidance emphasized the capacities of the four constitutional articles that are respectful of rights, while the conservative institutions such as the judiciary insisted on the religious and restricting aspects of the same articles. To constrain freedom of expression for the press, conservative authorities and institutions highlighted the conditional nature of these four articles based on observance of Islamic principles. Lack of clear legal delineation of a broad category such as "Islamic principles" gave the judiciary a powerful instrument to, for instance, shut down reformist newspapers, which had received permission to publish from the Ministry of Culture and Islamic Guidance, and haul their publishers to court based on a presumed threat they posed to Islamic values and principles. This legal vagueness, and the arbitrary implementation of whatever principle was violated, created a situation in which anticipating when the law was about to be violated became impossible.

Nevertheless, both reformist and conservative political camps emphasized the importance of the rule of law. While the reformists based their views on interpretations of Islam in line with their contemporary agenda, the conservatives implemented strict interpretations of Islamic laws to restrain freedom of expression. They insisted on the conditional provisions on various forms of freedom. Lack of precise definition for the notion of Islamic principles intensified tensions surrounding these conditional articles. For instance, in his Friday Prayers sermon in December 2000, Ayatollah Mohammad Yazdi, the former judiciary chief, reacting to the direction the Ministry of Culture and Islamic Guidance in its liberal interpretation of Article 24, which pertains to press freedom, stated:

> Our Constitution tells us that the press is free to write provided that they do not harm Islamic principles and rights of the public. . . . Now, if a newspaper owner is summoned to the court, others raise a hue and cry that [writing] everything is free. Our law tells us that they do not have the right to undermine the principles of Islam. You ask what is Islam? Is it the Ministry of Islamic guidance [that decides]? Can the Ministry explain Islamic principles? No, it is not qualified for this task.[14]

Similar disputes repeatedly took place between the judiciary and Khatami's cabinet during the eight years of reform. As a result, a number of issues and dynamics become evident:

- Clash of two distinct legal philosophies based on different foundations, hence creating a contest over interpretations of the law;
- Instrumentality of these clashing legal philosophies by the judges in implementing the law in line with their political views, often against reform; and
- Authority of the most powerful individuals and offices to implement various right-focused articles of the Constitution in favor of the rights and freedoms of the citizenry or to their detriment.

Given the lack of clarity as well as established precedent regarding the extent to which Islamic principles can abridge the rights of the people, the question then becomes whether in the existing legal framework of the Islamic Republic it is still possible to facilitate reform. At the political level, an affirmative answer to this question depends on whether those who think the Constitution has the capacity to reform control the most powerful sites of interpretation. Without a doubt control of powerful sites of interpretation is as important as, if not more important than, instruments used to offer alternative interpretations. At the same time, the Constitution offers at least two instruments that can be used in the competition for political control: the concept of *ijtihad* and the constitutional promotion of the use of "sciences, arts, and human experience advances."[15] Both of these in theory serve as capacities in the current legal framework of the Islamic Republic.

Ijtihad

In Islamic jurisprudence (*fiqh*), *ijtihad* is the practice of interpreting shari'a law and Islamic doctrine in accordance with the needs of people with respect to the requirements of time and location. This principle is the most fundamental characteristic of Shi'i jurisprudence to find its way into the Constitution. According to Ayatollah Seyyed Mohammad Mussavi-Bojnurdi, a Shi'i jurist,

> The issue of changing opinion of the faqih has existed in Shi'i fiqh from the beginning. This is one of the sources of pride in Shi'ism and is reflective of the dynamism of ijtihad. In Shi'i fiqh ijtihad is always alive, moving, and non-imitational. In Shi'i fiqh there is a freedom for a seminary student . . . to stand against all Islamic fuqaha and insist on his own creative reasoning and understanding. . . . In fiqh in general, the opinion of the one of leaders of religions is followed. But in Shi'ism fundamentally no such a thing exists. In Shi'ism, every faqih is obliged to practice what he interprets to be Islamic laws. It is for this reason that we consider the possibility of changing the opinion of a faqih, and not emulating it, to be a source of pride of Shi'i jurisprudence.[16]

The importance of *ijtihad* is explicitly stated in the Constitution. Article 2, Section 6 identifies the Islamic Republic as an order (*nezam*) that among other things relies on the "exalted dignity and value of man and his freedom coupled with responsibility" through recourse to the "continuous ijtihad" of the juriconsults (*fuqaha*) and use of the scientific and technical advancements of the human society at large. There is little ambiguity regarding the need to interpret Islam based on the requirements of time and place and through reliance on sciences and arts in order to secure the dignity of man.

Beyond the Constitution, a concept called dynamic jurisprudence (*fiqh-e puya*) has developed. This concept refers to the dynamism of *fiqh* that, if put at the core of legislature, could make laws compatible with cultural and social realities of the time. Some Islamic experts emphasize the ability of dynamic jurisprudence to make legislation compatible with the realities of the present time. For example, Mussavi-Bojnurdi states,

> We should not equate fiqh to "Islam." Those who equate fiqh to Islam are mistaken. Islam is not fiqh. Fiqh is a selection of those directives (*ahkam*) that include the interpretations of jurists throughout history. However, this is not to say that fixed instructions such as the number of units of prayer (raka'ats) also need jurisprudence. These directives are strictly fixed and cannot change.[17]

Thus, in contemporary Shi'i jurisprudence, legislation becomes an important instrument for distinguishing the flexible directives from the fixed ones. The fixed and unchangeable directives are called primary directives and the flexible ones are called secondary directives. The Leader is in charge of determining which problems and needs in today's society are not resolvable with primary directives. Upon the determination of such, primary directives related to the issue at hand are temporarily suspended in order to address the issue with an alternative law. Essentially, the temporary alternative law is classified as a secondary directive that is, by essence, flexible. However, once the problem or need is addressed through the implementation of the alternative law, the initial Islamic law that includes the primary directive—causing the issue to come about—once again becomes implementable. Thus, as Islamic scholar Mohammad Emami Kashani states,

> As a way to prevent disruptions in the Islamic Republic, it is possible to employ temporary and limited laws to address the challenges of the time—impossible to tackle with the initial Islamic laws that include primary directives. However, after the crisis is resolved the primary directive becomes, once more, strictly implementable.[18]

For this reason, a number of scholars and supporters of the rule of law believe that the Leader can indeed use the flexibility afforded to him by Shi'i jurisprudence to address domestic and international tensions facing the Islamic Republic. However, these existing capacities of Islamic law and *fiqh-e puya* do not automatically turn into practice; their implementation remains at the discretion of the Leader. Thus, it becomes important to examine the extent to which these capacities exist in relevant practices. To seek answers to this question, one must first explore whether there are obstacles on the path of using *ijtihad* to strengthen the practice of rule of law through reforming or passing new laws in the Majles.

The Constitution prescribes a restrictive control mechanism that prevents law-making based on legislative action. The Guardian Council is a powerful supervisory institution that approves all laws passed by the Majles. The criteria of the Guardian Council for approving bills passed into laws revolve around their compatibility with Islam and the Constitution. Hence, the Guardian Council has the discretion to reject new legislation by citing incompatibility with Islamic law and the Constitution.[19] In this manner, the veto power of the Guardian Council manifests itself as a serious obstacle in the path of timely revision of laws when the Council refrains from approving laws that are in accordance with the requirements of time and place. The Guardian Council particularly stands to play an obstructionist role if its six clerics do not emphasize the concept of *ijtihad* and refrain from considering the conditions of time and place while delivering archaic and outdated interpretations of Islam. Article 91, Section 1 of the Constitution states that "six just Islamic jurisprudents [*fuqaha-ye adil*], conscious of the present needs and the issues of the day, [are] to be selected [to the Guardian Council] by the Leader." Thus, the Constitution highlights the quality of the six just Islamic jurists of the Guardian Council as being "conscious of the present needs and the issues of the day." Therefore, if—a very big "if" that highlights the importance of political leadership in guiding the country toward rule of law—the Leader takes into consideration this essential quality for the six Islamic jurists of the Guardian Council while selecting candidates, the implementation of the theoretical capacities of *ijtihad* in interpreting Islamic laws could become a possibility in practice. Conversely, by selecting these clerics from among the circles of Islamic jurists who follow one specific version of Islamic jurisprudence, rather than practicing their right to *ijtihad*, the Leader can indirectly help impede the timely evolution of laws in Iran. In short, *ijtihad* is a theoretical possibility embedded in the Constitution that, if practiced, can serve as a facilitator for changing laws in a more progressive direction. However, complexities in practice could turn *ijtihad* into an instrument in the hands of those in favor of the status quo and intent on obstructing the adaptation of laws to evolving social norms.

Use of Sciences, Arts, and Human Experience Advances

Article 2, Section 2b of the Constitution not only emphasizes the use of "sciences and arts and human experience advances," it insists on the "effort to advance them further" in order to secure human dignity and freedom in society. No limitations based on Islamic principles and values appear in the article. This gives the *fuqaha* the opportunity to practice *ijtihad* in aligning the laws with the advancements of human civilization. The way Article 6 is written, *fiqh*, science, arts, and progression of human experience complement each other. Thus, a *faqih* of the Guardian Council is instructed to secure human dignity and freedom by taking into account progress in sciences, arts, and human experience. Considering that it is possible, in both theory and practice, to classify the internationally recognized human rights principle as one of the achievements of human society in the twentieth century, then the path is open to including those achievements in Iran's laws. Whether the Iranian legislature would begin to move toward such a classification has yet to happen. This is another theoretical capacity stated in the Constitution that, if adequately realized, could underwrite the gradual evolution of the laws in order to address the present needs and demands of the society.

In addition, most Shi'i clerics consider "reason" to be a source of *ijtihad*. In the words of Ayatollah Mohammad-Ebrahim Jannati,

> One of the public sources of human knowledge and learning, in all materialistic and spiritual aspects, is reason/wisdom. And in truth, revelation and tradition have come about in order to strengthen and help grow the authentic and sound thoughts of human societies in aspects that go beyond the human mind.[20]

Thus, from this perspective, *fiqh* is not to be static. Rather, it is to be updated, dynamic, and aligned with the modern evolving indicators of life and particularities of the society. In addressing members of the Guardian Council, Akbar Hashemi Rafsanjani, the chair of the Expediency Council, in a gathering on "Ijtihad in the Contemporary Era," stated,

> We cannot manage a society that is being led in the name of Islam with the principles and rules that are thousands of years old. In delivering these long standing principles and rules of Islam, ijtihad and the conditions and needs of the present time ought to be taken into consideration. These principles and rules cannot be directly applied without any attention to the wisdom and the expediencies and threats of the present time.

He further added,

> If attention is paid to the wisdom and intent of the Quran regarding ijtihad, at least in the major concerns regarding the management of the state, an assembly of jurists would be formed and if the jurists of Shi'ism and Sunnism collaborate in universities, then we could rely on the true capacity of Islam.[21]

These quotes are from an Iranian leader who has become a leading proponent of improving the use of *ijtihad* and dynamic jurisprudence for reforming laws. But they reflect the fact that the idea of active jurisprudence is part of public conversation in Iran. To further promote this belief, Hashemi Rafsanjani has even proposed the formation of a panel of jurists to solve the daily challenges facing society using existing sources and opportunities within the constitutional confines of the Islamic Republic. His position confirms that the concept of *ijtihad* can turn into a resource for reform if the individuals in charge facilitate the realization of its capacities in practice.

Impeding Reform through Rule by Law

Highlighting the capacity for legal reform is not intended to neglect the robust ways the conservatives have used law and order to weaken efforts to reform the Islamic Republic. A key component of their reaction to political reform was control via expansion and multiplication of security-oriented institutions and politicization of the judiciary. By dominating a key institution such as the judiciary, the conservatives effectively used the ambiguity and limiting aspects of the law to maintain and expand their power within the political system without explicitly denying the notion of rule of law.

Securitization occurred with the restructuring of the Islamic Revolution's Guard Corps (IRGC) and expansion of the Basij militia force, squeezing them into every aspect of social life in Iran ranging from bazaars to universities, schools, villages, neighborhoods, offices, and others. Thus, the Basij, which had previously functioned primarily as an institution for recruiting combatants for the Iran-Iraq War, was turned into a policing force.[22] This was the direct reaction to the Khatami administration's attempt to highlight Article 27 of the Constitution, which considers peaceful street protests against government policies legal and a right. The conservatives, who had essentially banned and repressed any such street demonstrations for two decades, were suddenly faced with an argument from within the establishment that considered demonstrations lawful and constitutional. Since they still wanted to appear as legitimate supporters of the rule of law, instead of challenging the argument directly, their method of choice was clandestine violation of law. They used the Basij force to send plainclothesmen to attack various gatherings and press offices in order to disrupt peaceful gatherings and demonstrations. Later, without acknowledging their role, hardline conservatives claimed that street violence of this nature was due to citizens attacking other citizens. These plainclothes groups became known as "pressure groups." Contrary to its constitutional responsibilities, the judiciary refrained from arresting members of the pressure groups and confronting supportive influential individuals behind their violence.

Effectively, with its refusal to take appropriate actions against pressure groups, the judiciary strengthened and approved violent actions against civil society and political associations. Furthermore, the policy of the judiciary gradually went beyond simply remaining silent. The politicization and securitization of the judiciary became the second path through which reform and rule of law were impeded. The partisan policies of the judiciary were so clearly in line with those of the conservatives that ultimately in 2003, the reformist-controlled Sixth Majles openly criticized the interference of the IRGC in judicial affairs. In a speech, Deputy Fatemeh Haghighatjoo stated, "Who is left unaware of the fact that IRGC has been behind the recent arrests and torture of a group of university students and religio-nationalist activists?" She added, "The investigation committee of the Majles visited detention centers and prisons of the country. However, it was not granted permission to visit the dreadful detention centers of IRGC."[23] In reaction, the IRGC wrote a letter to the Speaker of the Majles, Mehdi Karrubi, defending its actions. In its letter, IRGC insisted on its responsibility to resist corrupt individuals and criminals who act against the Islamic Republic. The reformist members of the Majles and like-minded groups continued to accuse the IRGC of ignoring the rights of citizens to criticize the government, and the IRGC, in turn, disregarded these accusations and proceeded with its approach relying on Article 150 of the Constitution, which gives the IRGC the responsibility of "guarding the revolution and its achievements."[24] In his letter objecting to the complaints against IRGC, Yahya-Rahim Safavi, the organization's commander, stated, "Any act IRGC has committed is lawful and there is no room for complaints."[25]

The securitization and politicization of the judiciary did not originate in the reform era. The Islamic Republic's judiciary has historically taken orders and instructions from the intelligence and military forces on politically sensitive cases. Still, the securitization of the judiciary became explicit and organized during Khatami's presidency. Parallel security and intelligence institutions had unofficially taken shape outside the Ministry of Intelligence and within the IRGC and even the judiciary for years, despite the fact that with the approval of the law to establish the Ministry of Information in 1983, the parallel activities of multiple intelligence services were to cease and instead unified under the Ministry. In the reform era, however, these parallel institutions became officially recognized in the aftermath of the murders of four intellectuals in 1998, which was ordered and organized by a group of hard-line intelligence agents.[26] Khatami's insistence on centralizing intelligence services and transforming the Intelligence Ministry into a proper intelligence-gathering agency in effect underwrote the legalization of parallel security institutions that, unlike the Ministry of Intelligence, were not headed by a president-appointed minister, but a minister who was appointed directly by the Leader or indirectly by his appointees. Consequently, parallel institutions became the most significant arenas of clashes between the hard-line conservatives and the reformists. These confrontations became so evident that

President Khatami's Minister of Petroleum, Bijan Zangeneh, announced in 2005 that there is evidence of the attempts of hard-line forces to wiretap correspondences and conversations within various ministries. In fact, during the eight years of Khatami's presidency, reformist officials repeatedly warned that the established parallel institutions had become instruments for monitoring the correspondences of Khatami's cabinet and ministries.[27] Thus, during this time the multiplicity and disparity of intelligence services had deepened so much so that one camp would use its intelligence forces against the other.

To further strengthen the encroachment of parallel institutions, the hard-liners called for the establishment of intelligence institutions even within the judiciary. While the head of the judiciary at the time, Ayatollah Mahmud Hashemi Shahrudi, welcomed this idea, the reformist Sixth Majles passed a bill based on which the intelligence services of the country were to become centralized. Disregarding the bill, the intelligence offices centered on the judiciary, the IRGC, and the Office of the Leader continued their work. The hosting institutions of decentralized intelligence services justified the presence of these offices within the institution as the guardians of their institutional independence.

The reformist minister of intelligence of the time, Ali Yunesi, repeatedly spoke about the topic of parallel institutions and insisted that these entities have no constitutional right to interfere with the work of the ministry. He emphasized that the minister is in charge of the coordination and management of all intelligence affairs of the country, to no avail.[28] Not only was multiplicity of security and intelligence organizations legalized but open partisan conflicts beset them. Some of the groups and individuals that were reformist or sympathetic to reform were detained and interrogated by these entities. After initial interrogations and detention, their cases were referred to the judiciary. Without acknowledging the unlawful initiation and processes of these cases, the judiciary took them on. In effect, for politically driven cases, the judiciary began to recognize parallel institutions as judicial appendages. Cases of this nature were referred to a select number of judges within the judiciary with partisan preferences in favor of hard-line conservative strategies and parallel institutions. One of these select judges was Sa'id Mortazavi, who became notorious for his repeated verdicts to suspend or shut down reformist newspapers.

The conservative reaction to the attempt to implement the rule of law during the reform era can be summarized as (1) the expansion and strengthening of the authority of parallel institutions, leading to a notable increase in the number of cases that were referred to the judiciary from parallel intelligence institutions; and (2) the highly partisan nature of the activities of parallel institutions as forceful instruments used by hard-line conservatives to weaken the reformist agenda by arresting reformist activists on charges ranging from action against national security to propaganda against Islam and the Supreme Leader. Despite their unlawful nature, these cases appeared legal as the judiciary took on an active role throughout the process to give them a lawful appearance.

Thus, the judiciary became the most important instrument for the weakening and elimination of the challenge that had risen within the political structure of the Islamic Republic in search of ways to implement some of the constitutional capacities of the system. The Sixth Majles was unable to respond to complaints of the people in the same way that then judiciary chief Hashemi Shahrudi could or would not respond to the complaints of either Khatami or the reformist Majles, whose Article 90 Commission is tasked to investigate constitutional violations.

Not all attacks against the reformists were successful. For instance, the decision by the judiciary to prosecute and arrest a deputy—Hossein Loqmanian—for his speech during a parliamentary session created uproar, as the Constitution clearly supports immunity for members of the Majles. Article 84 states, "Each and every member of the Majles is responsible before the whole of the nation and has the right to opine on every domestic and foreign issue." Article 86 adds, "Members of the Majles, in discharging their duties and in the expression of their views and votes, enjoy full freedom and cannot be prosecuted or arrested for views expressed in the Majles or votes they have cast in discharging their duties as people's representatives." In practice, the judiciary not only violated the principle of parliamentary immunity, it did so selectively by bringing charges only against reformist deputies.

This politicization of the judiciary was immediately noted in the reformist newspapers. An editorial in *Hambastegi* daily wrote:

> The news of the members of the Sixth Majles being called to the court in the past seven months seems to be one of the most important developments at the Majles. . . . The trend of rushing parliamentarians to court has created doubts and suspicion in the public about the political inclination of these prosecutions.[29]

Loqmanian was arrested after a speech he gave objecting to the arrest of opposition activists. But severe reaction from Khatami's cabinet as well as other Majles representatives led to his release after twenty days in detention even though he was initially sentenced to ten months of imprisonment.[30] In this case, persistence and rigor against a clear violation of rule of law worked and led to a conservative retreat. The uproar over the case intensified the confrontation between the conservative judiciary and reformist Majles, until Khamenei had to intervene to prevent the internal crisis from spiraling out of control. However, judicial harassment of deputies was not without impact. The arbitrary nature of the harassment strategy eventually made reformists fearful of having little or no immunity against the politically charged decisions of the judiciary. The potential threat made them grow more cautious, promoting self-censorship and even modification of policies.

Eventually, this cautiousness and the inability to bring about change led to the disappointment of the people in the Sixth Majles. Moreover, constituents began to think that they had overestimated the power of the reformists in standing up against hard-line conservatives in bringing about rule of law. However, in spite of the general disappointment in the limited power of the Sixth Majles, the reformists tried hard to realize some aspects of reform. But defining the rule of law was itself at the core of conflict. Reformists pushed for an understanding of rule of law that emphasized citizens' rights and due process, while the conservatives countered with an alternative viewpoint emphasizing state security and interest.

Torture and the Sixth Majles

The debate over torture illustrates the internal tensions leading to the confrontations between the reformist Majles and the conservative Guardian Council. Torture has been a common practice in both the prerevolutionary and post-revolutionary eras. What brought the discussion of the issue to the public realm was the revelation during the trial of the mayor of Tehran, Gholam-Hossein Karbaschi, that several officials in Tehran were tortured in detention in order to extract confessions from them against the mayor.[31] These revelations allowed the reformist press to discuss torture and violations of human rights in prisons. Despite the judiciary's denial regarding the use of torture in prisons, these discussions raised awareness regarding the ambiguity of laws in prohibiting torture. The debates shed light on the fact that while laws prohibit mental and physical torture in general, they remain ambiguous regarding some specific methods of torture. Consequently, with the reformists in charge of the Sixth Majles, the topic of torture reached the national legislature. In the legislation that was introduced and eventually passed, eighteen methods and behaviors that would constitute torture were delineated, including solitary confinement, a method commonly used to obtain forced confessions from those whose detention was politically inspired.

The bill on the prohibition of specific instances of torture was passed on December 15, 2002. However, the Guardian Council found faults with the legislation, the most fundamental of which was ignoring the prerogatives of the religious magistrate in Islam. Consequently, judges remain free to disregard the eighteen prohibited forms of torture listed in the legislation and the "absolute" ban on torture in general delineated in Article 38 of the Constitution. The reasoning offered by the Guardian Council was based on the argument that in Islam a judge is a *hakem-e shar'* (governing religious magistrate)[32] and in making decisions, at times he has to allow for a disagreeable or corrupt (*fased*) action in order to prevent the occurrence of an act or event even more disagreeable or corrupt (*afsad*).[33] This ruling led to reactions from a number of reformist clerics and legal experts who criticized the Guardian Council veto from a legal and juridical perspective. Nevertheless, the legislation detailing specific forms of torture to be prohibited was filed away without ever turning into law.

Despite rejection of the Guardian Council, it is still instructive to examine the way the Sixth Majles proceeded with the drafting and approval of the bill. In other words, based on which Islamic principles did the Sixth Majles make a case for banning specified forms of torture? Undoubtedly, the Sixth Majles was well aware of the Guardian Council's discretion in approving or vetoing such a bill. It was also aware that if it raised the issue of the incompatibility of any given bill passed by the Majles with Islamic and constitutional principles, the Guardian Council could exert its vetoing power. Yet, aware of the Guardian Council's discretionary powers, the Sixth Majles went ahead. A possible response to the question can be found in the content of Article 38 of the Constitution, which states:

> Any kind of torture used to extract an admission of guilt or to obtain information is forbidden. Compelling people to give evidence, or confess or take an oath is not allowed. Such evidence or confession or oath is null and void. Any person infringing this principle is to be punished in accordance with the law.

In its support of the bill, the Sixth Majles relied on (1) Article 38 giving constitutional justification for initiating legislation that would make its content regarding rejection of torture enforceable; and (2) presumed compatibility of legislation with principles of shari'a. In this case, both the Constitution and a tradition of Islamic jurisprudence that discouraged the use of torture were relied on. Indeed, among the opponents of torture were a few respected high-profile clerics. For instance, Ayatollah Mussavi-Bojnurdi, the head of the Islamic jurisprudence division of the Imam Khomeini Research Institute, insisted, "Torture is by nature indecent, is an unpleasant matter and should not become executable. Any and all matters that do not have rational justification, Islam does not approve of."[34]

Despite support from various high-ranking clerics and the seeming clarity of the constitutional ban on torture, the Guardian Council's veto illustrated that specific instances of torture, in practice, are open to interpretation. It further illustrated that the reformist Majles could not clarify the law, even in theory, without the will of the council. In fact, when the reformist Majles tried to clarify Article 38 by defining specific forms of torture, the Guardian Council used its constitutional power to reject the bill. The council based its reasoning for the rejection on shari'a law, according to which the judge cannot be constrained by the law in its investigation of the case. The leeway given to the judge in deciding to do harm in order to prevent an even bigger harm ended up providing legal justification for specific forms of torture, even though the general ban against torture remains in the Constitution. Rule by law was used to disregard Article 38 and maintain the supremacy of shari'a law. Even more disconcerting for the reformists was the fact that their attempt to clarify the practical implications of a constitutional amendment ended up further expanding the already robust discretionary powers of the judiciary beyond established law. The rejection, in effect, supported the practice of torture if sanctioned by a judge. The reformists accused the Guardian Council of abusing its powers and ignoring the letter and spirit of the law as delineated in the Constitution. Conservatives responded by referring to Article 98 of the Constitution, which identifies the Guardian Council as the only entity that is authorized to interpret the Constitution. They argued that the Guardian Council can use its power of interpretation even if to the reformists this interpretation was simply enforcement of conservative political preferences.

The Press Law and the Sixth Majles

The Sixth Majles also gave priority to the reform of the Press Law approved initially in 1986, and amended in 2000. This reform was to remove the obstacles against the freedom of press so that Article 24 of the Constitution regarding freedom of the press could gain relevance in practice. The Press Law entailed certain barriers in restricting the freedom of expression of journalists, authors, and those involved in the press. Relying on Article 71 of the Constitution, which establishes the Majles as the source of laws within the limits of its constitutional competence, the Sixth Majles began to review and reform the Press Law. But just as the Majles began its sessions and worked on the reform of the Press Law, the Leader sent a letter to the members of the executive board of the Majles.[35] The letter read:

> The press forms the nation's opinions and gives directions to the determination and hard work of the people. If the enemies of Islam, the Revolution and the current Islamic system of Iran manage to influence the press, the people will face a serious threat that will undermine their security, solidarity and faith. Therefore, I do not find it appropriate for myself and other colleagues to remain silent with regards to this vital matter. The current press law, to an extent, prevents the taking place of this threat. Amending this law based on the recommendations mentioned in transcript of the parliamentary commission is not legitimate for reason of expediency of the system and the country.

In ordering an end to these parliamentary discussions, the Leader disregarded both Article 24 and Article 71 of the Constitution. Nevertheless, Mehdi Karrubi, Speaker of the Sixth Majles, halted the parliamentary discussions to reform the Press Law. The abrupt closure of this discussion resulted in a heated debate in the Majles. Conservative parliamentarians along with the conservative press referred to Article 57 of the Constitution to highlight the discretion of the Leader in supervising the work of the legislative branch. While acknowledging the independence of the three branches of the government from each other, this article specifies that they all operate under the Leader's supervision.[36] However, those opposing the abrupt closure of the discussion worried that the events leading to it undermined rule of law. Ultimately, despite the opposition of many reformist representatives, the revision of the Press Law was removed from the agenda of the Sixth Majles.

The attempts of the Sixth Majles to revise the Press Law and the order of the Leader to stop the process demonstrated the alignment of the latter with the conservatives to halt reform. Furthermore, the principle used to stop the Press Law was *maslahat-e nezam*, which is awkwardly translated as "expediency" or "interest of the system" in English. The instrument used to implement expediency of the system is what has come to be known as *hokm-e hokumati* or state order, which can be issued only by the Leader and to which everyone must submit. This instrument as well as the *maslahat* principle was given legal power and legitimacy when the Constitution was amended in 1989, significantly expanding the powers of the Leader. The principle of *maslahat* had also been used by the founder of the revolution, Ayatollah Ruhollah Khomeini, in some of his key decisions and had been principally used in his 1988 ad hoc establishment of the Expediency Council, which was tasked to resolve conflicts between Parliament and the Guardian Council. But by incorporating the Expediency Council in the Constitution, the principle was effectively codified. Section 8 of Article 110—which deals with the responsibilities and powers of the Leader—specifically gives the Leader the power to resolve "the problems of the system which are not resolvable through normal means" through the Expediency Council. Other sections added to Article 110 give the Leader the power of deciding "the general policies of the system" after consultation with the Expediency Council, resolving conflicts and coordinating relations among the three branches,[37] and supervising "the implementation of the general policies of the system." These vague and broad powers have given the Leader the ability to step into all matters of concern with almost unlimited discretion and in the name of the "interest of the system."

The almost limitless powers given to the Leader had not become evident so long as there was no challenge to well-established practices of the Islamic Republic such as censorship or routine press harassments and closure by the government. But once there was a challenge by the Sixth Majles, these largely dormant but legally sanctioned powers became explicit and were given legal justification. The attempt to limit the arbitrary powers of judges to arrest and imprison journalists and contain institutions such as the Press Supervisory Board, which can shut down newspapers, not only failed but also brought into light much more powerful forces that the 1989 amendment of the Constitution had wrought. In other words, the reformist endeavor to use what they considered an existing constitutional capacity embedded in Article 24 of the Constitution on press freedom ended up revealing the reality of much more powerful constitutional limitations on that capacity.

The Family Protection Act and the Sixth Majles

Shortly after the Islamic Revolution of 1979, fundamental aspects of the 1975 Family Protection Act were amended in the name of Islam. The new amendments and revisions effectively eradicated the legal reforms made in favor of women during the Pahlavi regime. The reforms implemented during the Pahlavi era created special courts for family matters, abolished extrajudicial divorce, and increased the minimum age of marriage. These laws were revoked immediately after the revolution and replaced with discriminatory laws against women based on more conservative and rigid interpretation of Islam. But nineteen years into the Islamic Revolution, the Sixth Majles took notable steps to reform the family law in several areas.

First and foremost was the minimum age of marriage. The 1975 Family Protection Act had raised the minimum age of marriage for a woman to eighteen and for a man to twenty. After the revolution, Note 1 of Article 1210 of the Civil Code amended the age for maturity (puberty) for boys to fifteen full lunar years and for girls to nine full lunar years. Combined with another amendment of the Civil Code, ratified in 1991, which prohibited marriage before puberty, the age of marriage for both boys and girls was effectively lowered.

The Sixth Majles considered increasing the age of marriage a priority and decided to reform this law in favor of women. Consequently, it passed a bill that suggested sixteen as the minimum age of marriage for girls. However, the Guardian Council duly vetoed this bill, identifying it as incompatible with shari'a directives. Then two thirds of parliamentary deputies decided to vote in favor of the legislation again. As a result and according to Article 112 of the Constitution, which prescribes any topic of dispute between the Majles and the Guardian Council to be referred to the Expediency Council, the matter was forwarded to that council. Eventually, the Expediency Council made its own law and raised the minimum age of marriage for girls to thirteen and for boys to fifteen. The reformists did not fully get what they wanted, but on this issue there was enough consensus and solidarity to sidestep the conservative Guardian Council and reach a compromise through the intervention of the Expediency Council.

The Sixth Majles was also successful in bringing back elements of the prerevolutionary Family Protection Act. Article 12 of that act had given family courts the discretion to determine the custody of a child in the aftermath of divorce. These courts were to take into consideration only the interest of the child when making custody decisions. Accordingly, whichever of the parents was determined to be more competent would be granted custody of the child. In cases where the court determined both parents to be incompetent, custody was granted to another competent individual. In such instances, however, the court made the parents responsible for the expenses of the child. The revolution resulted in the revocation of this aspect of the law, again on the basis of Islamic directives. Consequently, Article 1169 of the Civil Code gained validity once more. According to this article, the custody of a male child is granted to the mother only until age two and that of a female child until age seven.

The Sixth Majles passed legislation in 2003 according to which custody of both male and female children was to be granted to the mother until age seven. After this age the custody decision was left to the opinion of the family court, which after their initial postrevolutionary abolition had become effectively reconstituted by the judiciary. The legislation was ratified by the Guardian Council. As in the prerevolutionary law, the interest of the child was once again brought back into Iranian laws, resulting in improvement of the law in favor of the mother. Here, both reformists and conservatives agreed on the useful and authoritative role the discretion of the judges of the family courts can play in acknowledging the special circumstances of every divorce. This significant change in family law can be considered a rare example of agreement between the Sixth Majles and the Guardian Council, one that resulted in concrete legal reform. This case illustrates a successful instance when the Sixth Majles used constitutional capacities to convince the conservative Guardian Council of the urgency of reforms in the child custody laws.

The Sixth Majles was much less successful in its attempt to persuade the Islamic Republic to join the Convention on the Elimination of Discrimination against Women (CEDAW). The convention, which was adopted by the UN General Assembly in 1979, defines discrimination against women as "any distinction, exclusion or restriction made on the basis of sex which has the effect or purpose of impairing or nullifying the recognition, enjoyment or exercise by women, irrespective of their marital status, on a basis of equality of men and women, of human rights and fundamental freedoms in the political, economic, social, cultural, civil or any other field."[38] For the first time in the history of the Islamic Republic, the female representatives of the Majles, all reformists, went to the offices and homes of high-ranking Shi'i clerics and reputable sources of emulation to discuss discriminatory laws against women. Their goal in engaging the clerics in an unprecedented dialogue was to persuade them to issue a religious edict (*fatwa*) that took into consideration the conditions of the modern Iranian society in favor of eliminating legal discrimination against women. But such attempts to coax high-ranking clerics to issue more progressive fatwas in favor of women faced systematic conservative resistance.

Eventually, the Sixth Majles did pass legislation in favor of joining CEDAW in 2003. But it was rejected by the Guardian Council for the incompatibility of this convention with the principles of Islamic shari'a law. The discourse of equality of men and women is a controversial one that triggers disagreements among conservative and more progressive Islamic jurists. For instance, a prominent jurisprudent, Ayatollah Mohammad Fazel Lankarani, insisted on the inequality of men and women, stating,

> Fellow Islamic clerics and wise gentlemen never say that we had a revolution and so there is no difference between men and women. Who has told you that there is no difference between them? There are, indeed, many differences. Now, we do not want to say that they [women] are incomplete when it comes to comprehension, wisdom and social matters. But, God has granted men advantages that have not been granted to women; and vice versa. In particular, [this should serve as a] warning to those sisters who now believe that they have become intellectuals and think that there is no difference between men and women.[39]

This point of view, rejecting equality between men and women based on the difference in their physical constitution, clearly dominated the Guardian Council as well. The argument is that because of their physical differences, men and women are meant to have different roles and duties, and therefore their rights must also correspond to those preconceived roles and duties. Despite this opposition, the Sixth Majles set a milestone in its persistence on the need to reform laws related to women and family protection. By doing so, it facilitated the deepening of a discourse concerning equality of men and women. While the reformists in the Majles did not deny the supremacy of Islamic principles and interests of the Islamic Republic, they shifted their emphasis to the necessity of considering the conditions of modern Iran in legislating. This elicited a strong conservative reaction on the ratification of CEDAW, but their persistence did have some positive results, such as in the case of the minimum age of marriage.

Conclusion

Our analysis of the reform era highlights institutional and partisan clashes between reformists and conservatives over various legal, judicial, and legislative issues. These instances illustrate the obstacles reformists faced in actualizing the capacities of the Islamic Republic to reform discriminatory laws. These obstacles, on one hand, highlight the great divide between theory and practice in the current Iranian body of laws and, on the other hand, point to an array of alternative interpretations of Islamic principles and law that can produce different approaches to the rule of law.

Our analysis suggests that if laws that are currently in the books are accepted and respected by influential political groups, reform is possible even within the limited framework of the current Constitution and laws. At the same time, these limitations cannot be wished away because they find their roots in a very conservative interpretation of Islamic law that gives Islamic authorities wide discretion in interpreting laws. The reformers in Iran were unable to fulfill their promise of the rule of law—which they interpreted as acknowledging the extensive rights given to citizens in the Constitution—because their efforts were undermined through frequent violations of existing laws. But they were also unsuccessful because their interpretation of the rule of law was repeatedly rejected by conservative officials and key institutions such as the Guardian Council. In essence, while reformists were able to challenge the conservative interpretation and implementation of the law by offering new interpretations of Islamic law and the Constitution in line with what they considered the present needs of society, they were mostly unsuccessful in convincing conservatives to endorse these interpretations. The reformists' inability to fulfill their promises rendered public opinion critical and disappointed about reform.

One way conservatives resisted the struggle for and Khatami's commitment to the rule of law was through their public support of the notion of rule of law. However, their definition of rule of law was opposed to that of reform. To ensure conservative dominance of the political and legal systems, they elevated two vague principles—the discretionary power of the judge and expediency of the Islamic Republic as defined by the Leader—into supreme law of the land. These two catch-all categories have been used to undercut important constitutional provisions that guarantee the rights of Iranian citizens. The anecdote at the beginning of this chapter demonstrates the degree to which even the revolutionary courts felt bound to act lawfully, at least in appearance, and protect their image as law-abiding judicial institutions. To do this, as the anecdote suggests, the judges often took measures to act respectful of the rights of the accused while basing judicial decisions on partisan preferences dismissing the prisoners' basic rights. Thus, Khatami's persistence on respect for the rule of law penetrated internal discussions among conservatives, spurring them to find ways around reformist interpretations of rule of law while protecting the legitimacy of their actions.

But the reformist push for a more democratic rule of law was not without impact. It did bring about change in a few laws and, more importantly, it helped generate spirited discussion in the public sphere. Through daily exposure to the reformist press, a larger number of Iranian citizens in urban areas became familiar with their rights within the religio-political structure of the Islamic Republic. This awareness led to increased demands. The conservatives saw these increased demands as a threat and, once they overcame their initial shock of witnessing reformist victories both in the presidential and parliamentary elections, they launched long-term resistance strategies against the promised reforms in the name of rule of law.

Nevertheless, Khatami's presidency left legacies that caused difficulty for his political opponents who took control after the reform era. Khatami relaxed regulations for legal registration of civil society institutions, allowing many nongovernmental organizations (NGOs) and groups to be established with ordinary citizens at their helm. Similarly, books that were published or films that were screened during his tenure would not have passed the more strict censorship regulations prior to the reforms era. Moreover, human rights and women's rights activists were able to work more openly despite all the obstacles that the judiciary threw in their path. Imprisonment did not stop these artists, activists, and journalists. In the meantime, attorneys, legal experts, socioeconomic experts, and the remainder of the reformist press resisted the discriminations and repressions imposed by conservative hard-liners. Although the latter publicly claimed to be guardians of the rule of law, in practice they further violated the rule of law as a result of resistance to their policies.

Meanwhile, Khatami's symbolic sociopolitical legacy outlasted his presidency and was passed on to the children who grew up during the reform era. As evidenced in the 2009 protests and then the 2013 election of a man who again promised a return to the rule of law and respect for the rights of the citizenry, irrespective of whether these promises can be fulfilled, the conservative counterreaction has been unable to make the generation that came to age in the reform era, both within Iran and abroad, abandon the ideas that animated the reform era and continue to hold sway.

Even though conservatives have been determined to eliminate talk of reform and reformists from the political scene of the Islamic Republic, the reform era brought about transformations that have proven impossible to undo in the collective memory of Iranian society, including the need for the rule of law and respect for people's rights. Undoubtedly, awareness about the capacities of the existing laws has rendered repression even more complicated for conservatives. Even though they continue to manipulate and violate the existing laws in the name of Islam and the expediency of the regime, they face the challenge of justifying their violations. Meanwhile, the bigger challenge for reformers remains the conservative refusal to modify their perspectives, decisions, and actions to meet at least some of the demands that were articulated during the reform era. If the conservatives decide to change their perspectives, they can rely on a different interpretation of the Islamic Republic's own Constitution. But as long as they dismiss the fulfillment of the desires of a large sector of the Iranian society as a vital factor in maintaining legitimacy, few democratic reforms can take place. As evidenced in the escalating level of repression during Ahmadinejad's presidency, the authoritarian aspects of the Constitution will tend to overpower its limited democratic potentials in the name of rule by law and order.

Notes

1. Maurits Barendrecht, "Rule of Law, Measuring and Accountability: Problems to Be Solved Bottom Up," *Hague Journal on the Rule of Law*, no. 3 (2011): 285–286.

2. Ibid.

3. Article 4: "All civil, penal financial, economic, administrative, cultural, military, political, and other laws and regulations must be based on Islamic criteria. This principle applies absolutely and generally to all articles of the constitution as well as to all other laws and regulations, and the jurisprudents [*fuqaha*] of the Guardian Council are in charge of discernment in this matter."

Article 72: "The Islamic Consultative Assembly cannot enact laws contrary to the principles and directives [*ahkam*] of the official religion of the country or to the constitution. It is the duty of the Guardian Council to determine whether a violation has occurred, in accordance to Article 96." "Constitution of the Islamic Republic of Iran," Foundation for Iranian Studies. http://fis-iran.org/en/resources/legaldoc/constitutionislamic.

4. Accordingly, Article 167 of the Constitution states, "The judge must judge each case on the basis of the codified law. In case of the absence of any such law, he has to deliver his judgment on the basis of authoritative Islamic sources and authentic edicts. He, on the pretext of the silence of or deficiency of law in the matter, or its brevity or contradictory nature, cannot refrain from admitting and examining cases and delivering his judgment."

5. Article 168 of the Constitution states: "Political and press offenses will be tried openly and in the presence of a jury in a court of law. The manner of the selection of the jury, its powers, and the definition of political offenses, will be determined by law in accordance with the Islamic criteria." While jury selection is premised on Islamic criteria, the Constitution is clear about the need for a jury, a fact ignored by the judiciary.

6. Said Amir Arjomand, "Civil Society and Rule of Law in the Constitutional Politics of Iran under Khatami," *Social Research* 76, 2 (2000): 283–301.

7. Islamic Republic of Iran Broadcasting (IRIB), Channel 1, May 11, 1997.

8. Robert Fisk, "Khatami Calls for Rule of Law," *The Independent*, February 12, 1999. http://www.independent.co.uk/news/khatami-calls-for-the-rule-of-law-1070295.html.

9. "Khatami Hopes for More Tolerance, Rule of Law in New Iranian Year," *Payvand News*, March 21, 2002. http://www.payvand.com/news/02/mar/1073.html.

10. IRIB, Channel 1, January 31, 2004.

11. IRNA, June 2, 2001.

12. *Aftab-e Yazd*, no. 296, February 23, 2001.

13. See note 2 for the content of these two articles.

14. Tehran Friday Prayer, *Paygah-e-Ettela'rasani-ye-Howzeh*, December 29, 2000. http://www.hawzah.net/fa/article/articleview/49418?ParentID=47893.

15. Article 2, Section 6b.

16. Seyyed Mohammad Mussavi-Bojnurdi, "*Naqsh-e zaman va makan dar taghir ahkam*" ("The role of time and place in the revision of directives"), *Majale-ye Kanun-e Vokala*, no. 10 (1376/1996–1997): 243.

17. Ibid., 241.

18. Untitled comments by Mohammad Emami Kashani, *Rahnemun Quarterly*, no. 6 (Fall 1372/1993): 22.

19. Article 96 of the Constitution of the IRI states, "The determination of compatibility of the legislation passed by the Islamic Consultative Assembly with the laws of Islam rests with the majority vote of the clerical jurisprudents on the Guardian Council; and the determination of its compatibility with the Constitution rests with the majority of all the members of the Guardian Council." The Guardian Council has twelve members, six of them clerics appointed by the Leader and six legal scholars nominated by the head of the judiciary and approved by Parliament.

20. Mohammad-Ebrahim Jannati, *Manabe' ijtihadi az didgah-e mazaheb-e eslami* (Sources of ijtihad from the perspective of islamic schools of thought) (Tehran: Keyhan Association, 1992), 223.

21. *BBC Persian*, December 22, 2008. http://www.bbc.co.uk/persian/iran/2008/12/081222_m_feqh_rafsanjani.shtml.

22. Mohammad-Ali Tofighi, "Rebuilding the Image of Basij," *Rooz Online*, January 7, 2011. http://www.roozonline.com/english/opinion/opinion-article/archive/2011/january/07/article/rebuilding-the-image-of-basij.html.

23. Fatemeh Haghighatjoo's speech in the 372nd session of the Sixth Majles, November 9, 2003, can be found in the archives of the Library, Museum, and Document Center of the Parliament. http://www.ical.ir/index.php?option=com_mashrooh&view=session&id=2584&Itemid=38.

24. Article 150 of the Constitution states: "The Islamic revolution Guards Corps, organized in the early days of the triumph of the revolution, is to be maintained so that it may continue in its role of guarding the revolution and its achievements. The scope of the duties of this Corps, and its areas of responsibility, in relation to the duties and areas of responsibility of the other armed forces, are to be determined by law, with emphasis on brotherly cooperation and harmony among them."

25. Safavi's harsh response was read in the 374th session of the Sixth Majles on November 12, 2003. http://www.radiofarda.mobi/a/362265.html.

26. Two dissidents, Dariush and Parvaneh Foruhar, were stabbed and killed in their home and, within a few days, two secular writers, Mohammad Mokhtari and Jafar Pouyandeh, were abducted and strangled, their bodies abandoned in remote locations. Eventually President Khatami formed a committee to investigate the murders. The investigation revealed that these killings were committed by a hard-line gang, identified as "rogue elements," within the Ministry of Intelligence. Ultimately, the ministry took responsibility and its minister was removed. But the effort to cleanse the ministry eventually led to the move of many intelligence officers to other institutions. For more information on these events, see Mohammad Sahimi, "The Chain Murders: Killing Dissidents and Intellectuals, 1988–1998," *Tehran Bureau*, January 5, 2011. http://www.pbs.org/wgbh/pages/frontline/tehranbureau/2011/01/the-chain-murders-killing-dissidents-and-intellectuals-1988-1998.html.

27. Arash Motamed, *"Hefazat-e ettela'at dar nahad-e riasat jomhuri?"* ("Counter-intelligence in the presidential office?"), *Rooz Online*, August 18, 2011. http://www.roozonline.com/english/news3/newsitem/archive/2011/august/18/article/-f99f02b330.html.

28. Mehdi Khalaji, *"Ijad-e nahad-e ettlela'ati-ye movazi ba vezarat-e ettela'at dar qovehye qazayi-ye"* ("Establishing parallel intelligence institution to the Ministry of Intelligence within the judiciary"), *Radio Farda*, August 26, 2002. http://www.radiofarda.com/content/article/1136425.html.

29. *Hambastegi*, January 18, 2001.

30. *Hamshahri*, July 28, 2004.

31. *Fath Daily*, no. 29, January 16, 2000.

32. The judges in Islamic/religious trials where the judge makes decisions based merely on his understanding and religious knowledge are called *hakem-e shar'* (governing religious magistrate). In the contemporary history of Iran, *hakem-e-shar'* has enjoyed an extensive influence in judicial decision making. Further, *hakem-e shar'* is historically not held accountable for decisions and their implications and consequences.

33. The legislation on torture in its original and amended forms and the arguments made by the Guardian Council to reject them can be found at http://hvm.ir/lawdetailnews .asp?id=45201 and http://www.hvm.ir/lawdetailnews.asp?id=45003.

34. *Noruz*, June 12, 2002.

35. Letter of the Supreme Leader to the Representatives of the Sixth Majles regarding the Press Law, August 5, 2000. http://farsi.khamenei.ir/message-content?id=3019.

36. Article 57 of the Constitution states: "The powers of government in the Islamic Republic are vested in the legislature, judiciary, and executive branches, which function under the supervision of the absolute velayat-e motlaqeh-ye amr [absolute guardianship of juriconsult] and the leadership of the Ummah and in accordance with the forthcoming articles of this Constitution. These powers are independent of one another."

37. Meanwhile, Article 57 of the Constitution was changed to take away the responsibility of creating links among various branches from the president. Article 57's current silence on who will create the links, along with the Leader's responsibility in coordination relations among the three branches, has buttressed the position that all branches of the government operate under the supervision of the Leader.

38. "Convention on the Elimination of All Forms of Discrimination against Women," *UN Women*, http://www.un.org/womenwatch/daw/cedaw/.

39. *Jomhuri-ye Eslami*, October 1, 1997.

7 The Green Movement and Political Change in Iran

Fatemeh Haghighatjoo

THE CONTESTED PRESIDENTIAL election of June 2009 unleashed the most serious mass protest movement since the birth of the Islamic Republic of Iran in 1979. The widespread unrest throughout major urban areas gave birth to what came to be known as the Green Movement, whose minimal initial demand was epitomized in the simple but profound slogan, "Where is my vote?" It was a movement born out of the anger of an electorate that felt betrayed by the tampered result of an election they were certain their candidate had won. It also emanated from the frustration caused by the unfulfilled aspirations of years invested in the reform movement during the presidency of Mohammad Khatami (1997–2005). The spontaneous organization of mass rallies lasted for several weeks, threatened the status quo, and brought about the repressive onslaught of the regime.

In this chapter I examine the transformation of the reform movement into the Green Movement after the presidential election of 2009. The Green Movement temporarily delegitimized the regime, but it could not sustain itself because of harsh state crackdown, weak organization, and the movement leaders' lack of will or ability to forcefully challenge the incumbent conservative elite when mass mobilization from below and the elite-led push for change converged. These challenges made the Green Movement a fragmented coalition of different groups and activists articulating diverse demands and pursuing different and often contradictory goals, a fragmentation that eventually underwrote its disappearance as an active movement. Nevertheless, its power continues to lie in a set of demands and a large enough constituency with the ability to reemerge when political opportunity becomes available. As the 2013 election of Hassan Rouhani as president showed, the Green Movement may not reveal itself in the same manner as before, but its demands and aspirations remain visible to Iranian leaders and seem still capable of influencing the balance of political forces inside the country.

The Green Movement's Antecedent

To understand the Green Movement and its limitations and tribulations, one must examine the reform movement during Khatami's presidency and how its successes and failures set the stage for the rise of the Green Movement. Khatami's unexpected victory in 1997 and the beginning of the reform movement brought to the forefront the persistent and inherent contradiction of the Islamic Republic: the republican element of the system, manifested in the elective institutions of presidency and Parliament, and the theocratic component, represented by institutions that embody the idea of the guardianship of the jurist—the Office of the Leader and the Guardian Council—that fall outside popular accountability. The platform developed by Khatami's strategists was political development (*tose'e siasi*), which in turn informed his key programs. Khatami's political agenda was grounded in expanding arenas of political contestation and fostering the representative component of the regime by expanding the power of elected institutions of the state and strengthening civil society. His strategy focused on elections as the key mechanisms for expanding participation and opening venues for greater change from within the system.

In the politically contentious years of his presidency, Khatami had to maneuver between demands generated by two sets of actors within his own camp. On one hand, the radical constituency of the reform movement questioned his minimalist agenda and accused him of submitting to regime pressure without putting up a fight and securing any political gains. This constituency wanted a more robust confrontation with unelected institutions through reliance on popular mobilization. On the other hand, a second group of Khatami supporters saw the fragility of the reform movement's power base and insisted on an incremental approach for advancing the cause of reform. For them, direct confrontation with unelected institutions, including the Office of the Leader, was a dangerous path that could backfire in terms of public support and loss of potentially natural allies from within the political hierarchy. Many moderate reformists were wary of the isolation of key segments of the political class and saw the antagonism that was brewing in different quarters as indications of possible blowback. In contrast, the more radical base of the reform movement, particularly student organizations, questioned this approach and claimed that Khatami and his associates were selling them out. To be fair, following the overwhelming Khatami victory, some sectors of popular sentiments also had unrealistic demands, fostered by an ungrounded sense of triumphalism, which in part led to the reformist leadership's inability or unwillingness to contain the radical demands of this assertive constituency. A case in point was how the reformist press treated former president Akbar Hashemi Rafsanjani not only by harshly criticizing him, but also by sidelining him as a potential ally.[1] Despite Hashemi Rafsanjani's stance, which assured that the election would not be rigged and Khatami could get elected, he was part of the status quo that the reformist and student movement, the latter of which I ended up representing in the Sixth Parliament (2000–2004), wanted to change. Instead of bringing him on board, we pushed him out.

In hindsight, the loss of Hashemi Rafsanjani as a potentially helpful inter-locutor interacting with the Leader Ayatollah Seyyed Ali Khamenei and other parts of the political establishment was a strategic mistake and a blow to elite realignment. Reflecting on my own experience as a member of the Sixth Parliament, I have come to believe that the reformist leadership in that Parliament on many occasions, perhaps unintentionally and not cognizant of the potential gains of broadening the political base of the reform movement, pursued a strategy that seemed not inclusive enough and resulted in the alienation of influential figures who could have contributed to a less threatening atmosphere as perceived by the hard-liners. By the same token, a more inclusive strategy could have helped establish more bridges to some hard-line elements of the regime, reducing their fear of the reform's antisystemic potential.

Along with conflicting impulses within his own reformist camp, Khatami also faced regime hard-liners who were suspicious of his agenda and never willing to bargain with him over the terms of the reform movement, practically blocking him at every juncture. The critical moment was the 1999 student protests and the decision by the security services to storm university dormitories in Tehran and Tabriz.[2] From then on it was clear that the authorities were determined to stand up to Khatami and his allies. His policies were deemed contrary to the essential character of the Islamic Republic. Faced with counterreaction, Khatami repeatedly shied away from seriously challenging not only the Leader but also the rules of the game set by the conservatives. At times, he vacillated in facing pressures coming from all corners, moving back and forth in an attempt to maintain balance between his constituency in the reform movement and the conservative establishment, a strategy that neither side found satisfactory. I believe that a more proactive leadership on Khatami's part could have developed better relationships and led to more trust between him and both radical reformists and the conservative establishment, including the Leader. A recalcitrant Leader, who was under pressure and perceived his office to be the ultimate target of the reform movement, and Khatami's own ambivalence regarding his role as the leader of a movement frustrated the radical reformist faction while exacerbating the gap between Khatami and his core conservative opponents.

Khatami's election ignited a genuine reform movement. At the same time, his failure to capitalize on the momentum generated by his election and his subsequent inaction in confronting the hard-line security establishment when it brutally suppressed the student unrest of 1999 signaled the decline of the movement and the rise of the conservative counteroffensive. His major legislative initiative to enhance the power of the presidency did not materialize, and the reformist Parliament's major political agenda to reform the Press Law was struck down by the Leader's interference.[3] Khatami's key political strategist, Sa'id Hajjarian, was physically disabled because of an assassination attempt, and many of his friends were arrested without his being able to confront the onslaught against the reform movement. He did have concrete achievements, including the curbing of the extralegal operations and indictment of rogue elements in the Ministry of Intelligence who were responsible for the serial murders of intellectuals. But Khatami did not actively lead the reform movement; neither did he embark on a serious negotiating and bargaining strategy from the top. He did not entertain the idea of mass mobilization from below, either, and he was fearful of its violent repercussions, thereby leaving the divergent factions of the reform movement on their own. The internal contradictions of the reform movement and the difficulty of garnering a coherent strategy to confront the authoritarian establishment produced two divergent constituencies, one loyal to the fundamental message of reformism promoted by Khatami, and the other pursuing a radical agenda demanding more profound and swifter transformations of the political system exemplified in the slogan of "moving beyond Khatami."[4]

Despite Khatami's shortcomings as the leader of reform, his most lasting institutional achievement was the enactment of the law pertaining to the city and village council election. The municipal council elections began a process of decentralization of power and the introduction of electoral accountability and a local democratic experience that would be hard to fully reverse. His long-lasting legacy on the broader political culture should not be underestimated either. His overall contribution was to shape the evolution of the discourse of accountability of political power and to plant the seeds of a democracy movement for the long haul. Khatami also demonstrated the possibility of using electoral cycles in Iran as political opportunity structures for pushing the envelope of change. Moreover, and despite all frustrations regarding failure to bring about desired changes, Khatami's reform movement introduced a young generation to activism and civil engagement and trained them in political mobilization and the art of election campaigning. Lessons learned and cadres and activists trained during the reform movement proved to be vital ingredients for the later successful mobilization of millions of voters in support of candidate Mir-Hossein Mussavi. These legacies were also instrumental in the birth of the Green Movement.

The Nature of the Green Movement

The movement toward democratization and openness in the Islamic Republic of Iran has been anything but linear. It has gone through cycles over the last twenty years, often with sudden and spontaneous action in the streets. The Green Movement was born out of the new cycle of protests, following the controversial presidential election of 2009. It was a movement for change with minimal demands epitomized in the simple but profound slogan "Where is my vote?" Before the election when the initial phase of the Green Movement began, it was still nearly impossible to separate the reform and Green movements as two distinct movements. Rather the Green Movement was widely considered a continuation of the reform movement or essentially identical with it, though with a different name.[5] After the election and widespread crackdown, debate began about the nature of the Green Movement and how it resembled or differed from the preceding reform movement.

As the postelection calls for a recount were faced with heavy-handed repression, people's demands expanded to include full political rights as stipulated in the Constitution. Many gradually even went beyond and called for changing the Constitution. The uncontrolled chain of events and the response of the state inaugurated intense debates within the emergent Green Movement concerning its nature and objectives as well as its strategy and tactics for success. Mussavi issued his first statement a day after the election on June 13, in which he set the goal for the Green Movement to be "combating a lie." In statements on following days, he said that the movement was based on religious teachings: "We will passionately continue our rational green wave derived from religious teachings and the nation's interests in Prophet Mohammad's family, we will fight against a huge lie that has overwhelmed the country and has smeared its face. However, we are not going to allow our actions to be blind and aimless."[6] He then tried to establish his solid revolutionary credentials and loyalty to the core principles of the Islamic Republic while maintaining his staunch opposition to the way the election was engineered. Warning the authorities that the blame for the ongoing street protests and their possible fallout squarely fell on the shoulders of officials, he said, "The protests around the country are not because of him [Mussavi], but because people worry about the new trend in political life that has been imposed on the country."[7]

After the June 15 rally, which included millions of protesters in Tehran, Mussavi stated, "We are engaged in peaceful protest against an unfair election process, seeking the objective of nullifying the election and redoing it based on mechanisms that would guarantee prevention of the previous disgraceful fraud."[8] He emphasized "peaceful methods and nonviolence."

By his fifth statement, Mussavi was warning against "dangerous paths" if authorities did not protect people's votes. He said, "if people's trust is not responded through protection of their votes, and if they are not allowed to show their peaceful and civil reaction in order to defend their rights, dangerous paths are predictable, the responsibility for which rests on the shoulders of those who cannot tolerate peaceful behaviors."[9] The narrative developed by Mussavi and the Green Movement leadership recognized the possibility of wider instability and its inability to contain the outbursts of violence and spontaneous escalation of demands and actions in the streets.

The Green Movement's primary goal was nullification of the election, but Mussavi predicted that if this would not happen, it would be seen as proof of the incompatibility of Islam and republicanism. On this point, it is clear that Mussavi did not want to cut his ties with the tradition of Islamic activism to which he belongs. He still maintains a profound conviction in a republicanism anchored in Islam. In fact, he and some of his associates had worked on a manifesto—published some time before the election—that aimed at locating their intellectual position as distinct from both the conservatism of the establishment and Khatami's reformism.[10] It was with this background that he reacted to the election in the way he did. He stated that "if the enormous extent of fraud and replacement of votes, which have tarnished people's trust, are represented as the proof for the absence of fraud, then the republican pillar of the system is destroyed, and it would practically prove the incompatibility of Islam and republicanism."[11]

Mussavi's call for reform entailed a return "to the pure principles of the Islamic revolution."[12] Immediately within the Green Movement, a consensus emerged as to the centrality of citizens' rights in these principles. This is why many analysts consider the movement a quest for fundamental rights.[13] Others, looking at the statements of movement leaders and the prevailing tactics used by the participants under relentless pressure argue that the core spirit of the movement points to the effort to reconcile the republican and Islamic elements of Iran's Constitution in search of a democratic solution. The explicit modernist religious utterances of movement leaders favored a return to an open interpretation of Islam that reconciles modern democratic governance with broad principles of Islam. Before the election, Mussavi and his associates had been working on a manifesto explaining their core beliefs. Concerns over the weakening of the republican aspect of Iran's Constitution likely motivated Mussavi to run as a candidate, believing that he could undo this disquieting development.

Still others, mostly residing outside Iran but some activists and ordinary Iranians inside the country as well, advocated a more fundamental restructuring of the Islamic Republic and believed that the initial demand regarding the nullification of the election facilitated the germination of a broad-based movement that aimed at changing the institutional basis of power and the establishment of a new constitutional democracy. While the movement went through a turbulent path following the election, this demand for reorganization of political life, though not necessarily coherent in organizational structure and specific strategies, gradually departed from Mussavi's agenda for reforming the Islamic Republic. The rift pitted reformism against the revolutionary objective of changing the regime. The nature and objectives of the Green Movement can be encapsulated in a major debate as to whether the movement was a continuation or rupture in the attempt to reform the Islamic Republic.

Continuity or Rupture?

Two opposing conceptions of the Green Movement, with variations within each one regarding demands and strategy, dominated the conversation among Green Movement activists after the 2009 election. The promoters of the first conception saw the movement as the continuation of the reform movement that began during Khatami's tenure. For the proponents of this argument, the impossibility of articulating sharp distinctions on key definitional criteria precluded meaningful differentiation between the two. Members of this group, best exemplified by Rajab-Ali Mazrui, who used to be a prominent member of the reformist political party Islamic Iran's Participation Front before it was banned and a former reformist parliamentarian now in exile, argued that the Green Movement was "another stage of an evolutionary process of reform movement born out of the experience of the reformist movement."[14] The Green Movement activists who adhere to this view saw no reason to include in the movement those who opposed the general objectives put forth by Mussavi and the other presidential candidate, Mehdi Karrubi. In other words, for these individuals, "the supporters of the dissolution of the regime do not really belong to the Green Movement; although they temporarily ride the tide to advance their own project."[15] They tried to highlight their commitment to reformism, strongly and clearly denouncing regime change as an objective and rejecting confrontational mobilization as their strategy.[16] Supporters of this definition of the Green Movement continue to be committed to the existing constitutional framework of the Islamic Republic and only object to the trampling of the civil and political rights of citizens, which was clearly manifested in the slogan "Where is my vote?" during the postelection demonstrations. For them, accountability of those who hold power, the protection of constitutionally supported individual rights, and electoral fairness were at the heart of the Green Movement's political agenda.

The second conception defined the Green Movement as a qualitative, not necessarily unrelated, departure from the reform movement. Mohsen Sazgara, who is one of the most well known and outspoken exiled opposition figures, argued that the Green Movement was a "fundamental departure to a rights-centered movement, a proof that democracy and freedom cannot come out of the Islamic Revolution." He agreed that the Green Movement would not have been born if there were no reform movement, but it went beyond asking for meager reforms and sought "fundamental constitutional change and liberal freedoms." For Sazgara, the Green Movement's "achievement was to make this important theoretical shift, while the reform movement could not break from the Islamic Revolution."[17] For those who separate the two movements, street protests proved that reform "within the structures of the existing political system was untenable and, as such, it was a new movement that incorporated the old movement rather the other way around."[18] In other words, for these analysts and activists, the reform movement of the Khatami era "no longer existed independent of the Green Movement," in theory as well as in practice.[19] Radicalization of the demands vociferously chanted in demonstrations across Iran after the election was enough to sway these observers and participants to believe that a whole new movement had begun.

The fundamental problem with the current regime, the second conception argued, stemmed from its inherently autocratic power structure in which the choices of citizens were respected only as long as they were not against the existing political structure and accumulation of power by the most powerful institution and individual. The Green Movement went beyond the reform movement in terms of demands and strategy, as the latter showed the inability and unwillingness of the Islamic Republic to reform itself. For people favoring this conceptualization, the Green Movement sought fundamental structural change, and despite its members' initial respect of Mussavi and Karrubi's leadership, they later felt neither could adequately represent their demands. Naturally because of repression and the absence of cohesion in the leadership, this group could not sustain any meaningful presence inside Iran, and if it did, it was primarily underground and in cyberspace.

A variation from within the spectrum that covered these two opposite poles is an approach that treats the Green Movement as a "coalition that encompasses different forms of reformism." Like any other coalition, the argument went, the Green Movement incorporated both maximalist and minimalist objectives, and depending on political opportunities and costs, "the rift between supporters of either set of objectives could widen or shrink."[20] The maximalist position demanded a complete overhaul of the regime and rejected any notion of reform that retained elements of the institutional or ideological makeup of the Islamic Republic. The minimalists, on the other hand, were interested in reform within the existing political structures and simply demanded more free and fair election. Alireza Alavi Tabar, who represents moderate and pragmatic reformists inside Iran, articulated a position that suggested a minimalist formulation and yet called for the importance of "unity and coordination" in the movement toward democracy.[21]

Abbas Abdi, a prominent reformist journalist, believed that the Green Movement had some strengths but its weaknesses could not be ignored. First, it acted mostly on emotions rather than prudence and rational calculation of means and ends. Secondly, its leadership did not manage or lead the movement well, as it was predictable that when accumulated popular demands and grievances were not properly addressed, the movement would radicalize in the streets. Nevertheless, Abdi contended that the objectives and slogans of the Green Movement were similar to that of the reform movement.[22] Abdi argued that the Green Movement was radical as far as its street manifestations were concerned, but "certainly the content, if not necessarily the language, of the statements of the Green Movement's leadership was not consistent with such radicalism."[23] For Abdi, the reform movement of the Khatami era was a failure and the Green Movement was itself a failed radical departure from reformist strategy and in response to the prior failures. That is why he did not consider himself a member of the Green Movement and proposed a "reformist strategy for the proponents of change."[24]

The line of argument that treated the Green Movement as an alliance or coalition seemed to be prevalent among the intellectual class and the seasoned mainstream reformists who were still interested in reconciliation, despite their pessimism toward such an eventuality. The political opportunity for them seemed to be predominantly domestic political variables such as factional balance of power, conservative bloc disarray and fragmentation, and heightened economic malaise.[25] They believed that, as a matter of principle as well as strategy, it is counterproductive to exclude those who demand radical change from the Green Movement, because radical demands have always existed but have eventually been marginalized. This interpretation did not want to exclude from the Green Movement those who advocated wholesale changes; instead, it recognized them without committing to their objective and strategy, hoping to persuade them to agree on a common and minimal goal of reform when and if occasion for accommodation arose. They argued that despite radical utterances by movement participants and advocacy for more confrontational strategy toward the regime, the more radical factions of the Green Movement were likely to be co-opted by the more accommodationist faction if reconciliation between the opposition and regime became a possibility. This was so, they argued, not only because the material and organizational resources of radical reformists were far more limited, but also because the benefits of accommodation resonated much more powerfully with the broad public. Such an optimistic understanding was shared by some of the movement's senior activists who were still in prison and eventually set the stage for their encouragement of people to participate in the 2013 presidential election in support of Rouhani.

People's Power and Electoral Politics

Although both Mussavi and Karrubi repeatedly asserted that they were not going to be silent regarding electoral fraud, their supporters' proactive demand for transparency and accountability propelled and inspired them to continue their protests. People were on the streets protesting an electoral fraud before Mussavi and Karrubi announced the June 15 rally. This was quite different from previous elections. In 2005, Karrubi and Hashemi Rafsanjani were candidates; both complained about the rigging of the election, and even Karrubi had a famous phrase in an open letter written to the Supreme Leader regarding vote counting of the

2005 presidential election. He wrote that "I was ahead of other candidates before I went to sleep at 5 a.m., and once I got up after two hours, it was like the Companions of the Cave awakening, I noticed the result of the election dramatically has been changed."[26] Still no street protests occurred, perhaps because most people assumed that the results were within the normal range of manipulation that usually occurs in Iranian elections and did not necessarily impact the outcome. Even during the 2004 parliamentary election, marked by the Guardian Council disqualification of more than 2,700 candidates, including 120 reformist MPs, protest was limited to a parliamentary sit-in by the disqualified members. This was the first time the Islamic Republic was faced with a significant street protest in reaction to an election. Once Karrubi and Mussavi saw such enthusiasm, they realized that people's power might transform the game.

The presence of a grassroots movement was an important variable that distinguished the Green Movement from the reform movement. Khatami had been criticized repeatedly for not relying on such power in his push for reformist policies and as an instrument of pushback against his conservative opponents. Now the Green Movement leaders were suddenly blessed with this spontaneous outpouring of support. But they seemed unable to lead continuously and effectively. The question of what constitutes effective leadership of social movements is an important one. Mussavi and Karrubi were constrained by both the spontaneity of the movement and pressures on them. They occasionally declared that they were just comrades of the movement and stood with the people. Some have portrayed these statements as disingenuous, but for many reasons including security pressures; detention of their campaign's staff, advisors, colleagues, and political activists; and lack of preparation, they could not organize and lead the movement. More likely, however, their ambivalence in taking up a more radical platform in tune with the demands that were being articulated in the streets also incapacitated them and eventually the movement itself. Thus they chose to rely on online social networks and initiatives of the youth and activists. But the question remained whether a more proactive leadership could have sustained the protests and, in turn, could have potentially convinced the incumbent elite to be more responsive to at least some of the protesters' demands. Many Green Movement activists felt that this was the only instance in the history of the Islamic Republic that an elite-led movement for change could have enlisted people's power from below—a dynamic different from the Khatami era, during which the reformist parties lacked the will to seize the opportunity to lead forces demanding change over a sustained period of time.

In the Khatami period, there was always a fear of possible consequences of popular spontaneous action and what it would do to the reform agenda in case it failed to spread out both geographically and among different social classes. The fear was also the result of the reformists' reading of the popular mood and the belief that spontaneous action could not be counted on. They believed that the people coming into the streets tended to retreat just as fast as they came out. In addition, they feared instability and violence if the repressive arms of the state were unleashed followed by possible bloodshed and cycles of revenge and retribution. None of the reformists was ready to embrace such an outcome.[27] Mussavi had the same assessment of the potentials of the street protests and the likely outcome of unmanaged protests that could quickly get out of hand. Paradoxically, the reform movement had a better and more coherent leadership, albeit certainly cautious about active street mobilization. But it had the organizational skills, cadres, and momentum to coordinate had such a bottom-up protest taken place. In short, incoherent leadership could not effectively use or control the streets to the advantage of the movement's objectives. Obviously this confusion was to some extent a reflection of the state's overreaction, but it was partly the result of fear, lack of determination, differences of opinion among the Green Movement leadership, and perhaps above all, the spontaneous nature of the movement, which the leaders had not anticipated and could not plan for in advance.[28]

As the popular expression of anger in the streets of Tehran and a few other urban areas surfaced, the chatter in the campaign headquarters was quiet about other aspects of mobilization. The critical question at the time, which became sharper later when the streets calmed down, was about the broadness of the social base of the movement. The class composition and geographic diffusion of the movement remained a handicap.

An Urban Middle-Class Movement?

Analysts and activists agree that the Green Movement was primarily a middle-class and upper-middle-class movement concentrated mostly in urban areas. The large-scale demonstrations in major metropolitan areas could not be copied in smaller cities and rural areas. But then the class composition of the Green Movement does not tell us everything. Iran has transformed significantly since the end of the Iran-Iraq War and the beginning of the Hashemi Rafsanjani–led "reconstruction period." The Hashemi Rafsanjani and Khatami presidencies changed Iran's social, political, and economic landscape, contributing to the emergence of new social movements. These changes in class and demographics are important in explaining the dynamics of social movement cycles in Iran. First is the growing population of the youth and young adults over the last two decades. This demographic accounts for more than 60 percent of the population that has been largely immune from the ideological socialization of the postrevolutionary period. Greater access to higher education and relative openness from the mid-1990s until the beginning of the reversal when the populist President Ahmadinejad came to power made this slice of the population the most significant and dynamic constituency of the reform movement.[29] Second, the declining population of rural areas to less than 30 percent meant that the locus of political mobilization became even more urbanized than before.[30] But the downside of the urbanization trend is that the bulk of the migrant population has not moved up the ladder of class structure to be part of the middle class and a natural constituency of the reform movement.

Therefore, urbanization created a sizable population of urban poor and lower classes for whom political demands such as freedom and free election were far less appealing than for the middle classes. This does not mean that the Green Movement had no support base among the poor and working class in rural and urban areas. On the contrary, throughout my political life as a student and a parliamentarian, I observed solid support and enthusiasm for the reform movement in the poor rural and urban areas of the country. But given its emphasis on political reform, the major proactive support for the Green Movement did not come from lower classes, especially given the seriousness of economic hardships these classes faced. Nevertheless, exclusive reliance on the class base of the Green Movement to evaluate its strengths and weaknesses, how it is connected to society organically, or how it may have led to transformative collective action is misleading, or at least subject to major dispute among analysts and organizers.

Ahmadinejad's populist agenda and his brand of welfare in the form of cash allowances granted him some popularity in rural areas and among lower classes. But then how significant were the rural areas for political mobilization or change? Analysts and activists inside Iran disagreed in this respect as well. Some argued that "the rural communities that became full-fledged supporters of the post-revolutionary established ideology are losing their weight relative to the city and urban communities and becoming weaker and weaker."[31] The reason for this, they argued, lay mostly in opportunities for social mobility among the poor villagers provided by the social development policies of the last three decades. Some sections of the rural population had access to educational opportunities and still maintained major family networks in their communities.[32] This seemed to be more so for rural communities that were closer to large urban areas. But some disagreed. Without necessarily disputing the urbanization trend, they insisted on the significance of rural areas when put in the context of "elections as political opportunity and mechanisms of mobilization."[33] For this group of activists and analysts, the rural sector, along with a significant portion of the informal sector, tended to buy into an Ahamdinejad-type of populist discourse or were still traditional enough to be effectively manipulated by the ruling elite.

But if history of the social movements in twentieth-century Iran is of any analytical or empirical value, one can take comfort in the fact that the rural areas, most of which belong to the lower classes, have had no significant role in most of these social upheavals. Thus to say that the Green Movement is a middle-class movement does not sufficiently explain the dynamics of change. The 2013 presidential election demonstrated strong support for the pragmatic candidate Rouhani in rural areas. This shows the critical impact of social categories such as youth and women on the outcomes rather than rural/urban split. Moreover, the demand for better economic opportunities and well-being seems to be more strongly tied to the performance of officeholders rather than blind acceptance of populist agendas of politicians by the economically distressed masses, whether in the cities or rural areas. Looking at the demographic composition and social consciousness of groups that have become the vital constituencies of the reform movement in general, and the Green Movement in particular, can give us a more accurate picture.

Youth and women's participation has been consistently crucial since Khatami's election in 1997.[34] These social forces, whose demands for inclusion cut across class and geographical cleavages, have intellectually and organizationally amplified the voices for peaceful change in Iran. The effects of social and cultural change have not been limited to the modern middle-class urban women and youth, but traditional lower-class and middle-class women have not been affected to the same level. Even if social and cultural changes have reached these classes of women, they have not necessarily transformed them uniformly in terms of demands and political discourse. Nonetheless, the rural-urban gap has narrowed considerably as far as social indicators for women are concerned. In political terms, the image of Zahra Rahnavard holding her husband Mussavi's hand during the presidential campaign was a vivid representation of dramatic change in even more Islamist segments of the population.[35] The presence of traditionally dressed women in postelection protests also demonstrated the support lent to the Green Movement by a significant portion of the traditional middle class. Therefore, neither the history of social mobilization nor the social transformation Iran has recently experienced made the Green Movement's class constituency as significant a drawback as some would like to suggest.

The mobilization of the working class and the labor movement could speed up the process of change by depriving the state of much-needed resources, a decisive element when the time comes and some sort of mobilization has already been launched. It could, furthermore, buttress the existing elite conflict and possibly enhance the voices of moderates or soft-liners who are interested in accommodation with the opposition. A successful transition in Iran is not feasible without the participation or active mobilization of the lower classes and the labor movement. Yet neither labor nor a significant portion of the poor joined the Green Movement. However, as observers and participants in the postelection protests have noted, considerable numbers of people came from the poorer areas of Tehran, although unrest did not take off in any measurable way in those areas.

Two major obstacles stand in the way of working-class political mobilization. First is lack of organization and solidarity infrastructures that could lead to collective political action. Labor syndicates have been either eliminated or co-opted into the broader regime-organized unions under state control.[36] Second, some segments of the fragmented working class concentrated in state-owned enterprises and large-scale manufacturing complexes have been partitioned by the regime's populist economic agenda. They are thus highly unlikely, given the costs of politically mobilizing the working class, to initiate significant action in the streets. Despite enormous economic pressures on the working class and increasing demand for political liberalization by them, the disunity of the working class has inhibited social movement organization of labor. Although "an important part of the organized working class has supported the popular demand for democratic reform," as a vocal and coherent movement, it has a long way to go.[37]

Whither the Green Movement?

From the start of the protests, the government unleashed its repressive arms ferociously with the aim of incapacitating the efficient organizational capacity that had been built in the months leading to the election. The organizational strength of the Green Movement was crushed in a short time with arrests and crackdowns on the means of communication and association. After the first week of large-scale protests, and by the end of the day on Friday, June 18, coordination and exercise of leadership became difficult. But the failure of the Green Movement was not solely the consequence of the harsh crackdown but could also be explained by organizational weaknesses caused by the multiplicity of election campaign structures that were put together hastily after it became clear that Mussavi was the lead reformist candidate.

Most importantly, no serious contingencies had been prepared in the event of massive repression. Activists were surprised that the regime would embark on such a dangerous course and would be willing to pay huge costs domestically and internationally to back Ahmadinejad's presidency. This was a shortsighted mistake on the part of the reformists, much easier to see in hindsight. It illustrated the usual reformist underestimation of the conservative faction's resolve and power in undermining any movement directed toward political change at any cost. The Green Movement had an advantage in the expansion of social media and their increasing impact on the movement's capacity to mobilize and confront growing restrictions.[38] These new modes of communication were invaluable resources to compensate for lack of direct and in-the-field leadership and absence of mass party organization. But none was enough to tilt the balance in favor of the movement. In addition, the state also managed to catch up with technology and employ countermeasures to circumvent the comparative advantage of tech-savvy youth. Still, reliance on new communication technologies to connect to the

Green Movement constituencies limited the presence of activists and the movement leadership to cyberspace.

This could be said equally about the leadership of the Green Movement. Mussavi and Karrubi, who became "accidental leaders" of the Green Movement, carried both revolutionary credentials and authenticity in the framework of Islamic Republic politics. But their credentials did not mean much when the survival of the political system was in danger. They were soon dealt severe punishment in the form of house arrest. It is easy to dismiss their leadership as simply nonexistent for analysts whose expectations of them were to change the system that they had helped to create.[39] But the Green Movement, in terms of its street protests and energetic action programs to stand up to the regime, was spontaneous and loosely organized. If we define a social movement as collective efforts to challenge existing power arrangements, "based on common purposes and social solidarities, in sustained interaction with elites, opponents, and authorities, the Green Movement was a movement that could not sustain itself and lacked sufficient organization, in spite of common purpose and strong solidarity among participants."[40] As the repression escalated and the leadership of the movement in the persons of Mussavi, Khatami, and Karrubi became restricted, the leaders were not leading anymore.

With all its aspirations and achievements, the Green Movement did not last long enough to change the balance of power in such a way to lead to either accommodation or wholesale change. The Green Movement failed to persist in the form of actively mobilized like-minded groups after 2010, but the ideas and demands presented, both spontaneously and systematically, during the turbulent months after the election continued to exist and would not go away. Divisions and bickering among different movement activists over proper objectives and strategies only deepened. After a while it became clear that the differences could not be reconciled, and, as one exiled activist suggested, "cooperation among contending factions are neither possible nor desirable since these groups have vastly divergent views on objectives and strategies."[41] At the height of Green Movement activism, I believed that forcible regime change or revolutionary transformation is not desirable. But I also thought that the critics of the regime have to go beyond the minimalist reform agenda and emphasize in more precise terms the imperatives for constitutional reform whereby the discriminatory components of the document can be revised. But continued disagreements among leading activists, increasing frustration in dealing with the regime's apparent consolidation, and the escalation of tension between Iran and the international community ended up opening even more fault lines among activists, particularly regarding the issue of whether the inability to challenge hard-line consolidation from the inside should open the way for cooperation between the Green Movement and outside forces that have also been in conflict with the current intransigent leadership in Iran.

International Linkages and the Question of Foreign Assistance

The role outsiders can play in promoting or stunting political change in Iran was part of conversation even before the outset of the Green Movement. Between 1997 and 2003, many gestures to improve Iran's relations with the West, particularly the United States, were not responded to adequately. The reformists' expectations that their domestic political leverage could be enhanced if the West's warming to Iran could move more seriously and expeditiously were not realized. The George W. Bush administration undermined the reform movement, either intentionally or inadvertently, by taking a hawkish stance toward Iran.[42] The toughening rhetoric against Iran and the invasion of Afghanistan and Iraq had reverberations across the political spectrum. For conservatives, the Bush administration's posture was more a proof of imminent threat against Iranian security and the potential of even adventurist military incursion into Iranian territory. Reformists were increasingly under the wrath of the conservative establishment and had little political capital to pursue whatever was left of their democratization agenda. Ahmadinejad's election and the conservative turn in Iranian politics changed the picture altogether, and the prospect for improvement of relations became bleaker in the ensuing years.

With the rise of the Green Movement, the presence of an active exiled opposition became more prominent. Various exiled opposition groups in Europe and the US became more vocal in supporting the Green Movement. These voices were not much different from those inside the country in terms of specific demands. However, they articulated a more radical vision of change that often collided with movement activists inside Iran. The exiled opposition typically represented the more radical constituencies of the movement and tended to seek regime change. This affected conversations inside Iran, making the subject of international support a contentious issue among activists and reformist leadership. Initially, given the euphoria over the possibility of dramatic change in Iran that dominated international media and policy circles, there was little open debate regarding the implications of international assistance for the movement among the opposition. Realizing that the US and other Western powers were also caught off guard and vacillated over proper policy, the quiet signals from Green Movement leaders and activists in Iran cautioned against lending support to the movement for fear of recrimination of collusion with foreign powers in fomenting unrest. Hillary Clinton mentioned the challenges facing the administration at the time in an interview with BBC Persian and commented that "it was a very tough time for us, because we wanted to be full-hearted in favor of what was going on inside Iran, and we kept being cautioned that we would put people's lives in danger, we would discredit the movement, we would undermine their aspirations."[43] Clinton's remarks pointed to the predominant position adopted by the Green

Movement leadership inside the country and the representatives of the reformist parties based in Europe and the US.

The failure of the Green Movement, the onset of the Arab Spring, and more importantly the removal of Muammar Qaddafi in Libya by NATO's military intervention opened new fault lines among Green Movement activists regarding the role of foreign assistance in facilitating change. The major divide was between organizations and figures supporting some forms of support by foreign governments and those rejecting them. Advocates of procuring foreign help were mostly based outside Iran, while leading Green Movement leaders and activists inside the country rejected material support by foreign powers. The Coordinating Council of the Green Path of Hope, which was close to Mussavi and reformist parties inside the country, opposed foreign intervention and rejected any notion of assistance. In reaction to Clinton's remarks that the opposition should request our help next time around, the Paris-based spokesman of the council Ardeshir Amir Arjomand said in an interview with BBC Persian that "certainly the request for such assistance would not be extended to any power. Our people are a proud people who have always tried to solve their problems themselves."[44] Others highlighted the centrality of "domestic forces" in defining the future of Iran and have warned the exiled opposition to be cognizant of their independence. Alavi Tabar argued that associating with foreign intentions and policies "could inflict irreparable damage to the legitimacy and popularity of the critics [of the regime]." He relayed the concern of many other activists in the Green Movement when he argued that "by committing to 'democratic patriotism,' the opposition and critics, independent of the methods and the approach of foreign forces, should confront any threat to the national interests and security by foreign forces alongside their effort for transition to democracy."[45]

As the specter of military intervention in Iran began to loom larger, the debate among the opposition became even fiercer. Some opposition figures outside the country asked for active and direct Western support for the movement and the application of coercive diplomacy that emphasized sanctions. Ignoring the Iranian political culture's sensitivities to notions of independence and foreign interference, these activists demanded a fresh look at the new international environment and changing concepts of independence and foreign assistance. Many advocates of requesting active foreign assistance argued that "acquiring support from the international community does in no way mean losing independence."[46] Some went further by criticizing those within the Green Movement who rejected foreign help as radical anti-imperialist intellectuals informed by an "America-bashing" discourse of leftist Islamists and Marxists whose ideas bring nothing but inaction in the face of the regime's brutal repression. Other opposition figures called on the West, particularly the US, for more robust support of the Green Movement and tighter economic and diplomatic pressure on the regime. Endorsing proactive foreign support short of military intervention, a Washington-based activist called on the US not to send wrong signals, "which would relieve the rulers of the Iranian government from international sanctions for violating fundamental rights of the Iranians."[47]

Although no prominent figure in the opposition supported direct military intervention, the possibility prompted many intellectuals and activists inside and outside the country to express strong opposition to any notion of foreign interference. A statement by a group of activists based in Iran underscored this sentiment by arguing that the fate of the Iranian people is determined by the people and "no foreign or domestic guardian" is needed.[48] This statement categorically rejected "any foreign interference, specially the military kind" as contradictory to the basic tenets of the Iranians' struggle for freedom. A statement by more than 120 Iranian intellectuals residing outside Iran also condemned any hint of foreign military intervention and cautioned foreign governments and the opposition forces against "resorting to notions such as humanitarian intervention or support for democracy to justify anti-Iranian actions or inhumane crimes."[49]

Disagreement among the opposition about foreign intervention or procuring assistance from foreign governments and NGOs stemmed from two major concerns. First was the fear that foreign intervention could exacerbate the existing chasm between the state and society and lead to dangerous instability. Many reformists believed that the legitimacy crisis of the state along with unfulfilled expectations from the Green Movement had created intense resentment and despair among a vast swath of the population. Under such circumstances and given the radical conservative faction's commitment to the survival of the regime, internal strife and long-term instability was deemed a real possibility if foreign governments pursued active interventionist policies. Khatami's explanation as to the wisdom of his voting in the parliamentary election of March 2012, the first election held after the contested 2009 election, referred to "repelling internal and external dangers and threats and safeguarding people's rights and interests" as the primary reasons for his decision to vote.[50] His decision to cast a vote was in part a reflection of his assessment of the hazards of foreign interference in Iranian domestic affairs and in the context of louder debates among the opposition regarding such a move. The debate did, however, further intensify cleavages within the Green Movement.

The second source of concern was loss of credibility among a significant part of the population and undermining of the potential of defection among some moderate elements within the regime. Mainstream reformists continued to believe that changing the balance of power between major players of Iranian politics would ultimately require the co-optation of some regime soft-liners. The critics argued that it was the hopeful strategy of the reform movement throughout Khatami's presidency to accommodate the hard-liners and their leader Khamenei in expectation of his shift to the center and a more even-handed approach. This strategy did not work, the critics argued, and eventually led to a more hard-line presidency. Because of the failure of the reformist era, the critics argued, the post-2009 period warranted a reassessment of the role of foreign assistance. Two fundamental changes in the political environment warranted this reassessment. First, the increasing repression of the state machinery left the opposition defenseless, and the moral imperative for foreign support became more compelling than ever. Second, the massive political imbalance in favor of the conservative camp was unlikely to change in the near future, and there was no indication that the Leader and his hard-line associates would ever change course. Given these realities, critics argued that there were areas in which Western countries could help the crushed Green Movement and the Iranians' yearning for freedom. But this argument was combined first with a categorical rejection of any form of military intervention and, second, an emphasis on foreign support for human rights. Military intervention or threat of military intervention was deemed as solidifying the ultraconservative hold on power, weakening the opposition and the constituency of democratic reform in Iran. Even supporters of foreign involvement felt that the more the threat of force was employed, the less the likelihood that the support base of the movement would expand or infrastructure of mobilization could be built. Instead, they argued, the focus of foreign assistance should be on human rights issues. Specifically, the use of coercive diplomacy—economic sanctions—should be more systematically and transparently tied to human rights promotion and against the regime's gross violation of people's fundamental rights.

Supporters of foreign pressure who resided outside Iran were placed in a difficult bind regarding the US-led economic sanctions. Knowing that the comprehensive sanctions imposed by the US probably harmed average Iranians rather than the regime itself, while by and large proving to be ineffective in changing Iran's foreign policy behavior, they argued that now that the sanctions were in place their easing should be tied to the improvement of the regime's human rights records and not merely its nuclear policy—advice that was difficult to heed given the format of and focus on nuclear negotiations. Furthermore, as the impact of comprehensive sanctions on the Iranian people became more evident, their support for any kind of economic pressure, even for the sake of human rights, was criticized even by Green Movement supporters inside Iran, further widening the space between opposition inside and outside Iran.

Authoritarian Consolidation?

The crackdown in the post–June 2009 presidential election also initiated debate regarding the question of whether the Iranian regime had changed to the point of no return toward authoritarian consolidation. Those who argued that authoritarian consolidation had already occurred pointed to several qualitative changes in the structure of power, including increased repression, the IRGC's enhanced role in the decision-making apparatus of the state and in assuming systematic responsibility in internal security, dissipated legitimacy of the system, and elimination of the reformist wing of the polity from the arena of electoral contestation. The center of political contestation shifted to the conservative camp and the intraconservative discord continued to be as ferocious as it was between the conservative and the reformists, they argued, but the range of contested political ideas had become so narrow as to leave little room for meaningful competition. In addition, the widespread belief even among the imprisoned reformist leaders that the regime had planned contingencies months in advance and the arrest warrants of a number of them dated three days before the June 12 election were proof of the intended electoral engineering and systematic crackdown.[51] These dynamics suggested defining reversals away from the reform of the 1990s and early 2000s and, in the words of one prominent activist, qualified at least as "authoritarian enhancement."[52]

Others questioned the possibility of the Islamic Republic moving toward full authoritarian consolidation. The persistent intra-elite conflict, or what Saʿid Hajjarian, a key theorist of reform, has called the "division of polity by two at any given time," provided permanent possibility for realignment of political factions and, if convergence of political opportunities and structural conduciveness allowed, the birth of a new equilibrium. In such circumstances, as was seen in Khatami's 1997 election, a reversal can always happen, they argued. Ideological cleavages within the system cannot and should not be underestimated. Moreover, the dialectical interplay of power and ideology makes it even more difficult to map out the trajectory of change in Iran, as its effects vary over time and in a cyclical manner and for different players. Paradoxically, the power of symbols and ideology continues to be a source of empowerment for forces agitating for change. This is perhaps why the leaders and many cadres of the reform movement, or even the Green Movement, continue to show their adherence to ideological principles of the revolution. Yet the same interplay of power and ideology and the ways the reformists have tried to capitalize on it created a handicap for unifying different forces within the Green Movement. The older generation of the Green Movement leaders and activists who were still emotionally connected to the founding father of the revolution, Ayatollah Khomeini, couched their message in terms of Islamist revolutionary discourse and argued that the Islamic Republic proper is what they advocate. Others wanted to break away from the past, seeing the reference to the "golden era of Imam Khomeini" as a regressive slogan that cannot lead to meaningful change, let alone democracy.

Another issue that created ambivalence regarding authoritarian consolidation was the continuously baffling question of who is in charge in Iran. How powerful is the Leader, and is consensus still the mechanism through which major decisions are reached? The political field and the polity itself have narrowed significantly, there was increasing personalization of power at the top, in Khamenei's hands. This phenomenon came about partly by design and partly by the force of uncontrollable events. But had the highly personalized form of power led to uniformity in decision making and coherence of policy outputs? How could the reality that inter- and intra-elite conflict persisted while Khamenei still enjoyed the unflinching support of core loyal groups, particularly in the security and military apparatus, be explained? An alternative explanation could be that the institutional arrangement of the system and the fractured and diffused nature of power in the Islamic Republic of Iran could not be easily supplanted, no matter how hard Khamenei insisted on achieving it. Neither he nor any other individual or institution could simply take the process of homogenization of the political system to its logical end without dangerously undermining the equilibrium and stability of the political system, something he probably realized as well.

Were there still possibilities for accommodation between the regime and opposition in the light of the failure of the Green Movement to achieve its objectives? Few factors seemed favorable to minimal accommodation. First, ironically, was the highly personalized nature of power. Khamenei's absolute grip on power could function as a double-edged sword. It made the polity more vulnerable and constricted but made him capable of mustering political consensus rapidly in the complex web of Iranian political structure. The political environment suggested that the possibility for reconciliation or a negotiated path rested largely on his shoulders. If he concluded that the survival of the system and his hold on power was in danger, he might signal a shift toward the center. The second favorable condition was the unresolved political crisis left from the postelection turmoil. The loss of electoral integrity and the perpetual fear of the government and the ruling elite that another crisis could emerge might end up being conducive to a change of heart and stepping back from relying exclusively on repression.[53]

The third factor was the divisions within the conservative bloc. The 2012 parliamentary elections vividly brought factional infighting within the conservative camp to the forefront, adding fuel to a sense that power remained more decentralized than the 2009 election suggested. The conservative bloc was divided into three factions: a radical conservative group supported by Ayatollah Mohammad-Taqi Mesbah Yazdi, mainstream traditional conservatives that ended up winning most of the seats, and independent conservatives. The more serious the rifts become among conservatives, the more room for forces promoting change to maneuver, and the more appetite for the core conservative establishment to rebalance the system.

Powerful hard-liners were still opposed to any formula that would embrace moderate reformists like Khatami in reconciliation efforts. They had vested economic and political interests that would translate into intense pressure on Khamenei not to pursue such a strategy. They would do everything in their power to sabotage any attempted accommodation.

Furthermore, oil rent has been the most important resource that has given the particular brand of Iranian authoritarianism flexibility and an instrument for survival. Oil resources have given the Iranian state enough of a cushion to not only drive a populist distributive agenda but also unleash a capable repressive apparatus. As long as oil rent exists, the state can both finance repression and afford patronage networks.

Finally, there was the intervention of international diplomatic and economic pressure. The economic sanctions and the threat of the use of force made the ruling elite more security conscious and weary of reformists and forces interested in meaningful change. But the escalation of sanctions and the intensified covert war conducted by the US brought forth the possibility of system accommodation toward more centrist or moderate conservatives at the expense of reformists and Green Movement leadership. Ironically, even a shift to the center, provided Khamenei allowed it, required a buy-in from the reformists and the Green Movement. No one doubted that the reformist parties associated with Khatami, Mussavi, and Karrubi would not be allowed to participate in the election. But even the election of a centrist candidate, if any was allowed to stand for election, would not have been possible without a deliberate decision by a vast part of the electorate that had voted for Mussavi in 2009. For the reformists close to the Green Movement leaders under house arrest, this meant a shift of position from being permanent doubters in the integrity of elections to becoming facilitators in the election of a centrist candidate. Accordingly, Khatami's decision to vote in the 2012 parliamentary election partly reflected his assessment of the political deadlock and the imperative to open up space if Khamenei contemplated a move to the center. Following the election of 2009, Khatami has walked a fine line between Green Movement aspirations and his own moderate brand of reformism. This ambivalence culminated in his voting in the parliamentary election, which led to fierce debate among activists from all political persuasions. Once again the political maneuver by Khatami exacerbated the debates over strategy and tactics among members of the Green Movement. Some praised his move as courageous while others saw it as a betrayal of Green Movement ideals and Khatami's own promise that he would not participate in the election unless his minimal demands are met.[54] His voting in the election nevertheless affected the Green Movement activists negatively and surprised even some of his ardent supporters and friends.[55]

By the time Khatami went to the polls, opening his path for the critical support he gave to Rouhani in the 2013 election, the opposition was in a ferocious fight over strategy regarding how to respond to possible overtures by the regime.

On one side were those who were adamantly opposed to any concession and regarded reconciliation as a betrayal of Green Movement aspirations. One can see this sentiment in the abundant condemnation of Khatami and reformists who were contemplating reconciliation.[56] On the other hand, prominent figures such as Abdollah Nuri, the Khatami-impeached interior minister who was later imprisoned for his activities as the managing editor of a reformist daily, despite being critical of Khatami's vote in the parliamentary election, stepped forward and implicitly signaled their openness to possible national reconciliation. Nuri's conversation with a group of students encouraged "rebuilding trust" among political forces inside the country and rejected "extremism" in articulating demands,[57] though the discord was at its height, further fragmenting the opposition and making the formation of even the semblance of a common platform very difficult. In the absence of an accommodation framework, some outside Iran even saw the possibility of full-blown implosion stemming from unbearable economic pressures on a large segment of the population, and mobilization of the masses by either a catalyst or active organization of the reformists. In both cases, the presence of a facilitating trigger and loss of elite cohesion and loyalty at the top were required. This scenario envisioned the more radical faction of the Green Movement finding an opportunity to take center stage. But given that they represented the least organized and the least resourceful among the broadly defined Green Movement coalition, they would have a daunting task in organizing and taking the lead. It was also a scenario that did not have many takers inside Iran.

Conclusion

The Green Movement, as we came to know in the aftermath of the election of 2009, no longer exists organizationally. But its powers should not be underestimated. As a spontaneous movement demanding electoral accountability and political inclusion, it galvanized a large swath of the Iranian population in 2009–2010 even if it did not survive or respond to the divergent demands of its multiple constituencies. The radical faction of the movement expected wholesale change of the Islamic Republic, while the reformist constituency wanted meaningful and constitutionally sanctioned freedoms and fair election. Neither achieved what it had hoped the movement would deliver. Fragmentation of the Green Movement and crackdowns further weakened the reform movement and closed the opening that some saw as the beginnings of a transition to a more democratic political arrangement.

But as a set of demands advocated by a large swath of the Iranian population and embraced by the largely repressed reformist parties and groups, the movement did not disappear. The potential to reorganize around the old reformist platform, or a reformulated agenda articulated by a coalition of reformists and centrists, could and at least partially did happen in the 2013 presidential elections. In the light of the 2009 crackdowns and widespread belief in authoritarian consolidation, the 2013 presidential election resulted in yet another surprise underwritten by Khamenei's decision to restore legitimacy to the electoral system by providing assurances for minimal political accommodation. Does this stunning turn of events indicate the beginning of another phase away from the authoritarianism exhibited after the 2009 election? It is too early to say with certainty, but a clear decision was made to restore the political equilibrium and, albeit reluctantly, respect the new political reality that included the events surrounding the 2009 election. The Green Movement failed to nullify the election's results through its street power, and its leadership did not and perhaps could not lead a sustained mobilization from below or engage in a give-and-take discussion in the height of the protests. What it did achieve, however, was powerfully present in the 2013 election. Many of Rouhani's yet unfulfilled campaign promises, including working for the release of Green Movement leaders and desecuritization of the political environment, were predicated on what he knew the electorate who voted for Mussavi wanted to hear. Furthermore, his decision to include key Mussavi advisors as his cabinet ministers signaled his disagreement with the attempt to sideline key reformists. Finally, Khamenei's decision to acknowledge and confirm the idea of voter preference was intended to reverse the lack of legitimacy the Green Movement protests had caused the electoral process. In short, both the 2013 election and the debates that have transpired since regarding the future direction of the country are testimony to the extent to which the Green Movement still weighs on the Iranian leaders' mind.

Notes

1. See, for instance, Akbar Ganji's series of articles about Hashemi Rafsanjani in the daily *Sobh-e Emruz*, which were later published in the collection of his essays *Alijenab-e sorkhpush va alijenaban-e khakestari* (Red eminence and gray eminences) (Tehran: Tarh-e No, 1378/1999).

2. Following the fifth Parliament's legislation to curtail the Press Law, *Salam*, a reformist daily, was shut down after revealing that members of the Intelligence Ministry were behind the legislation. Tehran University students protested, which led to a bloody attack on Tehran University and Tabriz University's dormitories. That midnight attack triggered more protests in Tehran. Iraj Gorgin, "Looking Back at Tehran's 1999 Protests," *Radio Farda*, July 9, 2008. http://www.rferl.org/content/Iran_Student_Protests/1182717.html.

3. See chapter 6 in this volume.

4. Moving beyond Khatami was the debate launched by journalist Abbas Abdi following his assessment that Khatami could not advance the cause of reform. His point was that the reformists must think about pushing their agenda further and beyond Khatami. For months the discussions, in many of which I was personally involved, within reformist parties and circles revolved around Abdi's controversial idea. His argument was that Khatami must use

the threat of resigning to force the conservative power block to accommodate him. The debate led to the first serious rift among Khatami supporters.

5. Author interview with a reformist activist in Tehran, September 30, 2011.

6. *Kaleme*, June 13, 2009. A compilation of all of Mussavi's postelection statements along with his other speeches and interviews can be found in *Chenin goft mir hossein* (Mir-Hossein said as such) (France: Kaleme and Kanun-e Doktor Shariati, 1391/2012). http://static3.kaleme .com/Chonin%20Goft%20MirHossein.pdf.

7. Ibid., June 14, 2009.

8. Ibid., June 17, 2009.

9. Ibid., June 20, 2009. For an illuminating discussion of Mussavi's statements and the evolution of the Green Movement's collective identify, see Arash Reisinezhad, "The Iranian Green Movement: Fragmented Collective Action and Fragile Collective Identity," *Iranian Studies* 48, no. 2 (March 2015): 193–222.

10. The title of the manifesto published in 2008 was *Olgu-ye ziste Mosalmani* (A Model of Muslim Living). It was published by the Jam'iat-e Towhidiyat vaTa'avon (Society of Monotheism and Cooperation).

11. *Kalame*, June 20, 2009.

12. Ibid.

13. See Abbas Milani, "The Green Movement," *Iran Primer.* http://iranprimer.usip.org /resource/green-movement.

14. Author interview with Rajab-Ali Mazrui, November 11, 2011.

15. Ibid.

16. Interview with Reza Khatami, "*Asl taghir-e siasathast va na taghir rais dolat*" ("The principle is change of policies not the head of the government"), *Noruz*, October 8, 2012.

17. Author interview with Mohsen Sazgara, October 12, 2011.

18. Author interview with a reformist activist living in Tehran, October 16, 2011.

19. Author interview with an advisor to Mussavi's presidential campaign, October 24, 2011.

20. Author interview with an academic living in Tehran who is close to the reform movement, October 8, 2011.

21. *Kaleme*, June 6, 2012. http://www.kaleme.com/1391/03/17/klm-102869.

22. Abbas Abdi, "*Jonbesh-e sab pasokhi beh zamingir shodan eslahat bood van a edame-ye an*" ("The Green Movement was a response to the bogging down of the reform and not its continuation"), *Ayande*, October 23, 2010. http://www.ayande.ir/1389/08/post_860.html#more.

23. Interview with Abbas Abdi, *Ayande*, October 22, 2010. http://www.ayande.ir/1389/10 /post_825.html#more.

24. See Abbas Abdi, "*Pishnahad-e yek rahbord-e eslah-talabaneh baraye tarafdaran-e taghir*" ("Proposal for a reformist strategy for proponents of change"), *Ayande*, April 16, 2012. http://www.ayande.ir/1391/01/post_1046.html.

25. See Nader Hashemi, "Religious Disputation and Democratic Constitutionalism: The Enduring Legacy of the Constitutional Revolution on the Struggle for Democracy in Iran," *Constellations* 17, no. 1 (2010): 50–60.

26. *Gooya*, June 19, 2005. http://mag.gooya.com/president84/archives/031422.php.

27. I recall many occasions when reformists debated organizing crowds even in closed environments such as stadiums and never actually tried to do so out of the fear of bloodshed or wider instability. And when at some point we decided to do it, it was too late in the process, with reformists losing leverage and not being given the permission to organize events.

28. Author interview with a senior Mussavi campaign staff member who lives in Tehran, December 15, 2011. In this interview he maintained that there was much anxiety about the

spontaneity of the street protests, particularly the largest one on June 15, 2009, and quite a bit of discussion about what to do. He maintained that it was total "panic" as the campaign perceived the situation to be getting out of hand.

29. See Djavad Salehi-Isfahani, "Poverty and Inequality since the Revolution," *Middle East Institute*, January 29, 2009, http://www.mei.edu/content/poverty-and-inequality-revolution.

30. The 2011 Iranian census data states that the rural population of Iran was 29 percent of the population. http://www.khabaronline.ir/detail/190093.

31. Author interview with a political scientist living in Iran who has conducted research and run election campaigns in the rural areas, September 21, 2011.

32. Eric Hooglund, "Thirty Years of the Islamic Revolution in the Rural Iran," *MERIP* 250 (Spring 2009). http://www.merip.org/mer/mer250/thirty-years-islamic-revolution-rural-iran.

33. Author interview with a student activist who worked in reformist presidential campaign in rural areas of Western Iran, September 25, 2011.

34. For an examination of the role of the women in the June 2009 election and the mass protests that ensued, see "Women in the Iranian Election Campaign and Protest," *Middle East Occasional Paper Series*, Woodrow Wilson International Center for Scholars (Fall 2009). http://www.wilsoncenter.org/sites/default/files/Women%20in%20Iranian%20Election.pdf.

35. For an examination of novelties in women's participation, see Ziba Mir-Hosseini, "Broken Taboos in Post-Election Iran," *MERIP Online*, December 17, 2009. http://www.merip.org/mero/mero121709.

36. See Mohammad Maljoo, "The Green Wave Awaits an Invisible Hand," *MERIP Online*, June 26, 2010. http://www.merip.org/mero/mero062610.

37. For a useful discussion of labor and social movements and the quest for democracy in Iran, see Farhad Nomani and Sohrab Behdad, "Labor Rights and Democracy Movement in Iran: Building a Social Democracy," *Northwestern University Journal of International Human Rights* 10, no. 4 (Spring 2012).

38. M. Hadi Sohrabi-Haghighat and Shohre Mansouri, "'Where Is My Vote?' ICT Politics in the Aftermath of Iran's Presidential Election," *International Journal of Emerging Technologies and Society* 8, no. 1 (2010): 24–41.

39. For an analysis of this effect, see Mehdi Khalaji, "Who Is Really Running Iran's Green Movement? Here's a Hint: It Is Not Mussavi, Khatami, or Karrubi," *Foreign Policy*, November 4, 2009. http://www.foreignpolicy.com/articles/2009/11/04/whos_really_running_irans_green_movement.

40. Sidney Tarrow, *Power in Movements: Social Movements, Collective Action and Politics* (Cambridge: Cambridge University Press, 1994), 4. Also see Reisinezhad, "The Iranian Green Movement," for a discussion of how the Green Movement fits within the frame of social movement theories.

41. Interview with Farokh Negahdar, March 12, 2010. Negahdar, one of the senior leaders of the Fadayian-e Khalq (majority faction), now lives outside Iran.

42. Text of President Bush's 2002 State of the Union address, January 29, 2002. http://www.washingtonpost.com/wp-srv/onpolitics/transcripts/sou012902.htm.

43. Interview with *BBC Persian*, October 26, 2011.

44. http://www.persian.rfi.fr/node/71213.

45. Interview with Alireza Alavi Tabar, *Jaras*, December 21, 2011. http://www.rahesabz.net/story/46165.

46. "Statement by Political and Civil Activists," *Gooya*, November 13, 2011. http://news.gooya.com/politics/archives/2011/11/131238.php.

47. Mojtaba Vahedi, *"Khanum-e klinton! Khun-e iranian ham qermez ast"* ("Mrs. Clinton! The Blood of Iranians Is Red Too"), *Gooya*, April 5, 2011. http://news.gooya.com/politics/archives/2012/04/138489print.php.

48. "Statement of a Group of Activists inside Iran regarding the Danger of Military Attack," *Gooya*, November 21, 2011. http://news.gooya.com/politics/archives/2011/11/131625.php.

49. "Statement of More than One Hundred Twenty Iranian Intellectuals Condemning the Ruling Regime's Repression and Foreign Intervention in Iran," *Gooya*, November 7, 2011. http://news.gooya.com/politics/archives/2011/11/130882.php.

50. Mohammad Khatami, "Reformist and Non-Reformist Will Stand Up against Foreign Intervention," November 13, 2011. http://www.khatami.ir/fa/news/1048.html.

51. See Mostafa Tajzadeh's letter to Khamenei, *Gooya*, June 11, 2012. http://news.gooya.com/politics/archives/2012/06/141939.php.

52. Author interview with a reformist activist, September 30, 2011.

53. Activists and reformist leaders in Tehran told me as early as 2012 that they believed the ruling elite were contemplating some kind of minimal accommodation and a move toward the center, especially in light of the disastrous experiment with Ahmadinejad.

54. For a praise of Khatami's action, see interview with Abbas Abdi, *Asr-e Ma*, March 21, 2012. http://www.asriran.com/fa/news/206377/%25. For a critical view, see Esmail Nuri-ala, *"Khatami, namad-e bartar-e eslah-talabi"* ("Khatami: the superior symbol of reformism"), *Gooya*, March 19, 2012. http://news.gooya.com/politics/archives/2012/03/137208print.php.

55. Ali Shakurirad, *"Baz ham Khatami!"* ("Khatami again!"), *Norooz*, March 13, 2012. http://norooznews.org/note/2012/03/6/1941.

56. See Mojtaba Vahedi, *"Aghaye Khatami! Shoma ham jaye motaham va moda'i ra avaz kardid"* ("Mr. Khatami! You too changed the place of the defendant with plaintiff"), *Gooya*, March 17, 2012. http://news.gooya.com/politics/archives/2012/03/137574print.php.

57. Nuri acknowledged that the conditions were not yet ripe for reconciliation but left open the possibility and warned against undermining Khatami as the leader of reform. *Jaras*, April 1, 2012. http://www.rahesabz.net/story/51943/.

8 "This Government Is Neither Islamic nor a Republic"

Responses to the 2009 Postelection Crackdown

Shadi Mokhtari

WHEN FACED WITH a crisis that threatens its survival, an authoritarian government often makes either knee-jerk or calculated decisions about whether heightened repression, "managed reform" according to limited concessions, or some combination of the two is more likely to *sustain* the life of the regime. In order to contain the considerable challenge they faced from opposition and popular forces following the 2009 presidential elections, Iran's hard-liners resorted primarily to heightened levels of coercion and repression. The use of such repression by governments is most often discussed in the political science and social movement literature as a constraint on the ability of opposition forces, civil society, or popular movements to challenge authoritarian regimes. Indeed, opposition forces in Iran have been constrained by hard-liners' turn to heightened repression. Yet there is also a flip side to repression and state violence. Under certain circumstances, repressive means such as the use of torture, imprisonment of political opponents, and crackdowns on media can serve as major catalysts for regime delegitimation, which may spur renewed contention.[1]

This chapter presents a composite of the elaborate response to the Iranian government's 2009 crackdown, which emerged from four sources: (1) the de facto leaders of the Green Movement, (2) a group of mostly high-ranking clerics, (3) jailed opposition and civil society activists, and (4) the broader population. It also considers the broader implications of this response in terms of regime delegitimation and prolonged public contention. Acknowledging that the political and public focus on the state's repression has waned since the first months following the 2009 elections, I argue that the issue as a grievance and source of delegitimation has never entirely disappeared from opposition discourses and public consciousness. This means that as both repression and opposition challenges to its deployment continue in Iran, the potential for political change, at least in part spurred by challenges to hard-liners' repression since June 2009, remains a possibility. As a more tangible gain, contention surrounding the coercion deployed has expanded the space for openly and explicitly describing the regimes' various acts of repression and increasingly labeling them as violations of human rights, a term hard-liners had long kept out of political discourse by relegating it to the realm of Western political agendas and cultural values.

Before proceeding, three caveats should be made. First, this chapter does not base its evaluation of the Iranian regime's legitimacy on any set of outside or internationally recognized rights standards, as most human rights assessments tend to do.[2] Instead it is interested in how the regime's repression is framed, interpreted, and evaluated from within Iranian society, and to what degree this weakens hard-liners' position and creates openings for political change and accommodation. Second, while the chapter limits its inquiry to the regime's repression, it recognizes the difficulty of pinpointing or quantifying the delegitimizing effects of the use of repression in isolation. Frequently, disapproval of several policies converges to create widely held perceptions of a government's lack of legitimacy. As a result, multiple grievances, only one of which is the use of repression, may accumulate to prompt cycles of protest, mobilizations, or significant pressure on ruling elites. Thus, while this chapter focuses on repression to highlight its importance as a variable influencing contentious politics in Iran, it also recognizes the limits of considering the variable in isolation. Finally, legitimacy, which can be defined as "a collective judgment that the exercise of power, through a policy or action, is valid even if it is unpopular,"[3] is a relative concept that is difficult to measure or operationalize.[4] The delegitimation effects being considered here are also dynamic, multifaceted, and shifting between actors and over time. These effects often move back and forth between the delegitimation of particular acts of repression, hard-liners who are primarily held responsible for these acts, and the entire postrevolutionary system viewed by some as enabling them through its prevailing ideology and institutions.

Repression and Rights in the History of the Islamic Republic

Although not unique, one of the ironies of contemporary Iranian history is that the use of repression by the Shah served as a major source of delegitimation of and popular grievance against his regime. The Shah's repression was deemed by the revolution's key architects as an indicator of its moral corruption and became a part of the justification for its ouster. Many of the Islamic Republic's leading figures used years of imprisonment and torture in the Shah's prisons as a way to both make the case for political change and bolster their own revolutionary credentials. The presence of freedom in the leading revolutionary chant "*azadi, este-qlal, jomhuri-ye eslami*" (freedom, independence, Islamic Republic) signified the important place of aspirations for liberties and rights, though it arguably stood in a crowded field of aspirations and was soon overshadowed by the centrality accorded to Islamism and anti-imperialism within prevailing ideologies of the era.

As a result of this discourse and the early influence of nationalist figures with liberal commitments, the Iranian Constitution enumerates a host of civil and political rights, though many are qualified with an "except when it is detrimental to the fundamental principles of Islam or the rights of the public" provision. Notably, however, recognition of freedom of belief and the prohibition on torture is not immediately qualified. Other provisions of the Constitution give the Supreme Leader/ jurisprudent (*vali-ye faqih*) sweeping powers, which include limitations on recognized civil and political rights. In the final analysis, as the product of a liberal-Islamist compromise, the Constitution simultaneously enumerates and limits rights meant to prevent the occurrence of the type of repression pervasive during both the Shah's and the Islamic Republic's tenures.

Following just a few months of relative political openness, the 1980s was a decade of high levels of repression in the history of the Islamic Republic. In 1988, thousands of supporters of the Mojahedin-e Khalq, a radical Islamist group, and leftist groups were killed in mass executions. A key (though limited) challenge to these executions was put forth by Ayatollah Hossein-Ali Montazeri, who was at the time the designated successor of Ayatollah Ruhollah Khomeini as Supreme Leader.[5] This intervention was widely viewed as a primary reason his designation as Khomeini's successor was revoked and he was sidelined, ultimately being confined under house arrest.

At this time, any significant criticism of the regime's repression could only be waged from abroad, and it was often done through the language of human rights violations. In response, the regime increasingly labeled human rights a Western, imperialist, and un-Islamic framework. Red lines were quickly drawn around explicit challenges to or even the mention of forms of state repression, and the space to invoke any notion of rights, especially human rights, virtually disappeared within Iran.

The 1990s saw the emergence of ideas and discourses that challenged the monopoly of key tenets underpinning the state-propagated conservative brand of Islamist ideology. The decade saw the prominence of the ideas of the Islamic intellectual Abdolkarim Soroush, namely theories surrounding diversity in interpretations of Islam, tolerance, and pluralism. As well, the decade witnessed the emergence of Islamic feminism, spearheaded from above by women related to the Islamic Republic's male elite and from below by activists, women's circles, and heightened gender consciousness among women from all social strata. Such currents set the stage for the surprise landslide election of reformist Mohammad Khatami, who campaigned and attempted to govern invoking a discourse largely focused on the asserted compatibility of Islam with notions of rights, tolerance, citizenship, and improving conditions for women. While the people's rights, the nation's rights, and citizen's rights were frequently invoked, reformists in Khatami's camp largely steered clear of invoking human rights for fear of hard-liners' charges that they were furthering a Western agenda. At the same time, discussions of rights were predominantly couched in Islamic discourses. Thus the accomplishment of the 1990s (which spilled over into the early 2000s) was the creation of the space to redefine rights as rooted in Islam and talk about rights violations within that medium.

Overall, centralized state repression and violence was less severe when compared to the 1980s and what was to come following the 2009 elections, particularly in relation to freedom of expression and the media. Nonetheless, several episodes of repression are notable. In 1998, Tehran mayor Gholam-Hossein Karbaschi, a reformist ally of Khatami's, was put on trial on corruption charges. His testimony and the testimony of several of his deputies at their televised trial included detailed accounts of their torture while in prison. As Elaine Sciolino points out, prior to the Karbaschi trial, only exiles spoke of torture in Iranian prisons. These accounts of torture from officials within the government, not only on Iranian soil but on national TV, in many respects "broke the torture taboo."[6] Other torture testimonials subsequently appeared in papers, and the Majles took up the question of torture.

During the same period, the serial murders of a number of Iranian dissidents and intellectuals garnered considerable attention and some popular mobilizations. In July 1999, hard-liners instigated a brutal attack on a University of Tehran dormitory that had been a site of protests following the closure of a reformist newspaper. The ensuing crackdown resulted in the imprisonment of over a thousand students who participated in the peaceful protests amid widespread reports of torture. Finally in 2000, an assailant shot in the head Saʻid Hajjarian, another prominent Khatami ally and advisor. Each of these episodes stirred significant though not mass popular disapproval and outrage.

As these battles over what is Islamic and what is un-Islamic with injections of episodes of severe repression took shape, important societal changes also occurred. As Asef Bayat describes, by invoking rights, Khatami (and later the Green Movement) tapped into growing popular aspirations for increased civil and individual liberties fostered by several important social transformations.

> This quest for individual rights partly reflects a broader process of individuation that Iranian society has been undergoing in the thirty years since the 1979 revolution. A creeping modernity has resulted from expanding urbanization (70 percent), increases in general literacy (80 percent) and college education, mobility, and the inescapable footprints of globalization.[7]

Thus, the years leading up to the 2009 elections could be considered a time of increasing popular rights consciousness in Iran.

The 2009 Presidential Election and Its Repressive Aftermath

As Holger Albrecht and Oliver Schlumberger have argued, all regimes "depend on a combination of legitimacy, repression and co-option."[8] Postrevolutionary Iran is certainly no exception. However, as Hossein Bashiriyeh has explained, the Islamic Republic "has faced more or less a chronic crisis of legitimacy."

> Four causes can be identified: (1) the rise of a more republican interpretation of the dominant Islamist ideology; (2) the contradictory nature of the constitution, in terms of seeking to combine theocratic and democratic principles of legitimacy; (3) an increasingly noticeable gap between ruling class practice and its legitimizing ideals and (4) a widening gap between public opinion and official ideology as a result of the increasing secularization of social values and attitudes.[9]

One of the few sources of limited democratic legitimacy the regime did enjoy was derived from the provision of relatively free and fair presidential elections once candidates were filtered through the regime's institutionalized undemocratic vetting process. The depletion of even this limited legitimacy with the announcement of a landslide victory for Mahmud Ahmadinejad amid widespread evidence of foul play presented the hard-liners in power with a severe and potentially explosive crisis of legitimacy. This was especially true given the open debates and discourse, high level of popular engagements, politicization, and mobilizations that materialized in the campaigning leading up to the elections. As Bashiriyeh argues, to maintain its stability, the regime sought to compensate for what now amounted to a "first degree crisis of legitimacy" almost entirely through coercion.[10]

In order to quell the unrest, hard-liners swiftly turned to a variety of tried-and-true repression techniques. First, they attempted to restrict the flow of information and communication by expelling foreign media, imposing restrictions on domestic media not seen since before the Khatami presidency, and limiting internet, texting, and mobile phone access en masse. Despite these measures, cell phone videos and minute-by-minute descriptions of the demonstrations from ordinary citizens nonetheless poured onto the internet, documenting the regime's indiscriminate violence.

At the same time, the government arrested thousands of individuals, some prominent political figures like former vice president Mohammad-Ali Abtahi and some protesters too young to vote or even bystanders. The government soon began airing scripted confessions from gaunt and dazed detainees followed by broadcasts of show trials in which dozens of imprisoned individuals were seated awaiting their turn to confess and apologize to the regime. During this time several death sentences were also issued, and in January 2010 two men were executed. Perhaps most significant, word of systematic rape perpetrated by security officials against detainees emerged. Kahrizak prison, where many allegations of rape put forth by victims occurred, soon became synonymous with state-perpetrated rape of prisoners. Both Mir-Hossein Mussavi and Mehdi Karrubi took up the issue of arbitrary detentions and allegations of torture publicly and formed committees to investigate and monitor detainee rights; however, Karrubi boldly also took on the rape allegations by publicly announcing on August 11, 2009, that detained protesters were being systematically raped, publishing the detailed account of a young male victim and threatening to go public with more accounts if the issue was not investigated. His campaign's Committee for Following Detainees and Injured compiled information on abuse cases, including photographic evidence of bruises caused by rape, telephone numbers of those who had been abused, and detailed videotaped victims' accounts. He presented evidence of the rapes and other torture before both a parliamentary committee and a judiciary committee charged with investigating the allegations.

Several cases early in the crackdown prompted considerable public outcry and attention. They included the cases of Neda Agha Soltan, a twenty-six-year-old woman who was shot by a Basij militiaman during the initial round of postelection protests, the life leaving her body vividly captured on a cell phone video and viewed by millions on the internet; Mohsen Ruholamini, the son of top conservative politician Abolhossein Ruholamini, who was tortured and killed in Kahrizak prison; Sohrab A'rabi, whose death at the hand of officials prompted protests and dramatic challenges to the regime by his mother; Taraneh Mousavi, of whom Karrubi initially spoke as a case of a young women having been raped and killed but that was later disputed; and student leader Majid Tavakoli, whose arrest for giving a speech criticizing the regime was accompanied by a picture of him wearing a female *hejab*. While occurrence of such highly dramatic cases largely died down by the start of 2010, the state's repression persisted largely unabated for some time. Aside from the February 2011 house arrests of Karrubi and Mussavi, perhaps the most prominent case of repression to emerge was the 2011 deaths of two of political prisoners, Haleh Sahabi and (to a lesser extent) Hoda Saber.

Opposition/Green Movement Response

A central tenet of the Green Movement's response to the 2009 elections and their aftermath was to challenge and ultimately weaken hard-liners by exposing and condemning their extensive resort to repression. The Green Movement's two de facto leaders, Mussavi and Karrubi, reacted to the violence and repression in several ways before they were placed under house arrest in February 2011.

The first strategy pursued involved collecting evidence of the state's violence and taking it directly to the public. Shortly after the elections, Karrubi and his aides undertook the most elaborate attempt to document and publicly disclose the regime's systematic use of torture and rape to take place from within post-revolutionary Iran. This act of compiling videotaped accounts of gruesome prison abuse, medical records, and pictures was an overt challenge to the regime's legitimacy. After compiling this information, Karrubi and his team took much of it to the public, presenting it along with repeated emotional appeals, which humanized the victims and highlighted the injustice they suffered. His statement on the report of the government's Three Person Committee provides an example of this.

> Oh God, what has Mehdi Karrubi seen and heard? What strange things! Would that he were not alive to see the days in which in the Islamic Republic, citizens would come to him and reveal that in an anonymous and unmarked building at the hands of people who are even more anonymous and unknown, any obscene or un-natural act was committed against them, from making them naked and seating them in front of each other, to obscene insults to urinating on their faces to leaving girls and boys blind-folded and hands tied in the middle of nowhere. All of this was not enough that news of the rape of girls and boys in detention centers reached me. I said to myself three decades after the Revolution and two decades after the death of the Imam, where have we arrived?[11]

Several factors made Karrubi's taking up of the rape accusations particularly significant. First, the fact that the allegations were being made by a former Parliament speaker with a long-held insider status and widely asserted allegiance to the Islamic Republic made them highly credible. Second, the detailed descriptions of the suffering of the victims and their families in demonstrating a systematic pattern of mistreatment had "the effect of dramatizing and publicizing previously hidden forms of state violence."[12] Finally, the fact that the accounts were not only of torture but of systematic rapes of young men and women made bringing them to light particularly damaging given the regime's asserted commitment to promoting Islamic morality and the elaborate lengths it has taken to regulate sexual behavior.

Beyond this initial documentation and publicizing of hard-liners' violence, both Karrubi and Mussavi repeatedly referenced the regime's crackdown, arrests, and abuse. Virtually every statement put out by Mussavi encompassed a list of demands centered on eliminating or redressing the repressive measures taken by the regime, namely the freeing of political prisoners, accountability for the torture and violence against protesters and dissidents, and the meaningful provision of freedoms of the press and speech. In their statements, speeches, and interviews, the two men frequently point to the repression being carried out. In one statement, Mussavi asserts,

> They say that the children of the revolution have confessed to ties with foreign powers and plans to topple the Islamic Republic of the Iran. I personally

listened carefully to what they had to say and did not find such meaning in their words. Rather, I heard a deep cry of sorrow of all that had become of them in the past fifty days; a crushed people who would have confessed to anything else that they were forced. Really, what other stories except of the pain they have endured would they speak?[13]

Both men and their outspoken spouses also repeatedly disclosed how they and their families were perpetually targeted and subjected to the state's violence in an effort to silence them. The most dramatic incidents revolved around the murder of Mussavi's nephew and the torture and threatened rape of Karrubi's son. Both leaders repeatedly called such violent episodes no worse than the fate being suffered by so many other Iranians and vowed to continue their resistance.

Second, the Green Movement's de facto leaders frequently engaged in explicit shaming of hard-liners through entwining secular, religious, and ideological discourses. The arrests, torture, and restrictions on speech and assembly were alternatively referred to as "vicious acts," "violations of the law," "violations of specific provisions of the constitution," "un-Islamic," contrary to the ideals of the Islamic revolution, worse than the Shah's repression, and "veering from the path of justice." For example, in his Statement Number Nine, Mussavi made a plea for a "return to Islam, honesty, reason, the law and the people."[14] In some instances the shaming was directed at high-level figures, for example in highly publicized and often public letters to figures such as former president Akbar Hashemi Rafsanjani and two heads of the judiciary in place since the elections, in which the allegations of crimes and violence were iterated and the leaders were asked to intervene. More often, the shaming was directed at the entire hard-liner camp.

The Green Movement leaders frequently invoked broad notions of justice. One example of this is the following statement by Mussavi:

> News of detainment of our dear brothers, Dr. Seyed Ali-Reza Beheshti and Morteza Alviri (both responsible for the committee investigating injuries triggered by recent events), and [former] Commander Moqadam (responsible for the Devotees Committee of my election campaign), have produced waves of doubt and shock in those devoted to the Islamic establishment. They are held captive while guilty of nothing but following the path of the revolution, demanding justice for unjustly spilled blood, and assisting the families of the innocents imprisoned after the election. Right now they are in prison, while those who committed the recent atrocities are free. Meanwhile, the officials responsible claim that they will categorically investigate the recent violence. Are they doing so by destroying the evidence of crimes committed and by imprisoning those who are pursuing the rights of the victims?[15]

Beyond appealing to the universal notions of justice, Mussavi and Karrubi invoke the rule of law and constitutionalism, holding that the regime is breaking the law. "Shooting into crowds, the militarization of city space, creating fear, and showcasing power are all the illegitimate offspring of an aversion to the law."[16] Similarly, various rights guarantees of the Islamic Republic's Constitution are repeatedly invoked. The argument offered is that none of the repression taking shape would be possible if the law and particularly the Constitution were faithfully followed. As Mussavi put forth, "our Constitution is full of unrealized potential."[17] In contrast to the hard-liners, the Green Movement is described by its leaders as committed to the law, for example, in explaining why the Green Movement repeatedly seeks to obtain permits to hold protests when it is clear that the requests will be denied by the hard-liners in power. Karrubi argued that doing so was motivated by a desire to demonstrate the Green Movement's intention to operate according to the law.[18]

A subsequent form of shaming and framing revolved around hard-liners' betrayal of the values of the Islamic Revolution and Khomeini. "That which has transpired these days is targeting the foundation of the Islamic Republic which is the legacy of our great Imam [Khomeini] and the valued martyrs [of the revolution]."[19] In this discourse, what the Green Movement strived for was in line with the values of the revolution. Mussavi argued that what people are fighting for now is the realization of the forgotten ideals of the revolution, namely "freedom, freedom of expression, freedom after expression, the freedom to be elected and to elect," slogans, which he pointedly noted were at the heart of the aspirations of Iran's Revolution but are now viewed as antirevolutionary.[20] In the same spirit, Karrubi not only humanizes the victims he describes but lays out their religious and revolutionary credentials and allegiances. This is seen in one statement where he describes his interactions with the father of one of the rape victims who brought his account to Karrubi. Karrubi quotes the father as saying, "We are Muslim and religious and why have they done this to us?" In an attempt to shame the Supreme Leader, he then recounts that the father took out a photo from his pocket. The photo was of another son who was pictured in the hospital recovering from wounds suffered from fighting in the Iran-Iraq War. Also pictured was then president Khamenei, who Karrubi reveals had been visiting the soldier.[21] Similarly, at one point Mussavi demands that the hard-liners "release the children of the revolution from prisons."[22] Further, the Green Movement leaders make parallels with the reviled repression of the Shah. For example, in one statement, Karrubi pleads for a public trial. "If you have honor and courage, at the very least, act as the Shah's government did. He persecuted tens of resisters with differing beliefs, at the very least their trials were made public in newspapers."[23]

Another form of shaming and delegitimization involved repeated assertions that the hard-liners' behavior was un-Islamic and lacking in Islamic jurisprudential foundation.[24] At one point, Karrubi expressed his frustration at the unwillingness of the judiciary to pursue the torture and rape allegations he was bringing forth by pointing to the institution's purported mission of upholding the justice of the revered Shi'i Imam Ali. "It is a disgrace as the commander of the faithful agonized over even having to remove an anklet from the foot of a Jewish woman and was the model of justice and once when he appeared in court in which a Jew had put forth a complaint and the judge addressed him informally, . . . [Ali] objected and said that in the course of judgment, he and I are equals."[25]

In addition to naming, shaming, and humanizing the victims, Mussavi and to a lesser extent Karrubi frequently invoked rights and the need to uphold human dignity.[26] A number of formulations were used regarding the rights being violated. Mussavi speaks of "fundamental citizenship rights," "the people's lost rights," and "the nation's rights." As the conflict with the hard-liners over the elections and the postelection crackdown drags on, he also invokes human rights. In his Statement Number Fifteen, Mussavi directly responds to hard-liners' attempts to delegitimize the human rights idea through anti-imperialist discourses.

> Do you not claim that expressions such as human rights, women's rights, minority rights and the like are excuses world powers hypocritically co-opt to beautify themselves? Why are they who are supposedly the original and primary owners of these values then far from [realizing] them? Is it that they seek to taint their school [of thought]? Why do you curse these concepts and render them the standard for heresy? A religion that has gifted a bushel of flowers for humanity with its mild teachings which are compatible with human nature. God forbid, we turn it into a bushel of thorns so that anyone who has contact with any corner of it is wounded—wounds like those our youth see in the streets.[27]

Later he further declares, "Today more than ever, people recognize the violation of the nation's fundamental rights and they are conscious of the repeated violations of human rights and human dignity in this judicial-security regime."[28] He then goes on to cite human dignity and human rights as the top value of the Green Movement:

> The first value of the Green Movement is the defense of human dignity and fundamental human rights irrespective of ideology, religion, gender ethnicity and social status. The establishment and guarantee of human rights principles as one of the most important achievements of humanity and the fruit of the collective rationality of all human beings is approved and emphasized by the Green Movement. These rights are God-given and no ruler, government, parliament or power can nullify or unjustifiably or arbitrarily limit them.[29]

Next, the two men repeatedly issue warnings to hard-liners and the leaders of institutions under their control such as the Islamic Revolution's Guard Corps (IRGC) that they risk losing or have already lost their legitimacy with the people.

In his Statement Number Four, Mussavi states, "I denounce the recent widespread arrests and warn that further such acts only reveal the ugliness of those opposing the people and increases the popular will to protest."[30] Elsewhere he warns, "Allow voices to refine and adjust their views through reason and debate in existing publications before these voices turn into shouts."[31] As the crisis progresses, the warnings turn to declarations that those in power have lost their legitimacy. "Unless we lose hope, this government will not enjoy legitimacy."[32] Elsewhere Mussavi rhetorically asks, "We can say that for a few days through arrests, violence, threats and the stifling of newspapers you create silence. How are you going to solve people's changed judgment about the regime? How are you going to make up for your destroyed legitimacy?"[33] Along these lines the two leaders assert that hard-liners are out of touch with popular sentiment while the Green Movement is in step with it. "In addition to strongly condemning the violent, inhumane and un-Islamic response, we warn you to remove the cotton from your ears and listen to people's voices," Karrubi asserts.[34] "The Kahrizak catastrophe and the murders of the 25th and 30th of Khordad and Hossein's *Ashura* will not be erased from people's collective memory and it should not be as it is a betrayal of the lives of the martyred and innocents. How can we forget the direct shots fired at people and the running over of people by police cars?"[35]

Finally, the Green Movement leaders aggressively engaged in and solicited interventions from influential clerics. One of the institutions the literature on democratization and political change recognizes as key to whether mobilizations for political change succeed is the military. This can take place through either defections at the top or refusals to follow orders by soldiers at the bottom. In fact, a great deal of the success of Iran's 1979 revolution has often been attributed to soldiers' refusals to crack down on protesters and carry out repression. Although in the 2009 crackdown there were isolated reports of defections rooted in outrage over torture and other repressive means, for a variety of reasons, military defections (both from the top and from below) were limited. Yet the structure of the Islamic Republic lent itself to another institution—the clerical establishment—playing a similarly critical role through deflections either from the top or from below. Although they do not have the crucial link to state violence of the military, because of the Islamic Republic's unique structure deriving considerable legitimacy from the clergy, such deflections can weaken the position of the hard-liners in power. Sensing this potentially pivotal role of the clergy, the leaders of the Green Movement repeatedly tried to persuade key members of the clergy to intervene on their behalf. They made repeated trips to Qom to make personal appeals and engaged in dialogue, deliberation, persuasion, and indirect shaming with high-ranking clerics. Like some of those languishing in jail, they wrote open letters asking clerics to issue rulings on the government's postelection actions, rendering the government's repression a matter of Islamic jurisprudence and religious morality.

The Clerics' Response

The clerical establishment and the Islamic Republic's ruling elite have a symbiotic relationship. The self-proclaimed Islamic state relies on the *ulama* in Qom to legitimate its claim to "Islamic rule," and the *ulama* rely on the state for maintaining an order that affords them a privileged position and ample financial backing of their key institutions. In the aftermath of the 2009 elections, most clerics found themselves in a precarious position. On one hand, they faced pressure from hardliners to sanction "the foreign conspiracy and internal sedition (*fetneh*)" version of events while turning a blind eye to the widespread assault on protesters and opponents. On the other hand, they faced pressure from the opposition and family members of political prisoners to condemn the violence and align themselves with popular sentiment. Only a handful of mostly high-ranking members of the *ulama* chose to publicly criticize or condemn the postelection repression. Another handful with close ties to the hard-liners validated the crackdown. The remaining clerics opted for the intermediary position of maintaining a prolonged silence amid unease over their associations with the regime.

While the number of vocal critics from among the ranks of the *ulama* was limited, two factors made their interventions highly significant. First, many of the regime's Qom critics were among the highest-ranking members of the *ulama*. Second, in their challenges to the hard-liners, these critics deployed increasingly bold and delegitimizing language. Many of these *ulama* critics themselves become subject to silencing and violence by the state. In October 2010, the websites of Ayatollahs Yusef Sane'i, Assadollah Bayat Zanjani, and Seyyed Ali-Mohammad Dastgheib were shut down. Pro-hard-line vigilantes repeatedly showed up at the homes of Grand Ayatollah Hossein-Ali Montazeri and Ayatollah Sane'i and ransacked their offices. Such measures shed light on how threatened hard-liners felt by these interventions.

The key challengers emerging from among the ranks of the *ulama* are worth briefly introducing. Grand Ayatollah Montazeri was widely regarded as the most senior Shi'i authority in Iran. A longtime critic of hard-liners, he quickly came to be viewed as the spiritual leader of the opposition whose death in December 2010 dealt a blow to the Green Movement. Ayatollah Sane'i has long put forth modernist interpretations of Islamic jurisprudence, but his challenges to the state became more overtly political following the 2009 elections. Ayatollah Bayat Zanjani had been one of the harshest critics of the absolute power of the leader among leading clerics. Ayatollah Mahmud Amjad Kermanshahi has reformist leanings and was dismissed from his local Friday prayer leader position for his refusal to close with a prayer for Khamenei's health. Ayatollah Dastgheib has been a vocal critic of Khamenei and postelection developments in the Assembly of Experts. Ayatollah Abdul-Karim Mussavi Ardebili served as the head of Iran's judiciary for most of the 1980s. Finally, the Assembly of Qom Scholars and Researchers consists of midranking clerics who had long weighed in on political contests on the side of reformists.

Clerics who have either directly aligned themselves with the Green Movement or were willing to provide public displays of sympathizing with and validating its criticism of the hard-liners did so in a number of ways. They issued religious edicts in response to questions posed by members of the Green Movement or imprisoned dissidents, wrote condolence letters to family members of those affected by postelection repression, gave interviews or speeches on the subject, and repeatedly met with members of the Green Movement and family members of those killed or imprisoned. Ayatollah Mussavi Ardebili is even reported to have visited Khamenei though he was sick and in a wheelchair, asking him to "release all of the prisoners of the recent events without any conditions and stipulations."[36] In Qom, Montazeri and Sane'i met to discuss developments and publicized the meeting as ending with a prayer for the release of innocent political prisoners and the country being saved from its current crisis.[37]

Perhaps the most forceful and elaborate challenge to the regime emerging from among clerics was the July 10, 2009, fatwa issued by Montazeri in response to a series of questions posed in a letter by exiled cleric Mohsen Kadivar.[38] Both Kadivar's letter and Montazeri's response address the regime's repression extensively. In particular, question three lays out a list of what Kadivar calls "cardinal sins" ranging from "ordering and causing the murder of innocent individuals" and extracting false confessions to "prevention of the circulation of false information and censorship of the news." Ultimately Montazeri's ruling is that such acts are un-Islamic and require popular and elite interventions to unseat those who are committing them.

The appeals take place within the context of decreasing legitimacy and popularity of clerics in Iran, a phenomenon many seem to be aware of. While most of the *ulama* who intervene have a history of modernist or reformist sympathies, several of them reference feeling ashamed or feeling the moral stigma of being associated with the regime's violence and repression. Dastgheib recounts one such exchange.

> While a young man was showing his wounds, his friend said, "Is this the definition of Islamic Republic? Would the same thing have happened during the time of the Shah?" Of course, the past was worse than now, but seeing this scene gripped me with shame and I did not have any answer to give him. Is this the right way to deal with Muslim and Shi'a people?[39]

In general, the discourse, arguments, and tactics of these dissident clerics intertwined Islamist and secular discourses and echo those of the leaders of the Green Movement but have their own orientation given the added element of religious authority. To begin with, sympathetic clerics are explicit in describing the repression taking place and the underlying injustice they encompass. "The innocent are killed. People's private and collective space is violated. Legal and fundamental freedoms that are most basic rights of every human being are violated such that fatigue and depression sits on the faces of young and old alike . . . lies and deception rule," Ayatollah Amjad is quoted as saying.[40] Ayatollah Dastgheib writes, "We witness the beating of innocent people, especially university students, the filling up of the prisons and extreme interrogations which are not hidden to anyone."[41] These descriptions are often highly emotional and sympathetic. For example, Ayatollah Sane'i puts forth, "If you do not have children you do not know what a child is . . . target their heart . . . and then call it meningitis or [say] that a contagious disease hit a prison. Who is responsible for a contagious disease? They are responsible."[42]

Several clerics speak of oppression at the hands of the Islamic Republic, playing on a central theme in the Shi'i tradition and the discourse of the revolution. Ayatollah Sane'i also responds to charges that those challenging the regime are sowing disunity: "They say why do you create division? The oppressors and the oppressed always have disunity."[43] Ayatollah Dastgheib states, "They said come and take part in the elections. They did and now they hit them in the head with clubs. Well, this is oppression. Then they say, don't say anything. Why should we not say anything? That which we see and that which we know, we should not say?"[44]

Elsewhere these clerics extensively invoke principles of Islamic jurisprudence and Islamic justice often derived from the practice of the Shi'i imams more directly. For these clerics, hard-liners' behavior is un-Islamic. Sane'i appeals to his audience to "tell people that Islam says that you cannot run matters with assassinations, torture, prison and murder"[45] and asserts elsewhere that "this type of authoritarianism is unprecedented in history. It knows no God, no prophet, no politics . . . this authoritarianism knows nothing."[46] In a meeting with families of political prisoners in January 2011, Amjad asks,

> How is it possible for anyone to be an Islamic scholar and speak about Islam, but be indifferent about what has happened? How can one be patient when one hears about the attacks on the universities in the middle of the night and the beating of innocent students? I have stopped all of my work and do not go anywhere, because I have no answer for such questions. Should I say this is Islam? That what has happened has been humane?[47]

Similarly, Dastgheib appeals, "Once again I ask you to listen to the legitimate and reasonable desires of this Muslim people. Abide by the Quran and the tradition (*sunna*) and the Constitution and stop all of this illegal and un-Islamic behavior in the name of preserving the regime."[48]

Challenging repression in turn becomes an obligation under the Quranic notion of "enjoining good and forbidding evil," which in postrevolutionary Iran has largely revolved around policing the *hejab* and rules about gender segregation in public. The principle is first invoked in relation to the postelection repression by Ayatollah Montazeri in his July 2009 fatwa, and others soon follow suit. After discussing the injustices resulting in the hunger strikes of political prisoners, Dastgheib calls on his fellow just *ulama* and *foqaha* to break their silence and engage in enjoining good and forbidding evil.[49]

The clerics also take up jurisprudential discussions of specific forms of repression. Bayat Zanjani puts forth that if we looked at the five-year rule of Imam Ali, there was not a single political prisoner. Dastgheib in a letter to the Assembly of Experts writes, "It is said that confessions in prison have been used as evidence of crimes. It must be said that no source of emulation would be able to give a fatwa endorsing such confessions. Thus as a matter of Islamic law, they do not constitute evidence."[50] Similarly Sane'i argues that Imam Ali has stated that confessions resulting from solitary confinement, imprisonment, or threats are invalid.[51] Bayat Zanjani states that in an Islamic government following Ali's path, as long a person's hand was not corrupted by blood, there was no right to detain or chase or pressure an opponent.[52] At one point Ayatollah Sane'i even states that "Listening to media that lies is against the Quran."[53]

Several of these clerics seem to view Islamic prescriptions and values as largely overlapping with human reason and global values. As a result, they often cite the Islamic Republic's Constitution, "the law," and various notions of rights. Mussavi Ardebili states that "it is regrettable and sad, however, that what is done by some in the name of defending Islam and Islamic government is against the religion, the law, morality, and human rights, and threatens the spirit of justice, search for the truth, and freedom that must be the basis for any government that is based on Islamic teachings."[54] Bayat Zanjani says that the many "strange" and "regrettable" ways in which confessions are obtained today have no legal or Islamic basis.[55] Elsewhere he states, "Human rights from the perspective of Islam and sacred shari'a is not a passive and peripheral issue. These rights have monotheistic and divine root."[56] Montazeri's fatwa also repeatedly invokes rights and refers jointly to the parameters of religion and reason in his indictment of the regime's repression.[57]

Finally, like the leaders of the Green Movement, this group of sympathetic clerics engaged in attempts to shame both the hard-liners in power and fellow clerics who have remained silent. Montazeri challenges the regime to "at least have the courage to announce that this government is neither Islamic nor a Republic and that no one has the right to object, present their views or criticize," arguing that what we see before us "is not the rule of the jurist, but the rule of the military."[58] Dastgheib writes to the Assembly of Experts: "It would be good for you to object to the illegitimate torture in prisons that produces a new corpse every day."[59] Pointedly directing its focus to fellow clerics, the Assembly of Qom Scholars and Researchers warns, "The destiny of the seminaries and the *ulama* is tied to the destiny of the regime. And if people come to view the regime as against them, they will undoubtedly come to view clerics and seminaries as against them."[60]

Again echoing Green Movement leaders, parallels to the Shah's regime were made along with claims that the regime was straying from Khomeini's path. "If it were possible to govern by creating fear and silencing and authoritarianism and oppression and filling up the prisons with the elite and those who desire freedom and opposing political groups, then the Shah's regime would have endured," Montazeri states.[61] Dastgheib says, "See what they did to people during the Pahlavi era. And now that it is an Islamic Republic, if people see that their source of emulation is silent in the face of their repression, it is clear that they will stop emulating and they will stop going to mosques."[62] Ayatollah Sane'i asks rhetorically if Khomeini ever aimed to target and shoot straight at people's hearts.[63]

It is difficult to assess the impact of the state's repression and these limited but forceful interventions on hard-liners, clerics opting for quietism within an Islamic state that purports to be ruled by jurists, and more devout segments of the population. One sign that clerics were uncomfortable with associating themselves with those at the helm of power came from reports that many high-ranking clerics were unwilling to congratulate Ahmadinejad for his asserted election victory and, more importantly, to meet with Khamenei in an official trip to Qom following the elections.[64] In fact, it is reported that Khamenei was forced to make several "unofficial" trips to Qom before he eventually made an official trip in which a substantial enough number of high-ranking clerics were willing to publicly meet with him.[65] Some clerics' growing unease with being associated with state repression is reflected in a report that after hearing the stories of political prisoners' families, Ayatollah Hossein Vahid Khorasani stated, "I have no relationship with these men and I have repeatedly issued warnings to their representatives who contact me."[66]

In the final analysis, the interventions by prominent clerics chronicled here would be significant in any Muslim world context but particularly in the Islamic Republic built around the idea of rule of the jurist. Religious leaders do not live in a vacuum from the wider social and political dynamics taking shape in their societies, and if the repressive measures taken by hard-liners against their most vocal clerical critics continue and expand, Iran's clerical establishment may be increasingly tied to future attempts to challenge their rule.

The Response from Activists

From the early days of the crackdown through the present, a long list of individuals falling in the categories of members of the opposition, journalists, lawyers, and an exponentially expanding number of individuals identified as "human rights activists" have been detained. As these detentions have dragged on, the plight of these individuals widely referred to as political prisoners has remained in public political consciousness through their own efforts and those of their families. These activists and their families created a third pillar of indictments of the state and its reliance on repression in the aftermath of the 2009 elections.

While the unprecedented postdetention efforts to document and record accounts of the occurrence of systematic torture and rape posed bold and unprecedented challenges to the regime, virtually all avenues for such activism from within Iran were quickly closed. Instead, as more and more activists were detained, their activism took the form of defiant hunger strikes and a voluminous body of public letters. Even activists who were not in prison sometimes took to penning a letter with the knowledge that their words could easily result in their imprisonment. Others wrote defiantly postimprisonment and between repeated detentions. While these public letters take several forms, what virtually all have in common is a description of the violence and indignities to which political prisoners are subjected and the various aspects of the injustices they endured. Some of the letters like that written by Mehdi Mohammadian are written almost as a human rights report in which, following an introductory verse from the Quran, an array of physiological, physical, and sexual violence perpetrated by officials and other (nonpolitical) prisoners with the knowledge and/or facilitation of officials is detailed.[67] Other letters offer vivid descriptions of torture and sexual abuse and engage in more unmistakable and direct forms of shaming. Perhaps one of the clearest examples of this is found in a November 2010 letter from Mohammad Nurizad, a former columnist for the ultraconservative *Keyhan* newspaper, to judiciary chief Sadeq Amoli Larijani, who had criticized British treatment of rioters in 2010:

> I suggest you that any time that you are in front of the mirror, you comb your hair and put on cologne, think of the heads of your country's political prisoners that have been dunked in the toilet bowls of their cells. I don't know if anyone has ever repeatedly slapped you on the face? Or has hit you in your chest or back with a shoe? Or has kicked you in your face with a foot? Or has spit between your eyebrows and your eyes?
> I confidently say that if you had slightly believed the savagery of our [country's] intelligence forces, you would set aside objecting to British police. I don't know if ever someone, in the middle of your being helpless and under rains of blows and kicks, has outrageously insulted your wife? Or has called your pure daughter a prostitute? Or has tainted your mother, sister or your other chaste family members with sexual comments? I don't think so; but some of the personnel of the ministry of intelligence, who are wearing the mask of soldiers of Imam Mahdi (the last Imam of She'a [sic]), did this to us.[68]

The writers tell of the abuses and violence they have experienced and what they have seen and heard perpetrated against others. While initially these prison letters were addressed to high-ranking officials short of the Supreme Leader, as the crackdown continued, more letters were addressed directly to Khamenei himself. By the beginning of 2012, the most galvanizing of those letters became a series written by Nurizad, who in vivid, emotionally charged language imbued with religious references proceeds to hold the Supreme Leader personally responsible for the repression, corruption and un-Islamic attributes of the self-proclaimed Islamic state.

In these letters, the notion that rights are being violated is either assumed or stated explicitly. An August 2010 letter by fifteen political activists who had staged a hunger strike in their ward begins, "We will continue to insist on our human rights and the basic rights of all prisoners. We pledge to continue to fight until all prisoners who are part of our beloved nation gain access to their full legal rights."[69] While Nurizad is perhaps the most unlikely candidate to deploy the language of universal rights given his lifelong immersion in conservative discourses, which designate the language of human rights as "Western" and "imperialist," he does so with considerable ease. This is evident in a December 2011 interview.

> I am saying that when it is accepted in the world that protesting is people's right, this protest will not necessarily lead to our downfall. We should understand this and not take this right away from people. This is not an invitation to revolt. It is the realization of the violated rights of these people. . . . These people should be able to breathe. A whole litany of rights has been denied to these people in these 32 years. Our intent is for these people to attain their inherent rights. I wrote to Mr. Khamenei in my Letter Number Fourteen that if you were in Mr. Mussavi's place, you could better judge how they should treat you. If they were to imprison you, how would you like them to treat you? You would want a fair trial in which you had the chance to defend yourself. So, why do you not make these provisions for others? It is their right to be free.[70]

Nurizad's statement speaks to both how far the "logic" and applicability of notions of rights has seeped into the Islamic Republic's political culture and discourse, and the contribution of activists to that end. But while for Nurizad there is no contradiction or conflict between Islamist commitments and human rights, in the end, the hard-liners' claim to upholding Islam renders their acts of repression most appalling to him. In another part of his 2010 letter to Amoli Larijani, Nurizad writes, "The British government, if it claims to respect human rights, has never claimed to be abiding by God, Quran, the prophet and holy Imams."[71]

Another set of public letters addressed prominent clergy, in effect sometimes inviting them, sometimes shaming them into intervening on their behalf. The letters contained questions such as, "Does solitary confinement constitute torture?" or "Is solitary confinement in an Islamic order such as ours forbidden or allowed?"[72] In their form, they solicit jurisprudential rulings, but in the tradition of Shi'i political activism revived by Khomeini and instituted by the Islamic Republic, they skirt the boundaries between religious rulings and politics.

Finally, a third genre of postelection public letters is those exchanged by political prisoners and their spouses, parents, and children. In these letters prisoners and their families express their love and longing for each other and put forth repeated indictments of their unjust predicament. If more politically (or even legally) oriented letters focus on the regime's brutality, these "love letters" focus on the victim in a way that humanizes them and allows readers to identify with them as mothers and fathers, spouses, or children, in effect taking a different path to highlighting the injustice of hard-liners' repression.

Beyond helping to publicize their letters, these activists' families brought their voices to the public in a variety of other ways. Activists' family members regularly staged protests in front of prisons, gave interviews to media, and tried to meet with and solicit the intervention of any prominent political or religious figures that would meet with them and then publicized the meetings and expressions of support that emerged. Early on, Abolhossein Ruholamini and the father of another protester who died at Kahrizak, Mohammad Kamrani, met with the Supreme Leader to demand an investigation. The mother of Sohrab A'rabi, who was shot after participating in protests, repeatedly and publicly challenged the regime's violence resulting in her son's death. She protested outside government buildings and prisons and spoke before the Tehran City Council, rhetorically asking, "For what crime was my son killed?" She also became a key member of the "Mourning Mothers," who, reminiscent of Argentina's Mothers of the Playa de Mayo, staged weekly protests in Laleh Park. Often the family members of detained political prisoners visited Qom to solicit interventions from the *ulama*. In December 2010, Nurizad's family met with six Ayatollahs—Mussavi Ardabili, Vahid Khorasani, Sane'i, Bayat Zanjani, Abdollah Javadi Amoli, and Mohammad-Ali Gerami. It was then reported that "the senior clerics sympathized with Nurizad's family and emphasized that inhumane treatment of prisoners is against the teachings of Islam."[73]

Viewed cumulatively, these efforts by activists and their families served the important function of keeping the flames of dissent alive. Still, from a critical perspective, there is the question of whether this activism and in particular the prison letters serve as what has been discussed as licensed, permitted, commissioned, or bought critique, all speaking to some form of the dynamic in which an authoritarian regime provides a limited outlet for accumulating public outrage through some public critique in order to prevent a larger explosion.[74] In a similar vein, Hamid Dabashi also notes a line of criticism that maintains that "the sorts of letters that Nourizad [sic] and others like him write to the Supreme Leader, in fact, perpetuate the cult of heroes and heroism, reducing collective political actions at a mass societal level to individual acts of defiance."[75] An in-depth treatment of each of these lines of inquiry is beyond the scope of this chapter. However, even if elements of each are present, the simultaneous and likely greater impact of the activism of these prisoners and their families is to generate public sympathy and retain a steady level of public consciousness of the injustice stemming from the regime's repression.

The Popular Response

Even in Iran's increasingly authoritarian setting, the fate of the hard-liners in power and the Green Movement as well as the status of clerics are intimately tied to popular perceptions of them and the extent to which their behavior impacts societal assessments of their legitimacy, including their adherence to prevailing social and religious norms. The Green Movement and opposition forces undoubtedly tried to use leverage from popular outrage and potential popular mobilizations to strengthen their position. Thus, it is critical to consider how that postelection repression was viewed and interpreted from below.

Repression can produce popular responses ranging from acquiescence to resistance. While it is impossible to predict where on this continuum the response to an act or episode of repression will fall, several factors can be identified as significant indicators of the outcome. One key factor is whether and to what extent repression comes to occupy the fore of public consciousness. Most repression resides in the periphery of public consciousness, where the population primarily coexists with it. Even when people contemplate and condemn the repression, they are not prompted to engage in public contention, which could render them victims of the repression. Public contention remains limited to a small number of activists. The repression may detract from regime legitimacy but is not a dominant factor in overall assessments of legitimacy. Yet at particular times, repression can be pushed to the fore of public consciousness, where it comes to dominate political discourse, becomes viewed as a grievance by significant segments of the population, and in some instances prompts public contention.

For most of its tenure, the Islamic Republic had successfully employed at times substantial, at times low, but always constant, repression to secure its rule. Since the early months of the revolution, people in Iran have gone about their lives with the knowledge that they did not live in a free society and that dissent entailed serious consequences, including stints at Iran's notorious prisons and physical violence. Yet they were able to push aside this knowledge and take on the daily grind without an intense focus on the repression under which they lived. While repressive means such as torture, arrests of opponents, and restrictions on media and free speech were generally not acceptable to many within the population, they structured their lives around the state's restrictions on political participation and expression and threats of violence to enforce these restrictions. There were many instances of outrage and reflection on the role or pervasiveness of repression, but there was not an impetus to engage in public contention over it. An underlying hope to which those who desired change clung as postrevolutionary politics evolved was that through their support of reformist candidates, the state's repression would incrementally subside. Yet the dramatic manner in which hard-liners demonstrated that the doors to incremental change through reform were largely closed and the equally dramatic surge in repression they undertook to drive home the point prompted the public to push aside their willingness to coexist with the repression they faced and actively resist it.

Thus, in the first few months following the 2009 disputed elections, acquiescence gave way to collective action. A handful of individuals emerged to publicly disclose egregious acts of repression committed by the state. Among them there was a sense that the truth about the regime's violence can no longer remain unspoken. Arash Hejazi, the doctor who tried to help Neda Agha Soltan, articulated the sentiment behind his actions, stating, "In every life, a moment comes that the integrity of some person would be tested, and I realized on that day this was the moment in my life that I had to choose whether to keep myself safe or prove my integrity."[76]

A similar sensibility is evident among the large numbers of Iranians who took part in some form of public contention. On multiple occasions between June and December 2010, they mobilized in the face of the state's repression. Not only did many participants seemed undeterred by the prospects of falling victim to such violence, such acts of repression seem to breed further indignation, outrage, and resistance. In some instances, the more drastic the repressive measures the state resorted to, the more appalled and defiant were the popular forces who did not expect such backslide into repression. This account of just one of the street battles that took place is indicative of the ethos of the early protests.

> In one of the first films to be circulated, students behind the gates of Tehran University can be heard taunting the surveillance-actions of the security forces. A young man raises his hand in a victory-sign and invites a close-up photo: "Filthy regime sell-out, take it." A notable aspect of much of the footage is that it is the cameramen seen working for the security forces that have their faces covered, be it from fear or shame. In this case, the masked cameraman draws back from the hand strapped in green ribbons, the campaign colors of Mir-Hossein Mussavi—the man millions of Iranians believe was the true winner of the presidential elections of 12 June 2009.[77]

Widespread indignation stemmed from each publicized case of deaths or abuse, and further from the string of imaginative explanations offered for them by the regime. In response to threats that he would be arrested and prosecuted for spreading lies about the regime, Karrubi declared that "the real trial is before the people." This was an apt characterization. In many ways the authoritarian state was put on trial by its subjects.

Popular contention did, however, subside after December 2009 because of a convergence of factors. Through an array of repressive measures, the state finally succeeded in closing off avenues for the type of mass protests that had marked the first few months following the elections. The traditional and even new (i.e., new media) mechanisms of mobilizing the public were severely hampered by the state. Security forces and regime supporters devised more effective ways of physically preventing people from accessing major squares where protests could take place. Finally, virtually all potential organizers were either arrested or under such strict surveillance that they were paralyzed. It increasingly became clear that the struggle with hard-liners was going to be a long-term one and people would have to attend to more basic duties. Mussavi seemed to have recognized this when he stated, "Resistance is a holy endeavor, but it is not perpetual. What is perpetual is life."[78] Finally, given their traumatic experiences with violence from repression and war in the 1980s, as it became clear that hard-liners were willing to engage in a sustained and bloody crackdown, the public retreated.

While significant forms of overt resistance could be seen in the letters and accounts emerging from prisons, prisoners' families staging protests, and statements from the Green Movement's leaders, popular resistance took increasingly hidden and anonymous forms. It is difficult to gauge the full scope of public discontent and grievance (and thus its delegitimizing effects) under the virtual police state conditions that remained in place, but the fact that people were not in the street protesting did not mean that hard-liners' repression did not continue to serve as a major public grievance. As Asef Bayat's analysis of street politics and the political street in the contemporary Middle East elucidates, in many authoritarian settings in the region, grievances are expressed and resistance takes shape not in formal public gatherings such as protests or organized meetings but in the conduct of everyday life and during the course of day-to-day interactions between individuals in what he calls the expanding public sphere—between street vendors, in the corner grocery, in taxicabs.[79] This analysis sheds important light on how momentum for public mobilization may accumulate with few visible signs. The central premise of the contention is echoed by Joel Beinin and Frederick Vairel, who also point to "the myriad silent refusals, bypassing of authority, day to day forms of resistance, evasion of power practices and other behavior in the authoritarian states of the Middle East and North Africa that does not fit neatly into the binary categories of resistance or collaboration."[80] Certainly, the 2011 Arab uprisings demonstrated just how much is missed by overlooking norms, discourses, and consciousness in the informal realm that run parallel to what is visible in more formal realms.

Grievances surrounding the regime's turn to increasingly more repressive and violent means since the elections continued to occupy Iran's "political street" well beyond the last mass protest in December 2009. Anecdotal accounts reveal regular references to the immoral and "filthy" lengths to which those in power are willing to go for their political survival in day-to-day exchanges in homes between family members and outside between strangers whose paths happen to cross. The leaders of the Green Movement and the clerics posing the most pointed challenges to the state frequently referenced what they see as the widespread "hatred" and resentment the regime's repression has created. Ayatollah Sane'i was among the first to point to the hidden expressions of discontent: "Whoa to a nation, whose daily conversations consist of pain, pain, the pain of the prisoner that is captive to today's oppressors . . . pain where confessions have been obtained through solitary confinement, the pain of not being able to say the *fateheh* prayer at the funeral of a loved one."[81] He further warns, "The more pressure you place on people, the more their awareness will grow, the more their hatred will grow" and later reiterates that few events in the Islamic Republic's history have spurred the level of hatred engendered by current events against some leaders.[82]

There are many other small indicators that the regime's repression left an enduring mark on public consciousness and political culture, which when viewed cumulatively point to the conclusion that the state's repression has remained a major grievance well beyond hard-liners' success in paralyzing the protest movement in early 2010. Among the most interesting was the publication of a satire piece in a reformist publication operating from abroad that was written in the form of a fatwa from hard-liner Ayatollah Mohammad-Taqi Mesbah Yazdi. In considerable detail, the fatwa was purportedly sanctioning the rape of political prisoners who challenged the Islamic Republic. Despite being initially published in the "fun and entertainment" section of the web portal putting it out, the "fatwa" quickly spread through e-mail and Facebook and became widely viewed as real news. The rumor took such extensive hold that on his website Mesbah Yazdi took to formally denying "the dirty rumor," noting that over the course of the previous year, he had received "a copious amount of inquires" relating to the rumored fatwa.[83]

Further indicators of the depths of the impact of the regime's postelection repression could be seen in jokes referencing Kahrizak prison, pictures of political prisoners embracing family members in court proceedings, satire pieces ridiculing the most ludicrous aspects of the forced confessions broadcast on state TV, and poetry, music, and other cultural productions centered on the regime's repression circulating in private conversations and through anonymous text messaging and internet exchanges. Just one example in the realm of cultural productions is found in underground music lyrics such as "Where does the Quran say to be corrupt and vile? Why does your clerical garb smell of blood? What are you trying to hide? Why did you crush this cry for justice? . . . Know that no government can hang on through hatred and violence."[84] All of these social and cultural phenomena referencing the repression indicated the depth of its social impact. As Lisa Wedeen notes in her work on Syria, "political parodies, feature films, and jokes are where Syrian political vitality resides and where critique and oppositional consciousness thrive."[85] As she further notes, "The point is not that such parodies threaten to generate collective action in the moment, but that they enable people to recognize the shared circumstances of unbelief."[86]

More overt signs of the continuing public preoccupation with the regime's repression or what Mark Sedgwick has called "small explosions"[87] are also occasionally seen. Nasrin Alavi describes one such instance:

> The elite implosion is occurring in the shadow of permanent social protest, albeit low-level compared to the spectacular demonstrations of 2009. If you have the chance to talk to everyday people *inside Iran*, or read the defiant and confident statements by imprisoned activists *inside Iran*, or even access blog entries and online chat from *inside Iran*—then you may get a glimpse of the ardour felt on behalf of imprisoned activists or those under house arrest, including the reformist leaders of 2009 (Mehdi Karroubi as well as Mir-Hossein Mousavi). The protesters who then filled the streets in search of their votes and voices may have been silenced, but their demands and aspirations remain and are finding different channels of expression.
>
> A small example is the funeral on 25 May 2011 of Nasser Hejazi, a legendary goalkeeper whose status in Iran is comparable to great sporting heroes such as Joe Di Maggio or Ferenc Puskas. Iranians mourned, and also used the opportunity to gather in relative safety to chant political slogans, demand freedom for political prisoners, and sing the student protest anthem about "overcoming injustice and tyranny." Some in the crowd wear the colours of Hejazi's *Esteghlal* football team. The chants include: "Mubarak, Ben Ali, now it's the turn of Seyyed Ali!"[88]

Both the hidden and the rarer but unmistakable public manifestations of grievances revolving around the state's repression that materialized in 2010 and 2011 suggest their rootedness and endurance as a source of public discontent.

The 2013 presidential election in which Hassan Rouhani was permitted to run and win on a platform largely centered on political reform also shed light on the ways in which the 2009 crackdown endured within political contests and consciousness. Throughout his campaign, Rouhani repeatedly referenced existing repression and took the stance that not only Mussavi and Karrubi but other political prisoners as well should be freed. While debates over whether to participate in the election given the regime's repression were heated among reformers and voters, in the end much of the population opted for the safer route of mobilization and resistance provided by strong support for Rouhani's candidacy over more overt and riskier forms of public contention. While the galvanizing incidents of repression that occupied the fore of public consciousness in the first six months following the elections had slowly started to lose the intense public focus with the passage of time, they never disappeared from public consciousness and political discourse. Some of the slogans chanted in the lead-up to the election and during victory celebrations in the streets are instructive. They included chants of "My martyred brother, I reclaimed your vote," "Political prisoners must be freed," and "Rouhani remember, Mussavi must be freed."

The regime's coercion had such a dramatic impact for several reasons. First, the repression perpetrated by state officials following the 2009 elections captured the attention of a larger portion of Iranian society than previous episodes of repression had. Revelations such as those surrounding the rapes and killings at Kahrizak prison exposed repression in an inescapable way. The way it emerged and was pushed onto the center of the political stage by Green Movement leaders, activists, and sympathetic clerics forced the wider population to focus on it, contemplate it, and ultimately pass judgment on it. Further, its circumstances allowed for the issue to move beyond more secular segments of the population who traditionally viewed the state's repression as an affront to secular moral codes to many in the more devout and ideologically committed segments of Iranian society. As Nader Hashemi and Danny Postel point out, "The Islamic republic retains ideological support in some poorer, rural areas of the country where people are more religiously pious and more dependent on state-controlled media instead of the Internet or satellite TV."[89] With public debates on the rapes in Kahrizah prison, even this group had access to at least some news of the repression, which could allow them to contemplate another face of the Islamic Republic and at least question the moral legitimacy of the acts of repression involved. For others who resided on a border between strong ideological commitments to the idea of an Islamic government (even a conservative one) and increasing doubts about the extent to which those currently at its helm were living up to the ideal, postelection repression could be seen as mimicking, not averting the torment and physical violence so integral to Shi'i narratives of oppression and victimization. Similarly, those with strong religious sensibilities found the rapes of men and women as well as the sexual vocabulary and blackmail of interrogation an affront to the religious values they may have previously thought the state more or less upheld. Certainly, this was not the first time in which sexual assaults took place in postrevolutionary Iranian prisons. In the 1980s, there were widespread reports that female political prisoners considered virgins were "married" and raped before being executed, on religious grounds. However at that time, the regime still benefited from other forms of legitimacy, and the sexual assaults could more easily be attributed to religious/ ideological fervor. Given the fact that most segments of Iranian society, secular and religious, had come to rely on the Islamic state's own rooting of its legitimacy in republicanism and elections, it became difficult to not associate the postelection repression with a ruling elite's quest to retain power rather than religious conviction or ideology. As R. Tousi, writing under a pseudonym from within Iran, states, "It is hard for ordinary Iranians to keep up with a rotating ideology that seeks to justify so much that looks indefensible."[90]

Another important factor that distinguishes popular perceptions of prior episodes of repression from popular perceptions of the postelection repression is how victims are viewed. While in the past victims were more easily relegated to the status of the "other" or the "enemy," the fact that victims today are current or former regime insiders or their close relatives makes it easier for people from a wider spectrum of ideological leanings to identify with them, identify them as victims, and view the violence committed against them as a grave injustice. Thus the oft-repeated opposition refrain that "people will not forget what they did to *our children*" has considerable popular resonance today.

All of the indicators discussed in this section suggest that while hard-liners' repression was successful in containing the protests and mobilizations that posed an immediate threat in the latter half of 2009, the repression can also be thought to have backfired to the extent that discontent surrounding hard-liners' use of repression in the aftermath of the 2009 elections continued to simmer and take shape as utterances of "what immoral acts have they left unturned" in homes and in thousands of atomized encounters on the street. Such exchanges and expressions of discontent simply could not be thwarted in the same way that public dissent such as organized protests could. In the final analysis, popular mobilizations and resistance in Iran were very public in the first few months following the elections; the state's heightened repression forced them into more atomized hidden forms, but the grievances did not disappear.

Conclusion

In the aftermath of the contested June 2009 elections, hard-liners tried to compensate for the legitimacy deficit with which they were faced almost entirely through coercion. This extensive reliance on repression backfired. David Hess and Brian Martin argue that there are two key prerequisites for an instance of backfire. First, they argue, "an audience must perceive the event to be unjust."[91] Second, "information about the situation or event needs to be communicated effectively to a receptive audience that are substantial enough that authorities must take their outrage into consideration."[92] Hard-liners' crackdowns on postelection protests were widely viewed as unjust not only by opposition figures but also by large segments of the Iranian population. Further, the steady stream of evidence documenting state killings, torture, sexual assault, and detentions ensured that compelling accounts of repression reached the broader population. Further, despite the fact that the repression succeeded in pushing protests off the streets, it was not able to eliminate scathing public denunciations from Green Movement leaders, activists, and a small but influential group of clerics, and private denunciations in homes, on the streets, and via new media. Ultimately, two key elements of the opposition narrative prevailed: the idea that the repression indicates the extent to which those in power have strayed from the Islamic Revolution's ideals, and that it amounts to a grave injustice and violations of some notion of inherent human rights. More than ever before in the history of the Islamic Republic, growing segments of the Iranian population seem to view those at the helm of government as neither adhering to the revolution's promise of politics guided by religious morality and the tenets of Islam, nor its promise of republicanism and rights, key sources from which those in power had tried to draw legitimacy since the 1979 revolution. Yet hard-liners weathered the storm at its early peak and have gradually achieved greater political stability since.

In a more immediate and concrete sense, the postelection contests unveiled the state's violence and allowed for it to increasingly be defined as constituting violations of human rights by more than just a small group of social elites and activists. All of the contestation and activism involving the crackdown on protests, arrests, confessions, torture, and rape transcended red lines and taboos around explicitly talking about and identifying such behavior as repression and authoritatively attributing it to the state within the public sphere. The public disclosures, often from former regime insiders, gave the repression a more real and less distant quality. At the same time, new space was created for deploying the language of human rights, a potentially powerful competing discourse built on moral judgment and stigma. Accordingly, an increasing number of political and social activists operating underground inside Iran and even larger numbers of exiles outside Iran identified themselves as human rights activists and engaged in efforts to document, publicize, and challenge the regime's repression.[93]

At the same time, the various statements made by activists, Green Movement leaders, and clerics are notable both for the lengths to which they go to indict those wielding power and for where they stop. Many of the voices critically weighing in on the regime's repression declare their allegiance to the Islamic Revolution, the Constitution, the concept of *velayat-e faqih*, and Khomeini. In his Statement Number Three, Mussavi prefaces an argument with "We, as those who adhere to the Islamic Republic and its Constitution and recognize the principle of guardianship of the jurisprudent as one its main pillars and pursue a political movement with the framework of the law."[94] Thus, in Iran, members of the opposition, either out of genuine commitment or out of strategic choices, operate within the parameters of maintaining an Islamic state and the key vocabulary of Islamist ideology.[95] Citing Barrington Moore, James Scott discusses the gradients "of radicalism in the interrogation of domination."

> The least radical step is to criticize some of the dominant stratum for having violated the norms by which they claim to rule; the next most radical step is to accuse the entire stratum of failing to observe the principles of this rule; and the most radical step is to repudiate the very principles by which the dominant stratum justifies its dominance.[96]

Iran's opposition challengers largely criticized the dominant stratum "for violating the norms by which they claim to rule," but they did not "repudiate the very principles by which the dominant stratum justifies its rule."[97] This adherence to so much that is institutionally at the heart of the current political framework can provide hard-liners with ammunition and weaken public willingness to take on the risks of collective action to challenge the status quo.

The repression that followed Iran's 2009 elections and the contention and discourses that it produced served as a watershed moment in contemporary Iranian politics. The episode may end up as simply an important chapter in the Islamic Republic's tumultuous history that has largely concluded. However, it contributed to political change through the election of Hassan Rouhani in 2013, and it may also turn out to be an episode with an even more enduring impact, its full effect yet to be realized.

Notes

1. David Hess and Brian Martin, "Repression, Backfire and the Theory of Transformative Events," *Mobilization* 11, no. 2 (2006): 249.
2. Following Oliver Schlumberger's discussion of legitimacy as an analytical category in "Opening Old Bottles in Search of New Wine: On Nondemocratic Legitimacy in the Middle East," *Middle East Critique* 19, no. 3 (Fall 2010): 233–250.
3. Mark Sedgwick, "Measuring Egyptian Regime Legitimacy," *Middle East Critique* 19, no. 3 (Fall 2010): 253.
4. Schlumberger, "Opening Old Bottles in Search of New Wine," 234.
5. Reza Afshar, *Human Rights in Iran: The Abuse of Cultural Relativism* (Philadelphia: University of Pennsylvania Press, 2001).
6. Elaine Sciolino, *Persian Mirrors: The Elusive Face of Iran* (New York: Simon and Schuster, 2001), 305.
7. Asef Bayat, "A Wave for Life and Liberty: The Green Movement and Iran's Incomplete Revolution." In *The People Reloaded*, edited by Nader Hashemi and Danny Postel (New York: Melville, 2011), 44–45.

8. Sedgwick, "Measuring Egyptian Regime Legitimacy," 252 (citing Albrecht and Schlumberger).

9. Danny Postel, "Counter-Revolution and Revolt in Iran: An Interview with Iranian Political Scientist Hossein Bashiriyeh." In Hashemi and Postel, *The People Reloaded*, 83.

10. Ibid., 92–94.

11. Mehdi Karrubi, "Statement on the Report of the Three Person Committee," *Aq-Bahman*, September 14, 2009. http://bahmanagha.blogspot.com/2009/09/blog-post_8566.html.

12. John Keane, "Refolution in the Arab World," *OpenDemocracy*, April 28, 2011. http://www.opendemocracy.net/print/59185.

13. Mir-Hossein Mussavi, "Statement Number Ten." *Khordad* 88, August 4, 2009. http://khordaad88.com/?p=94.

14. Mir-Hossein Mussavi, *Chenin goft Mir Hossein* (So said Mir-Hossein) (Paris: Kaleme and Kanun-e Doktor Shariati, 1391/2012), 299–301. http://static3.kaleme.com/Chonin%20Goft%20MirHossein.pdf.

15. Ibid., 371.

16. Ibid., 277.

17. Ibid., 349.

18. Mehdi Karrubi, "25 Bahman 1389 Statement," *Sahamnews*, February 17, 2011. http://sahamnews.net/1389/11/17061.

19. Mussavi, *Chenin goft Mir Hossein*, 294.

20. Ibid., 351.

21. Karrubi, "Statement on the Report of the Three Person Committee."

22. Mussavi, *Chenin goft Mir Hossein*, 299–301.

23. Karrubi, "25 Bahman 1389 Statement."

24. Mussavi, *Chenin goft Mir Hossein*, 349.

25. Karrubi, "Statement on the Report of the Three Person Committee."

26. Mussavi, *Chenin goft Mir Hossein*, 267.

27. Mussavi, *Chenin goft Mir Hossein*, 489.

28. Ibid., 904.

29. Ibid.

30. Ibid., 265.

31. Ibid., 267.

32. Ibid., 297.

33. Ibid., 510.

34. Karrubi, "25 Bahman 1389 Statement."

35. Mussavi, *Chenin goft Mir Hossein*, 904.

36. Reported in *Jaras*, February 8, 2010. http://www.rahesabz.net/story/9816.

37. *Haghighat News*, September 4, 2009. https://haghighatnews.wordpress.com/2009/09/04.

38. "Grand Ayatollah Montazeri's Fatwa," *Tehran Bureau*, July 12, 2009. http://www.pbs.org/wgbh/pages/frontline/tehranbureau/2009/07/grand-ayatollah-montazeris-fatwa.html.

39. Seyyed Ali-Mohammad Dastgheib, "Excerpts on Quranic Teaching," July 20, 2009. http://www.dastgheib.com/index.php?option=com_content&task=view&id=529&Itemid=55.

40. *Jaras*, June 16, 2011. http://www.rahesabz.net/story/38669.

41. Dastgheib, "Excerpts on Quranic Teaching."

42. Speech given by Sane'i in Gorgan, August 12, 2009. https://m.youtube.com/watch?v=wPsoAgjbi_U.

43. Ibid.

44. Seyyed Mohammad-Ali Dastgheib, speech regarding the elections, September 17, 2009. http://www.youtube.com/watch?v=KJAoPoSoUl8.

45. *Jaras*, December 9, 2009. http://www.rahesabz.net/story/5698.

46. *Jaras*, February 14, 2011. http://www.rahesabz.net/story/32457.

47. Muhammad Sahimi, "Ayatollah Amjad: Impossible to Ban an Islamic Scholar and Call this Islam," *Tehran Bureau*, January 28, 2011. http://www.pbs.org/wgbh/pages/frontline /tehranbureau/2011/01/ayatollah-amjad-impossible-to-be-an-islamic-scholar-and-call-this -islam.html.

48. Seyyed Ali Mohammad Dastgheib, message regarding the martyrdom of Mussavi's nephew, December 28, 2009. http://www.dastgheib.com/index.php?option=com_content& task=view&id=629&Itemid=55.

49. Dastgheib, message regarding the martyrdom of Mussavi's nephew.

50. Seyyed Ali Mohammad Dastgheib, message regarding the statement by members of the Assembly of Experts, July 26, 2009. http://www.dastgheib.com/index.php?option=com_content &task=view&id=531&Itemid=55.

51. Speech by Sane'i in Gorgan.

52. *Mardomak*, May 6, 2011. http://www.mardomak.org/story/61893.

53. Speech by Sane'i in Gorgan.

54. "Iran Snapshot: Another Grand Ayatollah Launches Major Criticism of Government," *Enduring America*, March 6, 2011. http://www.enduringamerica.com/home/2011/3/6/iran -snapshot-another-grand-ayatollah-launches-major-critici.html.

55. *Balatarin*, July 4, 2009, https://www.balatarin.com/permlink/2009/7/4/1646106.

56. *Jaras*, November 27, 2010. http://www.rahesabz.net/story/28067.

57. "Grand Ayatollah Montazeri's Fatwa."

58. Montazeri's response to the letter of 293 intellectuals and elites, August 26, 2009. http:// www.amontazeri.com/farsi/link.asp?TOPIC_ID=219.

59. Dastgheib, message regarding the statement by members of the Assembly of Experts.

60. Statement Number Four of the Assembly of Qom Scholars and Researchers of Qom Seminaries, protesting the Guardian Council's validation of the results of the Islamic Republic's tenth presidential elections, July 2, 2009. http://www.majmaqom.com/index.php/bayaniy eha/227-83.html.

61. Montazeri's reply to Mussavi's letter, September 22, 2009. http://www.amontazeri.com /farsi/link.asp?TOPIC_ID=223.

62. Dastgheib, "Excerpts from Quranic Teaching."

63. Speech by Sane'i in Gorgan.

64. *Deutsche Welle Persian*, October 10, 2010. http://www.dw.de/dw/article/0,,6099391,00 .html.

65. Ibid.

66. *Jaras*, February 14, 2011. http://www.rahesabz.net/story/32457.

67. Letter by Mehdi Mohammadian to Ayatollah Khamenei regarding the situation in prisons, May 9, 2011. http://www.irangreenvoice.com/article/2011/may/08/12948.

68. Mohammad Nurizad's open letter to the head of the judiciary (as translated on his website), November 19, 2010. http://nurizad.info/blog/1189.

69. Robert Mackey, "Iranian Prisoners Explain End of Hunger Strikes," *New York Times*, August 10, 2010. http://thelede.blogs.nytimes.com/2010/08/10/iranian-prisoners-explain-end -of-hunger-strikes.

70. "Interview with Mohammad Nurizad Regarding his Latest Letters to Iran's Supreme Leader," *Deutsche Welle*, December 9, 2011. http://www.youtube.com/watch?v=3dO6hV_4ZCA.

71. Nurizad's open letter to the head of the judiciary.

72. Nurizad posed twenty-five questions to several sources of emulation in July 2011 to which only Bayat Zanjani responded. See http://www.nurizad.info/blog/5889.

73. Muhammad Sahimi, "Update: Nourizad Still on Hunger Strike, Hospitalized; Family Briefly Detained," *Tehran Bureau*, December 16, 2010. http://www.pbs.org/wgbh/pages /frontline/tehranbureau/2010/12/extra-artists-plea-for-mohammad-nourizad-to-end-hun ger-strike.html.

74. See Miriam Cooke, *Dissident Syria* (Durham, NC: Duke University Press, 2007), 72, citing Lisa Wedeen and others.

75. Hamid Dabashi, "Letters to a Dictator," *Al Jazeera English*, December 29, 2011. http:// www.aljazeera.com/indepth/opinion/2011/12/2011122993232476296.html.

76. "A Death in Tehran: Interview with Arash Hejazi," *Frontline*, September 18, 2009. http:// www.pbs.org/wgbh/pages/frontline/tehranbureau/deathintehran/interviews/hejazi.html.

77. R. Tousi, "Voices of a New Iran," *OpenDemocracy*, December 11, 2009. http://www .opendemocracy.net/r-tousi/voices-of-new-iran.

78. Mussavi, *Chenin goft Mir Hossein*, 374.

79. Asef Bayat, *Life as Politics: How Ordinary People Change the Middle East* (Redwood City, CA: Stanford University Press, 2010), 11–14.

80. Joel Beinin and Frederick Vairel, *Social Movements, Mobilization and Contestation in the Middle East* (Redwood City, CA: Stanford University Press, 2011), 10.

81. Speech by Sane'i in Gorgan.

82. Ibid.

83. The formal denial issued on September 14, 2010, can be found on Mesbah Yazdi's website. http://mesbahyazdi.com/farsi/?news=249.

84. "Letters from Iran," *Al Jazeera Documentary*, 2011. http://topdocumentaryfilms.com /letters-from-iran/.

85. Lisa Wedeen, *Ambiguities of Domination* (Chicago: University of Chicago Press, 1999), 89.

86. Ibid., 90.

87. Sedgwick, "Measuring Egyptian Regime Legitimacy," 252.

88. Nasrin Alavi, "Iran, An Elite at War," *OpenDemocracy*, May 27, 2011. http://www.open democracy.net/nasrin-alavi/iran-elite-at-war.

89. Hashemi and Postel, *The People Reloaded*, xix.

90. R. Tousi, "Tehran, Glimpses of Freedom," *OpenDemocracy*, October 6, 2011. http:// www.opendemocracy.net/r-tousi/tehran-glimpses-of-freedom.

91. Hess and Martin, "Repression, Backfire and the Theory of Transformative Events," 251.

92. Ibid.

93. As openings for building a human rights infrastructure have shrunk inside Iran, efforts have expanded outside the country. There has been tremendous growth in the number of groups that monitor and publicize rights violations with relative professionalism and in a way that is relatively free of the political rhetoric of past invocations of human rights. At the same time, the level of collaboration between political activists and figures either inside Iran or with strong ties to the reform movement inside Iran and Western-based Iran-focused human rights activists is also on the rise. Just one example is Mohammad Nurizad's using the New York–based International Campaign for Human Rights in Iran to publicize state agents' confiscation of video material for one of his films. If these trends continue, challenges to the regime's repression and the discourse of human rights may bridge some of the gulf between divided domestic and diaspora opposition forces.

94. Mussavi later puts forth that he was not opposed to amending the Constitution, stating, "We must be aware that a good Constitution by itself is not the solution. We must move toward a structure that imposes a high cost on those who attempt to disobey or ignore the laws." Cited in Mohammad Sahimi, "The Political Evolution of the Islamic Republic" in Hashemi and Postel, *The People Reloaded*, 253.

95. This stands in contrast to Egypt, for example, where even Islamist parties with tremendous electoral victories speak of establishing a "civil state" and governing with "an Islamic reference."

96. James Scott, *Domination and the Art of Resistance* (New Haven, CT: Yale University Press, 1990), 92.

97. Ibid.

Epilogue

Daniel Brumberg and Farideh Farhi

W<small>HAT DOES A COLLECTIVE</small> assessment of these chapters tell us about the trajectory of Iran's politics in the coming decade and beyond? Do they portend continued centralization, or prospects for a reopening of the political and social field? These are not, of course, either/or propositions. Centralization and increased competition can unfold simultaneously, along different tracks and at different paces. Such dissonance would not be unusual for Iran's diffused semiautocracy, which had for decades managed contending political, social, and even ideological currents. Nevertheless, we sense that 2009 was something of a threshold. What came before cannot be fully duplicated, but it can be revived or recast in ways that will create new political and social dynamics. Although their content, nature, and direction cannot be predicted, these dynamics merit careful consideration.

In undertaking this task, our case studies were largely finished before Hassan Rouhani's 2013 election, an event that surprised many of our authors as much as anyone. While we must be careful about drawing definitive conclusions regarding the significance of that election, we are confident that it reflected more than momentary circumstances. Even if—as seems likely—hard-liners try to thwart the cautious bid of Rouhani and his allies to reopen the political, cultural, and economic fields, the deeper structural forces that gave rise to these pluralizing efforts will shape Iran's politics for many years to come, creating a complex interplay between dynamics of sociopolitical opening and contraction.

"Enforcer" or "veto" institutions will lead the effort to rein in the forces advocating for political détente at home and abroad. The security sector and Iran's Revolution Guard Corps (IRGC) in particular will flex their ample coercive and even ideological muscles. Thus we agree that the securitization, largely in reaction to the system's perception of threat from both inside and outside the country, of the 2000s ran deep, and that it will continue to pose difficult challenges for groups and leaders advocating greater political openness. Where we differ, however, is in our assessment of the capacity of the hard-liners in the IRGC and their allies in other institutions to denude Iran of its political and social effervescence and thus transform the Islamic Republic into a fully authoritarian system. On the contrary, this volume highlights the tenacious efforts of an array of social and political forces to sustain competition and even shape and reshape state policies despite, or because of, the securitization of the previous decade.

Paradoxically, the capacity of these forces and institutions to resist or even roll back further autocratization could partly hinge on the authority, power and role of the leading veto player, namely the Supreme Leader (*Rahbar*) and the vast bureaucratic office he occupies (*beit-e rahbari*). The institutional, economic, and judicial power the Leader has accrued gives him enormous capacity to thwart potential challengers, but it is also tied to an entrenched network of economic, clerical, and educational institutions all of which have a concrete interest in resisting change. As a result, and as Mehrzad Boroujerdi and Kourosh Rahimkhani's analysis suggests, seeking to retain his room for maneuver, the Leader has good reason to avoid binding himself too closely to any one faction. Indeed, Khamanei's decision to stand back from the political fray during the 2013 presidential election could reflect an effort to establish his authority as "Chief Arbiter" rather than "Chief Enforcer." Such a move would not be unfavorable to advocates of a domestic political détente. After all, they have little hope of even modest success absent a readiness of the Leader to speak, as former President Khatami used to put it, "for all Iranians" and the "System" itself.[1] Such an idea is, of course, anathema to hard-liners, who will surely claim Khamanei for themselves, even as they jockey for influence in anticipation of the inevitable struggle over his succession.

The huge stakes that attend this contest reflect the double-edged nature of the Leader's constitutional powers. As *Rahbar* he has the formal ultimate authority—although not a totally unconstrained capacity—to redefine the central principles of political life. He can uphold or take steps to change the system in ways both small and big in the name of the interest of the system (*maslahat-e nezam*). While there is zero chance that Khamanei will metamorphosize into a Pope Francis, the mere possibility of a future Leader-Innovator has probably alarmed his disciples. At the same time, aggregation of power in the Office of the Leader is not problem-free for a revolution-generated polity. One problem concerns the longevity of the term of the occupant, which is effectively lifelong without a guaranteed path for the transfer of power to a preferred successor. The second relates to the question of transition in that office after years of aggregated power. While many observers of Iran tend to reduce the Leader's office to the personality and ideological orientation of the officeholder, the much deeper problem is constitutional. The Iranian Constitution has created two executives, both with substantial powers but only one of which effectively has a life term while the other changes every eight years (and potentially even every four years). This imbalance has led to encroachment into the powers of the elected president, underwriting the deepest conflicts of the country first in the early years of the Islamic Republic and then in the second term of Ahmadinejad's presidency. Unless these two executives find a way to cooperate, their conflicts are bound to reverberate throughout the institutions of the Islamic Republic horizontally and vertically. Even assuming a smooth transition to a new Leader, made possible by a selection process in the Council of Experts, the aggregation of power that has been made possible by lack of rotation in the Office of the Leader is bound to unsettle the office unless its powers are more clearly delineated and legitimated before the time for transition comes.

Meanwhile the broader issues regarding political transition and the contest between forces of closure and opening will be shaped by many factors, including struggles over economic policy. As the studies by Kevan Harris and Payam Mohseni illustrate, the arena of economic policy making has always been contentious, fraught with public contests to shape the content and trajectory of welfare legislation, trade, and economic privatization. As the capacity of Iran's leaders to subsidize the economy through oil rents decreases in tandem with what could be a sustained opening of the country's market to more foreign investment and global greater trade—made possible by the July 2015 nuclear agreement known as the Joint Comprehensive Plan of Action (JCPOA) signed between Iran and five permanent members of the United Nations Security Council plus Germany (P5+1)—conflicts over economic policy will probably intensify, thus creating additional impetus within the ruling elite to find ways to negotiate the boundaries between state control and market forces.

Iran's experience, as elsewhere, has long demonstrated that such economic contests invariably carry political meanings that cannot be fully controlled or contained. That said, in noting how quickly economics slides into politics, we are not suggesting that greater market competition will favor pluralism—much less democracy. Indeed, as the experiences of many countries have shown (see China), economic reforms can magnify distributional conflicts in ways that make key social groups—including business and the professional middle class—amenable to the allure of order from above. This may be particularly so in a neighborhood besieged with instability and antisystemic violence. Nevertheless, the overall consequences of economic conflict in Iran has been to heighten the logic of—and need for—creating alliances and institutional mechanisms that can mediate disputes rather than let them tear at the fabric of the system. Our hunch is that the logic of negotiation, institutional and political, will intensify rather than diminish in the coming years.

The capacity of electoral institutions and processes to channel conflicts remains a key question. Yasmin Alem's study shows that the authority and influence of the Majles took a severe beating in the late 2000s and the ensuing decade. The exclusion of the Islamic left and subsequent assaults on both mainstream conservatives and the "republican right" (as Mohseni calls the business forces associated with Hashemi Rafsanjani and his allies) sapped Parliament of legitimacy while provoking disputes within the largest parliamentary faction (the principlists). But if the ensuing 2009 protests signaled widespread disillusionment with the electoral system, the 2013 surge of political mobilization suggested that a potential reopening of electoral competition could be a win/win for the regime and the wider society. This is certainly a lesson that many reformists have learned as they prepare for the 2016 parliamentary elections—and others to follow. A respectable showing might induce some mainstream conservatives to give reformists a measure of support rather than bandwagon with hard-liners. Small, calibrated electoral gains could prove more advantageous by comparison to the dramatic political transformation than many reformists sought to achieve in the late nineties and early 2000s.

Such calculations would echo one key lesson suggested by our case studies: leadership, choice, and agency can make a difference—even against a background that is structurally constrained. On this score, there is no doubt that the forces pushing for greater openness and pluralism at times stand accused of wanting to discard the Islamic Republic and its key institutions, including those controlled by clerics. The reformers' riposte that they merely want a gentler, more humane, permissive, and law-abiding Islamic republic and institutions makes sense only if such political transformation is possible within the confines of the Islamic Republic's constitutive ideas, powers, and institutions. Indeed, the reformers, along with forces that now identify themselves as moderationist (*e'tedalgara*), argue that reform is a process and not a project. It will take time; it has to be gradual; it must involve painstaking changes in every institution, not merely the ones at the political top, becoming more accountable and law-abiding. It also involves taking a stance against domestic and regional extremists who have wreaked havoc in Iran and neighboring countries.[2] This posture may be due to complacency generated out of lack of alternatives, especially in light of the violent turbulences that have gripped many of the countries in the wider Middle East. But it is a posture that helped elect Rouhani, and it is an approach that in the longer run may help advance a more inclusive politics.

The office and authority of the president could help determine the boundaries of political participation and negotiation. As the only directly elected national leader, the president occupies an office that is in structural tension with that of the *Rahbar*. However, because the president offers a vital instrument for managing the economy as well as elite tensions *and* securing popular legitimacy, he can also be asset to the Leader. For this reason we doubt that the presidency will be abolished. As elite and social conflicts intensify, the advantages of electoral competition in presidential, parliamentary, municipal elections, and the Assembly of Experts could increase to enhance the authority of elected institutions.[3]

The prospect of an even partial reinvigoration of electoral politics could invite retaliation from the Guardian Council and from the judiciary as well, many of whose courts and judges have become close allies of the hard-line factions. But as our studies of contests over the rule of law and human rights clearly indicate, the boomerang effects of widening regime repression in 2009 and beyond helped to sustain a concept of legality, constitutionalism, and rights that cuts across the ideological divide. As Shadi Mohktari shows, the notion that Islam in general or Shi'ism in particular condones torture and other abuses has been widely assailed by some prominent lay politicians and leading clerics, some of whom stand outside (if not in opposition to) the clerical establishment, but also by others who are part of the ruling elite. Whether proponents of the rule of law and constitutionalism will advance their case remains to be seen. The Islamic Republic's Constitution offers a dissonant vision whose rights provisions are conditioned by loopholes that strengthen nonelective institutions or the discretion of the Leader. Nevertheless, it has never figured as the constitutional equivalent of a Potemkin village. On the contrary, while the 1989 constitutional amendments did not abolish the Constitution's tensions, the public struggle over many of its key articles highlighted its enduring import as a point of reference for mediating elite struggles over basic political issues. While another round of amendments is unlikely, we agree with Mehrangiz Kar, Azadeh Pourzand, Fatemeh Haghighatjoo, and Mokhtari that the rights and rule of law discourse that developed wider roots in the 2000s could provide a powerful normative and symbolic resource in future contests to redefine the boundaries of political participation and expression.

That discourse finds a potentially mass audience within an expanding university population that constitutes the backbone of Iran's huge middle class.[4] Shervin Malekzadeh's argument that universities divert the energies of young people from politics into prolonged struggles for jobs and social advancement could prove true in the coming years. But the constraining effects stemming from the structural link between education and employment has been periodically disrupted by bursts of political energy and mobilization. With the prospects of a rekindled electoral field and the challenge of economic growth and reform, in the coming years Iran could see a reenergized middle class—one whose aspirations may not manifest themselves in a revived student movement per se, but one that could find other forms of intellectual, social, and institutional expression within the arena of university life.

The prospects for heightened activism and political energy will be affected by developments in the Middle East and the wider global arena. Unfortunately, global politics have enhanced the leverage of hard-line forces. Indeed, the most reliable studies of the IRGC demonstrate that the Guard's rising economic and political power was not a predetermined structural feature of the Islamic Republic; rather, it was propelled by a series of external threats, the first and perhaps most decisive of which was Iraq's invasion of Iran and the eight-year war that followed.[5] In the 1990s and even more so in the first decade of the new millennium, the US-Iranian cold war further constricted the space for political accommodation. Although our authors do not focus on international issues per se, many offer observations that illustrate the deliberalizing impact of regional and global tensions and the US-Iranian conflict in particular. On this score, Harris's chapter is telling, as it charts a link between the expanding power of the state on the one hand and the growing security, social, and economic challenges issuing from the Iran-Iraq War on the other. Moreover, alluding to the aftermath of 9/11 and the US military actions that followed, he notes that "Western intervention" has generated "high status anxiety among elites," forcing them together in ways that produce "far more durable ruling pacts than in times of normal intra-elite conflict." Such pacts, however, are not based on negotiated consensus but rather reflect the logic of coerced unity. Thus, Harris argues, "external threats tend to generate elite cohesion in Iran, but they also tend to centralize state power in more authoritarian forms." While Boroujerdi and Rahimkhani speculate that a US-Iranian "grand bargain" might abet the status quo, Alem, Haghighatjoo, and Mokhtari all provide evidence that suggests that intensified US-Iranian conflict has favored regime-imposed unity over negotiated pacts that might widen the political arena.

These observations, together with our own grasp of the empirical terrain, suggest that a diminishing of US-Iranian conflict will ultimately favor more inclusive politics. This is surely why hard-liners worry about reconciliation,[6] and why they see the nuclear accord between Iran and the P5+1 as a threat. If the JCPOA is implemented as planned, hard-liners may try to reimpose controls over the political and social arenas. But given the backlash precipitated by 2009, it is difficult to imagine a full-scale clampdown. More importantly, because of the political confidence gained through reaching an agreement with world powers—in a process of intense negotiation, bargaining, conciliation and compromise—the country's contending institutions and political forces are now expected to address internal conflicts through bargaining and conciliation rather than coercion and domination. In this news terrain, even the hard-liners might play a more subtle game, testing the capacity of advocates of political accommodation to forge and sustain alliances that might deflect hard-line challenges while keeping an eye on the prize.

That prize will not necessarily be a transition to competitive democracy. Liberalizing political pacts can spawn a myriad of political outcomes rather than leading to a democratic breakthrough. But a reinvigorated and widened politics that emerges through a measure of consensus and under the umbrella of Iran's diffused-power system could in time enhance citizen rights and the quality of political life. And it would certainly echo—if not build on—a dynamic that this volume amply illustrates, namely the enduring efforts of the Iranian political class and citizenry to engage in conversation and constant bargaining over how to address the domestic and external challenges facing the country. Many

Iranians appear to prefer this outcome to the uncertainties that might ensue with a bid for revolutionary change, particularly when they view the upheavals that have sparked internal conflict in the wider Middle East and North Africa.

In drawing attention to the forces and dynamics that might support a more open politics in Iran, we are happy to note that the insights provided by our authors are echoed by several recent studies.[7] Moreover, and returning to a theme raised in the introduction of this volume, our study demonstrates conceptual lessons extending far beyond Iran's borders. While its politics reflect forces, logics, and processes rooted in Iran's cultural, religious, and economic terrain, the ebb and flow of political and social contestation in the Islamic Republic have much in common with that of other semiautocracies.

These currents have a Janus-faced quality born of a system of diffused—but differentially concentrated—power politics whose fluid mix of formal and informal dynamics invites and at the same time limits the boundaries of competition. The concept of a diffused-power system is, of course, an ideal type that is never fully replicated in empirical practice. Moreover, it is also a matter of degree. Semiautocracies tend to vary along a continuum with formal power systems on one end and diffused power on the opposite. The former offer advantages, including a relatively coherent system of representative institutions and a mutually reinforcing set of constitutional rules and rights. Political forces—particularly political parties—can use these formal arenas to erode regime hegemony as well as to forge strong alliances and liberalizing political pacts in ways that increase—but do not necessarily guarantee—the chances for competitive democracy. In Mexico, for example, these dynamics helped to undermine a one-party machine in ways that eventually transcended the legacy of semiauthoritarianism.[8] By contrast, in more fluid systems alliance building and pact making are slippery and ever difficult to sustain, thus making it hard to fundamentally undermine what in Morocco are called *les pouvoirs*. Moreover, as the Moroccan case shows, the fact that power is not only diffused but can also be differentially concentrated in powerful "veto" institutions such as the monarchy and its allies (*les pouvoirs*) both invites dynamics of negotiation and works against a revolutionary redistribution of power relations.

Moreover, and on this score, it is not clear that a wholesale effort to separate ruling institutions and leaders from the state will advance the longer-term cause of democracy. As we have seen following the 2011 Arab rebellions, where state and ruling elite are closely tied, the assault on the latter threatens to collapse the former. The determination to prevent the hemorrhaging of the state is especially marked when its official or unofficial guardians see themselves as the ultimate protectors of some kind of collective ideology, scared mission, or narrow sectarian agenda. Under these conditions system enforcers often view the prospects of even a modest regime-opposition pact as a near existential threat. Facing such dire calculations, opposition elites might—if they are clever and patient—use the fluidity of diffused-power systems to deflect hard-line retaliation or mitigate its costs. But as the contrasting cases of Egypt and Iran suggest, such efforts require novel alliances that cut across ideological divides and/or efforts to partly accommodate hard-line forces. In 2012–2013, Egypt's Islamist forces resisted this strategic logic and paid dearly, while in Iran many leaders in the cacophonous opposition seem to have grasped its pragmatic and practical benefits.

Some activists in—but especially outside—Iran feel that such compromises are neither legitimate nor ultimately useful. But what they and many of Iran's leaders surely know (or have learned) is that political life in the Islamic Republic cannot long abide a system that seeks to eradicate the diverse voices, interests, and aspirations that animate Iran's vibrant society. By violating some of the very principles that many of the Islamic Republic's founders asserted were essential to its identity, and by undermining mechanisms that could foster accommodation and negotiation, a renewed drive to accumulate and centralize power will make a peaceful transformation of Iran's polity a dream deferred for all Iranians.

Notes

1. Daniel Brumberg, *Reinventing Khomeini: The Struggle for Reform in Iran* (Chicago: University of Chicago Press, 2001), 239.

2. While the term "moderate" has historically been used to describe a sector of Iranian elites by outsiders, it was not used to refer to any political faction inside Iran until recently. But the term has now been appropriated domestically and posited in opposition to "extremist."

3. Here we are also drawing attention to the possible importance of elections for the Council of Experts, which selects the Leader. Because the candidates will likely be limited to conservative forces, these elections will be the least inclusive. But even here we see the possibility for significant internal fissures, particularly when and if an attempt is made to mobilize popular votes to back particular candidates for the council itself.

4. In 2013–2014 Iran's universities had 4.68 million students. The total teaching staff numbered close to 71,000, while in 2012–2013 universities produced close to 720,000 graduates at a variety of levels. The data is from Iran's Institute of Planning and Research in Higher Education. http://irphe.ac.ir//files/site1/pages/Amar_1Negah/w-br-bruoshoor92-93.pdf.

5. Frederic Wehrey, Jerrold D. Green, Brian Nichiporuk, Alireza Nader, Lydia Hansell, Rasool Nafisi, and S. R. Bohandy, *The Rise of the Pasdaran: Assessing the Domestic Roles of Iran's Islamic Revolutionary Guards Corps* (Washington, DC: Rand, 2009), 24. For a discussion of the political discourse the war strengthened, see Farideh Farhi, "The Antinomies of Iran's War Generation." In *Iran, Iraq, and the Legacies of War*, edited by Lawrence Potter and Gary Sick, 101–120 (New York: Palgrave Macmillan, 2004).

6. The term "the worried" (*delvapasan*) is explicitly used inside Iran to refer to those who are critical of a nuclear accord between Iran and the United States. The term developed as many hardliners spoke of being worried about the accord and alleged nontransparent quid pro quos made between Iran and the United States.

7. See, for example, Negin Nabavi, ed., *From Theocracy to the Green Movement* (New York: Palgrave Macmillan, 2012); and Abbas Milani and Larry Diamond, eds., *Politics and Culture in Contemporary Iran: Challenging the Status Quo* (Boulder, CO: Lynne Rienner, 2015).

8. See Todd A. Eisenstadt, *Courting Democracy in Mexico, Party Strategies and Electoral Institutions* (Cambridge: Cambridge University Press, 2004).

Selected Bibliography

Books and Articles in English and European Languages

Abbasi-Shavazi, Mohammad, Peter McDonald, and Meimanat Hosseini-Chavoshi. *The Fertility Transition in Iran: Revolution and Reproduction*. New York: Springer, 2009.

Abbott, Andrew, and Stanley DeViney. "The Welfare State as Transnational Event: Evidence from Sequences of Policy Adoption." *Social Science History* (1992): 245–274.

Abdo, Geneive. *The Arab Uprisings and the Rebirth of the Shi-a-Sunni Divide. Brookings Analysis Paper*, no. 29 (2013). http://www.brookings.edu/~/media/research/files /papers/2013/04/sunni%20shia%20abdo/sunni%20shia%20abdo.

Abrahamian, Ervand. *The Iranian Mojahedin*. New Haven, CT: Yale University Press, 1989.

Abu Sharkh, Miriam, and Ian Gough. "Global Welfare Regimes." *Global Social Policy* 10, no. 1 (2010): 27–58.

Afshar, Reza. *Human Rights in Iran: The Abuse of Cultural Relativism*. Philadelphia: University of Pennsylvania Press, 2001.

Alamdari, Kazem. "The Power Structure of the Islamic Republic of Iran: Transition from Populism to Clientelism, and Militarization of the Government." *Third World Quarterly* 26, no. 8 (2005): 1285–1301.

Alavi, Nasrin. "Iran, An Elite at War." *OpenDemocracy*, May 27, 2011. http://www .opendemocracy.net/nasrin-alavi/iran-elite-at-war.

Alem, Yasmin. *Duality by Design: The Iranian Electoral System*. Washington, DC: International Foundation for Electoral Systems, 2011.

Alfoneh, Ali. *Iran Unveiled: How the Revolutionary Guards Is Turning Theocracy into Military Dictatorship*. Washington, DC: American Enterprise Institute, 2013.

———. "The Revolutionary Guards' Role in Iranian Politics." *Middle East Quarterly* 62, no. 4 (2008): 2–14.

Amir Arjomand, Said. *After Khomeini: Iran under His Successors*. New York: Oxford University Press, 2009.

———. "Civil Society and Rule of Law in the Constitutional Politics of Iran under Khatami." *Social Research* 76, no. 2 (2000): 283–301.

Anderson, Benedict. *Imagined Communities: Reflections on the Origin and Spread of Nationalism*. London: Verso, 1983.

Aryan, Hossein. "Commentary: How Schoolchildren Are Brainwashed in Iran." *Radio Free Europe/Radio Liberty*, May 27, 2010. http://www.rferl.org/content/Commen tary_How_Schoolchildren_Are_Brainwashed_In_Iran/2054304.html.

Bakhash, Shaul. "No Elected President for Iran?" *Iran Primer*, October 31, 2011. http:// iranprimer.usip.org/blog/2011/oct/31/no-elected-president-iran.

———. "Iran: The Crisis of Legitimacy." In *Middle Eastern Lectures: Number One*, edited by Martin Kramer, 99–118. Tel Aviv: Moshe Dayan Center for Middle Eastern and African Studies, 1995.

———. *The Reign of the Ayatollahs: Iran and the Islamic Revolution.* New York: Basic Books, 1986.

Bakhtiari, Bahman. *Parliamentary Politics in Revolutionary Iran: The Institutionalization of Factional Politics.* Gainesville: University of Florida Press, 1996.

———. "Parliamentary Elections in Iran." *Iranian Studies* 26, no. 3/4 (1993): 375–388.

Barendrecht, Maurits. "Rule of Law, Measuring and Accountability: Problems to Be Solved Bottom Up." *Hague Journal on the Rule of Law* 3 (2011): 285–286.

Bauer, Janet. "Poor Women and Social Consciousness in Revolutionary Iran." In *Women and Revolution in Iran*, edited by Guity Nashat, 141–169. Boulder, CO: Westview Press, 1983.

Bayat, Asef. "A Wave for Life and Liberty: The Green Movement and Iran's Incomplete Revolution." In *The People Reloaded*, edited by Nader Hashemi and Danny Postel, 44–45. New York: Melville, 2011.

———. "Tehran: Paradox City." *New Left Review* 2, no. 66 (2010): 99–122.

———. *Life as Politics: How Ordinary People Change the Middle East.* Redwood City, CA: Stanford University Press, 2009.

———. *Street Politics: Poor People's Movements in Iran.* New York: Columbia University Press, 1997.

Behdad, Sohrab, and Farhad Nomani. "What a Revolution! Thirty Years of Social Class Reshuffling in Iran." *Comparative Studies of South Asia, Africa and the Middle East* 29, no. 1 (2009): 84–104.

Beinin, Joel, and Frederick Vairel. *Social Movements, Mobilization and Contestation in the Middle East.* Redwood City, CA: Stanford University Press, 2011.

Bellin, Eva. "Coercive Institutions and Coercive Leaders." In *Authoritarianism in the Middle East: Regimes and Resistance*, edited by Marsha Pripstein Posusney and Michele Penner Angrist, 21–42. Boulder, CO: Lynne Rienner, 2005.

Boroujerdi, Mehrzad. "Iran." In *The Middle East*, 13th ed., edited by Ellen Lust, 478–506. Washington, DC: CQ Press, 2014.

———. "The Reformist Movement in Iran." In *Oil in the Gulf: Obstacles to Democracy and Development*, edited by Daniel Heradstveit and Helge Hveem, 63–71. Aldershot, UK: Ashgate, 2004.

Boroujerdi, Mehrzad, and Kourosh Rahimkhani. "Revolutionary Guards Soar in Parliament." *Iran Primer.* http://iranprimer.usip.org/blog/2011/sep/19/revolutionary-guards-soar-parliament.

Brown, Roland Eliot. "Notes from the Underground." *Foreign Policy*, August 31, 2011. http://www.foreignpolicy.com/articles/2011/08/31/notes_from_the_underground?page=0,1.

Brownlee, Jason. *Authoritarianism in an Age of Democratization.* New York: Cambridge University Press, 2007.

Brumberg, Daniel. "Transforming the Arab World's Protection Racket Politics." *Journal of Democracy* 24, no. 3 (2013): 83–103.

———. "Liberalization versus Democracy: Understanding Arab Political Reform." Working paper, *Middle East Series*, no. 37. Washington, DC: Carnegie Endowment for International Peace, 2004.

———. *Reinventing Khomeini: The Struggle for Reform in Iran*. Chicago: University Of Chicago Press, 2001.

Brumberg, Daniel, and Ariel I. Ahram. "The National Iranian Oil Company in Iranian Politics." Houston: James Baker III Institute for Public Policy, Rice University, 2007.

Carothers, Thomas. "The End of the Transition Paradigm." *Journal of Democracy* 13, no. 1 (2003): 15–21.

Chase, Anthony. *Rights, Reform and Revolution*. Boulder, CO: Lynne Rienner, 2012.

Chehabi, Houchang. *Iranian Politics and Religious Modernism: The Liberation Movement of Iran under the Shah and Khomeini*. London: Tauris, 1990.

Chehabi, Houchang E., and Juan Linz, eds. *Sultanistic Regimes*. Baltimore: Johns Hopkins University Press, 1998.

Collier, David, and Steven Levitsky. "Democracy with Adjectives: Conceptual Innovation in Comparative Research." *World Politics* 49, no. 3 (1997): 430–451.

Collins, Randall. "Social Movements and the Focus of Emotional Attention." In *Passionate Politics: Emotions and Social Movements*, edited by Jeff Goodwin, James Jasper, and Francesca Polletta, 27–44. Chicago: University of Chicago Press, 2001.

Cooke, Miriam. *Dissident Syria*. Durham, NC: Duke University Press, 2007.

Dabashi, Hamid. "Letters to a Dictator." *Al Jazeera English*, December 29, 2011. http://www.aljazeera.com/indepth/opinion/2011/12/2011122993232476296.html.

Daragahi, Borzou. "Broken by Prison, for a Cause All but Lost." *Los Angeles Times*, December 23, 2007.

Diamond, Larry. "Thinking about Hybrid Regimes." *Journal of Democracy* 13, no. 2 (2002): 21–35.

Ehsani, Kaveh. "The Urban Provincial Periphery in Iran: Revolution and War in Ramhormoz." In *Contemporary Iran: Economy, Society, Politics*, edited by Ali Gheissari, 38–76. Oxford: Oxford University Press, 2009.

———. "Round 12 for Iran's Reformists." *MERIP Online*, January 29, 2004. http://merip.org/mero/mero012904.

———. "Islam, Modernity, and National Identity." *Middle East Insight* 9, no. 5 (1995): 48–53.

———. "'Tilt but Don't Spill': Iran's Development and Reconstruction Dilemma." *Middle East Report* 191 (1994): 16–21.

Ehteshami, Anoushiravan, and Mahjoob Zweiri, *Iran and the Rise of Its Neoconservatives: The Politics of Tehran's Silent Revolution*. London: Tauris, 2007.

Ehteshami, Anoushiravan. *After Khomeini: The Iranian Second Republic*. London: Routledge, 2005.

Eisenstadt, Todd A. *Courting Democracy in Mexico, Party Strategies and Electoral Institutions*. Cambridge: Cambridge University Press, 2004.

Farhi, Farideh. "Constitutionalism and Parliamentary Struggle for Relevance and Independence in Post-Khomeini Iran." In *The Rule of Law, Islam, and Constitutional Politics in Egypt and Iran*, edited by Said Amir Arjomand and Nathan J. Brown, 123–152. Albany: SUNY Press, 2013.

———. "Rafsanjani Shut Out of Iran's Presidential Race." *IPS News*, May 22, 2013. http://ipsnews.net/2013/05/rafsanjani-shut-out-of-irans-presidential-race.

———. "The Revolutionary Legacy: A Contested and Insecure Polity." In *Viewpoints Special Edition: The Iranian Revolution at 30*, 29–31. Washington, DC: Middle East Institute, 2009.

———. "Crafting a National Identity amidst Contentious Politics in Contemporary Iran." *Iranian Studies* 38, no. 1 (2005): 7–22.

———. "The Antinomies of Iran's War Generation." In *Iran, Iraq, and the Legacies of War*, edited by Lawrence Potter and Gary Sick, 101–120. New York: Palgrave Macmillan, 2004.

Farokhnia, Hamid. "Azad University: A Schooling in Power Politics." *Tehran Bureau*, July 8, 2010. http://www.pbs.org/wgbh/pages/frontline/tehranbureau/2010/07 /a-schooling-in-power-politics.html.

Fathi, Nazila. "An 'Iranian Spring': How Iran's Youth Are Seeking Reform in a New Way." *Huffington Post*, February 23, 2015. http://www.huffingtonpost.com/nazila -fathi/iranian-spring-irans-youth_b_6664786.html.

Ferguson, Niall. "Complexity and Collapse: Empires on the Edge of Chaos." *Foreign Affairs* 89, no. 2 (2010): 18–32.

Fisk, Robert. "Khatami Calls for Rule of Law." *The Independent*, February 12, 1999.

Gandhi, Jennifer. *Political Institutions under Dictatorship*. Cambridge: Cambridge University Press, 2008.

Ganji, Akbar. "Rise of the Sultans." *Foreign Affairs*, June 24, 2009.

———. "The Latter-Day Sultan: Power and Politics in Iran." *Foreign Affairs* (November/ December 2008).

Geddes, Barbara. "What Do We Know about Democratization after Twenty Years?" *Annual Review of Political Science* 2 (1999): 115–144.

George, Marcus. "Ahmadinejad Grilled by Hostile Iran Parliament." *Reuters*, March 14, 2012. http://reuters.com/article/2012/03/14/us-iran-ahmadinejad-parliament-id USBRE82D0NK20120314.

Ghazian, Hosein. "The Ninth Parliamentary Elections in Iran: Challenges and Perspectives." Heinrich Boll Stiftung Foundation, February 21, 2012. http://www.boell.de /downloads/worldwide/Ghazian_The_Ninth_Parliamentary_Elections_in_Iran .pdf.

Gheissari, Ali, and Vali Nasr. *Democracy in Iran: History and the Quest for Liberty*. Oxford: Oxford University Press, 2006.

Gilbert, Leah, and Payam Mohseni. "Beyond Authoritarianism: The Conceptualization of Hybrid Regimes." *Studies in Comparative International Development* 46, no. 3 (2011): 270–297.

Gilley, Bruce. *The Right to Rule: How States Win and Lose Legitimacy*. New York: Columbia University Press, 2009.

Golkar, Saeid. *Captive Society: The Basij Militia and Social Control in Post-Revolutionary Iran*. New York: Columbia University Press/Woodrow Wilson, 2015.

———. "The Reign of Hard-Line Students in Iran's Universities." *Middle East Quarterly* 17, no. 3 (2010): 21–29.

———. "The Ideological-Political Training of Iran 's Basij." *Middle East Brief*, no. 44 (September 2010). http://www.brandeis.edu/crown/publications/meb/MEB44.pdf.

Gorgin, Iraj. "Looking Back at Tehran's 1999 Protests." *Radio Farda*, July 9, 2008. http:// www.rferl.org/content/Iran_Student_Protests/1182717.html.

Gough, Ian, and Geof Wood, eds. *Insecurity and Welfare Regimes in Asia, Africa and Latin America: Social Policy in Development Contexts*. Cambridge: Cambridge University Press, 2004.

Groiss, Arnon. *Iranian Textbooks: Preparing Iran's Children for Global Jihad*. Jerusalem: Center for Monitoring the Impact of Peace, 2007.

Guillaume, Dominique, Roman Zytek, and Mohammad Reza Farzin. *Iran—The Chronicles of the Subsidy Reform*. IMF working paper. Washington, DC: International Monetary Fund, 2011.

Habibi, Nader. "Allocation of Educational and Occupational Opportunities in the Islamic Republic of Iran: A Case Study in the Political Screening of Human Capital." *Iranian Studies* 22, no. 4 (1989): 19–46.

Haggard, Stephan, and Robert Kaufman. *Development, Democracy, and Welfare States: Latin America, East Asia, and Eastern Europe*. Princeton, NJ: Princeton University Press, 2008.

Haggard, Stephan, and Mathew D. McCubbins. "Introduction: Political Institutions and the Determinants of Public Policy." In *President, Parliaments, and Policy*, edited by Stephan Haggard and Mathew D. McCubbins, 1–17. Cambridge: Cambridge University Press, 2001.

Hafezi, Parisa. "Analysis: Ahmadinejad Seen Big Loser in Iran Election." *Reuters*, February 17, 2012. http://reuters.com/article/2012/02/17/us-iran-politics-id USTRE81G0MK20120217.

Hajizadeh, Mohammad, and Luke B. Connelly. "Equity of Health Care Financing in Iran: The Effect of Extending Health Insurance to the Uninsured." *Oxford Development Studies* 38, no. 4 (2010): 461–476.

Harris, Kevan. "The Politics of Subsidy Reform in Iran." *Middle East Report* 254 (2010): 36–39.

———. "The Brokered Exuberance of the Middle Class: An Ethnographic Analysis of Iran's 2009 Green Movement." *Mobilization: An International Quarterly* 17, no. 4 (2012): 435–455.

Hashemi, Nader. "Religious Disputation and Democratic Constitutionalism: The Enduring Legacy of the Constitutional Revolution on the Struggle for Democracy in Iran." *Constellations* 17, no. 1 (2010): 50–60.

Hashemi, Nader, and Danny Postel. *The People Reloaded*. New York: Melville, 2011.

Hen-Tov, Elliot, and Nathan Gonzalez. "The Militarization of Post-Khomeini Iran: Praetorianism 2.0." *Washington Quarterly* 34, no. 1 (2011): 45–59.

Hermann, Margaret G. "Content Analysis." In *Qualitative Methods in International Relations: A Pluralist Guide*, edited by Audie Klotz and Deepa Prakash, 151–167. New York: Palgrave, 2008.

Hertog, Steffen. "Defying the Resource Curse: Explaining Successful State-Owned Enterprises in Rentier States." *World Politics* 62, no. 2 (2010): 261–301.

Hess, David, and Brian Martin. "Repression, Backfire and the Theory of Transformative Events." *Mobilization* 11, no. 2 (2006): 249–267.

Heydemann, Steven. "War, Institutions, and Social Change in the Middle East." In *War, Institutions, and Social Change in the Middle East*, edited by Steven Heydemann, 1–30. Berkeley: University of California Press, 2000.

Hiro, Dilip. *The Longest War: The Iran-Iraq Military Conflict*. New York: Routledge, 1991.

Hoodfar, Homa. "Bargaining with Fundamentalism: Women and the Politics of Population Control in Iran." *Reproductive Health Matters* 4, no. 8 (1996): 30–40.

Hoodfar, Homa, and Samad Assadpour. "The Politics of Population Policy in the Islamic Republic of Iran." *Studies in Family Planning* 31, no. 1 (2000): 19–34.

Hooglund, Eric. "Changing Attitudes among Women in Rural Iran." In *Gender in Contemporary Iran: Pushing the Boundaries*, edited by Roksana Bahramitash and Eric Hooglund, 120–135. London: Routledge, 2011.

Howard, Marc Morjé, and Philip Roessler. "Liberalizing Electoral Outcomes in Competitive Authoritarian Regimes." *American Journal of Political Science* 50, no. 2 (2006): 365–381.

Huntington, Samuel. *The Third Wave: Democratization in the Late Twentieth Century.* Norman: University of Oklahoma Press, 1991.

———. *Political Order in Changing Societies.* New Haven, CT: Yale University Press, 1968.

Huntington, Samuel, and Clement H. Moore, eds. *Authoritarian Politics in Modern Society: The Dynamics of Established One-Party Systems.* New York: Basic Books, 1970.

Ibrahimipour, Hossein, Mohammad-Reza Maleki, Richard Brown, Mohammadreza Gohari, Iraj Karimi, and Reza Dehnavieh. "A Qualitative Study of the Difficulties in Reaching Sustainable Universal Health Insurance Coverage in Iran." *Health Policy and Planning* 26, no. 6 (2011): 485–495.

Iqbal, Farrukh. *Sustaining Gains in Poverty Reduction and Human Development in the Middle East and North Africa.* Washington, DC: World Bank, 2006.

Kamali Dehghan, Saeed. "Iran's President and Supreme Leader in Rift over Minister's Reinstatement." *The Guardian*, April 27, 2011. http://guardian.co.uk/world/2011/apr/27/iran-president-supreme-leader-rift.

Kamrava, Mehran. "Preserving Non-Democracies: Leaders and State Institutions in the Middle East." *Middle Eastern Studies* 46, no. 2 (2010): 251–270.

Kamyab, Shahrzad. "The University Entrance Exam: Crisis in Iran." *International Higher Education*, no. 51 (2008): 22–23.

Kazemi, Farhad. *Poverty and Revolution in Iran.* New York: New York University Press, 1980.

Keane, John. "Refolution in the Arab World." *Open Democracy*, April 38, 2011. http://www.opendemocracy.net/print/59185.

Keshavarzian, Arang. "Contestation without Democracy: Elite Fragmentation in Iran." In *Authoritarianism in the Middle East: Regimes and Resistance*, edited by Marsha Priepstein Posusney and Michele Penner Angrist. Boulder, CO: Lynne Rienner, 2005.

Keshavarzian, Arang. *Bazaar and State in Iran: Politics of the Tehran Marketplace.* Cambridge: Cambridge University Press, 2007.

Khatam, Azam. "Iranian Paradox: The Inverted Relation of University and Society." *Universities in Crisis: Blog of the International Sociological Association*, May 26, 2010, http://www.isa-sociology.org/universities-in-crisis/?p=480.

Kotkin, Stephen. *Stalin: Volume I: Paradoxes of Power, 1878–1928.* New York: Penguin, 2014.

Kristof, Nicholas. "In Iran, They Want Fun, Fun, Fun." *New York Times*, June 20, 2012.

Künkler, Mirjam. "The Special Court of the Clergy (*dādgāh-ye vizheh-ye ruhāniyat*) and the Repression of Dissident Clergy in Iran." In *Constitutionalism, the Rule of Law and the Politics of Administration in Egypt and Iran*, edited by Said Arjomand and Nathan Brown, 90–139. Albany: SUNY Press, 2012.

Kurzman, Charles. *The Unthinkable Revolution in Iran*. Cambridge, MA: Harvard University Press, 2004.

Levitsky, Steven, and Lucan Way. *Competitive Authoritarianism: Hybrid Regimes after the Cold War*. Cambridge: Cambridge University Press, 2010.

———. "Linkage and Leverage: How Do International Factors Change Domestic Balances of Power?" In *Electoral Authoritarianism*, edited by Andreas Schedler, 199–216. Boulder, CO: Lynne Rienner, 2006.

Linz, Juan. *Totalitarian and Authoritarian Regimes*. Boulder, CO: Lynne Rienner, 2000 [1975].

Linz, Juan J., and Alfred Stepan, *Problems of Democratic Transition and Consolidation*. Baltimore: Johns Hopkins University Press, 1996.

Litvak, Meir. "Iran: Jomhuri-i Islami-i Iran." *Middle East Contemporary Survey* 24 (2000): 213–218.

Loeffler, Agnes, and Erika Friedl. "Cultural Parameters of a 'Miraculous' Birth Rate Drop." *Anthropology News* (March 2009): 13–15.

Lyons, Jonathan. "New Justice Chief Faces Reform Battle." *The Iranian*, September 9, 1999. http://iranian.com/News/1999/September/chief.html.

Mahdi, Ali Akbar. "The Student Movement in the Islamic Republic of Iran." *Journal of Iranian Research and Analysis* 15, no. 2 (1999): 5–32.

Maloney, Suzanne. "Islamism and Iran's Postrevolutionary Economy: The Case of the Bonyads." In *Gods, Guns, and Globalization: Religious Radicalism and International Political Economy*, edited by Mary Ann Tetreault and Robert Denemark, 191–218. Boulder, CO: Lynne Rienner, 2004.

———. "Agents or Obstacles? Parastatal Foundations and Challenges for Iranian Development." In *The Economy of Iran: Dilemmas of an Islamic State*, edited by Parvin Alizadeh, 145–176. London: Tauris, 2000.

Markoff, John. *Waves of Democracy: Social Movements and Political Change*. Thousand Oaks, CA: Pine Forge Press, 1996.

McCann, Matt. "Youth in Iran: Inside and Out." *New York Times*, January 26, 2014.

McMichael, Philip. *Development and Social Change: A Global Perspective*. 5th ed. Thousand Oaks, CA: Sage Publications, 2011.

Menashri, David. *Post-Revolution Politics in Iran: Religion, Society, and Power*. London: Frank Cass, 2001.

Messkoub, Mahmoud. "Social Policy in Iran in the Twentieth Century." *Iranian Studies* 39, no. 2 (2006): 227–252.

Mettler, Suzanne. *Soldiers to Citizens: The G.I. Bill and the Making of the Greatest Generation*. New York: Oxford University Press, 2007.

———. *The Submerged State: How Invisible Government Policies Undermine American Democracy*. Chicago: University of Chicago Press, 2011.

Migdal, Joel. "Researching the State." In *Comparative Politics: Rationality, Culture, and Structure*, edited by Mark Lichbach and Alan Zuckerman, 2nd ed., 162–192. Cambridge: Cambridge University Press, 2009.

Molavi, Afshin. *The Soul of Iran: A Nation's Journey to Freedom*. New York: Norton, 2002.

Moslem, Mehdi. *Factional Politics in Post-Khomeini Iran*. Syracuse, NY: Syracuse University Press, 2002.

Nader, Alireza. "The Revolutionary Guards." *Iran Primer.* http://iranprimer.usip.org /resource/revolutionary-guards.

Nazemi, Nader. "War and State-Making in Revolutionary Iran." Ph.D. diss., University of Washington, 1994.

O'Donnell, Guillermo. "Tensions in the Bureaucratic-Authoritarian State and the Question of Democracy." *The New Authoritarianism in Latin America*, edited by David Collier, 285–318. Princeton, NJ: Princeton University Press, 1980.

O'Donnell, Guillermo, and Philippe Schmitter, *Transitions from Authoritarian Rule: Tentative Conclusions about Uncertain Democracies.* Baltimore: Johns Hopkins University Press, 1986.

Ottaway, Marina. *Democracy Challenges: The Rise of Semi-Authoritarianism.* Washington, DC: Carnegie Endowment for International Peace, 2003.

Saeed Paivandi, *Discrimination and Intolerance in Iran's Textbooks.* New York: Freedom House, 2008. http://www.rdfi.org/pdf/textbook.pdf.

Perlmutter, Amos, and Valerie Plave Bennett, eds., *The Political Influence of the Military: A Comparative Reader.* New Haven, CT: Yale University Press, 1980.

Pesaran, Evaleila. "Challenges Facing the Iranian Economy in Iran." In *A Revolutionary Republic in Transition*, edited by Rouzbeh Parsi, 41–59. Paris: Institute for Security Studies, 2012.

———. *Iran's Struggle for Economic Independence: Reform and Counter-Reform in the Post-Revolutionary Era.* London: Routledge, 2011.

Porter, Bruce. *War and the Rise of the State: The Military Foundations of Modern Politics.* New York: Simon and Schuster, 1994.

Postel, Danny. "Counter-Revolution and Revolt in Iran: An Interview with Iranian Political Scientist Hossein Bashiriyeh." In *The People Reloaded*, edited by Nader Hashemi and Danny Postel, 82–105. New York: Melville, 2011.

Przeworski, Adam. "Some Problems in the Study of the Transition to Democracy." In *Transitions from Authoritarian Rule: Comparative Perspectives*, edited by Guillermo O'Donnell, et. al., 47–63. Baltimore: Johns Hopkins University Press, 1986.

Przeworski, Adam, Michael Alvarez, Jose Cheibub, and Fernando Limongi. *Democracy and Development: Political Institutions and Material Well-Being in the World, 1950–1990.* Cambridge: Cambridge University Press, 2000.

Rahimkhani, Kourosh. "The Institutionalization of the Clerical Establishment in Post-Revolutionary Iran: The Case of the Friday Prayer Leaders." Paper presented at the biannual conference of the International Society for Iranian Studies, Los Angeles, CA, 2010.

Rezai-Rashti, Goli. "Exploring Women's Experience of Higher Education and the Changing Nature of Gender Relations in Iran." In *Gender in Contemporary Iran: Pushing the Boundaries*, edited by Roksana Bahramitash and Eric Hooglund, 46–61. London: Routledge, 2011.

Ringer, Monica. *Education, Religion, and the Discourse of Cultural Reform in Qajar Iran.* Costa Mesa, CA: Mazda, 2001.

Rivetti, Paola. "Student Movements in the Islamic Republic: Shaping Iran's Politics through the Campus." In *Iran: A Revolutionary Republic in Transition*, edited by Rouzbeh Parsi, 81–99. Paris: Institute for Security Studies, 2012.

Rodrik, Dani. "What Drives Public Employment in Developing Countries?" *Review of Development Economics* 4, no. 3 (2000): 229–243.

Rubin, Michael. "Can Iran be Deterred?" *Middle Eastern Outlook*, November 5, 2008.

Saeidi, Ali A. "The Accountability of Para-governmental Organizations (Bonyads): The Case of Iranian Foundations." *Iranian Studies* 37, no. 3 (2004): 479–498.

Safshekan, Roozbeh, and Farzan Sabet. "The Ayatollah's Praetorians: The Islamic Revolutionary Guard Corps and the 2009 Election Crisis." *Middle East Journal* 64, no. 4 (2010): 543–558.

Sahimi, Muhammad. "The Chain Murders: Killing Dissidents and Intellectuals, 1988–1998." *Tehran Bureau*, January 5, 2011. http://www.pbs.org/wgbh/pages/frontline/tehranbureau/2011/01/the-chain-murders-killing-dissidents-and-intellectuals-1988-1998.html.

——. "'Cultural Revolution' Redux." *Tehran Bureau*, May 11, 2010. http://www.pbs.org/wgbh/pages/frontline/tehranbureau/2010/05/cultural-revolution-redux.html.

Sakurai, Keiko. "University Entrance Examination and the Making of an Islamic Society in Iran: A Study of the Post-Revolutionary Iranian Approach to 'Konkur.'" *Iranian Studies* 37, no. 3 (2004): 385–406.

Salehi-Isfahani, Djavad. "Iranian Youth in Times of Economic Crisis." Dubai Initiative, Dubai School of Government and the Harvard Kennedy School, September 2010.

——. "The Revolution and the Rural Poor." *Radical History Review*, no. 105 (2009): 140–141.

——. "Poverty and Inequality since the Revolution." *Middle East Institute*, January 29, 2009. http://www.mei.edu/content/poverty-and-inequality-revolution.

——. "Iran's Third Development Plan: A Reappraisal." Working paper e06-4, Virginia Polytechnic Institute and State University, Department of Economics, 2006.

——. "Human Resources in Iran: Potentials and Challenges." *Iranian Studies* 38, no. 1 (2005): 117–147.

Salehi-Isfahani, Djavad, Mohammad Jalal Abbasi-Shavazi, and Meimanat Hosseini-Chavoshi. "Family Planning and Fertility Decline in Rural Iran: The Impact of Rural Health Clinics." *Health Economics* 19, no. S1 (2010): 159–180.

Sanandaji, Kaveh Cyrus. "The Eighth Parliamentary Elections in the Islamic Republic of Iran: A Division in Conservative Ranks and the Politics of Moderation." *Iranian Studies* 42, no. 4 (2009): 621–648.

Schedler, Andreas, ed. *Electoral Authoritarianism, The Dynamics of Unfree Competition*. Boulder, CO: Lynne Reinner, 2006.

Schirazi, Asghar. *The Constitution of Iran: Politics and the State in the Islamic Republic*. London: Tauris, 1997.

Schlumberger, Oliver. "Opening Old Bottles in Search of New Wine: On Nondemocratic Legitimacy in the Middle East." *Middle East Critique* 19, no. 3 (2010): 233–250.

Sciolino, Elaine. *Persian Mirrors: The Elusive Face of Iran*. New York: Simon and Schuster, 2001.

Scott, James. *Domination and the Art of Resistance*. New Haven, CT: Yale University Press, 1990.

Secor, Laura. "The Rationalist." *New Yorker*, February 2, 2009.

Sedgwick, Mark. "Measuring Egyptian Regime Legitimacy." *Middle East Critique* 19, no. 3 (2010): 251–257.

Sen, Amartya. "Mortality as an Indicator of Economic Success and Failure." *Economic Journal* 108, no. 446 (1998): 1–25.

Shavarini, Mitra K. "The Feminisation of Iranian Higher Education." *International Review of Education* 51, no. 4 (2005): 329–347.

Sikkink, Kathryn, and Thomas Risse. *The Power of Human Rights*. Cambridge: Cambridge University Press, 1999.

Silver, Beverly. *Forces of Labor: Workers' Movements and Globalization since 1870*. Cambridge: Cambridge University Press, 2003.

Singerman, Diane. "The Economic Imperatives of Marriage: Emerging Practices and Identities among Youth in the Middle East." Working paper no, 6, Wolfensohn Center for Development at Brookings Dubai School of Government, The Middle East Youth Initiative (September 2007).

Skocpol, Theda. "Social Revolutions and Mass Military Mobilization." *World Politics* 40 (January 1988): 147–168.

Slater, Dan. *Ordering Power: Contentious Politics and Authoritarian Leviathans in Southeast Asia*. Cambridge: Cambridge University Press, 2010.

———. "Review of Competitive Authoritarianism: Hybrid Regimes after the Cold War." *Perspectives on Politics* 9, no. 2 (2011): 385–388.

Sohrabi, Naghmeh. "The Power Struggle in Iran: A Centrist Comeback?" *Middle East Brief* 53 (July 2011).

Springborg, Robert. "Game Over: The Chance for Democracy in Egypt Is Lost." *Foreign Policy*, February 2, 2011. http://mideastafrica.foreignpolicy.com/posts/2011/02/02/game_over_the_chance_for_democracy_in_egypt_is_lost.

Thaler, David, Alireza Nader, Shahram Chubin, Charlotte Lynch, Jerrold Green, and Frederic Wehrey. *Mullahs, Guards, and Bonyads: An Exploration of Iranian Leadership Dynamics*. Santa Monica, CA: Rand, 2010.

Theodolou, Michael, "Iran Bans Two Leading Reformist Political Parties." *The National*, September 29, 2012. http://thenational.ae/news/world/middle-east/iran-bans-two-leading-reformist-political-parties.

Tilly, Charles. "War-Making and State-Making as Organized Crime." In *Bringing the State Back In*, edited by Peter Evans, Dietrich Rueschemeyer, and Theda Skocpol, 169–187. Cambridge: Cambridge University Press, 1985.

Tocqueville, Alexis de. *Democracy in America*, translated by George Lawrence. New York: Perennial Classics, 2000.

Tofighi, Mohammad-Ali. "Rebuilding the Image of Basij." *Rooz Online*, January 7, 2011. http://www.roozonline.com/english/opinion/opinion-article/archive/2011/january/07/article/rebuilding-the-image-of-basij.html.

Tsebelis, George. *Veto Players: How Political Institutions Work*. Princeton, NJ: Princeton University Press, 2002.

Tousi, R. "Tehran, Glimpses of Freedom." *OpenDemocracy*, October 6, 2011. http://www.opendemocracy.net/r-tousi/tehran-glimpses-of-freedom.

———. "Voices of a New Iran." *OpenDemocracy*, December 11, 2009. http://www.opendemocracy.net/r-tousi/voices-of-new-iran.

UNIDO. *Non-Farm Employment for Rural Poverty Alleviation: A Report on the Regional Seminar, Pilot Projects, and Country Papers*. Vienna: United Nations Industrial Development Organization, 1995.

Varzi, Roxanne. *Warring Souls: Youth, Media, and Martyrdom in Post-Revolution Iran*. Durham, NC: Duke University Press, 2000.

Waterbury, John. "Democracy without Democrats? The Potential for Political Liberalization in the Middle East." In *Democracy without Democrats: The Renewal of*

Politics in the Muslim World, edited by Ghassan Salame, 23–46. New York: Taurus, 1994.

Wedeen, Lisa. *Ambiguities of Domination*. Chicago: University of Chicago Press, 1999.

Wehrey, Frederic, Jerrold Green, Brian Nichiporuk, Alireza Nader, Lydia Hansell, Rafool Nafisi, and S. R. Bohandy. *The Rise of the Pasdaran: Assessing the Domestic Roles of Iran's Islamic Revolutionary Guards Corps*. Santa Monica, CA: Rand, 2009.

Weber, Max. *Economy and Society: An Outline of Interpretive Sociology*, edited by Guenther Roth and Claus Wittich. Berkeley: University of California Press, 1987.

Williams Jr., Nick B. "90% of Iranian Votes are Cast for Rafsanjani." *Los Angeles Times*, July 30, 1989.

Winters, Jeffrey. *Oligarchy*. Cambridge: Cambridge University Press, 2011.

Books and Articles in Persian

Abdi Abbas. *"Jonbesh-e sabz pasokhi beh zamingir shodan eslahat bood va na edame-ye an"* ("The green movement was a response to the bogging down of the reform and not its continuation"). *Ayande*, October 23, 2010. http://www.ayande.ir/1389/08/post_860.html#more.

———. *"Pishnahad-e yek rahbord-e eslah-talabaneh baraye tarafdaran-e taghir"* ("Proposal for a reformist strategy for proponents of change"). *Ayande*, April 16, 2012. http://www.ayande.ir/1391/01/post_1046.html.

Ahmadi Amui, Bahman. *Eqtesad-e siasi-ye jomhuri-ye eslami* (The political economy of the Islamic Republic). Tehran: Gam-e No, 1382/2003.

Babavand, Hamid. *"Ma ra az nazdik bebinid"* ("Look at us from up close"). *Moallem* (Mehr 1386/September–October 2007): 6.

Bashiriyeh, Hossein. *Jame'eh shenasi-e iran: doreh-ye jomhuri-ye eslami-ye iran* (A sociological study of Iran: The Islamic Republic era). Tehran: Ney, 1384/2005.

Emami Kashani, Mohammad. *Rahnemun Quarterly*, no. 6 (Fall 1372/1993): 22.

Esma'ili, Bahman. *Entekhabat-e majles haftom* (The seventh parliamentary elections). Tehran: Markaz-e Asnad-e Enqelab-e Eslami, 1384/2005.

Ganji, Akbar. *Alijenab-e sorkhpush va alijenaban-e khakestari* (Red eminence and gray eminences). Tehran: Tarh-e No, 1378/1999.

Hashemi Rafsanjani, Akbar. *Be su-ye sarnevesht: khaterat-e Hashemi Rafsanjani Sal-e 1363* (Toward fate: Hashemi Rafsanjani's memoir year 1363). Tehran: Daftar Nashr-e Maaref Enqelab, 1385/2006.

Jannati, Mohammad-Ebrahim. *Manabe' ijtihadi az didgah-e mazaheb-e eslami* (Sources of ijtihad from the perspective of Islamic schools of thought). Tehran: Keyhan Association, 1992.

Karimimobian, Zahra. *"Yadgiri be jaye hafezeh mehvari"* ("Learning instead of memorization-focus"). *Hamshahri*, October 5, 1386/2007.

Majles-e Showra-e Eslami. *Majles-e barrasi-e nahayi-ye qanun-e asasi-ye jomhuri-ye eslami-ye Iran, surat-e mashruh-e mozakerat-e majles-e barrasi-e nahayi-e qanun-e asasi-ye jomhuri-ye eslami-ye Iran* (The assembly for the final review of the Constitution of the Islamic Republic of Iran, details of the discussions of the assembly for the final review of the constitution of the Islamic Republic), 4 vols. Tehran: Edareh-e Kol-e Omur-e Farhangi va Ravabet-e Omumi-e Majles -e Showra-e Eslami, 1985–1989.

Mirdar, Morteza, ed. *Memoirs of Hojjatoleslam Valmoslemin Ali Akbar Nateq Nuri*, vol. 2. Tehran: Markaz-e Asnad-e Enqelab-e Eslami, 1384/2005.

Motamed, Arash. *"Hefazat-e ettela'at dar nahad-e riasat jomhuri?"* (Counterintelligence in the presidential office?). *Rooz Online*, August 18, 2011. http://www.roozonline .com/english/news3/newsitem/archive/2011/august/18/article/-f99f02b330.html.

Mussavi, Mir-Hossein. *Chenin goft Mir Hossein* (So said Mir-Hossein). Paris: Kaleme and Kanun-e Doktor Shariati, 1391/2012.

Mussavi Bojnurdi, Seyyed Mohammad. *"Naqsh-e zaman va makan dar taghir ahkam"* ("The role of time and place in the revision of directives"). *Majaleye Kanun -e Vokala*, no. 10, 1376/1997, 241–246.

Noruzzadeh, Reza, and Mojgan Mehrparvar, *Gozaresheh melli-ye amuzesh-e ali, tahqiqat, va fanavari 1389–90* (A national report of higher education, research, and technology 2010–11). Tehran: Institute for Research and Planning in Higher Education, 1391/2012.

Parchami, Davud. *"Sanjesh-e gerayesh-e mardom be basij"* ("Examination of the public's predisposition to the Basij"). *Basij Studies Quarterly* 18–19 (2003): 45–90.

Qadimi Zaker, Seyyed Javad. *Nezarat-e estesvabi dar dorehaye mokhtalef-e entekhabat-e majles-e shoraye eslami* (Supervisory approval in various Islamic consultative assembly elections). Tehran: Ravabet-e Daftar-e Tahkim-i Vahdat, 1378/1999.

Quchani, Mohammad. *"Tahlil-e entekhabat-e majles-e nohom"* (Analysis of the ninth parliamentary election). *Aseman Weekly*, April 15, 2012.

———. *Yaqeh sefidha* (The white-collars). Tehran: Naqsh-o-Negar, 1379/2000.

Rezaei, Mohammad. *Tahlili az zendegi-ye ruzmareh-ye danesh amuzeshi: Naresaeiha-ye gofteman-e madreseh* (An analysis of the daily lives of schoolchildren: The failures of school discourse). Tehran: Society and Culture, 2008.

Sahabi, Ezzatollah, and Hoda Saber. *"Forsat-e an do sal va tavan-e an shish sal"* ("The opportunity of those two years and the damage of those six years"). *Iran-e Farda*, no. 58 (1378/1999): 23–26.

Saili Kurdahih, Majid, *Sayr-e tahavol qavanin-e majles dar Iran* (Evolution of Parliament's laws in Iran). Tehran: Markaz-e Asnad-e Enqelal-e Eslami, 1378/1999.

Tahavori, Mohammad. *"Esteqrar-e demokrasi va hoquq-e bashar, shart-e sokut-e jonbesh-e daneshjui: goftegu ba abdollah momeni"* ("Establishment of democracy and human rights is the condition for silence of the student movement: A conversation with Abdollah Momeni"). *Gozaar*, July 1, 2007. http://www.gozaar.org/persian /interview-fa/3608.html.

Selected Websites and Weblogs Cited

http://www.aljazeera.com
http://www.alseraj.net
http://www.amontazeri.com
http://www.ayande.ir

https://www.balatarin.com
http://www.bbc.co.uk/persian
http://center.namaz.ir
http://www.csis.ir
http://www.dastgheib.com
http://www.dw.de
http://www.emdad.ir
http://www.enduringamerica.com
http://en.imam-khomeini.ir
http://etemadnewspaper.ir
http://www.ettelaat.info
http://gulfunit.wordpress.com
http://farsi.khamenei.ir
http://www.foreignpolicy.com
https://haghighatnews.wordpress.com
http://www.hawzah.net
http://www.huffingtonpost.com
http://www.hvm.ir
http://www.ido.ir
http://www.independent.co.uk
http://www.iranvij.ir
http://www.irib.ir
http://iranprimer.usip.org
http://irna.ir
http://www.isa-sociology.org
http://www.jameehmodarresin.org
http://www.kaleme.com
http://www.khabaronline.ir
http://www.mardomak.org
http://www.masjed.ir
http://www.mehrnews.com
http://norooznews.org
http://nurizad.info
http://www.nytimes.com
http://old.ana.ir
http://www.opendemocracy.net
http://www.payvand.com/news
http://www.pbs.org/wgbh/pages/frontline/tehranbureau
http://www.princeton.edu/irandataportal
http://www.rahesabz.net
http://www.rasanews.ir
http://www.roozonline.com
http://sahamnews.org
http://www.siasi.porsemani.ir
http://tarikhirani.ir

Contributors

Yasmin Alem is an expert on Iran's domestic politics and has written extensively on Iranian elections, factional politics, and civil society developments. She is the author of *Duality by Design*, a comprehensive study of the Iranian electoral system. She has been a nonresident Senior Fellow at the Atlantic Council and a consultant with a number of UN agencies.

Mehrzad Boroujerdi is Professor and Chair of the Political Science Department in the Maxwell School of Citizenship and Public Affairs at Syracuse University. He is a past president of the International Society for Iranian Studies; his publications include *Iranian Intellectuals and the West: The Tormented Triumph of Nativism*, *Mirror for the Muslim Prince: Islam and Theory of Statecraft* (edited), and *I Carved, Worshiped and Shattered: Essays on Iranian Politics and Identity* [in Persian].

Daniel Brumberg is Associate Professor of Government and Co-Director of Democracy and Governance Studies at Georgetown University. He is also a Special Advisor to the United States Institute of Peace. His books include *Reinventing Khomeini: The Struggle for Reform in Iran*, *Moyen Orient: L'Enjeu Democratique*, and *Islam and Democracy in the Middle East* (co-edited with Larry Diamond and Marc Plattner).

Farideh Farhi is an independent scholar and Affiliate Graduate Faculty at the University of Hawai'i at Manoa. Her publications include *States and Urban-Based Revolutions: Iran and Nicaragua*.

Fatemeh Haghighatjoo was a member of Iran's Parliament from 2000 to 2004. She is CEO of the Boston-based nonprofit Nonviolent Initiative for Democracy (NID). She is a former faculty member at the University of Massachusetts, Boston, and the University of Connecticut and has had fellowship positions at Harvard University and MIT. Her publications include book chapters and papers on the Iranian women's movement and democratic movement in Iran.

Kevan Harris is Assistant Professor of Sociology at the University of California, Los Angeles, and author of *The Martyrs' Welfare State: Politics and Social Policy in the Islamic Republic of Iran*.

Mehrangiz Kar is a writer, attorney, and activist specializing in women's rights and family law. She practiced law in the Islamic Republic of Iran for twenty-two years and has published books and articles on law, gender equality, and democracy in Iran, including *Crossing the Red Line: The Struggle for Human Rights in Iran*. Kar has received several international awards for her human rights endeavors including the National Endowment for Democracy's Democracy Award, the Ludovic-Trarieux International Human Rights Prize, and a Human Rights First Award.

Shervin Malekzadeh is Visiting Assistant Professor of Political Science at Swarthmore College. His research focuses on the politics of schooling and culture in postrevolutionary Iran. He is a regular visitor to Iran and an accidental participant-reporter in the 2009 Green Movement; his articles have appeared in *The New York Times, The Atlantic, The Washington Post, Time, Tehran Bureau,* and *Salon.*

Payam Mohseni is the Iran Project Director and Fellow for Iran Studies at Harvard University's Belfer Center for Science and International Affairs and Lecturer in the Department of Government. Mohseni's research focuses on the internal policy-making process of the Iranian state, the dynamics of factional politics in postrevolutionary Iran, and the Islamic Revolutionary Guards.

Shadi Mokhtari is Assistant Professor in the School of International Service at American University. She is the author of *After Abu Ghraib: Exploring Human Rights in America and the Middle East,* co-winner of the 2010 American Political Science Association Human Rights Section Best Book Award. From 2003 to 2013, she served as editor-in-chief of the *Muslim World Journal of Human Rights.*

Azadeh Pourzand, a graduate of the Harvard Kennedy School of Government, works as a deputy project director at a Washington, D.C.–based international development organization focusing on media, governance, and civil society in the MENA region.

Kourosh Rahimkhani is a Ph.D. candidate in political science at SUNY-Binghamton. *He began his career as a journalist in Iran in the early 1990s and worked for a number of reformist newspapers before moving to the United States.* He is the editor of *Perestroika va Eslahat* (Perestroika and Reform) [in Persian].

Index

CPSIA information can be obtained
at www.ICGtesting.com
Printed in the USA
BVOW09s0734120917
494639BV00004B/104/P